"*The Gates of Hell: An Untold Story of Faith and Perseverance in the Early Soviet Union*, written by Rev. Dr. Matthew Heise, is a true gem for a Christian's library. It is the result of a huge work of dedicated scholarship. And it is a book written for the common reader to enjoy and appreciate each page. It gives us an understanding of the nature of the persecution of Christians not only in Communist Russia but in any country that might be heavily influenced by Socialist or Communist ideas. It opens us to the treasures of the martyrs—their faith in the Lord Jesus Christ—and it teaches us to learn from their lives good lessons of faithfulness in persecutions. It teaches us to learn sympathy, love, and empathy from those who tried to do their best to help their persecuted brothers and sisters. It teaches us to be and remain strong and faithful even unto death in the Church Militant. The Gates of Hell helps us also to recognize the signs of the time, so that we are not lulled by songs of the world and the devil and caught in their traps unprepared."

—V'yacheslav Horpynchuk,
bishop, Ukrainian Lutheran Church

"The work of Matthew Heise is a precious work not only because of historical facts and his professional approach to their understanding, but also very precious with his inclusion of testimonies of individual people in their concrete reality. They bring a quiet yet insistent call for us to remain as faithful Christians in our present times."

—Ivan Eľko,
general bishop, Evangelical A.C. Church in Slovakia

THE GATES OF HELL

An Untold Story
of Faith and
Perseverance
in the Early
Soviet Union

THE GATES OF HELL

An Untold Story
of Faith and
Perseverance
in the Early
Soviet Union

MATTHEW HEISE

LEXHAM PRESS

The Gates of Hell: An Untold Story of Faith and Perseverance in the Early Soviet Union

Copyright 2022 Matthew Heise

Lexham Press, 1313 Commercial St., Bellingham, WA 98225
LexhamPress.com

The Prayer for Martyrs (page xvi) includes Psalm verses from the *New Coverdale Psalter in The Book of Common Prayer* (Huntington Beach, CA: Anglican Liturgy Press, 2019), copyright of the Anglican Church in North America.

Print ISBN 9781683595953
Digital ISBN 9781683595984
Library of Congress Control Number 2021947101

Lexham Editorial: Todd Hains, Elliot Ritzema, Erin Mangum, Mandi Newell
Cover Design: Joshua Hunt, Brittany Schrock
Typesetting: Abigail Stocker, Mandi Newell

To my parents, Walter and Betty,
whose unflagging devotion to my academic efforts
will always be appreciated.

And to my dear and loving wife, Raziyeh,
who inspires me daily in her walk with Christ—
my love for you is profound.

And to the martyrs of the faith
who stand as a host arrayed in white,
washed in the blood of the Lamb!

CONTENTS

CHRONOLOGY

Feb. 1917	Czar Nicholas II abdicates and a provisional government is formed
Oct. 1917	Four hundredth anniversary of the Protestant Reformation
Oct./Nov. 1917	Bolshevik Revolution overthrows the government and establishes a Communist government
Nov. 1917–Oct. 1922	Russian Civil War
Jan. 1918	Decree on the Separation of the State from the Church and the Church from the Schools
Dec. 1921	Dr. John Morehead of the NLC enters Russia to extend aid to Lutherans and others suffering from the famine
Sept. 1924	Leningrad Lutheran seminary begins classes
April 1929	Law on Religious Associations is decreed
Dec. 1929	Leningrad Lutheran pastors and Sunday school teachers are arrested
Sept. 1930	Leningrad Lutheran pastors and Sunday school teachers are sentenced
April 1934	Bishop Theophil Meier dies
1936	Dr. John Morehead dies; Bishop Arthur Malmgren immigrates to Germany
1937–1938	Joseph Stalin's Great Terror
Aug. 1939	All Lutheran churches in Russia are closed

ABBREVIATIONS

ACRRM	American Committee on Religious Rights and Minorities
ARA	American Relief Administration
DPZ	*Dom Predvarityelna Zakluchony* (House of Preparatory Incarceration)
GPU	*Gosudarstvennoe Politicheskoe Upravlenie* (State Political Directorate)
LWC	Lutheran World Convention
NKVD	*Narodniy Komissariat Vnutrennikh Del* (People's Commissariat for Internal Affairs)
NLC	National Lutheran Council
OGPU	*Obyedinyonnoye Gosudarstvennoye Politicheskoye Upravleniye pri SNK SSSR* (Joint State Political Directorate)

PRAYER FOR MARTYRS

IN THE NAME of the Father and of the Son and of the Holy Spirit. Amen.

BLESSED IS the one who has the God of Jacob for his help *
    and whose hope is in the Lord his God.   *Ps 146:4*
This God is our God forever and ever; *
    he shall be our guide, even unto death.   *Ps 48:14*
Dear in the sight of the Lord *
    is the death of his saints.   *Ps 116:13*

ALMIGHTY GOD,
you have knit together your faithful people of all times and places
into one communion, the mystical body of your Son Christ our Lord.
Grant us grace so to follow your blessed saints in all virtuous and godly living,
that, together with them, we may come to those unspeakable joys,
which you have prepared for those who love you;
through Jesus Christ our Lord,
who lives and reigns with you and the Holy Spirit,
one God, now and forever.
Amen.

PROLOGUE

JUNE 1918—AN IDYLLIC summer day in the Crimea, with trees blossoming and groaning from the fruit peculiar to that bountiful region near the Black Sea. Cherries, strawberries, plums, and mulberries blanketed the countryside. In the old German village of Neusatz it was a memorable day: the Hörschelmann family was marking the ordination of Friedel Hörschelmann, the eldest son of Pastor Ferdinand Hörschelmann Sr.

The Evangelical Lutheran Church of Russia and all Christian churches had recently experienced severe tribulation due to the Bolshevik Revolution of the previous fall, a revolution that promised a robust battle against what it considered outdated religious dogma. The Bolsheviks hadn't wasted time after taking power, crafting a law in January 1918 separating the church from the state and the school from church. Despite these forbidding signs, though, the church was far from dead. On this day, pastors from the surrounding region joyfully gathered along with their families to celebrate Friedel's ordination. They commemorated the occasion with a photo, which now appears on the cover of this book.

Despite the recent turmoil throughout the country, the fact that such a serene setting still existed in Russia must have comforted believers. But within twelve years of this gathering, both elder and younger Hörschelmanns would die in Soviet Gulag labor camps. Three of the other pastors in the photo, Arnold Frischfeld, Arthur Hanson, and Emil Choldetsky, would also walk the path to Golgotha that so many believers in Russia would travel. The young man lying in the foreground, a future organist for Sts. Peter and Paul Lutheran Church in Moscow, was the youngest son of Ferdinand Hörschelmann. He would also serve a stint in the Gulag and eventually be murdered when he was thrown from a train by Soviet criminals.

But on this day, all those tragedies lay in the future. The Lutheran Church was seeking to find some solid ground in the world's first officially atheist nation.

A WORLD IN FLUX

War, Revolution, and Reformation

LUTHERANS WORLDWIDE HAD been eagerly anticipating the year 1917. Celebrations marking the four hundredth anniversary of the Reformation had been in the planning stages for several years, and now, despite the cataclysm of a world war, they would be observed with fervor. One of the American planning committees had been formed as early as 1914 and had united representatives of the General Council, the General Synod, and the United Synod South. Another committee, the Reformation Quadricentenary Committee, was led by two Lutheran Church—Missouri Synod pastors, Otto Pannkoke and William Schoenfeld.[1] The Missouri Synod was in the process of commissioning a new translation of the Book of Concord that would ultimately be released in 1921.[2] The Missouri Synod's publishing arm, Concordia Publishing House, also printed a book on the Reformation in all its aspects, edited by William H. T. Dau and entitled *Four Hundred Years*.[3] An ocean away, the Evangelical Lutheran Church of Russia was similarly compiling a set of articles into a book edited by Theophil Meier entitled *Luther's Heritage in Russia*. The book chronicled the almost 350-year history of the Lutheran Church in Russia, the authors solemnly reflecting not only on the joys but also the persecutions of the past.

In St. Petersburg, the heart of the Lutheran Church in Russia, many events were scheduled to celebrate. At St. Peter's, the largest church in the center of the city, three evenings were planned. On the first, Rev. Wilhelm Kentmann presented on the basics of the Augsburg Confession, and during the following two evenings he read Luther's work on "The Freedom of the Christian." These were followed on Reformation Day by a morning service led by Pastors Kentmann, Paul Willigerode, and Karl Walter. There was also a celebration for the youth of St. Peter's Lutheran School (called the Peterschule), with Principal Erich Kleinenberg and his assistant, Alexander Wolfius, presenting, and the girls' choir performing. The day ended with a church packed full of all the German-speaking Lutheran congregations in St. Petersburg robustly singing the hymns of the Reformation.[4]

In Moscow, a fifteen-minute walk from the Kremlin at Sts. Peter and Paul Lutheran Church, Rev. Meier spoke of the dangers threatening Lutherans in Russia: "But has not much of our sacred heritage been born in the sounds of the Reformation? Thanks be to God, the echo of revolution is silenced in our hearts by the echo of the Reformation!" The congregation followed Meier's stirring words with the singing of "A Mighty Fortress."[5] Those words of Meier would sound a theme repeated by others in the coming years: the spiritual theology and musical strains of the Reformation versus the worldly politics and atheistic anthems of the Bolshevik Revolution.

The tragic events taking place on the battlefields of Europe that Reformation Day in 1917 would soon result in a peace that would allow the Lutheran churches of Russia and America to establish more intimate contacts. The Lutherans of both nations had much in common. Questions about the loyalty of ethnic Germans in Russia and America led to suspicion among those considered more "native." Due to the very language they used in their worship services, both groups were accused of being sympathetic to Kaiser Wilhelm II's imperialistic ambitions.

But now that the "war to end all wars" had exacted destruction on an unprecedented scale, the interest of American Lutherans was drawn to the shattered lives of their brothers and sisters beyond their borders. The fact that many immigrants from the Volga region had resettled in the American Midwest virtually compelled Lutherans to take an interest. They retained contact with their families overseas and would act on the consciences of their fellow Lutherans in America in the future. So as a result of the war, American and Russian-German Lutherans began a partnership that would only take on added meaning as the Bolshevik Revolution began its assault on religion and the Lutheran Church in Russia later that year. American Lutherans would come to appreciate the deeper meaning behind the biblical phrase, "my brother's keeper," and a remarkable man would soon step to the forefront and keep the plight of Russia's Lutherans foremost in their minds for many years to come.

As the Great War wound toward its conclusion, the European continent was reduced to a vast cemetery. British historian Michael Burleigh cited the plethora of cenotaphs, memorial arches, crosses, and obelisks that proliferated throughout the European landscape and reasoned that the loss of nine million men would force future archaeologists to ponder what had led Europe to such madness. Poets and writers like Rudyard Kipling, Karl Krauss (*The Last Days of Mankind*), and Erich Maria Remarque speculated on what it all meant, lamenting this "Lost Generation."[6]

In America, sympathetic Lutherans had already been coming to terms with the pressing needs of their own parishioners serving in the war. On October 19, 1917, the Lutheran Commission for Soldiers' and Sailors' Welfare was established. Its primary task was to provide spiritual succor through the employ of Lutheran chaplains at training camps for the army and navy. Along with its concomitant "seelsorger" activity, the existence of such an organization went a long way toward ameliorating the suspicion other Americans had regarding the loyalty of German-Americans.[7]

Due to the positive results of cooperation between American Lutheran church bodies, pastors Lauritz Larsen and Frederick Knubel felt compelled to create a more permanent inter-Lutheran cooperative agency.[8] This commission soon took the form of the National Lutheran Council (NLC), founded on September 6, 1918, in the Auditorium Hotel in Chicago.[9] At its April 15, 1919, meeting, the NLC described itself as representing the majority of Lutheran churches in America: "the United Lutheran Church, the Norwegian Lutheran Church, the Augustana (Swedish) Synod, the Joint Synod of Ohio, the Synod of Iowa and other States, the Buffalo Synod, the Suomi Synod, the United Danish Church and the Lutheran Free Church."[10]

As a national organization, the NLC sought to establish representation within the halls of government in Washington, DC, to facilitate its work overseas. As they became increasingly aware of the great suffering among European Lutherans, American Lutherans could no longer ignore the cries for help. Writing to US Secretary of State Frank L. Polk, NLC Secretary Lauritz Larsen pleaded for permission "to send a commission of not more than six members to bring greetings to the Lutherans of Europe, to study ecclesiastical conditions among them, and to give such moral, spiritual and financial assistance as may be found necessary to aid them in the rehabilitation and reconstruction made necessary by the destructive influence of the great war upon their church work."[11]

In reply, William Philip, Assistant Secretary of State, recommended that three representatives be sent to France, and then only temporarily. Afterward, dependent on conditions on the European continent, they might be allowed to expand their work and visit other countries. The three chosen by the NLC were Dr. John A. Morehead, Dr. Sven G. Youngert, and Rev. G. A. Fandrey. Morehead, the president of Roanoke College in Virginia, was the chairman of the commission. His assistant, Youngert, served as a professor at Augustana Theological Seminary in Rock Island, Illinois, while Fandrey was a pastor in the

Iowa Synod.[12] Summing up his perspective on his new duties, Morehead said, "I have felt compelled to respond to the call of the Council as the call of God. ... I am heart and soul in sympathy with your instructions for the pure faith of the Gospel as laid down in the Augsburg Confession."[13] Morehead and his colleagues soon received visas to visit Lutheran churches in Europe and begin reconstruction work. Most of the initial work of the NLC was focused on the Lutherans in European nations severely affected by World War I, ranging from France to Poland.[14] Despite that massive undertaking, though, soon events of an alarming nature would draw the NLC eastward.

Morehead was by all accounts a quiet, mild-mannered Southern gentleman, a scholarly type who had limited experience overseas. He had a knowledge of German since he had taken graduate studies at Leipzig University for one year, but the task of helping restore to life the Lutheran churches in Europe would be a formidable venture. His biographer, Samuel Trexler, put it this way: "The Europe which Morehead did so much to feed after the World War was as remote to him in his early life as Mars."[15] But Morehead was not entirely unaccustomed to the concept of reconstruction. Having been born in southwest Virginia in 1867, he grew up on a farm under the trying circumstances of a nation reeling from a devastating civil war. Soon enough, Morehead would see firsthand the destruction wrought by another civil war, this one taking place in Russia amid the conditions of a horrific famine.[16]

Indeed, over the next sixteen years Morehead would develop such an intense friendship with the bishops and pastors of the Russian Lutheran Church that he would do all in his power to keep it alive despite the severe persecutions of the Communists. His health would suffer as a result, but he would use all of his contacts and resources, including a United States president, to keep a seminary functioning and pastors serving their people. Through his leadership of the NLC and the Lutheran World Convention (LWC), these two organizations would become powerful sources of financial support for the decimated Lutheran churches of Russia after war and revolution had driven them to the brink of despair.

2

"THE CHURCH IS SEPARATED FROM THE STATE"

The Bolsheviks Take Power

HOW DID THE Lutheran Church appear in a land that had been so closely tied to the Russian Orthodox Church since Vladimir the Great adopted Christianity in 988? In the sixteenth century, desiring to modernize his country, Ivan the Terrible (1547–1584) carried on the tradition of his father by inviting educated and skilled European tradesmen into Russia. Lutherans were among these tradesmen, and as they began to settle in Russian cities and villages, they asked to build their own churches. Being theologically curious, the czar asked for a statement of what they believed. The Lutherans presented him with the Augsburg Confession, which the czar rejected violently.[1] Nonetheless, since European Lutherans were essential to the workforce, Ivan allowed them to live in the Nemetskoe Sloboda (German Settlement), an area just outside the Moscow city limits. In 1576, the czar permitted the first Lutheran church, St. Michael's, to be built in Moscow.

However, four years later he reneged on his permission, calling for St. Michael's to be burned down.[2] Thus began the precarious existence of the Lutheran Church in Russia. In future years, succeeding czars would be at times repressive or favorable to the Lutheran Church. Peter the Great and Catherine the Great, for example, were more than agreeable to the presence of the Lutherans, advocating for the benefits that they could bring to Russia. Catherine would submit a manifesto on July 22, 1763, inviting Germans into Russia to settle the land of the Volga River valley. As a result, fifty-nine Lutheran churches, thirty-three Roman Catholic, and twenty-three Reformed churches were built by the settlers of the Volga.

Although Germans would constitute the bulk of Lutheran believers in Russia, the remainder of Lutherans would come from various ethnicities: Finns, Swedes, Estonians, Latvians, even Armenians. (Ethnic Russians would not be allowed to leave the state Orthodox Church and become Lutheran until political reforms secured freedom of conscience in the early twentieth century.) Extending their influence throughout the Russian Empire, Czar Alexander I (1801–1825) invited German Lutherans to settle in what constitutes modern-day Ukraine and Georgia. His brother and successor, Nicholas I (1825–1855), brought the Lutheran Church under the state's more formal control when he signed a document making him titular head of the Church, much like the King of Great Britain at the time, William IV, was considered the head of the state Anglican Church.[3]

Russian czars, many of whom had partial German ancestry, respected the role that Lutherans played in civil society, from their schools with strong academic credentials to the service they provided in governing Russia. Famed Russian conductor Modest Mussorgsky was among the many notable citizens who graduated from St. Petersburg's legendary Lutheran school, the Peterschule.[4] A further example of Lutherans' positive influence can be found in Sts. Peter and Paul pastor Heinrich Dieckhoff, who was renowned for founding schools for the deaf and blind in Moscow in the latter half of the nineteenth century.[5] The Lutheran Church was also admired for other charitable institutions, such as homes for widows and orphans, and aid they procured for the poor and destitute. The outbreak of World War I, though, caused some

Russians to doubt the loyalty of Russian Germans, leading to violence. Eighty-four Lutheran pastors were imprisoned, some exiled to Siberia. Nevertheless, in 1917 there were still 3,674,000 Lutherans and approximately 1,828 churches and prayer houses scattered throughout Russia.[6]

SHORTLY AFTER THE anniversary celebrations of the Reformation in Russia were concluded, seething anger over a seemingly pointless war and a lack of bread led Russians to rebel against their ruler, Czar Nicholas II. The three-hundred-year rule of the Romanov family was abruptly brought to an end in February 1917 as the provisional government under Alexander Kerensky took power. In the beginning, Lutherans were encouraged, perceiving the revolution as a "liberating event" for the Church.[7] Despite having lived in Russia for centuries and demonstrating their loyalty to the state, German Lutherans were often considered a "fifth column" by the Czar's administration during World War I.

The official use of the German language was forbidden at that time, although as regards church services it only seems to have affected congregations in the Ukrainian region. Still, Bibles and books could no longer be imported and charitable institutions were forcibly requisitioned by the czarist authorities. When the buildings were returned, they were in such a deplorable condition that it would cost great sums to repair them. Pastors, especially those of Baltic German heritage, were deported because they had received mission funds from abroad. Rev. Richard Walter of Sts. Peter and Paul in Moscow had his home searched seven times all because he had shown concern for prisoners of war in Moscow.

The most horrible example of the czarist regime's anti-Germanism occurred when a pogrom was carried out against the German population of Moscow in May 1915. With the Moscow police force taking a laid-back approach, a three-day riot against Russian-Germans resulted in the plundering and burning of businesses and churches, and even led to several murders.[8] Given the deteriorating relationship between Russian-Germans and the czarist government, it could hardly be a surprise that they had high hopes after the February Revolution. They were not to be disappointed, either, as the Provisional Government immediately released prisoners and allowed banned Lutheran pastors to return.[9]

In the summer of 1917, Bishop Conrad Freifeldt of Saint Petersburg was allowed to hold a church conference with the hope of forming a new ecclesiastical structure. The Lutherans under Freifeldt desired to democratize their church, allowing more rights for the congregations. Latvians, Finns, Swedes, and Estonians also participated in the conference, with the stated goal of holding a General Synod in January 1918.[10] Lutherans in Russia were cautiously optimistic that the new government would allow them to return to normal church life.[11] But in October of 1917, those hopes were dashed. The Provisional Government was usurped by a new group of anti-government rebels, Communists known as the Bolsheviks. As philosophical materialists, the Bolsheviks were intent on eradicating all traces of religion from Russian society. While they would initially move in pragmatic manner, retreating when they encountered resistance, there was little doubt that they wanted the extermination of religion within the Russian Empire.[12]

As the state church of the czars, the Russian Orthodox Church suffered the full brunt of their blows. But since Lutherans had endured persecution under the czars, in the beginning they hoped that the Bolsheviks' more democratic tendencies might allow them to survive, albeit under the rule of a government averse to religion.[13] However, the first actions of the new government were not only directed against the Orthodox but were a concerted attack on all Christian denominations.

Shortly after taking power in October 1917, the Bolshevik government set about reversing the laissez-faire attitude toward religion that the Provisional Government had held. In a general decree issued on October 26, all land was nationalized including that held by the Church. On December 11, all schools were put under state control. Five days later, the Communist Party enabled local judges to issue divorces, to be followed on December 18 with a decree that the state would only recognize civil marriages. While churches could still conduct marriages, they lost their previous authority and subsequently were ordered to transfer their birth, marriage, and death records over to the state.[14]

But matters were about get worse. These initial actions of the government were but a precursor to the landmark January 20, 1918 Decree on Separation of Church from State and School from Church. This decree would prove to be the primary operating statement of the Bolshevik government toward religion throughout the 1920s. First, by separating church from state, old traditions like the use of religious oaths and Christian symbols in state institutions and buildings were forbidden. Second, by separating school from church, Christian schools were now outlawed. Historic Lutheran schools like St. Anne's in St. Petersburg were nationalized, the former teachers for the most part fired, and a new generation of teachers employed who no longer taught religion. St. Anne's was now labeled School Number 11.[15] Other Lutheran schools also could not teach religion. Sts. Peter and Paul in Moscow, for example, lost control of its school board and saw academic standards fall precipitously.[16] St. Peter's Lutheran school in St. Petersburg was unique in that its administration and staff was given a period of grace, and it survived until principal Erich Kleinenberg and the Lutheran teachers were fired in the late 1920s.[17]

Through this January decree and the nationalization of land and property, the notion of church property had become anachronistic. Congregations, now known as "religious groups," lost their legal status and had all their property confiscated. St. Peter's Lutheran in St. Petersburg had its property valued in several millions, so this was a considerable loss.[18] If a congregation wanted to use its own building, often property that had been built and maintained for centuries, permission had to be requested from the government.[19] Although the Bolsheviks in most instances allowed the use of the buildings, their message to Christians was clear: The government now owned the buildings and could use them for any secular or anti-religious purpose they chose.[20] To receive permission to use the church building, religious groups had to form a *dvatsatka* (the Russian number for twenty) of twenty parishioners operating along the lines of a church council. The *dvatsatka* would then sign an agreement with the local authorities, who would allow them to use the building as long as they maintained and insured it.[21]

The outcome of the Bolsheviks' actions was to take religion from being a public matter and relegate it to the private sphere. An inclination toward pragmatism may have led Vladimir Lenin and other moderates to first write in the January Decree that "religion is the private affair of every citizen of the Russian Republic." He soon replaced this phrase with "the church is separated from the state."[22] Later, in July 1918, Lenin would advocate using the phrase "freedom of religious and anti-religious propaganda" in the new constitution. This sounded as if religious believers were being given equal rights with atheists in Russian society. But due to the weakening of the church through the January 20 Decree, the Bolsheviks knew well that there was no real equality of expression. They held all the cards.[23]

One of the biggest cards was the Bolsheviks' wholesale theft of church property and funds. Unlike the state Orthodox Church, the Lutheran Church had amassed a large nest of funds and been self-supporting for centuries. Hospitals, schools for the deaf, homes for the elderly, and orphanages were examples of the work of the Evangelical Lutheran Church of Russia. But now former charitable institutions, founded and maintained by the Church, instantly became state property. Although indigents were allowed to stay in homes provided by the Church, the Church would have to find additional funds to pay for fuel and board since its treasury had been siphoned off as if by professional criminals.[24]

The clergy themselves were in dire straits. Not only were the congregations' sources of income emasculated, but the pastors were labeled as "non-productive elements" by the Bolsheviks. The reality of the clergy's reduced status included the following:

1. The right to vote was taken away.

2. Food ration cards were no longer given to them.[25]

3. The parsonages were either confiscated by the state or the number of rooms was reduced. To add insult to injury, they also had to pay rent.

4. They could no longer supplement income by teaching. Many pastors had previously taught German.[26]

5. Higher taxes were enacted on them and also on their children's study in state-run schools.[27] By 1923, the children of clergy would no longer even be accepted into schools of higher education.[28]

A good example of the troubled state of the Lutheran Church was conveyed to the NLC by Rev. John Mueller of Pittsburgh in May 1919. Translating documents given to him from Russian-German Lutherans, Mueller exposed the truth behind the new society developing in Russia and its dangerous implications for their fellow Lutherans. The author of one of Mueller's letters, a former Lutheran pastor in St. Petersburg who requested anonymity, described conditions up to his departure from Russia in September 1918. To begin with, he said, the Lutheran Church is bankrupt.[29] First, the nationalizing of the banks invalidated all of the Church's substantial capital. The relief fund of the Lutheran Church, one and half million rubles (approximately $750,000), was tied up in treasury notes that had now been absconded with by the Bolshevik government. Second, the government had expropriated homes that local congregations had owned and could rent out for income. Third, although wealthy parishioners initially tried to make up for lost funds, they soon lost their savings when the government confiscated their personal funds. The parishioners were reduced to selling their furniture, paintings, and other valuables to survive until this, too, was forbidden.

The result of these actions was that pastors and church officials could no longer be paid. The classless society and the violence the Bolsheviks used to create it led to an increase in the death rate. Rich and poor alike died in the streets. Many Lutheran pastors felt compelled to move to the Baltic states and Germany, leaving behind their furnished homes with what little they had saved from their meager salaries. Others were imprisoned or exiled to Siberia. Lutheran teachers were forced out of their homes into communal apartments, taking their meals in general kitchens.[30]

AT THE SAME time these troubles were occurring, Bishop Freifeldt was engaged in secret correspondence with German diplomats. In a series of September 1918 letters, he spoke of his surprise that, given the Germanophobia in Russia since the war, even a large sector of the ethnic Russian population could no longer support the rule of the Bolsheviks and looked to Germany for help. In fact, the treaty signed between Russia and Germany was disappointing to most Russian citizens like Freifeldt, who had hoped that Germany would be "the salvation from hell" for "our country."[31] The Bolsheviks' attacks on religion had up to this point concentrated primarily on the Orthodox Church and its outspoken Patriarch Tikhon. Tikhon had placed an anathema on the Bolshevik state, calling them "agents of Satan ... monsters of the human race."[32] The confiscation of church property and the brutal murders of both Bishop Vladimir of Kiev by drunken soldiers in late January 1918 and the Czar's family in Yekaterinburg in July had been an unmistakable demonstration to the patriarch of the Bolsheviks' wicked nature.[33] After the attempted assassination of Lenin in late August by a Socialist-Revolutionary Party anarchist, Fanny Kaplan, the "Red Terror" was unleashed on the presumed enemies of the government.

With this action, "prison hostages" could be shot, among them class enemies, former czarist officers, capitalists, and priests. The goal of the terror, though, seemed to be intimidation of the masses rather than simply exacting revenge on former enemies from the czarist regime.[34] Whatever the case, the Bolsheviks did not repeat the mistake of indecisiveness and timidity that had defined the provisional government under Kerensky.

One surprising result of the hardships encountered by all Christian denominations was the ecumenical comradeship that began to develop between Lutherans and Orthodox. On September 29, 1918, Freifeldt, using his ties to the German Ministry of Foreign Affairs, took a bold step by interceding for the Orthodox Church. Freifeldt wrote, "We are in the middle of circumstances of genuine persecution towards Christians. ... Protests by the clergy of all denominations are considered counterrevolutionary, and the current government is answering with terror, but in the beginning only towards the Orthodox Church."[35] While acknowledging that not one Orthodox priest had come to the defense of Lutherans during their time of persecution during World War I, Freifeldt opted to take the high road. He asked the German diplomats to intervene on behalf of their Christian brothers in prison, including thirty-four Orthodox priests and Metropolitan Veniamin of St. Petersburg, all of whom were arrested that summer. Metropolitan Veniamin and other Orthodox priests would eventually be shot along with their lawyer in August 1922, but Patriarch Tikhon accepted the Lutheran Church's note of sympathy with thanks: "Your friendly letter we receive and accept as a pledge of the readiness of Christians of all denominations to expend all of their strength for the good of the Motherland and as the husbanding of the 'full armor of God,' standing against the 'gates of hell.' "[36] Sooner or later, Bishop Freifeldt knew that the Bolsheviks would be no respecter of denominations and that the terror would strike the Lutherans, too.

GIVEN THE ATTACKS on all Christian churches in Russia, it's not too difficult to comprehend why the average Russian citizen expressed antagonism
toward the increasingly dictatorial actions of the Bolshevik government. A
civil war broke out in December 1917 between the Bolsheviks (known as the
Reds) and the Whites, including but not exclusively supporters of the czarist
regime. It would last until 1920, when the White armies effectively fled from
Russia.[37] Lutherans were stuck in a quandary, as they had suffered under both
regimes. They preferred to be left alone, an increasingly unrealistic option in
war-torn Russia. Through all these difficulties, the NLC continued to accumulate information, but due to the conditions in Russia could not send direct
aid. The new European Commissioner for the NLC, Professor George Rygh
of the Norwegian Lutheran Synod in America, shared a letter with supporters
that he had received from twelve Finnish pastors.[38] These pastors had fled from
Russia due to the malicious actions of the Reds, who had been robbing and
burning villages in the Saint Petersburg region, an area where close to 200,000
people of Finnish or Swedish ethnicity lived. Due to White General Nikolai
Yudenich's May 1919 assault on Saint Petersburg with 20,000 Estonian troops,
those of Finnish extraction were now considered suspect and forced to join
the Red Army.

As parents and their children suffered and died from the hunger and
cold, eight thousand Lutheran parishioners succeeded in fleeing to Finland.
Having joined these refugees, the Finnish pastors appealed to the NLC in
broken English, "We have the boldness to reach unto you the hand of the
Macedonian man. Come here and help us in the restoring of the churches and
parsonages instead of the destroyed ones in the day when the bolshevism there
shall perish."[39] A thousand dollars were immediately cabled to NLC representatives in Helsinki for distribution to the refugees with the promise of more
aid in the future. In their appeal to "help build the bridge of brotherhood
between the noble people of America and us unlucky people," the Finnish

pastors articulated the NLC's desire to be about "the Master's will in helping to feed the hungry, clothe the naked."⁴⁰ The fact that these Ingrian Finns and Swedes were Lutherans reminded American Lutherans that their close relatives in the faith were suffering beyond anything that they had experienced.⁴¹

Regions in the south of Russia, primarily the Ukraine but also the Volga region, were even more horribly affected by the civil war. Rygh had been informed of conditions in the Volga in December 1919 when he met with a Russian-German pastor in Berlin, Johannes Schleuning. Schleuning was born in the Volga colonies in 1879 and had served a congregation in Saratov since 1911. But in 1918, under threat of prison and death, he fled to Germany. As the head of the Verein der Volgadeutschen (Association of Volga Germans), Schleuning appealed to the NLC for help in rebuilding the Evangelical Lutheran Church in the Volga region, where he still believed it had a role to play in expanding the gospel among the peoples of the East. He even proposed opening a new seminary in the Volga region, a testament to his zeal but also to his lack of judgment given the conditions in the country.

Aware that there were hundreds of thousands of Volga Germans in America and citing the work of Russian-German Mennonites in America, Schleuning further proposed making an NLC-sponsored visit to America to familiarize Volga German immigrants with the misery of their kin in Bolshevik Russia. To ease the immediate needs of the five hundred refugees in Germany, the NLC dispatched 25,000 Deutsch Marks to Schleuning's Verein der Volgadeutschen in Berlin.⁴²

In March 1921, through mission contacts in Leipzig, the NLC received a highly detailed report of conditions in Russia during the civil war and its aftermath. For the beleaguered Russian-German Lutherans of central and southern Russia and the Ukrainian regions, conditions appeared to be worse than in other regions of Russia.⁴³ As a matter of fact, in those areas the battles were not only between the Reds and Whites, but also included anarchist groups of soldiers roaming the countryside. The leader of the so-called Greens was the notorious militarist Nestor Makhno. Makhno's band of about 40,000 soldiers was initially allied with the Reds, but shortly after Red General Leon Trotsky had appointed him a commander, he set out on his own due to disagreements. Makhno was a genuine anarchist, supporting the abolition of all state authority. Because of his inability to remain loyal to any authority, Makhno quickly became disillusioned by the activities of the Reds and their secret police, the Cheka, especially objecting to their forcible food requisitions from the peasants. However, Makhno was no friend to the Whites, either. He called for the extermination of the rich bourgeoisie, and that meant he was especially opposed to Russian-Germans who were wealthy farmers.[44]

If the NLC had had any doubts that it must quickly do something for Lutherans in Russia, this report would have dispelled them. At the end of World War I, German troops had remained in the Ukrainian regions, so the German community there felt well-protected. But when the troops withdrew, the civil war between Reds and Whites, as well as the bands of robbers under Makhno's control, decimated the countryside. Disease and epidemics followed in the wake of war, and with the dearth of doctors and medicine, the body count rose. For example, the Lutheran congregation of Rostov-on-Don would normally experience thirty to forty deaths a year, but this number rose to two hundred to three hundred in 1920. Villages could often change hands twenty times or more during the skirmishes. Those villagers who couldn't defend themselves would often be horribly abused, and those who lived on isolated and wealthy estates rarely escaped alive. German colonists learned to form their own self-defense units to survive the attacks from so many different quarters.[45]

Life in the church was also in decline due to the civil war. Pastors were used to traveling and serving congregations in surrounding villages, but those activities came to a standstill due to unsafe conditions on the roads. Given that most pastors had already lost their bread ration cards and their parsonages and could no longer obtain new shoes or clothing, they were in a desperate state.

Two stories paint a picture of increasing despair among the Lutheran villagers in the Ukrainian and central Russian regions:

A report from Sumi, a village in the Kharkov Province: "The year 1920 has dealt our Church many heavy blows. The heaviest blow of all for us was the death of our pastor, Felix Spörer. After almost 25 years of service, he succumbed to spotted typhus, sincerely mourned and greatly missed by the congregation. Under the economic conditions now prevailing it is impossible to call another pastor. It was not even possible to invite one of Pastor Spörer's colleagues to officiate at his funeral. A member of the Consistory and a friend of the family conducted the ceremonies at the grave. Soon afterwards the widow of Spörer and her children were evicted from their home, as the parsonage was put to other uses."[46]

A report from Voronezh: "Pastor J. Fastena of Voronezh was compelled to flee last October (1919) with his family. He fled to the colony of Riebensdorf, hoping to be able to return within a short time. But in the meantime the Whites had left the city and the Reds had again taken possession. All deserted houses were plundered. So the pastor lost all his possessions. The furniture and books were used for lighting the stoves. Christmas 1919 his wife became ill and died on New Year's Eve. Her unexpected death was a terrible blow. But this was only one of his afflictions. The youngest son was lost amid the tumult and confusion of war and no one knows whether he is alive or dead. The daughter is an invalid. All efforts to return to his congregation came to naught. At present Pastor Fastena is serving the vacant parish of Riebensdorf, whose pastor, Rev, Uhle, was compelled to flee; however, he is seriously thinking of removing to Riga."[47]

But if these reports were troubling, other news from the provinces was downright horrifying. In the village of Grunau, Pastor Hohloch, described as "one of the most charming and lovable personalities among the native Colonial clergy," was martyred in most horrific fashion.[48] As Makhno's troops readied themselves for more looting, the farmers of Grunau set up a defense force for protection. Pastor Hohloch's son was a former officer and took command of the village forces. After putting up a valiant resistance, the Makhno band was victorious and sought their revenge. Pastor Hohloch was tortured for hours and mutilated until he died from his wounds. The son, hearing his father's cries, shot himself to avoid the torture. Another son perished in the battle. The widow fled to the village of Berdyansk with her children.[49]

On November 14, 1920, the civil war officially came to an end, the overwhelming manpower and weapons of the Red Army too much for the Whites to overcome. Close to one million soldiers from both Reds and Whites died in battle, but over two million died from disease, malnutrition, cold, and suicide. Even more damaging to Russia, almost two million citizens emigrated abroad, most of them professionals and representatives of the intellectual class.[50] For the Lutheran villages and city churches, life would never be the same. Especially in the villages, a way of life had been destroyed—a harmonic relationship between fellow Lutherans that had been established since Catherine the Great invited Germans to settle the lands of the Volga region and southern Russia in the middle of the eighteenth century. Pastors, many of them of foreign origin, fled back to their historic homelands. Villages and churches were burned and destroyed. Of the 160 German Lutheran congregations remaining in Russia by March 1921, half of them were said to be without pastors. Church life had ground to a virtual halt. If anything of the former life was to be salvaged, a nation that had not been severely affected by the world war would have to provide aid. In other words, the NLC needed to find a way into Russia.[51]

"ANY PROOF OF BROTHERLY LOVE"

Finding a Way to Aid Russia

WITH THE END of the civil war and the land in ruin, starvation was on the horizon in the countryside. In an April 23, 1921 letter to Carl Paul, a professor at Leipzig University and the director of Leipzig Missionswerk, General Superintendent of the Evangelical Lutheran Church of Russia Theophil Meier spoke of the possibility of a bad harvest in the south. Since the pastors had little to no means of income for the foreseeable future, Meier wrote to Paul about his plan to support pastors and their families. Through the diplomatic pouch of the German Foreign Office, he proposed that they could receive funds from those of German Lutheran heritage around the world. His source would be Gustav Hilger (1886–1965), a German embassy representative based in Moscow. Hilger would direct the relief actions of the German Foreign Office for those suffering from the famine in Russia (1921–1922).[1]

Meier spoke about the "indescribable difficulties" that Lutheran pastors had experienced through the recent wars, so he was looking for "any proof of brotherly love." He proposed a great "help program" (*Hilfsaktion*) sponsored by Americans and interested parties from other lands like Germany. Since it was difficult to get clothing and goods directly to people, and cash would have been even more difficult, Meier proposed putting funds into a bank in a city like

New York. The pastors could then accumulate a pension and aid for depen-
dents if they died, contingent on their remaining in service to the Lutheran
Church in Russia. Although pastors wouldn't be able to receive the accumulated funds just yet, the fact that they had money secured in a safe bank would
help them remain at their posts until conditions improved.[2] Meier especially
appealed to the generosity of Americans, represented by John Morehead, but
the proposed action would have to be conducted in the strictest of secrecy. Still
smarting from foreign intervention in northern Russia during the civil war,
the Bolsheviks now labeled personal relations with foreign powers as a state
offense, subject to imprisonment. Meier cautioned that any correspondence be
kept to a minimum and be sent through Hilger. If any personal messenger was
to be sent to Paul from him, the password to be used would be *Pastorenhilfe*
("pastors help").[3]

While Meier's original plan of relief would ultimately not be enacted, in
time his idea of providing regular support for pastors and their families would.
Meanwhile, his password soon began to bear fruit, as he received *Pastorenhilfe*
from Fritdjof Nansen, a famous Arctic explorer, later that summer. Russians
had long admired Nansen, and this allowed him to assist through his aid organization, Nansenhilfe.[4] But despite his fame, he still was not able to create a path
for the NLC to enter Russia. Writing to NLC Secretary Lauritz Larsen earlier
in April, Nansen informed him that he had perhaps promised too much when
he said that he would negotiate with the Bolsheviks for the NLC's entry into
Russia.[5] Larsen appreciated his honesty and reassured Nansen that the NLC,
after consultation with the US State Department, was convinced that it was
not the proper time to enter Russia. Furthermore, Larsen also worried about
the strain such an undertaking would be for the fifty-four-year-old Morehead,
who would be working in "unsettled conditions." And yet, no doubt with the
March 21 report on conditions in Russia fresh in his mind, Larsen admitted that
the "thousands of innocent sufferers in that ill-fated land" were not far from the
thoughts of the NLC.[6] As a result, he wrote to General Superintendent Meier

and Bishop Freifeldt on May 13 that the Evangelical Lutheran Church in Russia was not far from their thoughts at the NLC, praying that "the Almighty Lord of the Church" would give them strength in their trials and suffering and persistence to remain faithful to "God's revealed truth." Although the NLC had decided it could not yet find a way into Russia, it was determined "to realize the plans of love and service as soon as possible."[7]

While Morehead was administering NLC aid to Europe, he made the acquaintance of Fritz Tömmler of Nansenhilfe. They met at the Hotel Adlon in Berlin on July 31, where Tömmler gave Morehead firsthand information on the conditions in Russia. Through the ministrations of Tömmler, who carried letters as he traveled back and forth between Berlin and Saint Petersburg (known then as Petrograd), Bishop Freifeldt was able to converse with those in the West without censorship. Morehead was also finally able to give NLC funds to Freifeldt through Tömmler. The 10,000 Reichmark gift was for clothing to be distributed to Lutheran pastors and their families in Petrograd.[8]

Freifeldt also wrote to Paul in August, thanking him for the assistance that the Leipzig Missionswerk had rendered to the Russian Lutheran Church through Tömmler. Two million Soviet rubles had been delivered to General Superintendent Meier in Moscow, although they had unfortunately paid three times the accepted rate to purchase those rubles in Berlin. (They had paid 10,000 Reichsmarks.) The funds had been sent to needy churches in the Yaroslavl and Samara regions, where a cholera epidemic as well as a potentially very poor harvest were making life exceedingly difficult.

Conditions were indeed very bad in the Volga region. Prices were spiraling out of control for basic foodstuffs and clothing throughout the country. As a result, expenditures were quickly dwarfing income. As prices rose, and especially prices for wood used as heating fuel, the coming winter looked grimmer than the previous one. Still, because of the help that had arrived, many pastors would remain at their posts. As a native of Estonia, Freifeldt even confessed that he had entertained thoughts of emigration, especially since he had a wife and four young children (only two were of school age, though, and he was seventy-four years old, celebrating his fiftieth year in the ministry in 1921!). But with the securing of American help through the NLC, Freifeldt now saw the "finger of God" urging him "to remain here longer."[9]

Writing to Larsen in German to express his appreciation, Freifeldt greeted him as he had been greeted, "You who were formerly unknown, are now known." Apologizing that he could not read English, Freifeldt reminded Larsen that they had a deeper language in common: the language of the heart that unites the children of God. Acknowledging the receipt of what came to two million rubles, he spoke of the "mountain of need" that had accumulated among the pastors and their families. But just when it seemed to overwhelm and bury them, from the hills came their salvation![10] These steps by the NLC would initiate a sustained program of aid that would last until well into the 1930s.

Adding to the hope of the NLC to alleviate economic conditions in Russia, the famed Russian writer Maxim Gorky now signaled to the Western world the Bolsheviks' willingness to allow aid. Although Patriarch Tikhon had already announced such an appeal, in late July the Bolsheviks allowed Gorky's "To All Honest People" to be published in the West. Gorky spoke of a crop failure brought on by drought—leaving out the forced food requisitions as well as the lax response of the Bolsheviks to the obvious signs of danger. In his appeal, he avoided mention of Lenin and Trotsky but did draw on Russian cultural figures whom Europeans and Americans admired, crying, "Gloomy days have come to the country of Tolstoy, Dostoevsky, Mendeleev, Pavlov, Mussorgsky, Glinka, etc."[11] As difficult and humiliating as it was to grovel to the West, the situation was perilous enough that the Bolsheviks had little choice. They knew that their country, and their hold on political power, could not survive without help. The way was now open for what would become a flood of foreign aid, and the NLC would play a key role working among their fellow Lutherans.

A quasi-private agency known as the ARA (American Relief Administration) had already been distributing over $150 million worth of food to children in

central, eastern, and southeastern Europe and the Middle East since the end of
World War I. The ARA was the brainchild of Herbert Hoover, a mining engineer who had been appointed to manage American food aid in postwar Europe
by President Woodrow Wilson. After contentious negotiations, Russian negotiator Maxim Litvinov and his American counterpart, Walter Lyman Brown,
signed on August 20 what became known as the Riga Agreement between the
Bolshevik government and the ARA. The Bolshevik government was obliged
to bear the costs for transportation, facilities, and supplies while the ARA provided money for the food. Litvinov did, however, insist that an official from the
Bolshevik government be allowed on the ARA's local food committee. This
would prove problematic in the future, especially for Lutheran pastors who
assisted with food distribution.[12]

Taking advantage of this open door, Morehead worked furiously to get
the NLC into Russia under the administration of the ARA. Hoover recognized the NLC's experience and allowed access to the ARA's warehouses and
food supplies.[13] The NLC would reimburse the ARA for the food for which it
had contracted. Furthermore, no private American organization would accept
clothing for shipment to Russia, but the ARA would. Morehead had been
waiting for this opportunity, so by November he was on his way to the Russian
border. At long last, he would personally experience the conditions that he
had read about in Russia.[14]

ON DECEMBER 10, Morehead arrived in Moscow in Colonel William
Haskell's private train compartment. Haskell was a 1901 West Point graduate
and a veteran of World War I. After the war, he had served under Herbert
Hoover in providing food relief to Romania and Armenia. Now the ARA's
primary task was to provide food for children, a duty in which the NLC would
also participate. The ARA had opened a kitchen in Petrograd on September 6,
but given the extent of the need, adults would soon be added to the number of

those served by food aid.¹⁵ As he had traveled through western Russia to Moscow, Morehead noted the extreme cold, wondering how the Volga Germans could survive such a climate, poorly fed and clothed as they were. Ensconced in the comfortable train compartment, Morehead read up on current conditions in Russia, perusing a recently published book by British journalist Arthur Ransome, *The Crisis in Russia*. Ransome was favorably inclined toward the Bolshevik experiment in Russia (but not in Britain), but Morehead was seeking to gather information from any quarter to wisely aid Christians in Russia.¹⁶

Morehead set to work gathering information, first from the ARA and then from Lutheran Church officials. The ARA knew where the famine was at its worst, so Morehead was able to divine from their records the probable situation of Lutheran citizens. Then Morehead met General Superintendent Meier, learning from him how many Lutherans were affected by the famine and where they were located. The congregations were scattered from Petrograd northward to the White Sea, then south to Odessa on the Black Sea, and finally out to the vast reaches of Siberia. Morehead came to appreciate that "Russia is a country of splendid distances." He recognized the impossibility of traveling two thousand miles from Moscow to Odessa and then waiting for instructions from the New York offices of the NLC on how to proceed. It would take at least six weeks, so he decided to become an affiliate of the ARA, requesting that three representatives be allowed on the ARA's Russian staff: himself, Pastor W. L. Scheding, and Pastor A. C. Ernst. Morehead then worked out a plan with Haskell: The NLC would devote approximately $15,000 a month to the feeding of children (the ARA's program), then use $17,000 for the feeding of adults.¹⁷ The money would be deposited in an ARA bank account in New York City. From that account, the NLC would draw the appropriate amount of money or food throughout the month. At the end of the month, the Moscow office of the ARA would cable the amount of NLC expenditures during that month, and the NLC would pay it. The plan required the NLC to keep the account in New York maintained at the level of $32,000.¹⁸

Included in the $17,000 for adults was the feeding of Russian pastors and their families. Morehead decided that a $10 food package, along with an additional monetary gift, would be given monthly to the remaining pastors to help them and their families survive. Since the Bolshevik Revolution in 1917, pastors had left in droves due to lack of material support, the Church had lost its property and thus a main source of its income to pay pastors, and persecution was widespread, affecting pastors' ability to teach and subjecting them to claims of espionage. In addition to these problems, Lutheran children were now educated in Communist schools, subject to atheist education. The concern for their children's future was the final straw for many pastors and their wives who had decided to leave the country. But since the NLC stipends had been put into effect, only one pastor had left Russia. For Morehead, the stipends accentuated the importance of the NLC's work in keeping pastors on the field.[19]

Volga German immigrants in America desired to send food packages, but they didn't trust the Communist government to deliver them. This had been one of the more contentious issues in the negotiations of the Riga Agreement between Litvinov and Brown. The Americans insisted on the right to deliver individual food packages, which had proved so successful in Central Europe. The Bolsheviks knew, though, that those packages would most likely be sent by those who had fled Russia during the Bolshevik Revolution. Valuing control of its citizenry, the Soviets were suspicious of permitting closer contact between their citizens and foreigners, especially those who had deserted the Communist experiment. In addition, the proposed program of a food remittance package would also be structured to profit the ARA. For example, each $10 food package would bring a $2.25 profit. ARA saw this as a way to funnel more funds into food procurement, although Hoover certainly was not above giving a good lesson in capitalism. The Bolsheviks were not amused.

After a week of tough negotiations, the Communist government signed on to the agreement after being assured that they could control the program and ultimately terminate it after three months. The program would work in the following way: A person would send a food package to the ARA, who would then locate the recipient through the post. The recipient would then go to a local distribution center in Russia and pick up his package. But for those giving to the NLC, the benefactor could sidestep the ARA and send a check to the NLC office in New York with the name of the recipient. Morehead or one of his assistants would then contact that person and make sure the package was received. Morehead would then draw on his account with the ARA in Moscow and the NLC would resupply their New York bank account, keeping it at the $32,000 level. The packages were no small matter for the recipients. It was estimated that each one would feed a family of three for one month. Package included forty-nine pounds of flour; twenty-five pounds of rice; three pounds of tea; ten pounds of fat; ten pounds of sugar; and twenty one-pound cans of preserved milk, adding up to 117 pounds in total! Although food packages could be delivered, many recipients during severe famine periods would rather go to the distribution point than trust the mail system. In the end, for most Russians the ARA became synonymous with food and therefore life.[20]

The effect of the food packages on the Lutheran pastors and their families was immediate. Pastor Arthur Kluck, serving in the village of Frank in the Volga region, had assisted in the distribution but now experienced the other side of American generosity. As he wrote to Ernst to express his thanks, he related how his own household was weakened by sickness and in need. His wife, Bertha, was nursing their firstborn. His father had just gotten over spotted typhus, while his sister was laid up with spotted typhus and inflammation of the lungs. The widow of a local pastor named Somelt was destitute. But now, through the generosity of the American Lutherans, all of them would survive. Kluck eloquently summed up the impact of these gifts:

> The world has never seen what the Americans in our hunger regions have done. It is hard to grasp it. ... But even more important than the physical is the spiritual, the inner help, that we have experienced from

our brothers in the faith. We now know that they are carrying us over there within their prayerful hearts; they want to help, to build up again the broken church, they come with faith and their Christian love ... and we gain new courage, new hope, receive new power ... then one can be comforted: in the Kingdom of God there is yet life. The cause of Jesus Christ will last into all eternity. But above all there is one thing: we will never forget that you didn't leave us lying in our own blood; you didn't put a price on the hunger and epidemics; you didn't let us doubt and die on the inside. No, on the contrary. You reached your brotherly hand across the wide ocean, you lifted us up in body and soul, you bound up our wounds, and you healed us from our pains. And even if thousands of obstacles are placed in our way, they can be overcome in the Faith that can set us high upon a rock. "This has been from the Lord and it is wonderful in our eyes."[21]

THIS HUMANITARIAN WORK was not without its politically motivated critics. The "Northwest Scandinavian Section of the Friends of Soviet Russia" criticized Hoover for "imposing imperialistic and reactionary conditions" on Russia through its program of food aid. Calling for "Famine Relief without Counter Revolutionary Conditions," the Soviet sympathizers appealed to not only feed those who were starving but to support the Russian workers' revolution.[22] Since they were seeking the support of Americans of Scandinavian background, Lauritz Larsen felt compelled to rebut them in a letter to the editor of *Skandinaven*, based in Chicago. Larsen spoke on behalf of Lutheran Americans of Swedish, Danish, and Norwegian ethnicity like himself. Decrying the impulse to inject politics into a humanitarian tragedy, Larsen informed the editor that the NLC was working with the only entity that could do anything in Russia at that time: the ARA. Anyone wanting to help the people of Russia was better off working with a truly American organization like the ARA.[23]

Criticisms of the ARA were part of a larger attempt by Communists in the United States to fool average Americans into supporting the Bolshevik regime in Russia. Dr. David Dubrowsky took over as the representative for the Bolsheviks in America when the so-called Bolshevik ambassador to the United States, Ludwig Martens, was deported. While Dubrowsky admitted to being a representative of the Bolshevik government, he would not admit that the Russian Red Cross was affiliated with the Communist state. He and other Soviet sympathizers fund-raised under the organization "The American Committee for Russian Famine Relief." On January 2, 1922, a meeting was held in Chicago in support of the starving in Russia, where the Communist beliefs of the participants were on display. Rousing cheers were heard for Lenin, Trotsky, and the Bolshevik government in Russia as well as the Communist Party of the United States (CPUSA). Isaac McBride, who worked for the American Committee for Russian Famine Relief, would funnel funds through Dubrowsky, who in turn passed the money along to the Russian Red Cross. As McBride asserted, "We are going to milk the bourgeoisie of this country, and they will help us to keep up the struggle against themselves."[24] The 1922 "Memorandum upon the Russian Red Cross" relayed all this information to Lauritz Larsen so that he could inform any potential supporters of NLC aid to Russia that not all relief organizations were committed to non-political goals.[25]

With Larsen taking care of the information war with the Communists in America, Morehead set out for the Volga in a special Russian Pullman car, accompanied by General Superintendent Meier and his wife Eugenie. Between themselves they conversed in German, which Morehead had learned in his days at the University of Leipzig. As Morehead's assistant, Meier was officially recognized as an employee of the ARA by the Soviet government. This association would prove troublesome for other pastors working with Morehead, and Meier may have suffered some consequences, but he seems to have been able to escape this scrutiny relatively unscathed before his natural death in 1934.[26]

Using a comfortable automobile secured for them by the Soviet government, Meier, Ernst, and Morehead drove to the Volga River Valley capital, Saratov, in February 1922. Nansenhilfe, the Swedish Red Cross, and Britain's Save the Children were also working in the region. According to government records, the percentage of those citizens suffering from hunger grew from 56.7 percent in August 1921 to 96.9 percent by the time Morehead made his first visit.[27] People would flood into cities like Saratov when the food supply was exhausted in the villages, crowding into government homes that were nothing more than unheated barracks. The temperature had plummeted to 16 degrees below zero on the day that he arrived. Numerous cases of spotted typhus were recorded in the barracks. The stench was overwhelming, yet the people remained because even in such dire conditions it was better than starving. Morehead commented on the scene unfolding before his eyes: "If Dante ever imagined a more horrible scene, he failed to include it in his Divine Comedy."[28] Indeed, what Morehead saw in Russia in 1921–1922 would remain with him for the rest of his life. It would motivate him to superhuman feats of perseverance whenever he became tired of the travel or Soviet perfidy.

While visiting the Volga Lutheran village of Krasnii Yar, Morehead and his entourage made the acquaintance of a not-untypical family. The husband had left three days before for Saratov to find work. The wife, an attractive woman thirty years old, attempted to greet them but fell back quickly onto her chair from exhaustion. One child lay dead on a cot while another lay sick with fever. Later, as they traveled further south to Kharkov in the Ukraine, they met Pastor Stender, a native of Courland (modern-day Latvia) and the twelfth of a line of pastors in his family going back to 1635. His congregation could no longer pay him, and two of his children had died of tuberculosis, while two of the four remaining were suffering from the same disease, along with his wife.[29]

This exhausting winter 1922 journey throughout the Volga, Ukraine, and Crimea would introduce Morehead to many of the extraordinary pastors populating the Lutheran village churches in Russia. In the moments of trial in the not-too-distant future, Morehead would do everything in his power to secure the pastors' freedom from imprisonment and provide support to their families. It was not an easy journey, with the danger of communicable disease (spotted typhus was especially prevalent) and crime ever present. As General Superintendent Meier said, "Whoever takes a long journey nowadays goes like a soldier onto the battlefield, not knowing whether or how he will come back."[30] The danger of travel in Russia during the famine would be conveyed to Morehead when he met with Pastor Georg Rath on his way to Crimea. Surprised by the bedraggled appearance of the pastor, who headed a large district of churches in the Ukraine, Morehead was at first taken aback. But after conversing with him about establishing a committee to distribute the food, Morehead offered him his extra set of clothes. Rath replied that he was not ashamed of his appearance, as thieves had robbed him of his best clothes two weeks before on a train while he was returning from a visit to a mission congregation. "But, oh, how thankful I am that you can give me a decent suit for this committee meeting."[31] Such experiences were not uncommon for Russians traveling in those days but were a revelation to Morehead.

General Superintendent Meier was soon forced to leave the Americans in Saratov, as he had to attend to his own large parish in Moscow and preparations for the Lenten season. Morehead then continued his journey farther south to the Black Sea port of Odessa. There he found about fifty thousand Lutherans in the Odessa district, including Latvians, Swedes, and Germans. He described the parishioners as "educated, developed, stable, earnest, conservative, faithful people."[32] One of the men who made a strong impression on him was Albert Koch, the pastor in the neighboring village of Grossliebenthal. Koch served on a committee appointed by Morehead that assured Germans in America that the funds they sent would get to their relatives in Russia.[33] Morehead would later describe Koch as "a lovable character, energetic in devotion to his work as a Christian minister, and fearless in the performance of his duties."[34] Koch would work closely with Morehead's coworker, W. L. Scheding, who would come on the field in autumn of that year.[35]

As he traveled to the Crimean Peninsula and the northern shores of the Black Sea, Morehead made the acquaintance of veteran pastor Ferdinand Hörschelmann.[36] Hörschelmann's dignified white mane testified to his long years of pastoral experience, having served the congregation of Neusatz in the Crimea since 1887. The father of eleven children (with only eight surviving at the time of Morehead's visit), Hörschelmann was born in 1855 of Baltic German stock in the vicinity of Reval (today known as Tallinn, Estonia). Hörschelmann matriculated at Yuryev University in Dorpat (1876–1882), the primary university for seminarians serving Lutheran congregations in Russia since its opening in 1801. Hörschelmann was a respected preacher who continued to boldly preach in German during World War I, when the German language was banned in sermons.[37]

Hörschelmann became a coworker with Morehead in the distribution of food and clothing to the thirty thousand Lutherans in the Crimea. On his own initiative, Hörschelmann established a congregational committee for the distribution of humanitarian aid and a free kitchen for those of any denomination.[38] While Hörschelmann worked, he saw that human nature was making the distribution of clothing more complicated. Writing to Scheding about the Christmas 1922 delivery, he lamented that in times of scarcity, the old adage of "one for all and all for one" quickly goes by the wayside. Too often the committee would succumb to giving support to those who were poor due to laziness or sluggishness. Hörschelmann believed it was unjust to do this. Meanwhile, the government was busy propagandizing the lower classes, telling them that they were being exploited by the kulaks, or bourgeoisie. Hörschelmann wanted his people to value hard work and thrift, so he advised the NLC to permit the pastors to manage the distribution of food and clothing as they would do it more equitably.

Perhaps nothing summed up the situation facing the pastors and parishioners in Russia better than a letter Pastor Alexander Streck of the Volga village of Grimm sent to Ernst in May 1922. In it, Streck carefully laid out the pressures that had been weighing on pastors like him since 1918. Without an organized church due to the October Revolution, the Communists had tried to set up a rival church in the Volga region under their influence. In November 1918, Streck and pastors Eduard Eichorn (Ust-Zolicha) and Friedrich Wacker (Norka) had been called to a special session with the Bolshevik authorities. The commissar, David Schultz, was to be the head of a Volga church that would have no connection to the General Consistory in Moscow under the General Superintendent, Paul Willigerode. The proposed church would ostensibly represent the interests of the people/parishioners, while the taler (pastoral collar) and the collection plate were to be forbidden as counter-revolutionary. When Wacker objected to the plan, he was kicked off the church committee. Streck himself was threatened with prison because he had engaged in secret communications with Willigerode. In short, a coup had taken place.

In 1919, the Russian civil war came to Streck's village when General Denikin's White Army had a major engagement with the Red Army and lost. After the battle, Schultz was called away further south to the village of Rosenberg and the proposed church in the Upper Volga region seemed to have been forgotten by the state for the moment. But the saddest effect of these troubled times was the people were losing faith in God and drifting away from the Church. Reflecting on all the vices becoming prominent in the Volga region— hatred, envy, wrath, broken marriages—Streck quoted Isaiah 1:5, declaring, "the whole head is sick and the whole heart is faint." But when conditions appeared to be at a nadir, the gifts from the NLC arrived: "But like lightning from the distant heavens came ... the gifts of love from American Lutherans, the gifts which should strengthen the body and will be accompanied by hopes and prayers that would contribute to the faith and love to the Church."[39] Since many pastors had fled the region after it had been flung into poverty and the civil war had raged about them, it would be difficult to deny that the American Lutheran aid had literally saved them.

As the feeding program continued to expand for the NLC, it decided to add another American worker: Gustav Beschorner, who was commissioned by the NLC as its official lay representative in the Volga region, effective January 16.[40] Born of German parents in 1880 in the old Austro-Hungarian empire, Beschorner made his way to America in 1902. In a typical American success story, he worked in the steel mills of Pittsburgh, learning enough English to study at a business college in Lincoln, Nebraska. There he earned his degree in 1904. More recently, he had been the circulation manager for a German-language newspaper, the *Omaha Daily Tribune*. While working at the newspaper, he became acquainted with the many Germans from Russia populating the Midwest and had been moved by their faith. Beschorner would be responsible to the ARA, who would manage the work of establishing kitchens in a particular famine area. The NLC, for its part, would provide the funds for the kitchen and also pay Beschorner as its employee. He in turn would travel throughout the Volga region, making sure the kitchens were operating effectively. The kitchens would be labeled: "American Relief Organization, maintained by the National Lutheran Council of America."[41]

After his long journey and return to Moscow from the Crimea, Morehead was feeling the effects of travel in a famine-wracked land. When he arrived, he had a fever and was vomiting blood, the result of an internal ulcer.[42] Although he soldiered on in Russia for several more months, it was evident that he would need to get medical care outside of Russia. So on May 31, Morehead and Ernst left Moscow for Western Europe. Having just completed yet another trip through the Ukraine and the Crimea, before he left Russia Morehead appealed to the ARA to raise the monthly NLC support to $43,000 until the harvest. This additional aid would be focused primarily on the Ukraine (the Odessa, Alexandrovsk, and Ekaterinoslav districts), the Crimea, Rostov-on-Don, and the northern Caucasus regions.[43] Ernst happily reported to the ARA that the five months of NLC operations in the Volga had been so successful that virtually no deaths were reported from starvation except for refugees. The old can-do spirit had revived among the Volga Germans as they returned to their fields, refreshed and apparently sowing twice as much land as the previous year. Ernst noted that even though horses and oxen had died or been eaten by many families, they themselves plowed the fields with a renewed spirit. The NLC could take pride in the fact that it had saved countless lives among the Volga Lutherans.[44]

4

A POWERFUL, INVISIBLE HAND FROM THE DARK

The Malevolent Might of the Cheka

WITH ALL THE Americans except Beschorner out of the field for the NLC, there was a need for additional personnel. NLC Secretary Lauritz Larsen set sail for Europe on July 29, providing temporary assistance until another pastor could be sent.[1] But since A. C. Ernst was also ready to return to America on July 21, in order to keep the work of feeding moving forward General Superintendent Theophil Meier offered the services of a seminary student named Kurt Muss.[2] Muss was a native of Saint Petersburg, born in 1896 to an ethnic German family that owned an engraving business. He had been educated in the highly respected Lutheran schools, attending St. Anne's school in his hometown before moving on to Yuryev University in Dorpat (1916–1918). After the Bolshevik Revolution and Estonia's subsequent independence from Russia, Muss was forced to leave Dorpat and return home. Desiring to continue his theological studies, he enrolled as an auditor at the Petrograd Orthodox Theological Institute in March 1922, making it clear that he was Lutheran and would not serve in the Orthodox Church. After two semesters, arrangements were made for Muss to continue his Lutheran theological education at the University of Leipzig for the winter semester. Bishop Conrad Freifeldt had even intended to ordain him as a pastor later that year, but Muss first agreed to replace Morehead and Ernst for the summer.³ Until his planned departure for Leipzig, Muss covered a significant region in southern Russia for the NLC.

Muss would prove to be an energetic, highly efficient worker, having a heart for people and genuinely committed to the propagation of the gospel. When the ARA official told him that there seven hundred food packages for both Rostov and the northern Caucasus, he had a decision to make. There was no official agreement to work in the northern Caucasus and Muss had only been asked to prepare for future work in that region, the plan being for Morehead to continue after his recovery. But as the need was growing and there was no help on the horizon, Meier gave Muss permission to distribute the food.⁴ They decided that alleviating the suffering of the people was more important than paper agreements.⁵ Unfortunately, this decision would attract the attention of the Russian secret police known as the Cheka.

AS LARSEN WAS crossing the border into Russia in August, he and an ARA courier seemed to be the only passengers in their car not traveling to a convention to celebrate the fifth anniversary of the Bolshevik Revolution. As they crossed from Latvia into Russia, the other passengers burst into a chorus of the Internationale (the Communist anthem) in twelve different languages. Larsen had recently attended an international conference for Protestants in Copenhagen before arriving in Russia. During that conference, the participants sang "A Mighty Fortress" in a variety of languages. Reflecting on these two incidents, Larsen summed up the coming spiritual battle in Russia and all of Europe: "The forces of Christianity are trying to get the Christians of the world to sing together. The forces of anti-Christians are trying to get their people and those who may still be Christians to unite with them in singing their godless, materialistic and revolutionary and orthodoxical songs." Addressing the board of the NLC, Larsen concluded, "And gentlemen, the struggle between these two forces is best understood after a visit to Russia."[6]

Morehead had already begun to see the danger of the Communist indoctrination of a new generation into their materialistic beliefs. He heard from a pastor in Alexandrovsk of the Ukraine that during school celebrations at Christmastime 1921, the new Communist principal of the former Lutheran school remarked how the children were accustomed to getting presents at Christmas. He then told them, "Kneel down and pray to your God for Christmas gifts." When none appeared after their prayers, he said, "Ask this Soviet government for Christmas gifts."[7] After the children had asked the Soviet government, "the curtains were drawn back and there was a beautiful Christmas tree and there were presents for all the children and there were songs." The Soviets were using every means to fight for the souls of future generations. The NLC would have to counteract their propaganda, doing everything in its power to help their fellow Lutherans stand firm in the faith.

As Larsen traveled around the Lutheran colonies, he increasingly saw the need to publicize the reasons for NLC activity in Russia. Because of this concern, he tended to chafe at the lack of acknowledgment for Christian support given to the work of the ARA. When he went to Colonel Haskell with his complaints, Haskell cautioned him to be patient. The ARA was already planning to leave Russia in August, and the NLC would need a separate agreement with the Soviet government to continue operations. The government would view with hostility any emphasis on their Christian faith.

Larsen described Soviet officials as "arrogant and self-satisfied," recognizing in them a determined foe.[8] The government was intent on controlling independent thought in the nation; during Larsen's brief tenure approximately 220 intellectuals were expelled from Russia (including their wives and children) in what British historian Lesley Chamberlain has labeled Lenin's "Paper Civil War." After a letter from Lenin to the leader of the Cheka, Feliks Dzerzhinsky, the secret police began rounding up and cleansing the country of influential philosophers, journalists, and historians in mid-August (when Larsen would have arrived in Russia). The "Philosophy Steamer" (so called because most intellectuals left the country via ship) included such brilliant intellects as religious philosophers Nikolai Berdyaev and Sergei Bulgakov, as well as Evgeny Zamyatin (author of the dystopian novel *We*, about an all-powerful state).[9] Similarly, the Catholic bishop of Petrograd was harassed and placed on trial for not agreeing to certain statements of the government. Although the bishop was eventually given a suspended sentence, the Orthodox Metropolitan of Petrograd, Veniamin, was not so fortunate. In the first major trial of church figures, Veniamin was accused of fomenting counter-revolution by agitating against the Soviet government. At this time, the government was seeking to confiscate church valuables in order to sell them for famine relief. Even though the Metropolitan had basically agreed to hand over church valuables, the Soviet government wanted to make an example of him and portray the Orthodox Church as a proponent of counter-revolution. Although Veniamin had not advocated violence, many of the Orthodox faithful were outraged by the charges and responded angrily to his arrest and those of other clerics. Nine separate Petrograd Orthodox churches met the Soviets with physical resistance when they came to remove church valuables.[10]

The issue of the requisition of church valuables dated to February 26 of that year, when the Soviet government issued a decree calling on the churches to give up all gold, silver, or precious stones under the pretext of assisting famine relief. Two days later, Patriarch Tikhon threw down the gauntlet, stating that this would be impossible for the Church.[11] In its defense, the Orthodox Church had hardly been indifferent to the people's suffering. Tikhon had in the summer of 1921 organized special collections for famine victims, including appeals to foreign countries for aid.[12] But when it came to the requisition of church valuables, he threatened to defrock priests and excommunicate laymen who turned over "consecrated vessels."[13] Things reached a boiling point on March 13 when Soviet officials raided an Orthodox church after a Monday service in Shuia, a small industrial town just north of Moscow. Parishioners responded with fury against the Soviet officials, driving them out of the church. Two days later, the Soviets returned with troops and fired on the large crowd of parishioners defending their church, reportedly killing four or five of them. Although accounts differ as to the numbers, it appears that approximately ten parishioners and five soldiers were seriously injured in the clashes. The result of the government's violent action was that 120 pounds of silver items were confiscated from the church.[14]

We now know from documents made public in the 1990s that Lenin seized on this issue to smash the Orthodox Church. Calling this moment "uniquely favorable," Lenin believed that with the famine at its height, people would not be sympathetic to a Church that hoarded its treasures or that could be portrayed as having done so. Making a direct appeal for violence, he rallied his comrades, saying, "We must now give the most decisive and merciless battle to the Black Hundreds clergy and subdue its resistance with such brutality that it will not forget it for decades to come. ... The greater the number of the representatives of the reactionary bourgeoisie and reactionary clergy that we will manage to execute in this affair, the better."[15] Although Patriarch Tikhon recognized the church's dilemma and offered to raise an amount of money equivalent to the church's valuables, this was not acceptable to Lenin. As a result, Tikhon was arrested in May and the issue of confiscating church valuables continued to foment disorder in the country, leading up to trials in Petrograd in August.[16] The Orthodox people were in a fighting mood, convinced that they were fighting for their Church's very existence. They would not be wrong.

The contrast with the Lutherans was striking. When Superintendent Meier was informed by the government that churches should submit their gold and silver valuables to the state, he called for a meeting of church members at Sts. Peter and Paul in Moscow. Feelings ran high against submitting to the government in this request. After all, the silver communion set had been in the church for over a hundred years. Morehead recalled the manner in which Meier addressed his parishioners, with "great love and tenderness": Paraphrasing Meier's words, Morehead said:

> My beloved people! My children in the Lord! Let us not resist our own government to which we are in duty bound to be loyal but let us obey the laws and deliver up these sacred vessels of the church as our sacrifice that the starving may be fed. Should they require us to give up, besides these sacred vessels, our church itself and even that sacred volume, the Bible in the pulpit; if the Word of God be held in faith in our hearts, they cannot rob us of our God and Savior and of our holy religion. If we were robbed of this historic building, the Church of our fathers and all it contains, the church of God among us would not be destroyed, for the true church is the workmanship of the Holy Spirit through Word and Sacrament; the true church is a temple built of human stones, the hearts and souls of those who trust and follow the Lord Jesus in sincerity and in truth. In all things pertaining to the order of this world, we must obey the law as good citizens, but in all things belonging to conscience and the essential things of the Christian religion, we must obey God rather than man.[17]

Meier's words were a forthright exposition of the Lutheran doctrine of church and state, God and Caesar. Church silver was not essential to the church's existence. The Church existed where its signs were present, word and sacrament. One could compromise on church silver but not on the word of God. Such a perspective would be helpful to Lutheran believers as their Church gradually lost more and more rights over the years and when Sts. Peter and Paul lost their church building in 1938. Meier's protégé, Kurt Muss, would echo similar sentiments in the future when confronted by the Soviets.

While the people were persuaded, eventually some families of the congregation provided a different solution. They raised double the amount required in order to save the church silver. To do this, they gave from their own household collections of silver ornaments, spoons, and plates. This possibility was offered to churches by the government in a decree issued on June 17, where it would be allowed in certain circumstances to offer a substitute payment in exchange for keeping the church valuables. Showing that their cynicism knew no bounds, while the government demanded double the price of the church valuables as the price for amnesty, it also reminded the churches that all church property and valuables actually belonged to the state anyway.[18]

THE SOVIET GOVERNMENT was also co-opting the Orthodox Church by using a group of dissidents known as "the Living Church," which sought reforms that would make the Church more democratic and sympathetic to the Bolsheviks. Several of their officials were summoned to incriminate Metropolitan Veniamin during his August trial. The Orthodox faithful now turned their anger on this group, also known as the Renovationists. During the trial, a woman struck Renovationist priest Alexander Vvedenskii with a stone, severely wounding him. But with other priests from the Renovationists testifying against Veniamin and his fellow priests, the court concluded its trial by condemning ten of the defendants to death. This was far beyond what the Renovationists desired. They then appealed to the government for clemency, Vvedenskii himself stating that the government had proven its case of counter-revolution. (The basis of the charge of counter-revolution was that the command of the Patriarch to excommunicate those who had given up church valuables had driven parishioners to violence). The government did relent to some extent, commuting the death sentences of six of the accused. But the damage had been done. The remaining four defendants were executed, including Metropolitan Veniamin. A famous photograph of Veniamin standing meekly yet boldly before his Soviet interrogators has since become iconic for Orthodox believers.[19]

That fact that Lenin had ignored an offer by the Vatican in May to pay the amount determined by the state for Orthodox and Catholic Church valuables laid bare the state's hypocritical claim that it was removing church valuables due to the country's need for funds.[20] To top off the state's duplicity, the Soviets had confiscated crown jewels from the czarist regime valued at close to one billion Russian rubles. *Izvestia* reported that by the end of the year the state had gathered a smaller sum from the Church, close to $4 million. Virtually none of that money was used for famine relief; reportedly, a little less than one million was supposedly spent on flour from Finland.[21]

The Living Church would never be fully trusted by the Russian people, the Petrograd Orthodox believers accusing them of having Metropolitan Veniamin's blood on their hands. Of course, the Soviet state could care less about the Living Church since it was committed to the eradication of religion anyway. It was simply a useful tool that would be discarded at the appropriate time.[22] In the not-too-distant future, the Lutheran Church would see its own pastors standing in the dock like Metropolitan Veniamin, giving faithful witness.

ONE OF THE ARA's biggest complaints was that its Russian employees were not immune from arrest. This had been one of the most vexing issues in the negotiations for the Riga Agreement, so the wording concerning Russian employees of the ARA had in the end been left vague. Unfortunately, some of the 120,000 Russian employees of the ARA were often subject to the charge of harboring an "anti-Bolshevik past," thus opening them up to a charge of espionage. For example, a reliable secretary in Moscow's ARA office mysteriously failed to show up for work on Thanksgiving Day in 1921. After ARA employee Farmer Murphy discovered that she had been arrested for espionage, he complained to authorities, seemingly to no avail. But to Murphy's amazement, and apparently not due to ARA intervention, she simply appeared at the office again one day in April 1922. This incident led Murphy to muse, "It is as if some powerful, invisible hand had reached out of the dark, quietly plucked someone from beside you and drawn her back into the dark."[23] That was the omnipotent power of the Cheka in Russia. All the ARA could do, which it did on occasion, was threaten to shut down feeding operations in particular regions if the Soviets did not respect their right to employ Russians without undue interference.[24]

Writing from his sickbed in Bad Homburg on July 8, 1922, Morehead urged Meier to have Kurt Muss write a report on his management of the feeding program in southern Russia and have it sent to him through the mailroom of the ARA in Moscow.[25] By August 2, he received Muss's report, which included photographs from his service that summer to those in the affected regions.[26] With regard to the famine in Rostov-on-Don, Muss wrote: "The famine in this section was not an act of God but was due entirely to the withdrawal of their reserves of grain from the farmers by the government." By the end of November, Muss had been arrested.[27]

Using his contacts, W. L. Scheding found out that the Cheka's attention was aroused when it saw a theology student handling large sums of money. That must have alerted them to the existence of a potential report, although Larsen had taken precautions. Scheding initially read the report in Riga, where Larsen had mailed his briefcase in the ARA mail pouch. Somehow, the Cheka must have opened the pouch.[28] They began to closely observe Muss's movements in October, even censoring his mail.[29] In November they finally struck, arresting Muss in Petrograd just as he was planning to embark for the University of Leipzig. His passports (for internal and external travel) were taken away. Scheding, who was hoping to use Muss as a translator in the south, went to Petrograd to visit Muss's mother and see what could be done. He approached ARA supervisor Don Renshaw, but was disappointed by his reluctance to help.[30] Renshaw, in fairnes, was considered a reputable ARA official. He had had his own dispute with Soviet authorities in February when they had opened his and his traveling companions' trunks and even attempted to open the ARA mail pouch. It caused a big brouhaha between the Soviets and Americans since there actually were some Americans bringing out large quantities of souvenirs (furs, rugs, jewels, etc.). The scandal was blown out of proportion by Soviet newspapers so that Representative Plenipotentiary of the Soviet government to foreign relief organizations, Karl Lander, took advantage of a promise once made by Colonel Haskell that allowed him to open ARA mail pouches and trunks. The NLC was not the only one using the ARA mail pouches to send sensitive information, as journalists, too, took advantage of the safe transmission of controversial articles.[31]

As Scheding dug deeper into the court case against Muss, he understood that he would be charged with "economic sabotage" due to the NLC allegedly having published his report in American newspapers. It wasn't true; the NLC had been very meticulous about not endangering any of its Russian Lutheran contacts.[32] Scheding fell into despair when he heard the charge. He had already gone to Haskell and other ARA officials with Muss's older brother Konrad, pleading for help. ARA official Cyril Quinn emphasized that the real problem was not so much the content but the fact that a Soviet citizen had written the report. Dr. Theodore Benze, who had just arrived in Russia to assist the NLC, carried their appeals all the way up to Lander, too. But Soviet promises to help were not followed up with any positive action.

Muss was soon transferred to Butyrka Prison in Moscow, and Scheding spent the next several months doing whatever he could for the family. When Luisa and Konrad Muss came to Moscow to visit their brother, Scheding bought baskets of food for them to give to Kurt. Since he was interacting with the Muss family, Scheding was aware that he was being watched by the Cheka (now known as the GPU). In order to protect Kurt, Scheding made certain that nothing of this financial assistance appeared on his books. It would have only justified the accusation that Muss really was an economic spy for America.

Scheding, like Morehead, believed that those at the NLC had to do every-thing in their power for Muss since he had suffered on their account.[33] Morehead called on his most influential contacts, pleading for them to intervene on behalf of Muss. One of those contacts was none other than Herbert Hoover, who had highly placed connections in the Soviet government and Washington. After making a thorough investigation of the Soviet accusation that Muss's report had been published in American newspapers, Morehead was convinced that it was filed confidentially and that there was no trace of it in the American press. He then asked Benze and Scheding to pass this information on to ARA official Cyril Quinn and have him convey it to Karl Lander. Sadly, all of his efforts were to no avail.[34] By April 11, 1923, Muss had been placed in solitary confinement. Furthermore, Scheding had also gotten word that his sentence would most likely be three years in a distant northern labor camp near Archangel. A little over one month later, when Scheding returned to Moscow from one of his trips to Rostov, he was met by a crying Luisa Muss. Finally, the judgment had come down via administrative order.[35] In a terse statement on May 18 given to ARA Executive Assistant Philip Matthews, a Miss Pokrovskaya answered on behalf of Karl Lander— "In reply to your letters from March 20 and May 2 we inform you that the Russian employee of ARA, Citizen Kurt Muss, on the basis of the charges brought against him, has been found guilty and sentenced to three years in a concentration camp."[36]

On being apprised of the charges, on April 28 Kurt Muss declared a hunger strike to the death.[37] Muss continued the hunger strike for eleven days while Scheding pleaded with him to give it up. His deportation to the Solovetsky Island concentration camp was delayed in the meantime, until June or July. When the time came to leave, Scheding feared that Muss might do something dangerous such as try to escape. When he had secured Muss's promise that he would not do so, Scheding set about purchasing items that would help him survive the three years in the Arctic north. Heavy shoes, underwear, woolen shirts, and a large amount of tobacco and cigars were purchased. Scheding knew that American tobacco would come in handy as an item for trade while Muss was in prison.

After Kurt left with the other prisoners for the north, Konrad and Luisa Muss visited Scheding in the Brown House, the ARA residence in Moscow where Scheding and Morehead lived while they were working in Russia. Kurt's siblings cried about their brother's fate while he commiserated with them. Scheding harbored guilt feelings yet realized that he had done everything possible for Kurt.[38] Meanwhile, Morehead never forgot Kurt Muss. They would be inseparably linked through the ARA and the NLC's work in Russia, and for the rest of his life he would petition for Kurt up to the highest office in the land. Most importantly, he and the NLC continually prayed for Kurt Muss's release and would in due time be amazed to see how God would answer their prayers.[39]

IN 1923, CHRISTMAS was celebrated on the same date, January 7, as the former state Orthodox Church. The Lutherans had generally followed this practice so that all Christians in the country would celebrate the holy days of Easter and Christmas together.[40] Pastor Scheding enjoyed his first Russian Christmas, noting the packed throng at Sts. Peter and Paul where close to four thousand people flooded into the cathedral for the Christmas Eve service. Although church attendance had decreased dramatically since the Bolshevik Revolution, on this night the people came. Seeing the two large Christmas trees and hearing the old familiar German Christmas carols resonating throughout the church, Scheding's experience provided evidence that the Christian faith was far from dead in Russia.

In his Christmas Eve sermon, Superintendent Meier referred to the gifts from "our brothers over the ocean" that had brought joy. All the poor in the congregation had been given food and clothing in time for Christmas. As Scheding spent Christmas Eve with the Meiers, he recalled Meier mentioning that he had never seen the church so crowded. While the Lutherans celebrated Christ's birth, the Communist Party made plans for a public burning of religious figures. The Komsomol (youth) Christmas would constitute a mock religious celebration replete with effigies of various divinities. As the bells chimed on the morning of Christmas Day, Scheding noted that there were few signs of a demonstration against Christianity. But as dusk set in and the darkness gathered, fires were seen in the city. Scheding himself didn't see any images burned, although he assumed that they probably had been. He also noticed that the people responded to the atheist provocations with a certain degree of apathy. Agreeing with Scheding's impressions, Social Democrat G. P. Fedotov wrote of how the entire population of Moscow, not only believers, was horrified and embarrassed by what they saw. Even though the participants tried to engage the onlookers in their blasphemous revelry, Fedotov said that "there was not a drop of popular pleasure in it." As a result, when the Twelfth Congress of the Communist Party met in March, a resolution was adopted that in the future atheists should refrain from offending the sensibilities of believers in such a manner. The party reasoned that a little more tact would be needed for the time being before the masses would accept atheism.[41]

5

THE "RELIGIOUS NEP"

The Departure of the ARA and the NLC's Struggle to Continue

BY EARLY 1923, the relationship between the ARA and the Soviet government had grown colder. The Soviets had been issuing new demands that the Americans pay for the housing of its personnel in Moscow and that it pay for Russian employees of the ARA. When the ARA's Cyril Quinn quoted the Riga Agreement, Karl Lander didn't contradict him but stated that the Soviet government didn't have the money for these expenses.[1] Local Soviet officials felt even more emboldened by the central government. Pressure and interference were increasingly being placed on the pastors involved in food and clothing distribution. Morehead noted how the Soviets called for the pastors' removal from distribution of food and clothing although the NLC trusted them and wanted to give moral support to the role of the Lutheran Church in the community.[2] Oftentimes, excuses were fabricated to get control of the distribution. For example, in Simferopol in the Crimea, the Soviet representative complained that the NLC only fed Lutherans in the villages. When Lander's office brought this accusation to the ARA's attention, W. L. Scheding explained to ARA official Philip Matthews that, first, the NLC often worked in villages that were 100 percent Lutheran. Second, since the NLC received its support from Lutherans in America, naturally they would feed Lutherans. But whenever there were non-Lutherans in a village, they would never neglect to feed them, too. It seemed obvious that the Soviets were more interested in controlling the NLC feeding program than in ensuring fairness in the distribution.[3]

Superintendent Meier further related that the Soviets were not averse to harassing and exerting physical pressure on the church. Rough Communist types and government employees would gather in the courtyard of his church and see how the distribution was being carried out, undoubtedly looking for some fault. At other times, crowds of young men would shout vile remarks from the courtyard toward the church during services, even throwing objects into the church building as well as at Meier. In response to these physical and verbal assaults, the police would do nothing. Since Meier's sister, Tilly (Mathilda), was primarily employed in the distribution of the goods, the pastor asked Scheding to intercede with the ARA in finding a different distribution point.[4] As a result, Scheding would seek a room for distribution in the ARA building, while Tilly Meier would become an official ARA employee on February 27th.[5]

In March, Scheding would give details to Morehead about the Soviet harassment, which included a demand for bribes from relief workers. President Schilling of the Odessa Synod, for example, was ordered to give 20 percent of the food delivery to the government. When Scheding arrived, he refused to pay a bribe. But on reflection, he reconsidered his refusal, realizing that his action would bring down the law on Schilling. So instead of direct confrontation, Scheding convened a meeting with an ARA official and his Soviet counterpart, and an agreement was hatched that would allow 20 percent of the food to go to a government children's home. The ARA official made sure the kids were being fed, but still, the Soviet representative was finding ways to interfere.

In the Alexandrovsk region in the Ukraine, District President Rath had an even tougher time. There the demand for a bribe was as high as 50 percent of the food the NLC had procured. Rath remained firm in not giving in to the Soviet representative, and the representative was supposed to have been recalled. A stamped copy of Rath's right to distribute food without cost was also to have been sent. But though the NLC appealed through the ARA all the way up to Lander, the Soviet representative remained on the job and continued to cause trouble. In light of these difficulties, and with the time of severe famine past, it was time to for the foreigners to go. The ARA made plans to exit Russia. As long as organizations like the ARA and NLC remained in Russia, they would be a reminder to the government that it was forced to rely on the hated capitalists for its survival.[6]

THE ARA HAD saved the lives of innumerable Russians, many of whom would never forget the largesse of the Americans. The Soviets estimated that 5 million deaths had occurred during the famine, while Quinn placed the number between 1 and 1.25 million. ARA employee Harold Fleming, trained in economics at Harvard and Oxford, estimated that hunger killed 1.5 million and that without ARA aid double that number would have died. In the end, the ARA spent approximately $50 million, with just under one million food packages being delivered.[7]

The NLC also had its own statistics to measure the help that had been given to Lutherans in Russia. By the middle of 1923, it had spent approximately $750,000 in clothing, food remittance packages, and food kitchen assistance in the Volga and southern Russian regions.[8] A professor from Odessa and a native Russian-German, Charles Glöckler, who traversed the Midwest with slides of Russia and the famine, estimated the number of lives saved at 100,000 men, women, and children. More importantly, Glöckler emphasized the spiritual regeneration that NLC aid had occasioned. During the famine, people had begun to lose hope, and with it their faith. Glöckler saw a deeper meaning behind the American Lutherans' assistance: "Imperishable are the bonds, tied by the generosity of American believers in the person of the National Lutheran Council, between themselves and the

Lutherans in Russia. Formerly we were only vaguely conscious of our brethren in America. All the more were we joyfully surprised and deeply impressed by their fraternal love towards us in our affliction."[9]

The leaders of the Evangelical Lutheran Church of Russia echoed his sentiments. In what would be his last letter to John Morehead, Bishop Freifeldt concluded:

> I cannot pass up the opportunity to give expression to my deepest gratitude that the American National Lutheran Council has saved our church from utterly perishing, not only through its magnanimous gifts of love in this time of distress and destruction of all that we formerly created in the spirit of faith and love, but also that its representatives in Russia, Prof. Morehead, Dr. L. Larsen as well as you [Dr. Benze] and Pastor Scheding, have shown such sympathy and understanding to us that the reception of these benefits has been made easier and refreshing. For that I will never forget you.[10]

Average parishioners also appreciated the support of the NLC. As Scheding returned from a trip to Odessa and the surrounding villages, he related this story: "The first home I entered in Grossliebental was that of a farmer. He has no relatives in America. When I had introduced myself, the Hausfrau ran into the other room and brought out a warm winter overcoat which she had received from America, asking that I convey her thanks to America."[11] The believers in the Grossliebenthal District were all grateful that the NLC gave freely not only to Lutherans but to all sufferers regardless of confession. Lauritz Larsen took from his visits the following message: "Thanks to the National Lutheran Council we are saved."[12] Countless others were recipients of the aid that not only saved the lives of children and adults, but also were a visible witness that the Lord had not forgotten them in their suffering and despair.

Scheding was constantly reminded of God's providence as he traveled throughout the Volga and southern regions of Russia. He would enter a village in a car lent to him by the ARA, usually scaring the living daylights out of people who had never before seen this modern contraption. The reaction of many people was to jump on or behind a fence to get out of the way. The children were more intrigued, curiously approaching the car trying to figure out what it was. In one comical instance, the car slid into a horse and sled, pushing the horse through a picket fence into someone's front yard. Thankfully no one was hurt, although Scheding wryly noted, "the horse driver shouted some compliments to our chauffeur, which we did not understand luckily."[13] Whenever introductions were made, Scheding's former work among Volga Germans in America usually resulted in some villagers having heard of him, whereupon he would mention the names of their relatives in America and pretty soon a lively conversation began. Of course, when they realized that he was there to bring aid, sometimes even from their family members, joy would overwhelm them.

Pastors were always happy to see him since some had not received a visit from a fellow pastor for years. Scheding could give them monetary support and talk about future plans for the reconstruction of the church, all of which encouraged them to no end. When Pastor Albert Koch of Grossliebenthal met Scheding for the first time, he threw his arms around his neck, hugging and kissing him for joy. All these incidents made a profound impression on Scheding and motivated him to persevere in his tireless work for the NLC.

Bringing medicine, too, was a godsend as many people were ill, some with malaria. Scheding lost track of how many quinine tablets he distributed. He was heartbroken whenever he heard a description of the daily routine: waking up, going to work all day, and finally returning home to the only meal they would have that day, a diet consisting of hominy grits, if they were lucky. And if they weren't, dinner was black bread and tea, or possibly cocoa. Suffering created a kind of complacency among the population. Children had ceased crying because it couldn't be answered. Most adopted a stoicism and a waiting for death. Scheding drew this picture for his readers in an article called "Life at Ebb Tide," imploring American Lutherans to care and show God's love to the suffering. Through the work of the NLC, they had been able to save a church and a people—for the time being. The names of Bishop Freifeldt and General Superintendents Meier and Malmgren were now more than just names on stationery—they were genuine friends and brothers in the faith.[14]

ON JUNE 4, 1923, Colonel Haskell announced the end of the ARA program, with its personnel to be withdrawn by mid-July.[15] The NLC now had some important decisions to make. Should it remain in Russia? Certainly, Morehead was more than ready to commit the NLC to future work in Russia. But how? The work of the NLC had always been predicated on more than just humanitarian aid, as essential as that was for the survival of the Lutheran Church.[16] Without the feeding program of the NLC, the parishioners of Russia's Lutheran Church would have fallen into despair. In essence, the Church would have died along with its parishioners.

Now that the people seemed to be revived in spirit and health, the NLC needed to turn its attention, toward the future development of the Church. It would soon lose its office space at the Brown House because the ARA had given a deadline of May 20 to move out. Since Colonel Haskell wanted to close up shop, that meant the NLC needed a working agreement with the Soviet government. The ARA could only promise to facilitate the NLC's operations until June 30.[17] So it was time not only to rent another facility but also to think seriously about what the NLC could do by itself under the Soviet regime. The ARA had been a lifeline of protection in times of difficulty, a resort to which the NLC would no longer be able to turn. For example, when Russian Lutheran pastors would not be allowed to distribute aid in a particular village due to the intransigence of local Soviet officials, Scheding would appeal to the ARA. The Soviets really didn't have a choice since they could only antagonize the ARA so much without losing their food aid. In this way, the NLC often had their "big brother" intervene successfully for them.[18] Like other organizations, the NLC had also relied on the ARA mail pouch, but now it would have to find a secure source to send its mail outside the prying eyes of Soviet censors. Morehead had likely foreseen the eventuality of ARA's departure already back in the summer of 1922 when the NLC sought through ARA's mediation a separate agreement with the Soviet government. But the day when the NLC would have to deal strictly with the Soviet government had now arrived.[19]

On April 9, Morehead wrote to Benze and Scheding that they should "kindly proceed with all speed in the making of the Special Agreement" with the Soviet government.[20] Morehead requested their frank assessment on a course of action for the future. What work in economic reconstruction was practicable? Should loans be offered, or materials like agricultural machinery and seed? What charity or relief work might be necessary after the next harvest?[21] There was also a fear that the Kurt Muss case might adversely affect any attempt to sign an agreement with the Soviet government for future work.[22] The pressure to sign an agreement increased when Karl Lander sent out a circular to international organizations that the Soviet Union would appreciate their continued assistance, but that there would be new conditions now. Beginning his letter with thankfulness for the help of the international organizations, Lander spoke of how the Soviet Union would value assistance in the future with agricultural reconstruction and homeless children. But then he cut to the point. The Soviet Union would not pay freight costs as it had during the days of the ARA. If an organization wanted to work in Russia, it would have to cover costs for all of its transportation as well as purchase all food products and other objects within Russia.[23] It was indeed a new day.

WHILE THE NLC was exploring options for continued work in Russia in the first half of 1923, American and Russian Lutherans were dealt a severe blow. Having returned home on December 9, 1922, after his extensive journeys throughout Russia that fall, Lauritz Larsen immediately set out on the road to tell the story of NLC aid to Europe and Russia. While speaking several times a day, combined with the physical exhaustion from traveling in Europe and Russia the previous five months, Larsen fell ill and succumbed to pneumonia on January 28. He was only forty years old. Superintendent Theophil Meier held a memorial service in Moscow in honor of Larsen the Sunday after his death. He also asked the NLC for a picture of Larsen that he proposed to hang in all the churches of the Evangelical Lutheran Church in Russia. On February 16, Morehead was called on to take up the duties of Larsen but with a new title as Executive Director. Morehead would now manage the operations of the NLC not only in Europe but also in America.[24]

Russian Lutherans, too, would descend into mourning when Bishop Conrad Freifeldt passed away after an operation at the age of seventy-six. It was not unexpected, as Freifeldt had been in poor health. He had delayed the operation until after Ascension Day so that he could attend the confirmation of his youngest daughter, fifteen-year-old Magdalina. Freifeldt had been the lone figure leading the 1.5 million-member Lutheran Church. When the Bolshevik Revolution had triumphed and he had the chance to leave Russia for Estonia, Freifeldt set a powerful example for hesitant pastors by remaining at his post as bishop. The son of an Estonian schoolmaster and a Swedish mother, Freifeldt had been educated in a German school and graduated from the University of Dorpat. Freifeldt's funeral was held in his parish, St. Anne's in Petrograd, a Rococo style church dating back to the days of Peter the Great. The two general superintendents, Theophil Meier and Arthur Malmgren, provided the sermons for the service. They would be the two leaders who would have to usher the Evangelical Lutheran Church in Russia through the harrowing days that lie ahead.

Malmgren chose John 21:18 as the text for his sermon. It was a theme aptly chosen as the elderly Freifeldt had, like St. Peter, been chosen by God to lead his church through fiery trials. Meier chose Proverbs 28:20, "A faithful man shall abound with blessings." Freifeldt had indeed blessed numerous Lutherans

with his service, Meier especially remembering him from his student days. After
the benediction, members of each of Lutheranism's ethnic groups read from
Scripture in their own language: German, Estonian, Latvian, and Finnish, with
Benze reading in English on behalf of the NLC. Benze especially treasured
his last correspondence with Freifeldt when, echoing St. Paul, he wrote that
although he would have liked to continue his work, "I am ready to leave this
in the hands of God."[25]

WITH BISHOP FREIFELDT'S passing, Meier and Malmgren would play
even more prominent roles in the Church. The atmosphere in which they
would work, while always stifling, had eased to some extent. In a joint decree
issued by the Commissariats of Justice and the Interior on April 27, all religious
organizations were given the right to hold provincial and central conventions
and to elect their own executive boards, subject to approval by the state. Exacting
its revenge against an old enemy, the state forbid the Orthodox Church from
holding a convention, although the Living Church (Renovationists) received
permission. For the Protestant church bodies, permission was generally given,
as they had been persecuted under the old regime.[26] Superintendent Meier
announced the new decree during the June 17 Sunday service, requesting a
congregational meeting be held after the service for the purpose of registering
Sts. Peter and Paul under the new state guidelines.[27]

June proved to be a bellwether for the new tone toward religion in Russia,
as Patriarch Tikhon was released from prison on June 27. He had been incarcerated since May 1922, but now exited prison a far meeker soul.[28] British Foreign
Minister Lord Curzon, along with the Archbishop of Canterbury, had led the
international outcry against Tikhon's treatment, demanding his release. While
it may seem that the Soviets capitulated, their action was to split the Church
even further, with Tikhon and the established church pitted against the upstart
Renovationists. The Soviet state released Tikhon and gave him relative freedom

in his residence at Donskoi Monastery, while at the same time releasing a propaganda film entitled *Tikhon after His Repentance*, depicting him as obedient to the state.[29] It is likely that the patriarch submitted to the Soviet state in order to save the Church from the Renovationists. Indeed, Tikhon was now free to speak out against them, and his credibility in the eyes of the government was furthered by his call for the Church to remain out of politics.[30] All in all, the state's actions turned out to be a masterstroke for promoting Orthodox disunity. The Renovationists, who had been used by the state to dethrone the old state Orthodox Church, were now severely damaged, and a large number of priests thronged back to Tikhon.

While this battle was taking place within the Orthodox Church, the Lutheran Church was enjoying what might be called a "Leninist thaw." The term "NEP" (New Economic Policy) had been coined when Lenin tried to grapple with the people's resistance to the abolition of money and trade. The economy had been completely nationalized during the civil war period and its immediate aftermath, a policy known as "War Communism." The NEP was Vladimir Lenin's strategic retreat from enacting full-blown communism by allowing elements of capitalism in order to revive the economy. Forcible grain requisitions had proved especially unpopular, so they were replaced with a grain tax. The adoption of the NEP in March 1921 had freed up the market and resulted in a burgeoning of economic activity and growing prosperity. The NEP would last until 1928, but Lenin made clear that NEP was only a tactical step backward for the time being. It was not envisioned to be permanent.[31]

There was a religious NEP as well. In 1924, the Thirteenth Congress of the Communist Party of the Soviet Union condemned the arbitrary closing of churches and crude propaganda efforts like those expressed at Christmastime in 1923.[32] Like the economic NEP, the religious NEP would last until 1928 and provide the Lutheran Church with time to recover from its losses during the years of war and revolution.[33] In the meantime, while the government was focused on undermining the influence of the Orthodox Church, the Lutherans were being allowed greater freedom. In fact, the Lutheran Church had often declared that it was not opposed to the powers that be. Meier's appeal to his parishioners to give up the congregation's communion ware clearly illustrated that the Lutheran Church hierarchy considered physical objects in worship in an almost adiaphoric sense. Meier stressed the permanence of the Word of God that could not be taken away as long as it remained within people's hearts and minds. It was a lesson that would bear repeating when objects more important than silver would be confiscated by the state.

Pastor W. L. Scheding had often discussed with Soviet officials the relationship between church and state during his visits to the Kremlin. As he wrote John Morehead in a confidential memorandum, "Time and again I tried to hammer it into many officials even in the Kreml [German spelling], that the Lutheran Church teaches loyalty to every existing Government and that they should show me one pastor who has risen against the Government. ... I remember distinctly how one of the Commissars grinned at this my statement, but he finally admitted ... I was right."[34] Superintendent Meier had likewise formed relationships inside the Kremlin and reiterated that the Lutheran Church was not anti-government. This helped him to get a hearing and opened doors that were now being closed to the Orthodox Church. Ironically, the persecution of the Lutherans under the old regime worked in their favor—for the time being.

The times were also bringing Lutheran churches into closer contact. In August 1923, the first Lutheran World Convention was held in the German city of Eisenach, site of Martin Luther's translation of the New Testament. The participants hoped to form an outward expression of Lutheran unity based on the Lutheran Confessions as the "indispensible foundation of the Lutheran Church." Four years of a dreadful world war and continent-wide hunger trailing in its aftermath had forged a bond between American and European Lutherans.[35] For Russian Lutherans, it was also an important moment because Meier received permission to travel to Germany for the first time.[36] The liberality of the Soviet government in allowing him a visa was no small matter when one takes into account Kurt Muss's arrest one year before. Meier consulted with Morehead about fresh possibilities for work in Russia due to the more liberal decree on organizing religious institutions. Meier's address was described by Morehead's biographer Samuel Trexler as the "most moving" of the convention: "I am sure none brought ... heavier luggage than I ... as the representative of the Evangelical Lutheran Church in Russia. I, of course did not have to pay excess baggage on the railroad, for my burden was not carried in trunks and traveling-baskets, but in my heart: and now I am here to unload it on other hearts."[37]

Returning home refreshed and energized on September 29, Meier immediately went to the Commissariat of Internal Affairs and secured a promise to permit an All-Russian Lutheran Conference in late January 1924. Regional church conferences were already being held in the Volga District in mid-June and the southern Russia congregations in Odessa in mid-September. Among the topics Meier proposed were: (1) a statement of the Lutheran Church's confessional position; (2) the external organization of the Church and the inclusion of the congregations into districts of the whole Church; (3) consultation on the filling of vacant congregations and the founding of a preacher's seminary; (4) the elaboration of instructions for carrying out the pastoral office in agreement with the Decree on Separation of Church from State and School from Church; (5) the election of a bishop and the remaining officers of the Church. This conference had been eagerly awaited since the dissolution of the Lutheran Church after the Bolshevik Revolution.

The biggest problem facing the Church, though, was the shortage of pastors. The Siberian regions had over 100,000 Lutherans, with only two pastors to cover the enormous distances. Furthermore, the Muss case had made it clear that students could not be sent abroad to study, and the Church could not expect that American and German citizens would be allowed to serve as pastors in Russia. Superintendent Malmgren had put into motion a proposal to form theological courses for "emergency preachers," but the Church had neither the money nor the teachers for that.

In light of the need for pastors, Meier felt compelled to begin negotiations with the Soviet government for the opening of a seminary. He planned to meet with the Commissar of Public Education, intending to find out what conditions were necessary to establish a seminary. If the answer was favorable, he would begin looking for a house to rent in Moscow or its suburbs that could accommodate up to fifty students and two teachers. He proposed that one of the two teachers be an American, already having told Scheding that Theodore Benze would be a good choice. The other position, he believed, should be held by a graduate of Dorpat University. Meier considered it imperative to unite the various language and ethnic groups within the Church, and a Dorpat graduate generally could converse in Latvian, Estonian, and German. If there was need for a third teacher, he proposed a pastor named Koch who lived in Vienna and was fluent in Russian. Braving a glimpse into the future, Meier hoped that Lutheranism might be preached among ethnic Russians.[38]

A more reticent pastor might have hidden from the Soviet authorities, but Meier charged ahead into the belly of the beast for the cause of the Lutheran Church. While he was successfully negotiating with some in the Soviet government, others exerted pressure on him in his own life. Since the early months of the year, he had been operating under the threat that he would be thrown out of his home, which included several rooms on the premises of Sts. Peter and Paul. Since pastors had no legal rights, he would be left with very little recourse. Furthermore, shortly after his return from Germany, he was called before the Cheka for an interrogation. After answering many questions, he and the organist of the church were allowed to return home. The unwanted consultation turned out to be nothing too serious, but it was a none too subtle reminder that Meier and his activities were constantly under the watchful eye of the secret police.[39]

AS 1923 DREW to a close, the NLC was still engaged in negotiations with the Soviet government for continued work in Russia. Scheding made the rounds in the Kremlin before his departure from Russia in November. He was obliged to work through the governmental office of Posledgol, an abbreviation for "Consequences of Hunger" (*Posledstviya Goloda*). Apparently, the NLC had missed the August 1 deadline set by Karl Lander for organizations to register with the government, because the ARA had inadvertently left it off the list of organizations with whom it worked. As a result, negotiations with Posledgol were only at the beginning stage in October.[40] Scheding's counterpart in the negotiations was Olga Kameneva, who was intimately connected with influential figures among the Bolsheviks. Her brother was none other than Leon Trotsky, while her husband, Lev Kamenev, was a member of the governing apparatus of the Soviet Union, the Politburo.[41] As Scheding arranged for the meeting in the Kremlin, he heard through her secretary that the Soviets desired that Luthco, the name that the NLC organization in Russia would take, should begin work soon. The secretary also informed Scheding that Posledgol had always had trouble with the NLC's distribution of goods, a point that Scheding countered by saying that it was generally due to the obstruction of local Soviet officials.

By mid-October, Scheding had conducted two meetings with Kameneva and had a better indication of what the Soviets required from Luthco for it to operate in the country. She suffered from headaches and poor eyesight, and would undergo a serious operation by the end of the year. Nevertheless, Scheding got the impression that she would be willing to make some compromises for the Soviets and Luthco to work together effectively.[42] Scheding especially emphasized the need for Luthco to have control of its own funds and the ability to choose the areas where it desired to work, naturally in Lutheran regions since American Lutherans were providing the financial support. Despite Kameneva's assurance that Luthco would have freedom to operate within Russia, Posledgol would renege on the agreement, including the promise to cover half of Luthco's transportation costs. As Scheding prepared to leave Russia, Kameneva promised a visa should he return to do the relief work in Russia.[43]

By the end of 1923, by God's grace, the NLC had rescued an almost three-and-a-half century old Church from physical death during the famine. But the spiritual destruction of the Church would not be long in coming if the pastoral shortage was not addressed.

6

A FIR TREE WITH TWO PEAKS

The First All-Russian Lutheran Synodical Convention

OVER THE PREVIOUS ten years the Lutheran congregations had lived through world war, revolution, civil war, and famine. To say that they were impoverished would be an understatement. A Church that had numbered over 3.5 million parishioners at the outbreak of World War I now numbered slightly more than 1 million.[1] Counting the superintendents Meier and Malmgren there were only 81 pastors serving in the USSR in 1924 compared to the 198 serving in 1914. In the vacant congregations, either dedicated lay readers or imposters took over the administration.[2] Of the 180 pastoral positions available only half of them were filled.

The pastoral shortage was the biggest problem facing the Church. Some areas had not seen a pastor in nine years. This is perhaps best exemplified by the story of a couple who took a two-and-a-half-day train journey to Moscow just to get married by a Lutheran pastor. Lutherans were also going without the sacraments, mostly in Siberia. As a result of the pastoral shortage, Lutherans were either falling away from the faith or going over to the Baptists, Methodists, Adventists, or whatever church would send missionaries their way. Meier concluded that the Lutheran Church would disappear if it did not take urgent measures immediately. He had hoped to get visas for pastors from Germany or

America to come and serve, but the governmental attitude toward foreigners had only worsened. Even if Meier could secure visas, though, the lack of language skills and the general difficulties of life in Russia made it unlikely that a foreigner would remain for long.[3]

THIS WAS THE STATE of the Evangelical Lutheran Church of Russia in 1924 when it held the first synodical convention in the almost 350-year history of the Church. Superintendent Malmgren believed that the Lutheran Church was already one in spirit, faith, and confession, but now that unity would be publicly expressed.[4] In order to gather the most influential servants of the Church, the NLC provided the funds for the convention in the spacious Sts. Peter and Paul in Moscow. Scheduled for June 21–26, Superintendent Meier planned to follow the agenda in the basic format that the Soviet government had approved in April.[5] But on what should have been a happy occasion, when the convention began on Saturday, June 21, tension was already brewing between the Meier supporters in Moscow and the Leningrad advocates for Malmgren (with Lenin's death in January 1924, Petrograd was renamed Leningrad). Malmgren had taken offense that Meier had written up the protocol for the convention without any input from himself or the pastors in the Leningrad region. Only when the Temporary Church Administration met in Moscow in January were Malmgren and others able to add their input.[6] The dispute, though, was really related to Meier's temperament rather than arrogance. An energetic, impulsive man, he recognized that he would need approval from the government. The corridors of power were familiar to him since he lived in Moscow, and so he went about getting that approval without consulting Malmgren. He probably didn't consider until afterward that there might be some hurt feelings and disagreements since he had acted without the consultative body of the Church. Unfortunately, the damage had been done. Allies of Malmgren's like

John Tuneld, a Swedish engineer and layman at St. Katherine's Lutheran in Leningrad, felt that Meier had overstepped his bounds. He resented the fact that Meier alone represented the Church in Eisenach before the LWC the previous summer, although it wasn't his fault that the death of Malmgren's wife had precluded his accompanying Meier. Tuneld wrote to Archbishop Nathan Söderblom in Sweden that Meier was trying to set himself up as the natural successor to Bishop Freifeldt with the help of "poorly informed Americans." Writing to Meier before the convention, Malmgren chided him, "I'm going to speak to you the same words that Luther spoke to Melanchthon from the Coburg when he continually tried to change and reword the Augustana: 'Philip, it is not your work, but the Church's.'"[7]

In light of the tension, there was no better servant in the Church to begin the convention by leading the devotional service than the highly respected pastor in the Crimea, Ferdinand Hörschelmann. The following day, the fifty-six delegates (twenty-seven pastors and twenty-nine laymen) gathered for the opening divine service as the two general superintendents led the festal procession into the church. The summer weather allowed the church to be festooned with palms, laurels, and flowers. After the opening hymn ("Come, Holy Ghost, Our Hearts Inspire"), Superintendent Malmgren gave a short address from the altar. The old tradition of a preparatory sermon before a communion service was conducted by Pastor Ernst Holzmayer from Nizhniy Novgorod, followed by "A Mighty Fortress," accompanied by organ, trumpets, and a seventy-five-member choir. This Lutheran standard would be sung often in the next few days. Superintendent Meier offered the sermon, preaching on the text from Psalm 118:24–26, "This is the day which the Lord hath made; let us rejoice and be glad in it." With an eye toward the inclusion of various ethnic groups in the Church, Latvian representative Pastor Schanzberg and Pastor Selim Laurikkala of the Finnish-Ingermanland congregations assisted with the liturgy and prayers.

In the evening, the business of the convention got underway with Superintendent Meier reading a statement (translated into Russian) thanking the Soviet government for allowing the Lutherans to gather for their first all-church convention in history. After giving the obligatory thanks, Meier defined the parameters of their gratefulness:

> The Synod notes with peculiar joy that freedom of conscience has been proclaimed by the constitution of the Union of Socialistic Soviet Republics and that freedom of faith is guaranteed by law. ... This is the first meeting of a Synod since the foundation of Evangelical Lutheran congregations in Russia in the sixteenth century. It is only the separation of the Church from the State, which carries with it the recognition of the equal rights of all confessional groups that has offered the possibility of the convocation of this Synod. The confession of the Evangelical Lutheran Church places the obligation upon every member in his relationship as a citizen to respect authority and the existing constitution, to fulfill the decrees of the government, and to discharge all the obligations laid upon citizens, including that of military service. Therefore, the people confessing the teachings of the Evangelical Lutheran Church have always been loyal and always will be.[8]

The resolution highlighting the separation of church and state would have sounded strange to Orthodox believers given their close association and reliance on the czarist state in the past. Russia's Lutherans were willing to take advantage of the newfound freedoms accorded them, although they were aware that they were riding the proverbial tiger. Still, a Soviet official reading the resolution would have found very little objectionable in its content, given that it allowed Lutherans to serve in the military (something Baptists didn't allow, for example) and defined them as citizens of the Soviet state. The resolution was unanimously adopted at the convention.[9]

After offering thanks to those Lutherans throughout the world who had provided aid to Russian Lutherans during the famine, the first act of the convention was to decide whether it would affirm the Lutheran confession as stated in the Eisenach Preamble at the 1923 Lutheran World Convention. Superintendent Meier explained why the Church must stand by the Lutheran Confessions, the assembled multitude following his presentation by singing the hymn "By This Foundation Will I Stand." Afterward, the people in unison confessed the words of Luther's Explanation of the Second Article of the Apostle's Creed. The Eisenach Preamble contained the following: "The Lutheran World Convention confesses the Holy Scriptures of the Old and New Testaments as the only source and infallible norm of all Church teaching and matters and sees in the Confessions of the Lutheran Church, in particular the Unaltered Augsburg Confession and in the Small Catechism of Luther the genuine reproduction of the Word of God." The convention decided to overwhelmingly back Meier and his more traditional stand on the Lutheran Confessions, though there was a faction led by Pastor Woldemar Reichwald that believed Church authority was too centralized.[10]

THE MOST DELICATE matter of the convention would be choosing a bishop to lead the Church. Pro-Meier and pro-Malmgren factions existed, so who would defer to the other was an open question. In retrospect, both remembered giving in to the other in order to secure peace, but it appears that Hörschelmann was the real peacemaker who helped avoid a contentious fight. According to Pastor Johann Völl, there were long debates, and both sides stuck to their candidates. Then Hörschelmann remarked that in his homeland of Estonia, he had often seen fir trees with two peaks. "Why can't the Evangelical Lutheran Church of Russia also not have its two peaks, its two bishops?" The issue was settled after Hörschelmann's suggestion.[11] It could hardly be imagined that the Orthodox or Catholic Church would designate two patriarchs or popes to rule, but the decision provided a good example of a spirit that did not place the unbridled authority of one man above conciliation in the Church.

Now the delegates set about hammering out the details for sharing power between the two bishops. Although initially the division of duties between Malmgren and Meier was a little unclear, by the time a follow-up conference in October was held there was a forthright delineation of each bishop's responsibilities. In principle, it was decided that Malmgren would represent the Church in educational matters while Meier's duties would be focused on the administrative level. In actuality, though, Malmgren would represent the Church before foreign Lutheran churches; he would also be responsible for pastoral education, providing organization and leadership for the seminary that it was now decided would operate in Leningrad; lastly, he would provide oversight for the four Synod councils located in the northern Russian regions. Meier's duties entailed representing the Church in relationship to the government; he was also responsible for the inner spiritual care of the Church, providing leadership for the district presidents and the activities of the Synod councils (except the four northern districts that belonged to Malmgren's sphere); lastly, he was the President of the High Church Council. Both bishops would conduct their offices in the name and under the instructions of the High Church Council.[12]

The last major order of business concerned the Church constitution, which pit the traditional allies of a strong, centralized Church (here Malmgren and Meier were in accord) against those advocating more congregational authority. The traditionalists most feared 'unrestrained parliamentarianism with its elections, intrigues and party quarrels.' They sought to choose bishops for life (which they successfully achieved for Malmgren and Meier), desiring quiet and orderliness that centralization of authority would provide. The opposition thought that congregations should be more active participants in the management of Church affairs within their districts and at the General Synod level. They also felt that congregational and synodical principles were more con-ducive to the times in which they lived (as opposed to the old czarist, tradi-tional ways).[13] Most likely in the background of this discussion was the growth of Protestant sects like the Congregationalists in Siberia and the Volga region that often denigrated the Lutheran Church as simply a "bishop's church." They were competing for the souls of traditional Lutherans who had not seen pastors for some time. Due to the decline in the number of pastors, some Lutherans were calling for keusters (teachers of religion) to carry out the duties of a pastor in emergency situations. Meier, for his part, recognized the need for immediate pastoral help in these far-flung places and proposed making short-term courses available to those who had had some theological training before the Bolshevik Revolution.[14]

Given the stark nature of opposing views within the Church, the discus-sions for the constitution would take a few days. But in the end, a spirit of compromise prevailed. Individual congregations would be granted the right to form their own councils. Above them would be Synodical districts with their presidents, and finally the General Synod [of all congregations] with its High Church Council would be the ultimate authority. The High Church Council would consist of the two bishops, a representative of the non-German people groups (Latvians, Finn/Ingrians and Estonians) and two secular Lutherans.[15] There would be 12 synodical districts of German congregations while 3 sepa-rate districts total would be formed for the Latvians, Finn/Ingrians and the Estonians. A 13th district would be formed for the scattered Siberian congre-gations of German ethnicity. A census in 1926 would record close to 900,000 Lutherans in the Soviet Union.[16]

Despite the spirited sessions at the convention, there were also moments of poignancy and reflection. The memorial service held on Monday evening, June 23, provided just such an occasion. The participants listened to Malmgren invoke the names of the twenty-five pastors who had died during the years of turmoil, 1917–1924. He read a short biography of each pastor while Pastor Emil von Bonwetsch of Pyatigorsk preached a fitting sermon based on Revelation

2:10 ("Be faithful unto death and I will give you the crown of life"). One of the names was the former General Superindentent and pastor of Sts. Peter and Paul, Paul Willigerode. Willigerode had suffered a nervous breakdown after the traumatic events of the 1917 revolutions (February and October) and sought to emigrate from Russia. He was imprisoned for his faith in 1919 and may have committed suicide in prison due to his confused state of mind. His was among the more tragic stories of those days.[17] The first convention had taken great steps to reconstitute the Evangelical Lutheran Church in Russia, so it was fitting that a concluding service thanking God for all of their blessings be held on the final day. Professor Bartholdy of Leningrad, a teacher at the Peterschule connected to St. Peter's, had been elected president of the convention, and now he publicly expressed to the satisfaction of all that a Church Constitution and Church Orders had been agreed on. The three most senior clergymen, Pastors Hörschelmann, Bonwetsch, and Althausen (Oryol) then presented Superintendents Malmgren and Meier as bishops elected by the General Synod. Pastor Paul Kuhlberg of Marxstadt (the former Katherinenstadt) delivered the final sermon with Bishop Malmgren giving the closing prayer and Bishop Meier blessing those gathered with the Aaronic benediction.

UNFORTUNATELY, THE CHEKA marred what should have been a joyful conclusion to the convention. During the closing service, Bishop Meier was issued a summons to appear the very next day at Lubyanka, the Cheka head-quarters located a few blocks from Sts. Peter and Paul. There he was subjected to a two-hour inquisition and finally let go with a warning. So despite being given the freedom to hold the convention, the Lutheran Church was given an unmistakable reminder that Caesar was carefully watching that which belonged to God.[18] Odessan District President Schilling summed up the situation of the Church presciently in a letter to Scheding a few months before: "It is still pretty dark around us, and we beg the American brethren to remember us in their prayers and in their brotherly hearts, because it is in the hand of God alone to preserve our dear Church."[19]

With the completion of the Church's reorganization, an opportunity to register new congregations was provided, as in the case of the first, exclusively Russian-speaking congregation in Leningrad, which was registered with the government on September 14, 1923. The registration process with the state set forth the goals and practices of the congregation, which the parishioners stated as holding worship services, Bible studies, confirmation classes, spiritual music performances, and so on. A congregation had to stipulate in its charter that it would not engage in any political activities or commentary in its sermons, conversations, or speech. Undergirding the document was the agreement that the congregation would abide by the Decree on Separation of Church from State and School from Church (1918), thus acknowledging that wherever it held its activities was in effect government property.

A total of fifty-eight people signed on as members. Though it called itself an Evangelical Lutheran and Reformed congregation, the Evangelical Lutheran Church of Russia offered it membership in the Church, which it accepted on October 2. (By then there were seventy-four members). In all probability, any concerns the Lutheran Church had about a "mixed theology" were rendered moot as only local Lutheran pastors had agreed to lead the congregation: Helmut Hansen, Arnold Frischfeld, Paul Reichert, and Wilhelm Fehrmann.

Historically, an ethnic Russian was automatically considered a member of the Russian Orthodox Church and any attempt at proselytism was considered illegal. But after the Bolshevik Revolution, any complaint registered on this score by the Orthodox Church fell on deaf ears.[20] So now the congregation's use of Russian was not only for those who had lost the ability to converse in their ethnic tongue but also for ethnic Russians who would be inclined to join them. Konstantin Andrievsky, a forty-six-year-old Russian lawyer who was the son of an Orthodox priest, was just such a convert. He would become an influential figure within Lutheran circles in the future.[21] Perhaps because of their unique nature the congregation chose the name "Jesus Christ Lutheran Church" over the more traditional Lutheran moniker of St. Paul's.[22]

BACK IN THE UNITED STATES, Scheding was itching to return to Russia, missing the thrill and satisfaction of doing mission work in such a historic time. He even proposed bringing his family over so that he could serve there as a pastor. While his heart was in the right place, the situation in the country had changed and Morehead seemed reluctant to bring him back to the field in a full-time capacity. Morehead saw no need for a permanent representative in Russia, recommending at most two visits a year. He was no longer willing to trust in the good will of the Soviets.

The registration of Luthco seemed to be in trouble, as it and the visa application for Oscar Mees were moving very slowly. Morehead had proposed sending Mees to Russia on behalf of the NLC to investigate conditions for future work, but paperwork was holding up his arrival. The motives behind this delay were answered by Bishop Meier in a letter to Morehead near the end of 1924. It now appeared that any Soviet citizen working with foreigners was being watched so closely that even Meier had to be careful about close associations with his fellow foreign Lutherans. Because of these concerns, he didn't feel that he could work closely with Mees, nor could Mees travel with him to Siberia. Either way, Meier knew that Morehead would understand the necessity of avoiding public criticism of the Soviet government, especially when writing about the oppression of the Lutheran Church. Criticism would only draw attention to Russian Lutherans and make them appear disloyal to the state.[23]

In an irenic yet determined spirit, Morehead continued the exchange of letters with Soviet official Olga Kameneva. In a November 28 letter to Morehead, Kameneva requested from the NLC the specific amounts of money to be spent, in which regions it might be spent, and what form the relief would take. Morehead answered her on December 12 that the NLC could make no commitments until it sent its representative, Mees, to scout out the situation in the country. Morehead guessed a sum in the neighborhood of $100,000 was what the NLC would spend, but he reiterated a desire for freedom of travel to support those of "our blood and faith." Morehead described their proposed work as "purely philanthropic" and in the spirit of the work that they had previously performed with the ARA.[24] Despite the changed political environment since the days of the ARA, everything seemed to be in order and Mees expected to receive his visa soon. Frau Schmieden, Luthco's clerk in Moscow, expected as much, too. Writing to him on January 27, Schmieden mentioned that the Kremlin promised "that there will be no delay in obtaining your visa."[25] But Mees received an unpleasant surprise on February 5 when he learned that his visa had been refused.[26] Schmieden immediately went to the Foreign Commission office and found that a more specific proposal of the amount of money to be spent in Russia was required for Mees to get a visa. Advising Mees on the wording to be used, Schmieden assured him that the delay was not out of the ordinary and that Kameneva would approve his visa soon.[27]

But Kameneva's previous positive relationship with the NLC did not appear to be enough to counteract the prevailing political winds. Conditions that previously allowed for a foreigner's quick entry into Russia were no longer extant. It would no longer be coerced into holding contentious discussions with foreigners bearing gifts. On February 19, Mees received a tersely worded telegram from Kameneva: "Sorry, your application to enter Russia refused. Kindly send your proposals by letter." As Mees was already in Riga, he answered her the same day, perplexed as to what had gone wrong. The NLC had already gathered $50,000, hearing from their sources that there would be great need in the coming spring. He was hoping that they could reach an agreement with the Soviet government to provide free transportation for the distribution of clothing. The clothing was already being gathered in Hamburg, preparing for shipment to Russia.[28]

One week later, Kameneva replied—definitively. "Your conditions ... refer to the situation in the Union of SSR such as it existed in the years 1921–1923."[29] The former conditions under the ARA were now radically changed. Where previously the NLC could use its pastors to distribute aid, now the government would choose its own local people to oversee the distribution. Where formerly the government paid transportation fees, now Luthco would be required to take on that expense. Similarly, customs duties, excise fees, and cost of living for personnel were no longer covered. Due to those customs and excise fees, Kameneva recommended bringing only cash so that Luthco could purchase all items within Russia. A few days later, a forlorn Schmieden cabled Mees with the bad news: "On proposed conditions—no hope."[30] In fact, Schmieden had read the handwriting on the wall before Kameneva's February 26 letter to Mees. On February 24, she began to ask for direction as to where to send the office's furniture and stationery, concluding that Luthco would soon be closed. Likewise, she now requested references for future work.

On the one hand, conditions in the country had changed somewhat favorably toward religion, but the government was simultaneously viewing with increasing paranoia and suspicion the relationships between foreigners and Russians. Perhaps Bishop Meier's concern about a Soviet bureaucrat's fear of close association with foreigners was behind Kameneva's sudden coldness? But Kameneva was also clear that she had communicated these new conditions to Scheding before he left, so even his good relationship and intervention with her would probably not have affected the outcome for the better. Disappointed, Mees returned to New York on March 30th after three months of fruitless efforts to enter Russia. Meier, for his part, was not surprised. Another way to send aid would have to be found. Luthco, in essence, would turn out to be stillborn.[31]

SERVANTS IN HIS VINEYARD

A Bible School Is Born in the USSR

AS EARLY AS 1923, the traumatic situation of the Lutheran Church in Siberia weighed heavily on then-Superintendent Meier's heart. A Lutheran population of over 100,000 had only two pastors (Reichwald and Gorne) serving an area the size of North America, and they were far from the population centers where the majority of Lutherans lived. The years of war and revolution had allowed for virtually no contact between the Siberian congregations and the Church's center in Moscow. With the dearth of pastors, beautiful old cathedrals in Omsk, Tomsk, Irkutsk, Krasnoyarsk, Chita, and Tobolsk were lying dormant. Congregations felt forced to choose preachers from within their midst, most of whom were theologically uneducated or unprepared to lead a congregation. Meier worried that Lutheranism would soon die out in Siberia if drastic measures were not taken.

Meier had initially hoped to make a summer visit to Siberia in 1923, but the invitation to Eisenach for the Lutheran World Convention was more pressing at that time. Nonetheless, Siberia still occupied his thoughts, so Meier appealed to John Morehead in May 1925 to finance a Siberian summer journey. No official of the Church had traveled there since Alexander Fehrmann, who had served as

Vice President of the Moscow Consistory (1902–1913), and he had only traveled as far as the western Siberian city of Omsk. Meier planned a more extensive journey of two to three months, traveling as far as Lake Baikal. His wife Eugenie would accompany him and make house visits to the sick and to the children. He had also gathered three crates of New Testaments and catechisms from Morehead and others that he hoped to distribute. Accompanying him would be a young pastor, Friedrich Deutschmann, who had recently finished a course for preachers under Bishop Malmgren in Leningrad and done his practical work under Pastor Karl Arthur Hanson in the Crimea. Meier planned to ordain the recently wed Deutschmann for service in Siberia.[1] It was an ambitious travel plan for a sixty-year-old bishop whose zeal at times was greater than the concern for his own health. With Morehead sending over $3,000 to finance Meier's travels, the long-awaited journey began on May 30 after a special service in Sts. Peter and Paul in Moscow.

In Siberia, Meier was impressed with the spiritual hunger among the people. If they had no cathedral, they built prayer houses; at times, as for example in the village of Dönhof, the people lavishly decorated a gigantic barn that served as a church. The believers would barely allow him time to rest, continually plying him with requests for services and conversations. He also visited Latvians and Estonians, conducting services in Russian wherever possible. Meier was also taken with the natural beauty of Siberia. He marveled at the majesty of the Yenisei River after a long journey. Once, at the conclusion of an all-day church festival in Orlovskoye, Meier and his company watched the sunset from the summit of a mountain. Looking to the north and seeing the steppes laid out, and then looking at the mountains to the south, was an hour in Meier's life that he would never forget. The Lutherans of Siberia had impressed him as robust people, but a flock desperately in need of shepherds. His trip had roused him to do something about it so that there would be a future for the Lutheran Church in Siberia.[2]

PERHAPS THE MOST pressing issue of the Evangelical Lutheran Church in Russia, even before Meier's journey to Siberia, was finding a means to replenish the congregations lacking pastors. Due to death and emigration, at least half of the congregations needed pastors.[3] Without help, they would turn to other Protestant denominations, fill the vacancy with someone in their own midst who was unqualified, or simply fall away from faith. As long ago as 1922, Meier had begun to broach the topic of a seminary with Morehead.[4] Bishop Arthur Malmgren had likewise been concerned with the lack of pastors. Through the Petrograd Church Office, in fall 1922 he began what became known as a *Schnellkurs*, an accelerated seminary course. After an appeal by a Swedish engineer working in Petrograd, John Tuneld, support arrived via the Lutheran Church of Sweden and Archbishop Nathan Söderblom. Initially, Meier was somewhat skeptical of this *Schnellkurs*, seeing it only as an emergency measure. But after his journey to Siberia, he would gain a greater appreciation for the qualifications of the *Schnellkurs* students. A 1925 graduate, Friedrich Deutschmann, had ably accompanied him on that journey.

Meier's plans for a seminary began to crystalize in 1924. Morehead was skeptical as to whether the Soviet government would allow a Lutheran seminary to open, but the times were now different since the advent of the "religious NEP."[5] Since the Evangelical Lutheran Church of Russia at its June 1924 convention subscribed to the Lutheran Confessions as laid out by the LWC Conference in Eisenach, Morehead saw no reason why the LWC or the NLC could not financially support the proposed seminary. According to the decision reached by the Lutheran Church Conference in June, Malmgren was chosen to head the seminary with its location slated for Leningrad. Leningrad was more appropriate as a site than Moscow because the local conditions were more favorable. A potential roster of professors lived in the city, and St. Anne's Lutheran Church could provide sufficient schoolrooms as well as an adjoining building where dorm space could be found at a reasonable rate.[6]

With potential funding in place, Malmgren went to the Soviet authorities and on April 15, 1925, received permission to open a "Bible school" in Leningrad that fall. Morehead was a little skeptical of the proposed title for the seminary and asked Malmgren to clarify the reasons for registering the seminary as a "Bible school." Was the title "merely the adaptation of the name to the psychology of the country" or would it "make it impossible to give adequate scientific training for the ministry?"[7] Malmgren answered that the term "theological" was not accepted because they lived in a land where God was not recognized. As for the name "seminary," it, too, was rejected because it reminded the government of the prerevolutionary institution that the Lutheran Church operated in Dorpat.

In fact, the Russian Orthodox, Baptist, and Evangelical Christians were only allowed to open "Bible schools" as well. Nonetheless, Malmgren assured Morehead that the Bible school would operate like any university in the Western world, teaching all the subjects that a theological faculty would offer. Furthermore, the neighboring building where the students would be housed had adjoining rooms. The rooms were now vacant, the building itself having formerly belonged to the Church until it was nationalized in 1918. Unfortunately, the rooms were in such a state of disrepair that the housing administration of the city couldn't pay for repairs. Repairs would cost 21,500 rubles, approximately a little over $10,000!

Displaying his negotiating skill, Malmgren worked out an agreement with the government so that Lutherans would pay for only half of the repairs ($5,000) and in return be allowed to occupy their rooms rent-free for three years. Due to the housing shortage, this was a beneficial arrangement, all the more so as the agreement would ensure that rent would not be raised for the next few years. When Morehead wondered whether it might be more efficient simply to purchase a building, Malmgren reminded him of the complicated circumstances under which he was operating. The Soviet government owned all property! The Church had no rights and only used its property at the government's good pleasure. The Soviets could easily take any building back, no matter whether one had purchased the property outright. To expedite funding, Malmgren suggested it would be best to send the funds through the German Consulate in Leningrad by way of the General Consul Herr Schliep.[8]

As rector of the Bible school, Malmgren assembled a capable staff: The dean of students would be Friedrich Wacker, who had served as a pastor in the Volga region village of Norka. Otto Wentzel, a graduate of the theological department in Leipzig, would hold the position of student overseer. Professor Brock would teach the classical languages, while local pastors Alexander Juergensonn, Paul Reichert, Helmut Hansen, and Arnold Frischfeld would teach the remaining subjects. Former student Johannes Lel later remembered Frischfeld as being exceptionally literate. He read Greek and Hebrew as fluently as his own native German. Lel recollected that when teaching, he only had a small sheet of paper with some notes on it. His memory was exceptional. In fact, it appears that the level of instruction was quite high, as student Bruno Toryassan would remember Hebrew verses to the end of his life in 2009! General instruction for the courses would be given in German, but the other ethnic groups represented in the Bible school (Estonian, Latvian, Finnish/Ingrian) would be allowed to do practical work in their native tongue. The plans were to form a first-year class of thirty students who would range in age from eighteen to thirty-five. The course of study was planned to last three years.[9]

There was one matter that troubled Morehead as he sought to raise support for the Bible school, and it concerned a problem that Meier had encountered in Siberia and the Volga. Congregationalists were engaging in "sheep-stealing," enticing Lutherans away from their Church. The problem surfaced likewise in the American Midwest, where a large number of Russian-Germans had settled. *Die Weltpost*, a secular newspaper based in Lincoln, Nebraska, described life back in the Volga region, so the NLC kept tabs on the conversations generated by its articles. Recently, Morehead had become aware that the proposed seminary dean, Wacker, had letters published in *Die Weltpost*. Morehead was concerned that Wacker seemed to be appealing for seminary support through Jacob Volz, a well-known Congregationalist active in the Volga region. This was concerning to Morehead for two reasons. First, he knew that the Soviet authorities could easily gain access to public information about seminary plans. It was no secret that Bolshevik agents were actively engaged in the United States. Second, Morehead raised funds among firmly convinced Lutherans and knew that they would not countenance a unionist or mixed seminary in Russia. The NLC also had always been concerned with those duplicating efforts at fund-raising in America. Morehead found it simpler and more transparent to operate through Church channels rather than individuals whose motives might be suspect. (Morehead did acknowledge, though, that he believed Volz to be a good man.) For these reasons, there was also some enmity toward the Iowa and Missouri Synods for attempting to work outside the structure of the NLC.[10]

When Malmgren was made aware of Wacker's actions, he was surprised and disappointed. After quizzing Wacker, though, he was relieved. It seems Wacker had relatives from the Missouri Synod with whom he often corresponded. They were interested in the Volga region where he served, as they were from that region themselves. Apparently, some of his letters had been passed along to *Die Weltpost* without his knowledge. It was no doubt surprising to the Russian-Germans in the Soviet Union that there was such interest in America about their lives. Wacker reassured Malmgren, who in turn assured Morehead, that Wacker would not solicit funds from Congregationalists. The irony, of course, was that Morehead, of the United Lutheran Church, was defending the construction of a purely Lutheran seminary in Russia, something with which Missouri Synod Lutherans would also be in sympathy.[11]

FINALLY, ON SEPTEMBER 15 the hard work came to fruition as the seminary opened its doors with an inaugural service at St. Anne's.[12] The first-year class registered twenty-four students out of a total of sixty applicants, ultimately numbering eighteen students as six had to decline for family reasons or military service. The students came from various regions throughout the country: the Crimea, Kherson (Ukraine), the Caucasus and other southern regions, not to mention the Leningrad region. Although fourteen students were of German ethnicity, there were also three Latvians and one Russian studying. Malmgren described them as "full of zeal and desire to equip and educate themselves so that they could give a good witness for their Savior and be servants in His vineyards."[13]

A normal day at the seminary began with devotions at 8:30, followed by a small breakfast usually consisting of coffee and butter bread. The daily lectures would then begin at 9:15 and last until 2 p.m., with a fifteen-minute interval between classes. A two-course lunch would follow at 2:30 p.m. (a three-course meal on Sundays and holidays) and then the students would have free time from 3:00 to 5:00, where many would go for a walk. After the break, study time commenced with a light dinner at 7:30, followed by evening devotions. Music lovers had access to the piano until 11 p.m., and all lights were expected to be out and students in bed by midnight.

The subjects taught were what was expected from a seminary in Europe at that time. Alongside Greek and Hebrew, students began with Introduction to Theology and Introduction to the Old Testament. Related to the language classes were exegetical lectures on Genesis and the Gospel of Matthew. As a reflection of those times, a course on Albert Schweitzer's *The Life of Jesus* was offered, as were practical subjects like Homiletics and Catechetics. For history courses, A General History of Religion, History of the Ancient and Medieval Church, and the History of Dogmatics were the subjects covered. The biggest problem for the seminarians was the lack of textbooks. For example, the materials for *The Life of Jesus* and Introduction to the Old Testament consisted of one teacher's copy for all the students. For the Hebrew textbooks, three or four students had to share a copy. The seminary would need more books in the future, but at least a beginning had now been made.[14]

No one at that time knew how long the seminary would be able to operate freely, but in the middle of the 1920s it appeared as though the Lutheran
Church just might be able to survive the restrictions of the Communist regime.
While it was a time of rapid change in the country, it was also a time of hope
for Lutherans. Edith Müthel's description of the ordination of her father, Emil
Pfeiffer, paints a picture of a Church that was still full of spirit despite all the
hardships of the previous eight years. His ordination took place at St. Anne's
in Leningrad on a bright, sunny June day in 1925. Müthel has remembered all
her long life the garlands of flowers, the smell of roses permeating the packed
church where not one space was vacant, the pealing of the organ, the blend-
ing of the rich voices in the choir, the sun beaming through the stained-glass
windows. She and others could have been forgiven for thinking, "Surely the
Lord would never let such a Church die?"[15]

"HOLD FAST WHAT YOU HAVE"

The Status of the Lutheran Church in 1926

AS THE CONGREGATION of Sts. Peter and Paul in Moscow prepared to celebrate its 300th anniversary and the Evangelical Lutheran Church in Russia its 350th in 1926, Bishop Meier in a secret report described for foreign Lutherans the status of his own congregation and the Lutheran Church in the Soviet Union. Likening the Church to the broken tabernacle that the prophet Amos saw, Meier pondered how long it could survive given the oppressive conditions. At the beginning of World War I, Sts. Peter and Paul had numbered 20,000 parishioners, with 300 baptisms, 225 confirmations, 200 marriages, and 350 burials each year. This enormous church held space for 2,500 people while its three secondary schools plus other lower-level schools numbered over 1,500 students. There were three pastors serving the congregation with one part-time pastor. In the words of Meier, though, this congregation was not only badly damaged but "completely ruined." The nationalization of the property led to the church losing about 3 million rubles, or the equivalent of $1.5 million of property and funds. Now only a third of its former parishioners remained, as many had left for the Baltic states. By 1926 it was reduced to 100 baptisms, 75 confirmations, 80 weddings, and 85 deaths a year. Only one pastor served the congregation, and at times he was even forced to fill in at St. Michaels.

Yet despite all the obstacles, the perseverance of the Church and its parishioners was remarkable. For example, in the past the Church had relied on its
property and funds to undergird a variety of charitable institutions and its
pastors. Now that the Communist state had taken that away from them, there
was a reduction in income and the number of parishioners attending church.
Yet despite the decline of Sts. Peter and Paul to about a third of its previous
level, parishioners tithed more money now than they had previously. People
seemed to recognize that they had a treasure in their church and seemed to
value it even more than in the past. Many city congregations had even added
Saturday evening services, and in the case of Sts. Peter and Paul, they were
very well attended. Looking over the circumstances of the Lutheran Church
in the Volga region, Meier saw reason for cautious optimism. Attendance was
up and pastors were ministering to larger crowds than they had in the years of
war and famine. The sixty-three-year-old Volga District President, Nathaniel
Heptner, was kept busy on Sundays and throughout the week, holding services
in villages and cities throughout the Volga region. One congregation regularly
numbered five hundred to a thousand attendees but could also reach numbers
in excess of 1,500! Heptner wore a pedometer during one communion service,
calculating that he walked twelve kilometers in the altar space! During the week
of Pentecost in 1926, he traversed the Volga River villages, confirming more
than 1,500 girls and boys.[1]

Heptner's restoration to the pastoral ministry was nothing short of a miracle. He had been charged with political crimes for distributing food for the
NLC and was sentenced to prison for a term of five years and four months. His
initial response was to reject any accusation of guilt, but due to poor health he
apparently broke down and confessed. It is more than likely that he simply confessed that he was not opposed to the Soviet regime (as most Lutheran pastors
would) and was then freed under the terms of a July 10, 1924 amnesty law passed
by the Communist Party of the Soviet Republic of the Volga Germans. Meier

played a role in Heptner's liberation, too, as he interceded with none other than the President of the Soviet Union, Mikhail Kalinin. Whatever the reasons for his release, a revitalized Heptner was doing the work of a much younger man. His family's zeal to serve the Church at any cost would be illustrated in the fall when his son, Bernhard, decided to enter the seminary in Leningrad.[2]

Heptner's situation was not the only good news the Church received about those imprisoned for their faith. Morehead had never given up on his efforts to free Kurt Muss. Writing to Meier on March 25, 1924, he recalled that Muss "undertook his mission for me when I was ill with the full approval of the American Relief Administration and his papers were countersigned by the representative of the Soviet government. He made reports to this office, just as others made them. His reports have never been published in America and will not be published. His imprisonment seems to us to have been a great injustice." Morehead asked Meier if there was anything that could be done for Muss.[3] Now word came to Morehead in August 1924 that Muss had been freed from prison after 1.5 years. Unlike the liberation of Heptner, in this case Meier had exerted no influence. This made sense to Morehead, for he always believed that Muss's freedom was God's answer to the continued intercessory prayers of those who had not forgotten him or his sacrifice. After Muss's liberation, he was sentenced to exile in the Yaroslavky region without the right to live in either Moscow or Leningrad.[4]

While in the Yaroslavsky region, Muss made the acquaintance of a famous Russian scientist, Nikolai Morozov, who took a liking to the inquisitive young man and would continue corresponding with him and his family for many years. Due to Morozov's intercession, in June 1926 Muss was allowed to return to Leningrad where he immediately took the exams necessary to be received into the ministry of the Lutheran Church. On September 16 he began serving at St. Peter's under the guidance of his old classmate at Yuryev University, Helmut Hansen. And so, like Peter unexpectedly walking out of

his jail cell due to the Lord's intervention, Kurt Muss returned to freedom
and would take up the pastoral duties at Jesus Christ Lutheran Church in
Leningrad the following year.[5]

THE LUTHERAN CHURCH was far from dead in these regions where pastors
worked tirelessly with little pay to meet the spiritual needs of their people. In
the Crimean District, District President Ferdinand Hörschelmann was being
kept constantly on the go by the religious demands of parishioners. The vigorous seventy-year-old joked that he was riding a virtual merry-go-round that
past spring and summer, having just finished one round of pastoral visits only
to embark on another throughout the Crimean districts. Further proof that
age was no obstacle to a dedicated servant of God, sixty-five-year-old Northern
Caucasus District President Emil Bonwetsch's travels extended to Baku on the
Caspian Sea, an estimated journey longer than a trip from Europe to America!
Meier was also pleased that Siberia was beginning to get the pastors that he
had promised. Four new pastors had been sent, including his travel companion
from the previous year, Friedrich Deutschmann. Deutschmann now ministered from Slavgorod to seventy preaching stations while another, Siegfried
Schultz, covered ninety preaching stations from his base in Omsk. In addition,
four pastors traveled to Siberia in June to assist the ministry to the scattered
congregations in Siberia.[6]

The state of the Lutheran Church in 1926 could not only be described by
the revival of congregations throughout the country; it could also be seen in
the restoration of institutions like the seminary. In September the seminary
began its second year of studies, having added six more students than it antic-
ipated for the first-year class. Combined with the second-year students there
were thirty-four students total. Bishop Malmgren would need to find more
accommodations for the students, because they would not have enough room
in their current student dorms. With regard to costs, the Lutheran Church had

been able to run the seminary in its first year (1925–1926) for basically $10,000, with the local Russian Lutheran congregations raising an additional $2,650.

All in all, Meier discerned "a process of clarification and sorting out" taking place in the congregations. "Those that still retain their Christian faith are today probably more conscientious and deeper Christians than the average church members during former years. ... We notice this especially in the younger generation." Meier noted that the Church was most robust in the Volga settlements, where the old "German rustic nature" would not give up its old traditions despite the changing culture of the Soviet Union. There young and old held together in strong Lutheran communities, rarely if ever renouncing the faith in light of the persecution of religious believers.[7]

AND YET THE picture was not entirely rosy. There was confusion among some believers stemming from active proselytism on the part of Protestant "free preachers" as well as certain cultic groups in the villages. The free preachers were working in tandem with Congregationalists from America, who tended to financially support their "sheep-stealing" endeavors among the traditional Volga Lutheran communities. However, where the local Lutheran pastors exhibited a strong presence, these Protestant groups rarely made inroads among the population. At times, religious revivals took place through the influence of cultic groups. For example, during the stressful civil war and famine years (1920–1922) in the Volga region, chiliastic teachings led to excesses and only died down after reasonable living conditions returned. But recently a local lay preacher had begun preaching that Christ's return was imminent. In order that they not be found sleeping when Christ came, the ecstatic gatherings of this group were punctuated by a "mad-like dancing," prompting the nickname *Tanzbrudern* (Dancing Brothers). There were additional groups like the *Abendlichter* (Evening Lights), as well as the Irvingite cult in Volhynia (western Ukraine).

In Meier's estimation, although the Church faced dangers such as these within the Volga communities and other regions, the unification of Lutheran congregations in the Soviet Union held out hope for a future of strong, confessional Lutheranism. While he did not want to minimize the persecution of the Church, Meier also felt that it was not facing "destruction or abolition." His hope was that the older generation would preserve its Lutheran heritage for the younger generation, whose day he believed he wouldn't see but would come when the Lord "will in time re-erect the fallen church."[8]

While he contemplated the existence of the Church in the future, Meier experienced daily struggles. When the state nationalized church property in 1918, Sts. Peter and Paul lost the pastor's home on the church grounds. Previously, the ten- room, two-floor home housed three pastors, but now Meier and his family of four had access only to the lower floor. Meier and his wife occupied one room, his son the second room (which also served as the only kitchen and living room), his daughter the third room, the church organist the fourth room (which was also the church office) and the church groundskeeper and his wife the fifth room. Fourteen or fifteen people now lived on the upper floor, employees of a local factory.

As a member of the clergy, in essence a "non-person," Meier had to pay three hundred rubles (approximately $150) to rent his family's rooms. This did not include heating, lighting, or water. Try as it might, the congregation could only raise about 30 percent of the costs associated with the expenses of the parsonage. To further complicate the situation, Mr. Raudkepp, the church organist, had died in 1925, and now to keep his room the congregation was obliged to pay thirty-five rubles a month (approximately $17.50). Meier was certain that eventually he and the other church workers would either be forced to pay even higher rates or be kicked out of the home. After all, as a member of the clergy, he was singled out by good Soviet citizens as one of the "former people" (*biivshe lyudi*), the phrase used in derogatory fashion for those who were considered representative of the old czarist regime.[9]

As complicated as the housing situation was for Meier and other pastors, a far more shocking event occurred August 27 in Siberia that would have a chilling effect on any pastor serving a congregation in the Soviet Union. A recently commissioned pastor, Siegfried Schultz, had just completed a sermon in the Siberian town of Tara, three hundred versts north of Omsk, when a radical Estonian Communist by the name of Puusepp accosted him on the street. Puusepp shot Pastor Schultz three times in the back in broad daylight, killing him on the spot. At his trial, Puusepp declared that he hated priests with a passion and that this pastor in particular had disturbed his anti-religious propaganda.[10] Schultz had a five-year old son and his wife was expecting their second child at Christmas. The Church had also lost an energetic, able servant, as Schultz spoke three languages fluently and had been covering ninety widely scattered preaching stations from his base in Omsk. Schultz had been beginning to organize congregations in the region, so his sudden loss was a great tragedy for the Church.

Bishop Malmgren felt keenly the loss of Schultz since he had ordained him five years before. Morehead was likewise deeply saddened because the LWC had commissioned Schultz for Siberian mission trips and saw his pastoral service as only the beginning of a restoration of the Lutheran witness in Siberia. Now his widow was left destitute. She was pregnant with a young child at home and the congregation was two months behind on the pastor's salary. Malmgren appealed to Morehead, "Who can help us here?"[11] Morehead agreed with Malmgren's request to establish a fund not only for the widow Schultz but also for other church employees who were in dire straits.[12] That assistance would be needed for the widow of yet another veteran of the Siberian missions, because after his mission journey that summer the 63-year-old Bishop to the Estonians in Russia, Oskar Palsa, passed away on October 29. Known for his strong constitution, he continued to serve under difficult conditions that summer in the Minusinsk region of Siberia despite being very sick. As soon as he returned home, his energy having been sapped, he slowly sank away after being bedridden for two months. Palsa's death was a severe blow to the Estonian contingent of the Lutheran Church in Russia, who had lost Bishop Gruenberg only three years before.[13]

IN HIS REPORT to Lutherans in Russia on the state of the Church in Siberia in 1926, Bishop Meier prefaced his comments with a quotation from Revelation 3:11: "I am coming soon. Hold fast what you have, so that no one may seize your crown." The Christian church was becoming increasingly threatened throughout the world, he warned. Earnest Christians needed to recognize that they were living in the Last Days, the time of the great falling away from Christianity. In a sermon at the October celebration of Sts. Peter and Paul's three hundredth anniversary, the pastor in the Volga River city of Marxstadt, Arthur Kluck, echoed similar themes. Encouraging his parishioners to stand by the Christ of the apostles and martyrs in these challenging times, Kluck asked the congregation, "Do you also want to leave this [faith]? No, no, no! We will stand with the apostles. ... 'Lord to whom shall we go? You have the words of eternal life.'"[14] All Meier, Kluck, or any other Lutheran pastor would have to do is observe the religious situation in the Soviet Union and apocalyptic images would immediately present themselves.

Kluck's words at Sts. Peter and Paul summed up the situation as it existed in Siberia as well. A beginning had been made in efforts to restore the Church, but those gains among Lutherans in Siberia had to be sustained by the Church. Morehead's thoughts on this matter reflected a sober outlook, admitting to Malmgren on learning of Palsa's and Schultz's deaths, "In the battle we are waging, ... we must expect casualties and losses."[15] But Morehead could never remain pessimistic for long. He continued, "But He that is with us is greater than those who are against us." It was a call for encouragement to those who, despite the positive gains made in 1926, knew that there were devils loose in the land and they would stop at nothing less than the annihilation of Christianity.[16]

Despite the trials challenging the Church in Siberia, the spirit of the pastors continued undaunted. When asked at a Moscow conference in October who might take the place of Pastor Schultz, more pastors put up their hands than could possibly be sent for the planned summer mission visits of Siberia in 1927. Furthermore, when Dean Wacker announced the death of Schultz to the seminarians, four students immediately expressed their desire to be sent to Siberia on completion of their studies. Such responses encouraged Meier that Schultz's position in Omsk would not remain vacant for long.[17] Despite the difficulties of operating in an officially atheist land, the state of the Lutheran Church was better than it had been since the Bolshevik Revolution. But that didn't mean that the dark shadows of persecution were not visible and that further trouble didn't lay ahead.

9

"UNBELIEVABLE ELASTICITY"

Managing Relations with Church and State in 1927

THE NOOSE WAS tightening around Bishop Meier in Moscow. The State Communal Housing Administration had been charging rent to a factory whose workers were living in the other rooms, but now the government decided to give the property to a local school administration. The former Lutheran girls' secondary school next door to the parsonage and church had already been converted to a Soviet school, and Meier was convinced that the school administration would soon take over his rooms as well. So, the proposed plan to build on the land also would not make sense because the school administration ultimately would own anything built on "their land." Seeking ways to avoid trouble with the authorities, Meier and the High Church Council concluded that purchasing a home on the border of the city was the best answer to his dilemma. There one could rent a home for $1,500 a year, as opposed to the $3,500 that was the going price in the center of the city where Sts. Peter and Paul was located. The idea was to get a large home that could house both the bishop's family and the High Church Council offices. With the new bus and tram lines, one could travel to the city center in thirty minutes.[1]

While he was speculating on all the possibilities, Meier was ordered to appear in a Soviet court on May 13 to defend his right to his longtime residence. In response, the bishop decided to dig in. He would not leave his rooms after all. If he left the rooms, his successor at Sts. Peter and Paul would never be able to effectively carry out the ministry without the apartment next to the church. Working with the government, as he lamented to Morehead, required "unbelievable elasticity." Furthermore, Meier decided he could not carry out his duties as bishop and serve as the pastor of Russia's largest Lutheran congregation. Recognizing the burdens on him, the congregation agreed to call another pastor. Unfortunately, the called pastor could not leave his congregation for another year, and Sts. Peter and Paul didn't want a different pastor. As a result, Meier was forced to remain in these uncomfortable living conditions with the added pressure from the school administration to vacate the home he had lived in since 1911. He could not leave his people without a spiritual shepherd in these perilous times, even if his health would suffer as a result.[2]

Though Meier would stay in the parsonage for the time being, Morehead gave of his own personal funds toward the goal of having a separate house for the High Church Council and the bishop. As they sought to raise further funds, Meier worried about what the congregations might think when they learned that such a sum was to be spent, even though it was important for the whole Church. He knew that his people were suffering and possessed so little. Part of the problem was that the Lutheran congregations historically did not have to pay for their pastors. Even though the Lutheran Church suffered persecution under the czars, pastors were paid employees of the state. So, although the Lutheran Church in the Soviet era had more freedom in its affairs, the congregations still were not accustomed to gathering funds for the preservation of their Church. Nevertheless, through Meier's influence, they were slowly but surely learning how to support the Church. Meier hoped that they might even gather $1,500 for the Church office in Moscow that year as well as contribute $2,500 for the seminary in Leningrad. Given the economic and political conditions in the Soviet Union, it is evident that the Lutheran parishioners were doing what they could to keep their Church alive. But intimidation from anti-religious activists also existed, as well as the government itself, which at times would forbid locals from gathering funds for the Church.[3]

With pressure encompassing him on all sides, Bishop Meier took advantage of his dacha (summer cottage) in Golizyno, a one hour and ten-minute ride from Moscow. There, in the peace and comfort of this forested area, he could plan for the coming General Synod and retreat from the old parsonage that had now become, in his words, "a living hell." He would come into the city on Saturdays and Sundays to conduct worship services, but during the week Nizhniy Novgorod District President Holzmayer would represent Church interests in Moscow, along with Ferdinand Hörschelmann, who would provide temporary assistance beginning June 1.[4]

Burdened by his efforts to keep up a busy work schedule, Bishop Meier suffered a serious physical breakdown that forced him to his bed that summer. He admitted to suffering from depression, a natural response given the attention that the Soviet state had accorded him. Fortunately for Meier, his neighbor in Goliznyo was the famous Dr. Kramer, known for his service to Vladimir Lenin a few years before. Meier's prognosis was favorable, although it was recommended that he remain in Golizyno and convalesce for two months. His work would also be curtailed due to a problem he had with his eyes. He was having trouble reading with even the sharpest of eyeglasses, and his wife had to read to him. His son Traugott, who couldn't enter a Soviet university because he was the son of a pastor, would also provide care for him in Golizyno. On August 4, Meier attempted to return to activity by simultaneously writing to Carl Paul, Bishop Ludwig Ihmels in Leipzig, and John Morehead in America. He confessed that he could no longer carry on the work of bishop and pastor due to his health. He struggled with the additional concern as to how he would support his family since the congregation had covered utilities and room and board for the Meiers. (He did not receive a salary from the congregation). His daughter Elisabeth was a great help since she was working at two Moscow universities after receiving her PhD in Germanic languages and literature in

1924 at the University of Leipzig. She provided much of the family's financial support, although she was at the moment in Germany for academic purposes.[5]

DUE TO THE worsening economic situation in the Soviet Union despite the liberalized economic policies promoted by the NEP, parishioners were giving less and less. Dedicated High Church Council members like Paul Althausen and Arthur Gernsdorff were receiving only small compensation for their work, yet they soldiered on for the good of the Church. Althausen was working on the first Church journal, known as *Unsere Kirche* (*Our Church*). *Unsere Kirche* had been in the works for some time but due to the obstruction of Soviet censors had yet to be published. Meier announced that after six months' delay, the first three issues were being submitted for what appeared to be the final review of the censors. Initially, the first two issues were rejected in their entirety, but the Lutherans were able to redact the issues to the satisfaction of Soviet censors. Now Meier and the Church were awaiting the publication of a journal that would provide information about the Church to Lutherans throughout the Soviet Union. Meier was certainly ready for this good news, remarking somewhat incisively that it was "a special day of joy in a dark time." Concluding his letter to his good friends in Germany and America, Meier joked, "I have done more than enough for today. My wife and son, my loyal co-workers have gone on strike."[6]

Looking ahead to engaging Meier and Malmgren more directly in conversation about the issues at hand as the Chairman of the Executive Committee of the LWC, Morehead invited them both to a meeting in October to be held in Budapest. Given the stark reality of censorship in the Soviet Union, they could never be as open with each other as they could talking face to face in a free country. Meier's visit to Dresden the previous year had allowed them to discuss issues that could only be broached in a veiled manner through letters. Their apprehensions about the censors were not unfounded. The Soviets were likely wary of potential conversations between the two; they refused Malmgren a visa the previous year and rejected this invitation as well. As he invited Meier to the Budapest conference, urging him to accept only if his health was better, Morehead expressed his concern about the bishop's extraordinary work schedule: "May I speak to you as a brother a word of caution? Never again dare you commit yourself … to undertake so much work as in the past nor to work with such ceaseless and energetic intensity." Morehead understood him all too well. He also suffered from the same commitment to overwork leading to the brink of exhaustion.[7]

While Bishop Meier had been resting that summer, High Church Council member and lawyer Paul Althausen was corresponding with Morehead, happily noting that permission had been received to import a large number of Luther's Small Catechisms along with Bible history books. Even better news was that the books were not only in German but also Latvian and Estonian.[8] Since April 1926, Morehead had been advocating for the printing of Bibles, catechisms, and other Christian literature. The door for this mission opportunity had been blocked, but Morehead was trusting "that in God's own way and time the way may be opened."[9] This permission appeared to offer a sign that possibilities still existed to do ministry in the Soviet Union despite obstruction from the authorities. Maybe God's time for the church had now come?[10]

The import of Christian literature in various languages was a positive development for unity. Bishops Malmgren and Meier were aware of the need to show that their Church was not simply an enclave of German nationalists. Getting permission to import religious literature in many languages was a start. To continue on the path of reconciliation, though, the seminary would need to graduate more than ethnic German pastors. One of the biggest hindrances to this goal was that the level of general education for the other ethnic groups was lower than that of the Germans. Furthermore, the professors and most students were ethnic Germans, making it imperative that the language of instruction be German.

In his report to the LWC given in Dresden in 1926, Meier sounded exasperated as he tried to balance academic standards and the need to admit more non-Germans to the seminary. At the time there was one Finnish-speaking student (the Ingrian Paavo Haimi) and two others who would eventually serve Latvian-language parishes. There were no Estonians, as they generally were not conversant in German.[11] The potential existed for a further distancing of Germans from other ethnic groups in the Church since pastors who had been educated at Yuryev University in Dorpat were getting older. Bishops Meier, Malmgren, and the late Freifeldt and Palsa were all educated at Yuryev and were able to converse in German, Estonian, and in certain cases Latvian. Now that Latvia and Estonia were separate countries, though, their ethnic brethren in Russia were cut off from them and the Leningrad Seminary was the only means for theological education for those residing in the Soviet Union. To rectify this unequal representation in the Lutheran Church, Malmgren appealed to Morehead to provide financial support for a plan to teach prospective students from among Latvians, Estonians, and Finns/Ingrians. Malmgren foresaw preparatory classes of general education for these students, but he strongly affirmed that these classes were not to be considered seminary education. The seminary trained pastors; these students, whom he hoped would then apply to the seminary, were not yet prepared for classes that included such academic subjects as Hebrew and Greek. They would need preparation if they were to succeed in the seminary. The government had given its oral approval, but Malmgren needed to wait for the more formal and essential bureaucratic approval. By the spring, Malmgren had assembled ten Finns/Ingrians and Estonians for just such a preparatory course.[12]

Morehead foresaw no problems with the plan and was in "full agreement," although the money was not yet in hand. The NLC would without doubt come through as it had so often in the past, but Morehead was inclined to pressure the European Lutherans so that the support of the Lutheran Church in Russia would not be so one-sided.[13] Because of his desire that the support of Russian

Lutheranism be a joint effort with Europeans, Morehead always took special pleasure when informing Malmgren that support for the seminary had come from Lutherans outside of Germany or America: for example, Poles, Czechs, Hungarians, or Yugoslavs.[14]

IN KEEPING WITH the desire to create conditions for the Lutheran Church to be available to all language groups, Malmgren ordained Kurt Muss on March 27, 1928, as the pastor of Jesus Christ Lutheran Church in Leningrad. Muss would become the first Lutheran pastor in the Soviet Union who ministered full-time to an exclusively Russian-speaking congregation.[15] Morehead was emotionally overcome by the news. "It is impossible for me to express the joy which is mine on learning from your letter that Kurt Muss has been released from prison and that he will be ordained to the ministry of the Evangelical Lutheran Church. I have suffered much sorrow and regret on account of the punishment he has had to endure in connection with his service of the National Lutheran Council as my representative." Lauding them for the "progressive spirit of the Evangelical Lutheran Church of Russia in these new times," Morehead hoped the Lutherans of Russia would replicate the American practice of using the native language of their country. Just as American Lutherans were moving from German or Scandinavian languages to English, the Lutherans in Russia would eventually need to prepare candidates for the pastoral ministry in Russian. Muss's service would be a positive step forward, and the Church couldn't have chosen a more suitable candidate.[16]

The congregation was growing steadily, although they lacked their own space and had to meet in the evenings. Soon the Sunday and Wednesday services were gathering five hundred persons, and there was a children's service that a hundred regularly attended. Muss began youth Bible studies and attempted to upgrade and expand the old hymnal from 106 to 230 hymns, some newly translated. In the fall of 1928, Muss contacted Morehead to see if he could provide some aid so that the congregation could move into its own building. The children's service at times had to be canceled because of special services scheduled by the Finnish Lutheran church (St. Mary's) where they were meeting. Moreover, there was no meeting hall in the Finnish church for confirmation classes, something that Muss understood as an essential element for any congregation.

Muss looked to reconstruct an old German Reformed Church building where the congregation could meet exclusively. The German Reformed congregation had shrunk so that they could no longer pay for upkeep of its building. Muss stressed that his congregation could pay for the care of the church, but the building was now in such a state of disrepair that they needed about $2,500 for reconstruction. The indefatigable Muss saw God's hand in all that was going on. Even while informing Morehead that the state had proclaimed the uselessness of the clergy by charging higher and higher rent rates, Muss had hope. He noted that there were three apartments within the church, and that would take care of the housing situation for pastor and staff.[17]

Morehead was always open to those engaged in missionary activity, and couldn't easily resist any appeal that Muss made because of his great sacrifice for the NLC during the famine years. He hoped that the congregation could gather the money or loan necessary for temporary use of the building, which would give the LWC time to supply a considerable amount of the cost needed.[18] Since its registration as a congregation in 1923, the congregation's receipts had increased. In fact, church council chairman Alfred Zietnick urged the people, though they were poor, to give more to the pastors. Whereas previously the visiting pastor would receive three rubles per sermon, that number had increased to nine by 1926. Zietnick was a strong leader, encouraging his fellow worshipers to follow the example of the first Christians so that it could remove its defects and grow as a normal congregation. Given the circumstances in which they were living, Zietnick's reference to the early church would often be cited in the coming years as persecution from the state mounted.[19]

THE THIRD SEMINARY YEAR (1927–1928) opened with a total of thirty-three students. While Morehead was disappointed that a new class did not matriculate, Malmgren calculated that the seminary would need an additional $7,000 as there were simply not enough dorm rooms for the prospective students. At any rate, another classroom would still need to be procured for the current students. The lack of living space combined with the animosity of Communists would make these requests even more problematic. It is impossible to underestimate the malevolence of Communists toward Christian believers in those days. For example, Malmgren had wanted to make use of the local gymnasium as his students lacked physical exercise after sitting for long periods of time. The local Soviet school, which formerly was St. Anne's own Lutheran school, refused to allow the students to use their old gym![20]

Morehead was not the only one concerned with getting as many students as possible and as quickly as possible into the Lutheran parishes. Malmgren had already compromised on his desire for a four-year theological education, reasoning that with the shortage of pastors the Church would be forced to offer only three years of study to its first few classes. As a result, only the incoming class of 1928 would be offered a four-year study program. Meanwhile, the students' schedule had remained the same except for evenings, where Malmgren felt the need, due to the younger students' Soviet schooling, to add lectures on literature and history. In the school year of 1927–1928, he decided that the seminary would add lectures on art history and church music as well. Furthermore, acceding to the instructors' and students' wishes, Latin would be added as a subject.

When the school year came to an end, the Leningrad Lutheran seminary celebrated its first legitimate milestone since beginning operations in 1925. On June 14, 1928, the first fourteen graduates successfully completed their theological education. Among the graduates were Jan Migle, Wilhelm Lohrer, Johannes Schlundt, Heinrich Behrendts, David Kaufmann, Woldemar Rüger, Georg Rendar, Theodor Fehler, Jakob Scharf, Konstantin Rusch, Paul Hamberg, Christian Sept, Friedrich Bratz, and Ernst Boese. A student named Lazhis Bluhm would take his exams later in September and be sent to the Latvian-German congregation in Mogilev in what is now Belarus. Gotthold Sterle would, due to illness, only be able to finish his course work in 1929. After that he would assist Helmut Hansen at St. Peter's in Leningrad until he was placed under arrest at Christmas in 1929.

Morehead had assumed that six students would be sent to Siberia, but when the final calls were made only Wilhelm Lohrer was sent, temporarily serving in Omsk under Pastor Friedrich Merz, who had been one of the summer circuit preachers in Siberia. Five students would be called to the Volga region: Boese, Kaufmann, Scharf, Rusch, and Schlundt. Fehler and Sept would go to the Transcaucasian Lutheran Church, which would be united to the Evangelical Lutheran Church of Russia in the fall. The others were called to specific areas and people groups: Migle would serve at the Latvian Synod president's behest; Rendar would go to Volhynia; Hamberg to the Crimea; Bratz to Yekaterinoslav in Ukraine; and Rüger to St. Michael's in Moscow. At age thirty-six, Heinrich Behrendts, the son-in-law of Bishop Malmgren, was older than most students, having started what might be described as a "second career" after working as a lawyer. He was slated to take some final courses in the university, whereupon he would replace Professor Otto Wentzel as the lecturer in Hebrew around Christmastime.[21]

The report of fourteen new pastors was received with pleasure by Morehead, but then Meier informed him that nine pastors would be retiring and asked if he could provide some assistance to them in retirement. Morehead's reply betrayed an exasperation that was unusual for him. "I must confess to some considerable sense of distress that so large a number as nine aged or elderly pastors have under consideration the immediate retirement from the active work of the ministry. ... Must these nine brethren ... all retire from the work of the ministry when pastors are so much needed? ... Are they all feeble or in poor health?" While he understood normal physical limitations when one reached an advanced age, these were extraordinary times for the Lutheran Church in Russia. Could these elderly pastors not fill a need in vacant congregations? He had spoken to American congregations about the self-sacrificing spirit of these pastors in Russia. How could he now defend this request?[22] Perhaps combined with the fact that a new class had not been formed in fall 1927, Morehead worried that vacant congregations would not be filled quickly enough to make a difference to a Church that was facing continual pressure from Communists and the growing atheist movement.[23] In his reply, Meier elaborated on the difficulties of doing the work of the Church in the Soviet Union. Under his own set of pressures, though, the request for retirement funds for elderly pastors seems to have been forgotten.[24]

As a matter of fact, everyday life in the Church was becoming more and more difficult. The so-called Religious NEP, despite the relative freedom it offered, had never offered a problem-free atmosphere for the Church, and sustained persecution was just around the corner. Every single one of the class of 1928 would be arrested in the future, one (Rendar) would escape across the Polish border, while another (Scharf) would leave the pastoral ministry within a few years. All but three would eventually be shot.[25] Although they certainly would have had no illusions as to the potential danger that lay ahead, on graduation day in 1928, they celebrated. A few months after their graduation, Theodor Fehler and Konstantin Rusch would become the first to be arrested.[26]

ON NOVEMBER 15, 1927, Meier officially stepped down as pastor of Sts. Peter and Paul. The younger Hörschelmann, Ferdinand Jr., would fill the pulpit temporarily until Alexander Streck, who had accepted the call, relocated from Astrakhan. Streck would migrate north from the Caspian Sea region and begin work at Easter in 1928. Despite gradually worsening economic conditions, the parishioners provided Meier with a 100 ruble/month pension (approximately $50). Not to be outdone, the ladies of the church separately gathered 720 rubles (approximately $360) so that Meier could take a summer visit to a resort in Germany for his health. Meier was touched and even requested that Morehead personally thank them, providing encouragement from a respected figure abroad who had done so much for their Church.[27]

While preparations were being made for Meier's successor, his housing situation was rapidly moving toward a resolution. A house had been found for the bishop and the High Church Council in the fall of 1927. The offer was for seven years' rent at the price of $7,750. With $9,000 in the bank from funds previously sent by Morehead for housing, it appeared that the funds were on hand for the move. To purchase furniture for the church office and to cover moving costs, an additional $1,000 would be necessary.[28] With the Meiers moving out of the parsonage, four rooms yet remained. As a state employee at the university, Elisabeth Meier would be able keep one room since she was given reduced rental rates. The remaining three rooms would be handed over to Streck, his wife, and two daughters. Church deaconess Tilly Meier and Streck would then have office space in the basement of the church, which would be reconstructed for that purpose. The funds would come from the parishioners themselves, albeit at great sacrifice.[29]

On February 14, the Meiers moved into their new home in Moscow. The bishop's relief was evidence of the harried and cramped living conditions many Russians had to endure from the introduction of communal living arrangements throughout the Soviet Union. Meier blessed the house with the words of Solomon on dedicating the temple: "That Your eyes might be open night and day toward this house." Offering prayers of thanks to God, Meier especially remembered Morehead and those who had provided the funding for the house.

On being happily sequestered into his new two-story home and office, Meier now received the unwelcome news that the school administration had raised the rent for his former rooms to $330 a month (it had been $1,500 a year). The long-suffering congregation submitted a formal protest and had hopes of winning, but the move was ominous nonetheless. Despite these threats, Meier believed that Streck was arriving at a propitious time. The congregation had become more conscious of its duties during the struggles of the past few years. Hardened from their battles, they were determined to support Pastor Streck.[30]

10

"THEY WOULD NOT SEE HIS FACE AGAIN"

A Last Synod and Mission Festival

IN SEPTEMBER OF 1928, the Lutheran Church prepared to hold its second synod in the Soviet Union. This would allow the pastors and bishops to discuss issues like what to do with the journal *Unsere Kirche*, because things weren't going well. Although the journal had been subject to continual interference from the Soviet bureaucracy since its inception, the Church hadn't expected that it would have to fight for the content of every issue. As an example, on February 3, 1928, John Morehead was still awaiting the Christmas 1927 issue, which the censors had not yet allowed to be published.[1] Theophil Meier tried to put an optimistic spin on the situation, writing to Morehead, "With the publication of the church journal we are running into great difficulties, which we thought would be the case in the beginning."[2] Translating from the German to Russian took a long time, but afterward the censor would frequently strike out a large portion of the text. The resulting delay would often mean that the next issue would not come out for weeks or months. The Christmas 1927 issue finally appeared in February 1928, but that pushed the publication of 1928's first issue back to the end of April. Under such conditions, Meier mused,

perhaps it might be better to print the journal in Kharkov, not Moscow.[3]
In fact, only three issues of *Unsere Kirche* would make it out of the censor's
department in 1928.[4]

On September 2, forty-three delegates and eighteen guests filed into Sts.
Peter and Paul for the opening service. As the High Church Council reported
on its activities for the last four years since the first synod, it was evident that
there had been great gains made in the face of constant pressure from the
authorities. But no doubt most were aware of Joseph Stalin's successful accu-
mulation of political power that would result in the introduction of his First
Five-Year Plan beginning in October. The good news, though, was that while
the Communists had been busy fighting each other the past four years for
influence in the party, the resulting political vacuum had allowed the Church
opportunities to restore itself after the initial brutal years of Bolshevik rule.

High Church Council representative Robert Derringer wrote to Morehead
describing the success of the synod. He lauded the harmony on display as many
nationalities were in attendance and had their own leaders officially designated
by the Church at large: Alfred Juergenson became the official bishop of the
Estonians, while Selim Laurikkala of the Finns/Ingrians and Mikhail Lapping
of the Latvians were recognized as *probst* for their respective peoples, having
rejected the title of "bishop." (*Probst* would be akin to "director" or "president.") One of the highlights on the agenda of the synod was the status of
the Transcaucasian Lutheran Church that had operated separately from the
Evangelical Lutheran Church of Russia since its inception 118 years ago. It had
taken a wait-and-see approach during the General Synod in 1924, but afterward requested to join the Evangelical Lutheran Church of Russia. Twenty-
eight congregations from the Transcaucasian region voted to become members,
but only if they would be allowed to retain their internal structure. With this
request granted, the synod recognized Pastor Emil Reusch of Annenfeld as the
representative for the new district of Transcaucasia.[5]

THE HISTORY OF the origins of Lutheranism in the Transcaucasian region was extraordinary. The Church initially consisted of Germans from Württemberg who were Lutheran Pietists. They had become disillusioned with the state church in Germany and its penchant for control, desiring freedom of worship and a piece of land to farm. They were also not necessarily enamored of the state church's formality, especially as reflected in the liturgy. As a result, many of these Lutherans decided to leave what they called this "House of Babel."[6] Drawing on an end times theology that added up the mathematical calculations and predictions of an early eighteenth century preacher, Johann Bengel, many of these Württemberg Lutherans now sought a place of hiding, identifying the woman from Revelation 12:14 as the true community of Christ fleeing a coming antichrist who would be even more terrible than Napoleon. They hoped to find a secluded, mountainous region where God would preserve a holy people for the last days. The basis of their interpretation was Jesus' words in Matthew 24:16: "then let those who are in Judea flee to the mountains."

These Lutherans concluded that the proper place for their community to settle should be somewhere near Mount Ararat (in modern-day eastern Turkey).[7] Into this history now stepped a devout evangelical Christian, the German baroness Juliana von Krüdener. In the summer of 1815, von Krüdener managed to arrange several meetings with the Russian czar Alexander I. Alexander was at that time the most admired man in the world, having just led allied troops to victory over the despised Napoleon. Europe breathed a sigh of relief after Alexander's troops took Paris and brought peace to the continent. The meetings between the czar and baroness were providential for the plans of the Württemberg Lutherans. At this time in Russian history, Alexander I was intrigued by the growing evangelical movement in Europe and Russia, and his interest was reflected in the founding of the Russian Bible Society in 1813. The Lutherans found a kindred soul in the czar whose mother, Maria Feodorovna, was a native of Württemberg.

The Gates of Hell

Juliana von Krüdener convinced him to sponsor the immigration of the
Württemberg Lutherans to Russian territory. As the journey began in 1817 and
the first ships floated down the Danube River, flags fluttered in the wind with
words spelled out in gold: "Czar Alexander: Called by God as the Defender of
the Faith." Hundreds of German families immigrated to this "mountainous
place" in the Russian Empire, which was on the historic territory of Georgia.[8]
Von Krüdener herself, like visionaries before her, never made it to the promised land. She died on the journey, reaching as far as Odessa. However, scores
of families arrived in late 1817 and early 1818 and established six communities in
what is now Georgia and Azerbaijan.[9] It was the congregations that were established by these immigrants who now decided to join the Evangelical Lutheran
Church of Russia.

OTHER ITEMS FOR discussion resulted in some surprising decisions for a
relatively conservative Lutheran church body. With regard to weddings, it was
agreed that where one spouse was Lutheran and the other a Muslim or Jew, or
even of no faith, it was permissible for the pastor to marry them. This action,
though, would be dependent on whether the non-Christian parent was willing
to allow the child to be raised Lutheran. Given the reality of divorce after the
Communists liberalized the laws on marriage in 1918, the synod decided that
as long as the marriage was a civil ceremony one had to wait at least one year
after the divorce in order to be remarried by the pastor.[10] More than likely this
was to illustrate the folly of the Soviet "postcard divorce," where one spouse
could at any time inform the registration office of his or her desire to dissolve
the marriage. The divorce would be signed immediately, with the other spouse
then informed by postcard.[11]

Despite these concessions to the reality of an increasingly secularized society, the synod refused to accept Friedrich Deutschmann's request to allow
non-ordained persons to conduct emergency weddings and baptisms. Since

Deutschmann served in Slavgorod, his proposal reflected the reality of pastoral life in the vast expanse of Siberia. The synod relented somewhat, permitting baptisms only if the district church council approved. In a related matter, Gustav Birth's call for giving laymen the right to offer communion in emergency situations was also rejected. Driving many of these issues was frustration over how to provide pastoral care for far-flung congregations as well as those that were collapsing due to the pastoral shortage. One potential answer to the shortages was to train keusters for ordination. Keusters historically played a prominent role in Russian-German communities, working as teachers of general education who also taught religion. Knowledgeable of the Bible, keusters frequently taught confirmation classes or conducted Bible classes to assist overworked pastors. The synod confirmed that the keusters could be used to help alleviate the dearth of pastors, hoping that at least a small number might be eligible to serve in about four years' time after their supplementary education was concluded. Meier added that he would more clearly delineate the role and duties of the keusters in the near future.[12]

Another vital issue for discussion at the synod concerned the proper age of the student for confirmation. Confirmation had proved to be one of the thorniest and most uncertain issues confronting the Church throughout the 1920s. Officially, the government had decreed on June 13, 1921, that it was forbidden to give religious instruction to organized groups of boys or girls below the age of eighteen.[13] Since the Lutheran Church had generally believed that a child could be confirmed from the age of fifteen and up, a conflict with the law was inevitable. The late Bishop Conrad Freifeldt had generally operated within the parameters of the law, yet his fifteen-year-old daughter Magdalina was confirmed shortly before his death in 1923.

Synod delegate Pastor Johann Völl had concluded that confirmation lessons provided the religious instruction that would make the difference between children who could consciously express their Christian faith and to those who might possess a more cultural view of their faith. With governmental pressure to raise a generation of atheists pressing on them, Völl and his congregation in Grunau (Ukraine) sought a way to instruct the children. As Völl later put it, confirmation instruction "should make the young people spiritually independent, so that they would stand on the foundation that remains immovable when the earth and heavens shake."[14] That belief had taken on greater meaning in 1923 when the Communist authorities in his region officially forbade Völl from instructing children under eighteen. Two days before he was to confirm a new group of students, the local Communist Party official called him to their headquarters for a five-hour cross-examination. "Confirmation itself is a cultural matter," the party official informed him, "we can't prohibit it, because the foreign countries will be watching what we do."[15] However, from then on Völl could no longer officially give confirmation instruction to those under eighteen. he was still permitted to teach younger children, but only in groups of three.

Völl was stuck in a quandary because he would usually confirm two hundred students a year. How could he continue to instruct so many students in small groups of three? The year that this rule came into effect, 1924, the desired goals of the Communists had its effect. Völl confirmed no one. And yet despite the prevailing ethos in society, the parents wanted their children confirmed. In 1925, Völl came up with a new idea. He would prepare his students for confirmation via catechism sermons. Children's services were not allowed by law, but the children could come to regular church services with their parents or related adults. Völl offered three catechism services during the week, although he always believed that the parents got more from these sermons than the children.

Despite the restrictions placed on him, Völl was relatively pleased with the results. One child, an orphan who could neither read nor write, was once asked by one of the atheist-oriented League of the Godless spies what the pastor was teaching him. He replied, "That we should come to Jesus." Even though the orphan couldn't say much more about his instruction, Völl knew that the child had understood the gist of his teaching. On Confirmation Day in 1925, 444 students along with their relatives packed into the village church. Due to the absence of a confirmation class in 1924, Völl now had the equivalent of two classes to confirm. The students and their families occupied all the places so that even the Communist spies couldn't get into the church. Angered, they took to the newspapers to accuse Völl of agitation, wondering how long he would be allowed to get away with actions like these.

Still, Völl was not satisfied with the catechism sermons, so the next year he gathered the confirmands in the government-approved small groups. From Easter until Pentecost, he instructed the students from 7 a.m. to 8 p.m., and sometimes, even longer. He found this a far more satisfying option, as he could hear from their own lips what each of the students understood. He also urged parents to follow Luther's understanding of the role of a parent in teaching his child the faith. He asked them to familiarize their children with the Small Catechism, explaining Luther's idea that "all proper Christian education has its beginning, middle and end in the family." The parents gave his plan their blessing, and so Völl would continue this practice until his arrest in 1930.

Völl was convinced that even if his students forgot the lessons, the word of God would remain in their hearts and bear fruit at the proper time. This theme was echoed by pastors like Kurt Muss and Helmut Hansen, who pushed the boundaries of what was permissible in the realm of religious matters in Soviet Russia. Years later, when he was living in West Germany, Völl would hear from many grateful students who had retained those confirmation lessons all their lives. Even in the short term, the parents were also satisfied because those children who were confirmed at an earlier age generally did not join the Communist youth organizations. In contrast, those congregations that waited until eighteen to confirm their children frequently saw more of them join the Communist youth group, the Komsomol.[16]

Given the importance of confirmation, the General Synod decided that some clarification about confirmation instruction should be agreed on. Was the proper age for confirmation instruction fifteen years old or eighteen years and above? A petition would be sent to the government to ascertain the rules for confirming members. With the conclusion of the General Synod, participants on the whole proclaimed it a success since it clarified issues and provided pastors a forum to discuss questions of great import for the Church.[17] No one knew it at the time, but this would be the high point of the Church for many decades to come—and the last synod.

The delegates were not ignorant of the atheist movement's growing power and the efforts of the OGPU (the secret police agency that had succeeded the GPU in 1923) to support it. While the delegates were gathering, they shared their concerns of spies in the midst of their congregations who reported to the OGPU. It was difficult to determine who the spies were, as parishioners would be threatened with a bullet if they even discussed with anyone that they had been compromised by the OGPU. Völl did have some parishioners who told him that the OGPU had forced them to get information on him, so they decided together what questions they should ask him. He was impressed that his parishioners trusted him more than they feared the dreaded secret police! The OGPU's goal apparently was to wear out the pastors with continual questioning while creating a climate of doubt among their threatened parishioners.[18] While conversing with his fellow pastors at the General Synod in 1928, Völl couldn't shake the sensation that he was practically the only one who hadn't yet been called in for an interrogation with the OGPU.[19] The pressure on bishops Malmgren and Meier was enormous, and it would only grow in the coming years. At least Meier was able to avoid an interrogation with the secret police after this synod, unlike in 1924. He and his wife took advantage of the kind gift offered by their parishioners and went to a *Kurort* (vacation resort) in Bad Oyenhausen in Westphalia for a well-deserved rest.[20] They would need it, because these actions by the Communist authorities were beginning to create an atmosphere of dread among the Lutherans in Russia.

IN THE LATE summer of 1928, plans were made to hold a large festival in the village of Warenburg on the Wiesenseite of the Volga River. The festival, scheduled from August 24–30, was to be led by the elderly itinerant preacher Heinrich Peter Ehlers. Ehlers was the most renowned of the traveling evangelists belonging to a pietistic movement known as "The Brothers." Believers and Lutheran pastors in the region had respected Ehlers because, unlike those inclined to Congregationalism, he worked with rather than against the interests of the Lutheran Church. Sensing that the times were changing and that Christians were on a collision course with atheism, Ehlers sent out handwritten invitations for the festival to people as far away as Siberia. Such a gathering would most certainly not have received state sanction, but in 1928 it was still possible to push the parameters of state limits on religious expression in the provinces. In the years to come, this festival would be remembered as a demarcation between the golden years of relative spiritual freedom and the deadly persecution that would follow.

As the summer drew to a close, thousands of German believers set out from the Black Sea, the Caucasus, and even from Lake Baikal in Siberia for the Volga region. Traveling primarily by horse and wagon, they made the long trek realizing it might be Brother Ehlers's last exhortation to the people to hold fast to the faith of their forefathers. Following the old traditions from their Bible and Mission festivals, the Volga Germans offered up their farmyards to brothers and sisters in the faith. The gates were opened wide to friend and stranger alike so that they could overnight in the courtyards of locals. All gathered to celebrate their faith and pray to God for his presence during the coming days.

Johannes Grasmück of Brunnental opened the festival by leading the participants in a worship service at the large Lutheran cathedral in Warenburg. Despite the size of the cathedral, not all could fit inside.[21] Grasmück was a pastor who had been receiving regular support from the NLC (and now via the LWC) for some years. At first, he had been unaware of just who was supporting him, wondering in a letter to the German-language *California Post* (Fresno) why an anonymous donor would give his family gifts of $40. John Morehead assumed that the High Church Council had already explained to the Lutheran pastors who was supporting them and why. After hearing about Grasmück's letter, Morehead took the opportunity to inform him and other pastors like Woldemar Reichwald that the money was a gift from American Lutherans to enable them to remain at their posts during these difficult times.²²

Now this Lutheran pastor who had remained at his post due to NLC support mounted the pulpit. Using as his text 2 Chronicles 20:15b, he preached, "Do not be afraid and do not be dismayed at this great horde, for the battle is not yours but God's." Grasmück paraphrased the words of Jehoshaphat, who ages ago had exhorted his people to stand for the Lord, imploring the believers to "remain unshakeable in the eternal foundation of God's Word, as it has been made manifest to us in Christ and has been renewed through Martin Luther." ²³Those present believed that "A Mighty Fortress" had never been sung, even during the Reformation, with more gusto. As the four thousand voices inside the church sang,

> Take they our life;
> Goods, fame, child and wife;
> Let these all be gone;
> They yet have nothing won;
> The kingdom ours remaineth,

surely Luther's words never rang truer. Some present had already experienced these losses in the initial phase of Stalin's collectivization. Others foresaw that they, too, would soon lose all that they treasured.

The daily events for the festival followed a detailed program: 5 a.m. morning prayer; 9 a.m. divine service; 2–5 p.m. prayer time; in the evenings, Bible study. Brother Ehlers had organized the entire festival, sensing that it would be his last chance to address the people and earnestly desiring to prepare them for the deadly persecution he feared was coming on the land. In his last devotion, Ehlers used as his text Acts 20:17–38. Especially poignant were the words of Paul from verses 36–38: "And when he had said these things, he knelt down and prayed with them all. And there was much weeping on the part of all; they embraced Paul and kissed him, being sorrowful most of all because of the word he had spoken, that they would not see his face again." These words not only reflected the fact that many would not see Brother Ehlers again. In reality, they would not see each other again.

The following year, Pastor Johannes Grasmück would be arrested and sentenced to twenty-five years of hard labor in the gulag camps of the far north. He was last seen wrapped in rags, requesting some old clothes. He was never heard from again. His wife and two daughters were expelled from Brunnental, condemned to a life of begging. In the future, there would be no Religious NEP. Behind their hardened leader, Stalin, the Communists would show no sympathy for these relics of a bygone era who had to disappear if the Soviet state was to move forward boldly into an atheistic future. The way of life that the Lutherans of Russia had known for centuries was about to change—forever.[24]

11

"A DECLARATION OF A RELENTLESS STRUGGLE"

The Battle Against Religion Is Joined

THE YEAR 1929 would prove to be fateful for the Lutheran Church in Russia. Until that year, the Lutheran Church had survived most of the turbulent changes in the country reasonably well, especially since the early years of Soviet rule would have led an astute observer to think that the Church would soon be extinguished. The emigration of large numbers of pastors followed by a devastating famine, along with persecution of religion in general, did not bode well for the Church in the initial years after the revolution. And yet it survived, because despite these problems the Evangelical Lutheran Church of Russia was no longer limited by the Russian Orthodox-dominated czarist state. General synods for the Lutheran Church had never been allowed in Russia in the past, but when the Soviet state proclaimed freedom of religion and atheism, new possibilities opened up. The Lutheran Church held two general synods in 1924 and 1928, and this despite the fact that pastors were categorized with the so-called *biivshe ludii*, the "former people" of the old czarist regime.

Not only that, when borders changed after the 1917 Bolshevik Revolution and Estonia became an independent country, Russia had lost its only Lutheran seminary, which had for years been located in Dorpat. This new geographical reality turned out to be a blessing in disguise because it forced the Church to request permission from the Soviet state to establish its own seminary. In 1925, the Lutheran Church of Russia officially opened the doors to a seminary on the grounds of St. Anne's Lutheran Church in Leningrad. So naturally, most Lutherans could be forgiven for assuming that they would be able to weather any changes and continue to hold on to the Church of their forefathers, a Church that dated back to the sixtenth century.[1]

But the relative freedom that the Church had experienced would in 1929 be curtailed by the dictates of the state. Specific decrees directed against religious freedom would be enacted, as opposed to the arbitrary actions of individual atheists and die-hard Communists. Reading the letters of bishops Malmgren and Meier to Dr. John Morehead in America, one can discern a change in tone from guarded optimism to growing pessimism. While both bishops would fight for the Lutheran Church's survival to the bitter end, it was clear that they were coming to the conclusion that the inevitable triumph of the state over the church was only a matter of time.

JOSEPH STALIN HAD solidified his power base by 1929, first by allying with Nikolai Bukharin, the so-called Rightist Bolshevik. Together they were able to purge the Leftist Bolsheviks from the party. As Leftist Bolsheviks, Grigory Zinoviev, Lev Kamenev, and Leon Trotsky had advocated a more aggressive campaign of industrialization and collectivization of agriculture. Stalin used the articulate Bukharin to great effect, defending Lenin's NEP as a reasonable policy for the time being on the road to socialism.[2]

Once their victory was secure, however, Stalin did an about face in 1927 and began implementing forced grain requisitions in the countryside, much to Bukharin's chagrin. Bukharin felt that Stalin was going too far in alienating the middle peasant, but he would lose out in a power struggle to Stalin. His protests increasingly unheeded before the party faithful, Bukharin and his allies would lose the argument with Stalin and ultimately be stripped of their positions of authority by 1930.[3]

With his challengers to power out of the way, Stalin now embarked on an ambitious plan to dramatically transform the country. The year 1929 would eventually become known as the year of the *Veliky Perelom*, the Great Turning Point.[4] Others would refer to it as the Stalin Revolution.[5] Stalin used his power to begin a program to rapidly collectivize agriculture and industrialize the economy so that Russia would be dramatically changed from an outdated, manual-labor-driven society into an industrialized economic superpower. The first of Stalin's Five-Year Plans began implementation in October 1928, with its formal adoption in the spring of 1929.[6]

The arguments of historians as to whether this was a revolution from above or below would ultimately become a moot point for those Lutherans who lived through this new "cultural revolution." Historian Robert Tucker described industrialization and collectivization only as "focal processes," pointing out that in the arena of culture Russian society underwent a massive upheaval, affecting the entire social structure, church life included.[7] Indeed, even Emelian Yaroslavsky, head of the League of the Militant Godless, would announce his own Anti-Religious Five-Year-Plan in late 1928.[8]

Stalin recognized that the church was too often associated with images of Russia's czarist past and that in order to truly change the mindset of Soviet citizens and build socialism, religion had to be eradicated. Malmgren, associating Stalin with a Leftist Bolshevik point of view, referred to 1929 as the "year of crisis." In his view, Stalin set forth a new goal: "Above all, he proclaimed religion to be a superstition that had to be overcome and uprooted, and the church smashed and destroyed as a patron and defender of superstition. And this, in the shortest period of time possible, in the process of the First Five-Year-Plan."[9]

IN RETROSPECT, THE SIGNS of danger for the Lutheran Church were already on the horizon before the onset of the First Five-Year Plan. With the month-to-month problems due to government obstruction weighing on him, Malmgren had written in 1927, "The thunderclouds are coming together on our horizon and in the distance, we hear the rumbling."[10] The rumbling of those thunderclouds and the coming catastrophe for the Church came closer in 1928 with the closing of St. Michael's Lutheran in Moscow. St. Michael's was the oldest Lutheran congregation in Russia, its origins dating back to 1576 when Czar Ivan the Terrible allowed the first Lutheran church building to be erected in Moscow. The name itself appears to have come later in honor of Czar Mikhail Romanov, officially being established in the 1630s.[11] In 1926, a service of celebration was held at St. Michael's in honor not only of the 350-year anniversary of the congregation but of the Lutheran Church in Russia itself.[12] Since St. Michael's had long been held to be the symbol of Lutheranism in Russia, when in November 1927 a special commission called for its closing and the transfer of its building over to the Central Aerodynamics Institute (CAI), Moscow's Lutherans were rightfully alarmed.

The official reason given for the transfer of the church to CAI was that its security personnel could not check all of the parishioners coming to church on Sundays. Since the church was on the territory of CAI, it was feared that these valuable laboratories could be subjected to sabotage or espionage. CAI was involved in the military defense of the Soviet Union, so St. Michael's pleas had little chance of success. As a result, the church was "liquidated" on January 14, 1928, by a secret order of the Presidium of the Moscow Soviet, signed by the head of the Moscow regional police force.[13] Bishop Meier broke the bad news to John Morehead in a letter dated February 3, 1928. Meier told Morehead that Moscow's Lutherans would continue to fight to the end for the building, but realistically he deemed it a losing cause. The property where the church had long stood was no longer its own since the Decree on the Separation of Church from State in 1918. Two years before the order to close St. Michael's, CAI had begun to build a factory on church territory until it decided at last to take over the church building itself.[14] (In 2013, pastor of Moscow's Sts. Peter and Paul in Moscow, Dmitry Lotov, recalled that his grandfather worked in the aerodynamics factory and could still make out the basic outlines of the church building.)[15]

Meier remained true to his principles of fighting for the rights of the Lutheran Church in the Soviet Union. He wrote to the Communist Party about the historic meaning attached to St. Michael's for Lutherans throughout the centuries. In addition, hundreds of letters of protest came in from parishioners pleading the cause of their building.[16] In fact, more than eight hundred signatures were given on a protest sent to the government from parishioners not only of St. Michael's but also Sts. Peter and Paul and the High Church Council.[17] In the end, though, Pyotr Smidovich, the chairman of the All-Russian Central Executive Committee, decided in favor of CAI. The congregation of St. Michael's was allowed to move to the former Reformed church's building in central Moscow, sharing the church with evangelical Christians and Baptists until the congregation was finally shut down in 1936.[18]

In Leningrad, a 1926 report of a citizen antagonistic toward religion was a harbinger of troubled times to come. This unnamed witness reported to the OGPU on Pastor Helmut Hansen of St. Peter's Lutheran. Troubled by his gatherings of young people for religious purposes, this person wrote, "Pastor Hansen gathers boys and girls in his apartment every Wednesday at 7 p.m. where they sing spiritual songs. He even has a teacher who teaches them, and he pays her as if in a school. Is this really allowed? And his wife gives singing lessons there and at 1 p.m. on Sundays they have a children's gathering where they sing songs and teach Christianity under the guise of a church service. And then every Monday and Thursday at 5 p.m. in the church building they teach the children. Does the *dvatsatka* of the church know about this and allow them to do it? Or do they not know?"[19] This accusation would accurately describe a violation of the law concerning religious activities with children, but it was a law that was rarely enforced.

The pressure was turned up in 1928 as opposition to Hansen's activities was aired in a public forum. In an article entitled "Coffee Evenings" from May 9, 1928, *Leningradskaya Pravda* spoke ominously of a conspiracy forming at St. Peter's Lutheran on 25 October Avenue (historically and currently known as Nevsky Avenue), the main street in the center of town. Pastor Hansen and his colleague Kurt Muss, pastor of Jesus Christ Lutheran Church, were accused of creating anti-Soviet cadres. An extensive quotation of this article gives a flavor of the bitter criticism now being leveled against activist Lutheran pastors in Leningrad:

> In the center of the city, a revolution is being hatched next to the Marxist seminary ... in an ancient church, paint peeling off its walls, just like 400 years ago. Gloomy mysterious services, sermons howled out by Helmut Hansen, the bellicose preacher and wily philosopher. He quotes Luther, Calvin, Nietzsche, Confucius, and about God, even Marx. He calls for war, preaches openly anti-Semitic sermons and counterrevolution. This is what this good pastor inculcates in the children. His counterrevolutionary work is joined by the young Pastor Muss. This notable subject was sent to a labor camp for three years for espionage, having sent intelligence data to England. ... Pastor Hansen has still not gone underground [with his activities] in order to "preach and fight." He lives rent free in his own apartment in the house of the Finnish Consulate ... where they hold religious services ... and gather all who are offended by Soviet power. ... Let's refer these shrewd preachers to the prosecutor's office, so that they can defend us from the counterrevolutionary hissing sounds coming out of the bilious mouth of Pastor H. Hansen.[20]

This article alerted Hansen and his wife Erna to the inherent danger of carrying out activities associated with normal church life, and Erna later admitted that it had alarmed her and her husband. Because of this, she would pass lists of the confirmands, notebooks, and biblical texts for children and the programs of musical church concerts over to Sunday school teacher Elisabeth (Elsa) Freifeldt, daughter of the late Bishop Conrad Freifeldt.[21] Freifeldt confirmed that Erna, fearing a search of their apartment, handed her the papers sometime in 1929, most likely earlier in the year.[22]

Helmut Hansen, however, said that his wife had handed over these papers to Ilsa Wassermann, Margo Jurgens, and Elsa Freifeldt after the printing of the article. When he learned of his wife's actions, he demanded that she get the papers back, but apparently his wife didn't carry out his request immediately.[23] Erna would get the papers back in October 1929, and then only because Elsa Freifeldt had gotten into an argument with their neighbors, Ivan and Boris Anichkov. The brothers, no doubt aware of the pastoral activities taking place in their building, had threatened to bring the law down on them. Perhaps fearing for Elsa more than herself and her family, Erna took the papers back. But in November 1929, she handed them back again to Elsa. (Elsa would burn the so-called compromising materials on Wednesday morning, December 19.)[24] The OGPU would eventually represent all of these actions in sinister form, as if Hansen was engaged in conspiracy and in a panic, expecting imminent arrest, had these papers hidden by parishioners.[25]

Next door to St. Peter's stood the Peterschule, established in 1712 and long admired as a model school in Russia with famous graduates such as the composer Modest Mussorgsky.[26] The church and school had operated in conjunction for centuries, and despite the Bolshevik Revolution, those ties remained to some extent, though the school was now known officially as Soviet School Number 41. For example, Peterschule schoolteacher and member of St. Peter's *dvatsatka*, Alexander Wolfius, had, according to church member Evgeny Hoffman, allowed Hansen's youth groups special privileges. They were allowed use of the school gymnasium for games, even if the youth were not actually students at the school.[27]

Previously, the Peterschule had escaped most of the Sovietizing tendencies that had been brought to bear in Russian schools. While the teaching of religion and biblical languages had been forbidden after 1918 and co-educational classes had been introduced, most of the teachers had remained on staff, including the principal, Erich Kleinenberg and his assistant, Wolfius.[28] They were probably able to influence the students with their Christian faith, although they had to be wary.

But the Peterschule now employed other teachers who had no ties to the Lutheran Church. In May of 1928, a social sciences teacher by the name of Mrs. Weinstveig, an immigrant from Germany and a member of the Communist Party, decided to publicize the fact that members of the senior class of students had been confirmed at St. Peter's. A younger student named N. P. Ulyanov afterward remembered that the older students themselves hadn't taken special notice of their confirmation. Obviously, though, enemies of religion had. Weinstveig's accusation was apparently taken as a signal to act because some aggressive Communists soon formed a commission to investigate the school and accusations were lodged against it in the local newspapers.[29]

Despite all this commotion, nothing was found to be criminal or irregular in the school except the fact that the students habitually addressed some teachers as Frau and Herr! Nevertheless, Kleinenberg and Wolfius were dismissed along with a large percentage of the teachers, all having in common that they were pre-Communist graduates of the Peterschule. Such people were no longer fit to move the school in the direction that the Communists desired. Some teachers, like biology teacher Alfred Forsman, took advantage of the relative liberality in emigration laws and immigrated to Finland. Anatoly Lunacharsky, the Commissar of Enlightenment, had openly debated Wolfius at the Peterschule back in 1925 on the topic of the existence of Christ, and not very effectively, from one account. Now he publicly proclaimed that a Christian teacher was a contradiction in the Soviet state and measures should be taken to replace them with atheist teachers.[30] Whereas previously the teaching in schools had not allowed mention of God or religion, in May 1929 at the Congress of Soviets Anatoly Lunacharsky announced that the government would institute measures to more actively promote atheist education. Textbooks would be changed to focus on religion's incompatibility with science, a materialistic outlook would be promoted, and excursions to anti-religious museums planned.[31]

At the Peterschule, though, the changes had already begun in 1928. The new directors were hardline Communists who immediately imposed their regime on the school, stating that they would lead the charge against "the enemy spirit of the former times."[32] The new principal, M. C. Yeletsky, was noted as a particularly cruel character, while the director of academic affairs was none other than Leon Trotsky's first wife, Alexandra Bronshtein. His fall from power and exile from the Soviet Union would not bode well for her, either, as she would perish eventually during Stalin's Great Purge (1937–1938). Assisting Yeletsky in establishing the new order in the school was the steward, Ilya Pechatnikov. A former Chekist, Pechatnikov seems to have been quite a character, noted for his long bangs and habit of carrying a revolver in his pants' pocket. With these partisans of the Communist Zeitgeist in charge, it was now abundantly clear that the old days where St. Peter's Lutheran Church was closely associated with the Peterschule were gone for good.[33] Schools in Stalin's Soviet Union were to be venues only for atheist propaganda.

THIS WAS THE context when, on January 24, 1929, Stalinist ally and Secretary of the Central Committee of the Communist Party Lazar Kaganovich signed a decree "On the Measures for Strengthening Antireligious Work." When the decree was sent to local party committees in February, the party cadres were urged to identify religious organizations as the "only legally counterrevolutionary force" acting in society. The directive admonished Communists to speed up the anti-religious struggle against the clergy and opponents of socialism.[34]

That same month, the Secretariat of the All-Russian Central Executive Committee formed a separate commission to insert changes into the constitution of the USSR. The new wording allowed for "freedom of religious confession and anti-religious propaganda," a change from the constitution that had been accepted in 1918, which had called for "freedom of religious and anti-religious propaganda." Initially, the committee had agreed on language acquiescing to freedom of "religious convictions," but ultimately found that language a little too broad and open to interpretation in favor of religious believers. The phrase "religious confession" would soon be interpreted to include only activities taking place within church buildings. When pastors like Kurt Muss would later cite the rights of a citizen to believe and act on his faith, these new provisions in the constitution would contradict their interpretation of the law as anachronistic.[35]

While the Soviet state was turning up the heat on Christians, John Morehead of the LWC was planning for the year 1929. With typical American optimism, he encouraged Bishops Meier and Malmgren to increase their outreach opportunities among the many peoples and religious groups within Russia. Meier regretfully answered him, "We live and work here in Russia under such extraordinary circumstances that it is hard for a foreigner to understand what is possible and what is not possible." Morehead, in his desire to reach the lost with the gospel, had been asking for information on the possibilities of doing outreach among Muslims, Buddhists, and atheists in Russia. Meier responded that the Communist authorities would immediately be alerted to anyone trying to do mission outreach, so it would be best to concentrate on the inner life of the church for the time being until "the Lord opens up a door."[36]

In his correspondence with Morehead, Malmgren likewise regretted that twelve years after the Bolshevik Revolution, the Russian Lutherans had not taken further steps to support themselves and become weaned off foreign aid. Shame and embarrassment came through in his letter even as he acknowledged that persecution had grown stronger and the pressure greater on the parishioners, as well as the seminary. Steadily increasing taxes made it more difficult to run the church.[37] In economic matters, ration cards for bread were distributed to ordinary citizens but not to pastors or seminary students. They could only get bread after citizens had purchased their fill, and that at double the price. In an attempt to get around these restrictions, the seminary bought flour and baked its own bread.[38]

Despite these obstacles, Morehead urged the bishops to do what they could to attend the Lutheran World Convention to be held in Copenhagen in June. He knew that no one could so clearly explain the situation of the Lutheran Church in the Soviet Union as the bishops. At the Lutheran World Convention held in Eisenach in 1923, Meier had done just that, impressing all who heard his eloquent pleas for assistance to the Russian Lutheran Church.[39] But this was no longer 1923, when a Lutheran bishop could travel without too much hindrance to a religious conference. There was no longer any discussion within the government about taking a tactical step back with regard to religion. Stalin was in full attack mode.

Responding to Morehead's letters of January 5 and 16, Malmgren on February 15 said that he would do everything in his power to get the visa permit for Copenhagen. But the increasing pressure of anti-religious propaganda would probably make it more difficult for anyone to get a visa for a visit that concerned religious matters. Morehead, for his part, was not entirely unaware of the current conditions in the Soviet Union. He responded to Malmgren on March 15, "We have heard from many sources that conditions are more unfavorable than usual at the present time for religion and the Church in Russia." Sympathizing with the bishop, Morehead continued, "May God grant grace, a strong faith, and an unfaltering courage to all His people in Russia and we pray that in His own time and way He may deliver them from all their difficulties and restore unto the Church of our Fathers in Russia freedom, growth and prosperity in the great work of witnessing to the Gospel of Christ and developing the cause of true religion among the people."[40]

BUT WHILE AMERICAN and Russian Lutherans were busy exploring what was possible for the church in the Soviet Union, a crushing blow to religious freedom came to all Christian believers on April 8. A new law entitled "Concerning Religious Associations" would basically determine the parameters of the relationship between church and state until 1990.[41] Its importance can be attested by the fact that the officials for the NLC and LWC obtained a translation of the law for their archives. When they read the translation of that law, any hopes that they could expand missions and church work among Russian Lutherans must have been dashed.[42]

The new law was aimed at practices that Lutherans and other Christians were pursuing with the goal to strengthen and grow Christian communities. Undergirding the new law was the reminder from the 1918 Decree on Separation of Church from State and School from Church that the church still did not own property but was granted the use of property by the state. All activities and meetings in the church would now have to be approved and the secretary's notes sent to the local Soviet authorities. The most devastating of the sixty-eight paragraphs in the new law was paragraph 17. It stipulated the following:

> Religious associations may not (a) create mutual credit societies, co-operatives or commercial undertakings, or in general use the property at their disposal for other than religious purposes; (b) give material assistance to their members; (c) organize for children, young people and women special prayer or other meetings, or, generally, meetings, groups, circles or departments for biblical or literary study, sewing, working or the teaching of religion, &c., or organize excursions, children's

playgrounds, public libraries or reading rooms, or organize sanitaria and medical assistance. Only books necessary for the purposes of the cult may be kept in the buildings and premises used for worship.[43]

The regulation that the church building could only be used for services and not for teaching would outlaw Sunday school, catechism classes, youth gatherings, and Bible classes for all groups. In doing so, the state was now saying that the church could not carry out the normal functions that would allow it to educate its members. Bishop Malmgren recognized this danger immediately, calling Paragraph 17 the worst of the regulations: "This paragraph's goal is to enfeeble the entire life of the worshiping community and allow only church services."[44]

That was indeed the goal of the Soviets. At the Congress of Soviets on May 22, the July 1918 constitution was amended to reflect the new law on religious associations. Those interpreting the new law observed that a Christian believer could no longer answer in response to public attacks on his faith.[45] Although technically the teaching of Christianity to children had been forbidden in 1918, the law had not been strictly enforced. Throughout the 1920s in the countryside, for example, religious life carried on as it had for many centuries with only minor interference, depending on the zealousness of local Communist Party officials. Now, the law specifically stated that confirmation instruction could not be given to anyone under eighteen years of age, nullifying the former allowance for confirming those who had reached fifteen years of age.[46] Furthermore, in 1928 at the General Synod of the Evangelical Lutheran Church of Russia, it had been reported that the government was restricting the time frame for confirmation teaching to two weeks. With the addition of this new law, regular confirmation instruction would be virtually impossible and depended on the willingness of the pastor to flout the law.[47] This could be more easily accomplished in the countryside, where traditional Lutheran villagers would defend the pastor and the local party officials would have less respect. But in a crowded city with the ever-expanding practice of spying on one's neighbor, the risk would be much greater. Pastors Helmut Hansen and Kurt Muss of Leningrad would begin to take that risk in the fall of 1929, looking for loopholes in the law in order to teach children the Christian faith.

Paragraph 17 would also restrict the right of congregations to assist their fellow members financially. Charity for parishioners had been a common practice in the past for the Lutheran Church as evidenced by its own hospitals and poor houses. Even though those institutions were outlawed and taken over by the state in 1918, Lutheran churches still found the means to help their own elderly and poor. For instance, Hansen had arranged for musical concerts at St. Peter's and sold tickets by lottery in order to use the proceeds for the benefit of the poorer members of the congregation. The new law allowed the church to take freewill offerings but only for the upkeep of the church, the clergy, and administrative bodies. In addition, Paragraph 12 clarified that these offerings could not be "organized," which of course was the only way that the concerts could be held in the first place.[48]

In Paragraph 11, a short reference to the forbidding of publishing or printing religious materials would now provide further legal obstacles to the publication of the church journal *Unsere Kirche*. When Bishop Meier announced the publication of this journal in August 1927, hopes were still high that the Lutheran Church would be able to carve out a sphere of influence, however restricted, within the USSR. Now Paragraph 11 promised to dash that optimism, affecting not only the Lutheran but also Baptist and evangelical journals as well.[49] Steadily and surely, the Soviet authorities had been emasculating the journal through censorship to the point that every appearance of the publication only came about after a contentious struggle. Sometimes they would forbid an article outright while at other times they would mercilessly strike out portions of it. Even if the author tried to write carefully and agreed to change the text as the censor required, the article would frequently be rejected in the end. In the end, the August issue would be the last. The Soviets had achieved their goal through relentless pressure and chicanery.[50] The Lutherans were not being singled out, though, as Baptist and evangelical journals were banned in 1929.[51] And what was the official reason given by the Soviets for the banning of religious journals? A lack of paper.[52]

The pressure on the Lutheran Church would only get worse toward the end of the summer. Finnish and Estonian Lutherans had previously been able to get Christian books across the border with the approval of the government, albeit with a charge of five hundred rubles added to their account. But by late summer, there were ten thousand hymnbooks that couldn't be sent into Soviet Russia. At first, the Lutherans had been given the go-ahead by the government, but in an abrupt reversal the Soviet authorities now refused to allow the hymnbooks to cross the border. Furthermore, the Lutheran Church had requested the right to publish a simple wall calendar with the festival days of the church year indicated. That, too, was refused. Bishop Malmgren succinctly summed matters up: "The anti-religious direction is sharper than before."[53] These actions by the government showed that Paragraph 11 was more than mere words on paper. Those Christian tracts that Morehead had hoped to send to Russia in 1928 would not legally see the light of day.[54]

Paragraph 19 also restricted the activities of pastors and teachers to church buildings or the places where members resided. With this law in effect, the mission trips that Meier had taken to Siberia would now be illegal, although he would test this with a summer mission trip in 1929. With the dearth of pastors in regions like Siberia or the Volga, those pastors serving in the vicinity had been committed to traveling to surrounding villages to serve vacant Lutheran congregations. This, too, was now outlawed.[55] The Communist state was closing every loophole in the law that had allowed religious life to flourish. Bishop Malmgren bluntly summed up the new law as "a declaration of a relentless struggle, where possible, up to and including extinction" of the church.[56]

Officials at the German consulate in Leningrad, through whom Morehead as chairman of the LWC had been sending money and with whom Malmgren was in constant conversation, also had a gloomy take on the new law. They noticed that the anti-religious propaganda in the press, on the streets, and in the schools and factories was increasing in its stridency.[57] The journal of the League of the Godless, *Bezbozhnik*, called for doing away with Easter since it was an expression of Christian anti-Semitism, blaming the Jews for the crucifixion of Christ. In contrast, they said, the international movement of Communism was struggling to unify all working peoples by emphasizing their common human-ity irrespective of nationality.[58] As if to emphasize their new aggressiveness in the struggle against religion, in June 1929 the League of the Godless would morph into the League of the Militant Godless at its convention.[59]

BUT WHILE GOOD Communists were out on the streets celebrating May Day (May 1) and participating in parades, a small group of Lutheran youth was being led on an excursion outside Leningrad.[60] On a holiday where everyone had the day off to celebrate the Communist state, Helmut Hansen took them thirty kilometers outside the city to Pavlovsk, the palace of Emperor Paul I.[61] In fact, Sunday school teacher Ilsa Wasserman remembers Hansen saying after a rally that "people gallivant about with red rags instead of praying."[62] Hansen's excursions on Communist holidays would later be presented in menacing terms by the OPGU.[63]

Easter was celebrated that year on May 5. The following day was Confirmation Day at Jesus Christ Lutheran Church, and Pastor Kurt Muss's orations fell on the ears of the secret police as the battle against religion grew in strength and tenacity. Muss believed that one could still be a good citizen and a Christian, a view that was becoming increasingly untenable in a society intent on throwing out the gods of the past. Local officials did little to dis-courage confirmation classes in the past, but the May confirmation at Jesus Christ Lutheran would be the last one allowed there.[64] Perhaps sensing the pressure on Christians to conform to society's new norms, Muss laid down the gauntlet against atheism at St. Peter's in the center of Leningrad, where his Russian-speaking congregation now met. According to eighteen-year-old parishioner Dagmara Schreiber, Muss preached boldly. His words clearly had an impact on her, as she would recall them word-for-word after her arrest. Muss began:

> Today is a day of joy. You have long waited for this day. We know that the Almighty created this day. If He hadn't defended and blessed us, would we have even seen this day? There are people today captivated by new ideals, thought up by professors in their offices, rejecting everything from the past. They say that we are confused, but could they not be the ones who are mistaken? Because if the scientists themselves are mistaken, who's right? In earlier times scientific people proved that God exists. How can we know but that perhaps the time will come when these new ideals, falling like manna from the offices of professors, will make us smile? Maybe they will be seen as mistaken?[65]

Warming up to his theme, Muss reminded his listeners:

> I have long explained to you the goal of life. I familiarized you with the person of Christ. When Pilate stood before the uncontrolled, bloodthirsty mobs and said, "What will be done with Christ?" they shouted out in response, "Crucify Him!" As with Pilate in his time, you, too, now stand in his place. Pilate began with small steps but the more he moved in his mistaken direction, he eventually allowed others to crucify Christ. But how will you respond to Him? Don't forget that you are responsible before Christ for this answer! They will persecute you for His name just as they persecuted Him, because they did not know of that coming miraculous day when every Christian will have the occasion to rejoice. Still, in the meantime there will be gloomy days. We are now just a few people remaining. Just as with the ten lepers only one of them returned, we once who were numerous have now seen that many have left us.

Noting that their opponents labeled them as "dreamers," Muss called for the confirmands to remain firm. "Today as you children return to your normal lives, will you find any support for your faith? Will you be able to be sailors on the stormy seas?" Not content to call his confirmands to a firmness of faith against the atheism of the day, Muss rallied them to an active faith: "Tonight there will be an organ concert for support of the church. If we don't take advantage of the possibility we have to support our church, will we then simply remain silent and give it back [to the state]? Our generation will then ask: Where were you, Christians, when you gave back your church?"[66]

In the same month that Muss was preaching boldly to his parishioners, Soviet Minister of Culture Anatoly Lunacharsky was declaring to a session of the All-Russian Soviets that the "building up of the culture must accompany a battle against the churches and religions in any of their forms."[67] Despite his public challenge to the confirmands to stand for Christ against the powers of the age, Muss remained free for the time being. The Soviets were not yet prepared to attack all pastors and churches openly. Bishop Malmgren noted in a letter to Fritz Rentdorff on July 2 that the April 8 law had not come into force just yet. But in the next few weeks, he expected it would become binding.[68] He further acknowledged that while the church would naturally continue to fulfill its calling, it was obvious that the work would become more difficult and even dangerous. "We are dealing with an opponent who has openly expressed his desire to annihilate us and he will not back off from using any means in order to carry out that goal."[69] In the autumn, the attacks against Christians would heat up considerably.

BUT FIRST, MANY Lutherans in Leningrad had a chance to enjoy one more summer of freedom. That summer, in defiance of the new law on religious associations, Muss and Hansen continued activities as they had in the past with children from their congregations. They would rent a dacha (summer home) and offer summer camp activities in the Baltic resort of Strelna. Hansen had served as a pastor there before being called to St. Peter's. At times, Muss and his sister Luisa would help out at the camp, but sixty-one-year-old Amalia Meier was the primary caretaker for the children. She had been a member of St. Peter's when Hansen took the call to serve there in 1924, and when she fell on hard financial times in 1926, he took her into his apartment as the nanny for his three children. It was natural, then, for her to serve as the caretaker for the camp children. In gratitude, Hansen allowed her two grandchildren to attend the camp for free. Her respect for the pastoral spirit of Helmut Hansen was aptly displayed when she was arrested the following year and interrogated by the OGPU.[70]

The camp was not just a time of relaxation after a busy school year, though; educational opportunities were provided for the children. Those who attended were usually students whose parents couldn't take them to their own dachas or who needed special help with academics. Elsa Freifeldt joined seminary students Otto Tumm, Konrad Gerling, and Peter Mikhailov in providing German and Russian language classes, as well as arithmetic. It seems the children did not have religion classes, but each day would end with the singing of hymns and prayer. There were about twenty children, ranging in ages from seven to sixteen. In photos, the children seem happy and carefree. Given their poverty, they obviously treasured the opportunity to spend a good portion of their summer at one of the Baltics' nicer resort areas. As far as we know, this would be the last camp held in Strelna by the Lutheran Church.[71]

Hansen was concerned about the moral upbringing of the children, and there were serious concerns about the steep decline in moral values even among Communists. The prudishness of the early Bolsheviks gave way to a new cultural phenomenon by the end of the 1920s, and what we might call "family values" was now seen by youth as outdated and bourgeois.[72] In an ironic twist, the Communist attack on traditional Christian morality backfired when youth began to adopt Western popular culture, best exemplified by the foxtrot and jazz music. No less than cultural heavyweights like famed novelist Maxim Gorky and Commissar of Public Enlightenment Anatoly Lunacharsky led the assault on jazz. On April 18, 1928, Gorky published an article in *Pravda* entitled "Music of the Gross." Sounding much like an American fundamentalist of that era, Gorky decried the uninhibited sexuality unleashed by jazz rhythms. At the First All-Russian Musical Conference held in Leningrad in 1929, Lunacharsky echoed Gorky, expressing the need to counter this capitulation to bourgeois capitalism. He called for an attack on decadent jazz and the foxtrot, and in their place advocated a form of expression that preferred collectivism to individualism.[73]

Despite the pleas of these prominent figures of Soviet culture, many youth were inclined to see marriage as "a bourgeois holdover." Instead, they gravitated toward a lifestyle of drinking, partying, and sex without the benefit of marriage.[74] Influential Communist Alexandra Kollontai approved, expressing the materialistic ideal of "free love" this way: "We have intercourse for the same reason that we drink a glass of water, to slake our thirst."[75] Even in the countryside, young girls started using powder and rouge, and the old folk dances were replaced by the tango and foxtrot. Prostitution, venereal disease, and hooliganism were on the rise.[76] The fact that abortion had been legal since 1920 could only contribute to further cultural decline and irresponsibility in matters pertaining to sexual behavior.[77]

Despite the threat from the new law, Hansen could not refrain from preaching to young people a different lifestyle. His wife Erna admitted that her husband's sermons would touch on the immorality of the times, including the increasing number of young people disavowing marriage. His heart was drawn to the children and wives who had been literally "thrown away." The summer camps allowed him the opportunity to spend time with the children and cultivate within them a Christian spirit, a spirit contrary to the times in which they lived.[78]

At the end of the summer, in August, thirty-three-year-old Kurt Muss married twenty-one-year-old Elena Cherneshyeva at St. Peter's. Elena had joined Kurt earlier in the summer to help out at the summer camp.[79] But while Hansen and Muss were enjoying what would be their last summer of freedom, the forces of atheism were advancing. In June, the League of the Militant Godless had proclaimed that it was time to conduct class war against "the last bastion of reaction hindering the building of socialism." This call to the barricades by atheists was having an effect in the organs of government. Both bishops Meier and Malmgren were refused visas to travel to the LWC conference in Copenhagen that summer. Meier did not allow this refusal to deter him from his work and took a missionary journey into the south of Russia. However, even though the people yearned for them, the local authorities did not allow him to conduct worship services in some of the colonies. Undeterred, in keeping with his character, he took advantage of whatever opportunities were granted to him in central Asia, including holding a worship service in the Lutheran church in Tashkent.[80]

12

"HE ... SHALL THINK TO CHANGE THE TIMES AND THE LAW"

Stalin's First Five-Year Plan Gets Underway

AS IF THE new law passed on April 8, 1929, were not enough of a warning to Christians that their activities would now be severely curtailed, the government declared its intention to change the times and seasons as well. A decree issued on September 24 introduced a new five-day workweek. The typical worker would work four days and then get one day of rest. Then he would go back to work the following day and repeat the process of four days of work, one day of rest. The normal months were still observed, but traditional Sunday worship services were affected since not everyone had the same rest day. The effect on church attendance was catastrophic, not to mention the effect on other church holidays throughout the year.[1] Pastors were forced to offer church services on Sunday evenings, not only because most workers would be at their place of employment during the daytime, but because of the stigma now being attached to churchgoing in general.[2]

The authorities' actions made clear their commitment to wean Russians off observing time according to the old church calendars. Even the names of the days were changed, with the goal to do away with religious-oriented names like Sunday (*Voskreseniye* in Russian, meaning "resurrection") and Saturday (*Subbota* in Russian, meaning "Sabbath").[3] Only the festive Soviet holidays (such as May Day and the anniversary of the October Revolution) would be rest days for all of the workers.[4]

Naturally, Lutheran parishioners were alarmed at this development. In his response, Pastor Kurt Muss realized that this was a defining moment of truth for the church. Muss declared that the canceling of religious holidays was actually God's punishment, since too many parishioners had not taken the Lord's Day seriously. This was God's plan to wake up his church because it did not consist of dead but living stones. So "the Lord was creating within the hearts of the people, temples, as we Christians actually await the day when there will no longer be churches, as the Apostle John wrote."[5] Muss was most likely referring to Revelation 21:22: "And I saw no temple in the city, for its temple is the Lord God Almighty and the Lamb." The church should, therefore, not be caught up in the minutiae of "passing days" but understand time as being held in God's hands. With such a perspective, Christians could look forward to a bright future while others would set their own limitations to time, focusing on "five years," for example (a clear swipe at the Five-Year Plan). The one who believed in a living God who acts from century to century could look joyfully to the future because God would achieve his objectives with humankind in his own time. To those who doubted God's omnipotence and feared that he had left his people, Muss encouraged them to remember Christ's words that the kingdom of God is among them. Anything that serves to benefit people by eliminating differences between them is a seed planted for the kingdom of God. Muss was clearly contradicting the ideals promoted by Stalin and his fellow Communists, who were inclined rather to foment distinctions among the people by using contrasting terms like "proletariat" and "kulak."[6]

The April 8 law on religion and the changing of the workweek were the initial powerful attacks in 1929 directed toward the weakening of religious faith in the USSR. Bishop Arthur Malmgren, while writing to John Morehead, admitted as much. The hostility toward all of Christendom by the Soviet state could be seen "in the new law on the church and the cancellation of Sundays." There would, unfortunately, be more attacks. But still Malmgren would humbly and faithfully conclude, "It pays once again to heed the plea of the disciples, 'Lord, increase our faith!'"[7]

WITH THE COMING of autumn, there would be a more indirect but equally devastating attack on the church in the form of Joseph Stalin's drive for collectivization of agriculture. Already from June to September the number of collective farms had nearly doubled from an initial base of one million.[8] The intention was that private enterprise in farming be completely eradicated in five years, with the small, traditional labor-intensive farms transformed into large, state-run collectives furnished with the latest machinery and espousing scientific principles for farming. But there was little enthusiasm for this radical remaking of the countryside among the farmers.[9]

Lutheran pastor Otto Seib, who served parishes in the Ukraine, wrote to Morehead about the effect of collectivization in the countryside. No farmers were inclined to join the collective of their own free will. Outrageous taxes were levied against farmers who refused so that the sale of their crops, household appliances, or home would be insufficient to pay the government its stipulated fee. As a result, the property would be auctioned off at rock-bottom prices to poorer farmers. If the farmer decided to walk away from it all with what little property remained to him, he would not be allowed to join any other commune and would soon be imprisoned. According to Seib, his was already the fate of thousands, no doubt including many of those who had been warned about the times to come in the last mission festival along the Volga in the summer of 1928.[10]

The situation forced some of these Volga Germans to cry out for help through intermediaries like German von Schmidt, the editor of a newspaper in Berlin. Writing to the LWC, Schmidt appealed for the formation of a *Hilfsaktion* to assist the Russian-German Christians. Former Russian-German pastors now living in Germany could lead the committee, as they had contacts and knew the nature of the Soviet government. To accentuate the urgency, he went on to describe the heartbreaking story of the typical Russian-German farmer. One night, the farmer would be awakened at 10 p.m. by the OGPU and brought before a commission and told that he must deliver two thousand poods (1 pood = 36.11 pounds) of grain within three days. The farmer would protest and say that he had only five hundred poods and needed to save some income to buy seed for planting in the coming year. The commission would then raise the fee to three thousand poods and ask, "Then why don't you sell your cattle, or house goods, or home, in order to buy seed for the coming year? Is it because you are a counterrevolutionary or betrayer of the working people?"

Through the work of their spies, the commission knew what possessions the farmer held, so he couldn't fool them. Being an obedient sort, he would gather what money he could from friends and relatives and sell his cattle and horse, thus collecting the amount requested of him. In response to his willing-ness to meet their terms, the commission would then say, "You give us three thousand poods' worth? That means you could gather yet another five hundred poods!" When he clearly could gather no more, the farmer would be psycho-logically broken and ready to join the collective. He would be pressured to sell all that he had at a loss and be forced into the collective of his own "free will," with only the clothes on his back. His children could also be taken from him and given to atheistic Communists to raise or be sent to an orphanage. This situation was repeated not only in the Volga region but also in the Ukraine and in western Siberia.[11]

Unjust actions like these were also taken against ministers like Rev. Ferdinand Hörschelmann Sr., who had assisted Morehead with distribution of food supplies to Lutherans during the 1921–1922 famine in the Crimea. In the summer of 1929, he was required to turn over several hundred poods of grain to the Soviet authorities as a tax payment. Bishop Theophil Meier, who was visiting Hörschelmann at the time in order to ordain his son, Ferdinand Jr., noted that the amount of tax came to the equivalent of 1,800 rubles. Since Hörschelmann didn't own land or work as a farmer and received what bread he could from his parishioners, the government's request was virtually impossible to fulfill.[12] Furthermore, Communist journalists went on to accuse Hörschelmann of hoarding powdered milk and other supplies that were to have been given to those affected by the famine in 1922. Now, they sniffed, he hadn't distributed those products but had stolen them.[13] Hörschelmann's own poverty made the charges appear as ludicrous as they sounded. In fact, the day after Meier had left, the seventy-four-year-old Hörschelmann was forced to sell all of his household appliances at a ridiculously low rate and was forced to sleep on the floor on a straw mattress (as his bed had been sold, too!). Only in this way was his tax obligation fulfilled.

A sympathetic parishioner had compassion on his pastor and purchased Hörschelmann's bed back for him, but it was taken from him again and resold. Other pastors were taxed at a similar rate, and not only them but also those parishioners who held positions on the church councils.[14] In Meier's congregation of Sts. Peter and Paul in Moscow, seven of the ten church council members stepped down because of just such economic pressure applied by the Soviet authorities. The men, as family breadwinners, felt compelled to leave the church council while mostly women remained. Yet Meier retained some degree of optimism, recognizing in their circumstances the theology of the cross that the apostle Paul knew so well: "We are treated as ... dying, and behold, we live!" (2 Corinthians 6:9).[15]

Given such brutal actions by the government, it is no wonder that violence accompanied much of the forced collectivization throughout the USSR in 1929. Not everyone would willingly accept the new conditions that the Stalinist authorities were placing on them. Arsons and murders spiked during this time, too, especially during the fall as commissions tried to extract from communities of farmers their land and goods. Soviet officials, considered to be outsiders by the villagers, were often attacked. But local peasants who served as activists for the Communist Party were also targeted, as were those who informed on other peasants.[16] Apocalyptic language and images found expression throughout the countryside, as they often had in Russia's past. In the central Volga region in 1929, the rumor was spread that "Soviet power is not of God, but of Antichrist." Many felt that they would be stamped with the mark of the beast for joining the collective. Rumor fueled rumor as the agitated peasants, dreading the day of judgment inaugurated by the beast of Revelation, resorted to violence and riots in order to stave off collectivization.[17]

While the evidence is still scanty regarding particulars of revolts in the countryside, it doesn't appear that the Lutheran villages were complicit in such violent reactions. As much as Lutheran pastors were appalled by the actions of the government, they were not theologically inclined to support violence against the authorities that God had instituted. Instead, many Lutherans decided to avoid violence by voting with their feet and traveling to Moscow in order to secure travel documents to emigrate. Karoline Glöckler, the sister-in-law of NLC worker Charles Glöckler, wrote that most villagers in the Kharkov region of the Ukraine were ready to leave, but Moscow was overflowing with people and most would be sent back. Still, there was little hope for her village of Ryabovo, because although the harvest had been good, the proceeds would go to pay for the "frighteningly high taxes." "Whether it will be difficult to begin [in America], at least one will have his own property. Here one is not allowed to live anymore."[18]

IN FACT, EMIGRATION from the Soviet Union, while difficult, was not as hopeless as it would later become. The Soviet state in 1929 was not as adamantly opposed to allowing its citizens to leave as it would be in the 1930s. Edith Müthel, daughter of Lutheran pastor Emil Pfeiffer, recalls that her father was given the opportunity to immigrate with his family to America in 1929. As a former teacher of languages (including English), he could have resettled his family in the United States without too much difficulty. She was excited about the possibility of going to America and being able to attend school regularly, but he ultimately decided against the move. She remembers him saying that God had called him to serve the people of Norka, a village on the western banks of the Volga. He could not justify leaving his people or his call.[19]

Along with the Lutherans, thousands of Russian-Germans, including Mennonites and Catholics throughout Russia, left their homes and possessions behind on their way to Moscow in hopes of procuring visas to Germany or America. A precedent had been set in 1918 when many Mennonites had successfully immigrated to North America, so when they now left their villages to make the trek to Moscow, other Christians took note and followed them. The number of potential emigrants encamped around Moscow's suburbs may have numbered as many as seventeen thousand, while an observer from the office of the German ambassador in Moscow counted close to 2,500 Lutherans. This did not sit well with the authorities, who were praising collectivization and claiming that it had the unstinting support of the people.[20] Furthermore, the Western press had awakened to the calamity developing in the USSR and vehemently protested the government's actions. In the December 1929 issue of *Bezhbozhnik*, the atheist movement's monthly magazine, the proponents of a godless worldview felt it imperative to answer "the worldwide bourgeois press" on account of such "scandalous attacks against the USSR." Press reports portraying the emigration of the Mennonites as "the flight of the peasants from collectivization" was simply not accurate, *Bezbozhnik* author Heinrich Friesen countered.

Friesen asserted that several thousand Mennonites did arrive from Siberia and petition the government for emigration. The government, he said, had given permission for them to go to Canada but it was the Canadians who refused them entry. The German Red Cross called for help and even German

President Paul von Hindenburg signed one of their pleas. The Germans themselves really didn't want to allow their fellow ethnic German Mennonites entry into Germany, Friesen claimed, so the German authorities proposed German African colonies or Brazil as settlement options. Three hundred people managed to leave the USSR and the rest were sent back to their villages. In other words, Friesen said that the Soviet government was being reasonable in its attempts to deal with the Mennonites; everyone else, though, was callous and was using the would-be emigrants as pawns in their ideological battle against the Soviet state.

Accusing the Mennonites of being opposed to the October Revolution from the beginning, Friesen claimed that they were kulaks, part of the pre-revolutionary wealthy class of farmers who fought on the side of the Whites in the Russian Civil War. Friesen thought it reasonable to assume that the Mennonites were opposed to collectivization and wanted to leave when conditions were no longer advantageous for them. Accusing the Mennonites of inculcating an ideology of the kulak-religious worldview among their people for centuries, Friesen set forth the following argument: Their preachers declare that collectivization is godless. They are leading a class war against the politics of Soviet power. The preacher supports the kulak, because the religious culture among them is strong. And so, the religious-kulak influence is great and the Communist Party influence is weak among them.[21]

On the contrary, German citizen and journal editor German von Schmidt claimed that many of those Russian-Germans camped out in Moscow would be refused emigration papers because the Soviet government feared that they knew too much and would vent anti-Bolshevik propaganda if allowed to leave for the West. These, Schmidt said, were the exact words a colonel among Soviet officials expressed to a leader of the Russian-German colonies.[22] As late as February 1930, Meier confessed that not a day went by without some poor German from the colonies showing up in Moscow, trying to get a visa but always without success.[23]

However, the Gustav-Adolf-Verein (an aid society based in Germany) reported that some had successfully been spirited out of the Soviet Union. In its publication *Die Evangelische Diaspora*, the Verein acknowledged that six thousand Russian-German refugees who had made it to Moscow had eventually ended up in Germany. By the end of 1929, they had been temporarily placed in refugee camps throughout the country. Germans of all political persuasions, except those of the Communist Party, felt a responsibility to their ethnic brethren in Russia even while the government recognized the difficulties of resettling so many people. Contradicting *Bezhbozhnik*, *Die Evangelische Diaspora* asserted that at least some of the refugees would remain in Germany while those with relatives in America would resettle there. But it wondered about what would be done with the yet one hundred thousand or so who remained in Russia, still desiring to leave.

The majority of those who made it to Germany were Mennonites, but Lutherans and Catholics from the villages also were among the grateful ones who exchanged the hopelessness of any future in Soviet Russia for a refugee camp in Hammerstein, Prenzlau, or Mölln. They arrived at the camps virtually penniless, as those who had even managed to save a little money had it taken from them by Soviet authorities at the border. Now these former independent farmers were forced to rely on the charity of the German government, in addition to the German Red Cross and Brüder in Not (Brothers in Need), an evangelical aid organization that the Gustav-Adolf-Verein also supported. The Hammerstein camp authorities even erected an altar for church services to provide spiritual comfort for the refugees.

The refugees knew that the future was bleak for an ethnic German farmer in Soviet Russia, as the German Communist paper in Moscow *Die Zentralzeitung* bluntly explained in its November 13 issue: "There is no more place for the kulak in Russia; he has been condemned to death."[24] But at least those in refugee camps in Germany had made it to freedom. The unfortunate ten thousand or so refugees remaining in Moscow were taken by the OGPU and sent back either to their old villages, which held little prospect for them, or shipped to the Gulag labor camps in Siberia.[25]

THE ECONOMIC TRAGEDY affecting these farmers was bad enough, but collectivization was more than just a reorganization of the rural economy. From the outset, Stalin had proclaimed that the culture of the countryside would be changed, too, and that meant the destruction of the religious character of the peasantry.[26] Emboldened Communists went about the countryside determined to show that a new ideology was in force, for example, turning churches into garages housing tractors.[27] In the November 1929 issue of *Bezbozhnik*, V. Sarabyanov explained that it was only the poor and middle peasants who truly believed in God; the kulaks were just hypocrites, using religion to keep the poorer peasants in bondage. If the state hoped to carry out the Five-Year Plan effectively, it had to create the conditions that would raise the material and cultural level of life among these lower-class peasants. Since these peasants were deluded by religion, the religious influence surrounding them had to be weakened. The Communists would begin the winnowing process by exiling the more influential kulaks. At the same time, the priests and enemy sectants (a code word for Protestants) were cited for disrupting the work of collectivization, because "they clearly understand its socialist and anti-religious character."[28]

While atheist journals like *Bezbozhnik* portrayed the peasants as naive and gullible adherents of religion lacking class consciousness, many of the German peasants who left their villages for Moscow were in reality strong Christian believers who cited religious persecution as their reason for emigrating. They even asked their pastors for their baptismal certificates so that they could prove to those in their new homelands that they were never atheists or Communists. Sadly, these documents attesting to their Christian faith served to incriminate those who did not escape the USSR, and that included those ten thousand who had made it to Moscow but no further.[29] In a long letter to Morehead, Seib described how the anti-religious movement accompanying collectivization was succeeding in strangling the Church. "The five-year-plan ... is intended to brush away entirely the little bit which is left of the church and religion, and the quicker the better, since the church is considered the seat of the counter-revolution, and its representatives and adherents, counter-revolutionists."[30] Seib spoke of preaching to congregations of ten or twenty parishioners, mostly women, because the men and young people feared losing their jobs if they attended church. The high taxes were another burden that could not be met by congregations given the effects of collectivization on parishioners' personal wealth. The new workweek also had its effect on attendance, and the next step after the churches were emptied would be the confiscation of the buildings. Seib knew that Ukrainian Lutheran churches in Nikolayev, Elizavetgrad, Ekaterinoslav, Poltava, and Kiev were on the list for confiscation. Once those churches were taken away, Seib guessed that no one would then rent a hall or place for church services. The religious believers would need government approval to rent a building for worship services, and thus alert the officials to their religious convictions—with inevitable results.

Conditions were reaching the point of hopelessness. People avoided greeting Seib on the street; parishioners no longer called on him. And even if people did pack the pews, a local official could simply cancel a service; this had already occurred that summer when Meier was not allowed to conduct a service in a Ukrainian village church. Seib recalled people coming from fifty miles to the village church in Schlangendorf, where he had agreed to do some baptisms and confirm the youth. Although the worship service was conducted successfully, the people left the village secretly to avoid detection. And yet despite such precautions, the local authorities accused Seib of holding an illegal meeting and participating in a "religious demonstration." What, in their opinion, constituted a demonstration? Apparently, the fact that Seib led twenty-five confirmands to the church from the home in which they had gathered before the service, singing "Jesus Still Lead On!" Seib went on to give an account of his last two months of pastoral service:

> I was driven by force from the village of Neuheim, presumably because I tried to prevent the congregation from delivering to the government the required amount of grain. For this offense the death penalty can be imposed. In another village I escaped arrest only because I had succeeded in finishing the divine service and official church acts and left the place two hours before the writ for my arrest was issued. From other congregations I received cancellations upon receipt of my announcement of scheduled visits together with warnings and heart-rending descriptions of their situation. The church district of Kronau sent a call. A month later, however, I received a letter from them requesting me not to come, as none of the farmers would be allowed to offer shelter to a pastor.[31]

Seib was no malcontent wanting to flee at the first sign of struggle but one of the long-suffering pastors who had endured throughout the persecutions of the past: the anti-German propaganda of World War I, the civil war, the famine of the early 1920s, and the twelve years of revolution. But now, his strength was sapped. Concluding his letter of November 29 to Morehead, Seib appealed to him: "There is only one salvation possible for our Lutheran people of German descent ... to help them get out of present-day Russia, because they will die as a people of German extraction and more so as a Christian people. ... Please save us, the pastors and our children from this misery and from this communistic prison. ... We and our children will thank you for it for the rest of our lives."[32]

"FAITHFUL TO HIM TO THE GRAVE"

Inspiring a New Generation of Believers

AS THE LUTHERAN seminary in Leningrad began its fifth year of operation in fall 1929, the disruption in the economy brought about by collectivization and the end of the NEP adversely affected its budget. Bishop Malmgren, after thanking John Morehead for the recent LWC gift of $1,000 for the seminary, explained to him the current economic situation in the USSR and its troubling implications for the seminary. In a letter dated October 12, Malmgren reminded Morehead that the state grocery stores were off limits for pastors and church organizations, with the result that they had to pay substantially more than the average citizen at the free-market stores. There had even been a rumor that beginning October 1, the military would cordon off the cities from the farmers in the countryside. As in the early days of the Bolshevik Revolution, farmers were fearful that they might be prevented from selling their produce as freely as they had been able to do.

The rapid tightening of the noose around the seminary forced Malmgren to confess, "We will not worry but commend ourselves and our work into God's hand. He has up until now helped us and sent us friends from throughout the entire, wide Lutheran world. He will help us further because we desire nothing other than to build His kingdom."[1] Morehead was not oblivious to the changes taking place in Russia, relating to Malmgren that Paul Hutchinson, editor of *Christian Century*, had described his recent visit to the churches in the USSR in alarming terms. Furthermore, Morehead had gotten word that the local government in Leningrad was threatening to force the seminary to give up its residence in the city. What was going on, he wanted to know?[2]

Bishop Malmgren answered him on October 24 with assurances that the seminary had been given a reprieve for the time being. Morehead's information had been correct, though, for in the summer Malmgren had been advised by the government to have the students vacate their dorm rooms in the building next to the seminary so that workers could be resettled there. He had been given two weeks' notice to find living space outside the city. Malmgren was certain that if this request had been carried out, he would have had to close the seminary. The evangelical Christians in Leningrad had just been forced to close their seminary or "preachers' college" (*Predigeranstalt*) under similar circumstances.

But due to his persistent efforts and complaints, the authorities retreated on this request. Although Malmgren possessed an official document testifying to the seminary's three-year lease on the students' apartments, he had no illusions as to the authorities' ultimate goal. The Communist Party had reiterated that whoever was not of the party or serving the party would be banned from the city. With the constant pressure of the Communists weighing on him, he assured Morehead, "Nevertheless we have learned to take seriously the Lord's words, 'Don't worry about tomorrow.' For the moment it is enough that we can work unmolested, but what will happen in the next half year we confidently place in God's hand. He has helped us so far and He will continue to help us." Malmgren's faith would be put to the test much sooner than perhaps even he had imagined.[3]

AS THE NEW school year began, the attempt to continue holding Sunday school classes as in the past would have to be carried out in a manner that would draw less attention from the OGPU. Due to the April 8 Law on Religious Associations, the church could no longer teach the Bible to children within the confines of the church building. Pastors Helmut Hansen and Kurt Muss decided to pursue a loophole in the law so that their Sunday school teachers would be able to conduct classes within the apartments of the students on Sunday mornings. Bishop Malmgren had warned Hansen that the consequences of such actions might be unpleasant, but he replied in the words of the apostles Peter and John that he was compelled to obey God rather than man.[4]

Hansen would regularly gather the Sunday school teachers in his apartment on Friday evenings and review the lesson for the coming Sunday. Ilsa Wasserman noted that the number of teachers attending would normally range anywhere from thirty to thirty-five, but on two occasions the number of attendees actually reached fifty! (Interested friends of the teachers also attended from time to time). With such a crowd in the small Soviet apartments of that time, and in the very center of the city, it would have been impossible to hide their activities from neighbors and spies.[5]

Hansen usually had the basic lesson plan typed out for each of his teachers by a young lady named Margarita Blau.[6] Blau was a friend of Kurt Muss's sister, Luisa, but was not a frequent churchgoer and claimed that she did the work in order to get "a piece of bread." She didn't see anything anti-Soviet in her work, but simply typed quickly without paying too much attention to the contents.[7] Elsa Freifeldt was one of Hansen's Sunday school teachers and explained how Hansen would instruct them. He stuck exclusively to biblical themes, explaining the meaning of the text of the week. Afterward, the teachers would relate the instruction to their students according to their age and level of understanding. The foundation of his teaching, she declared, was that truth and love would be victorious on earth. The content of the lessons, she noticed, were something he exhibited in the way he lived his own life.[8]

Hansen had begun gathering teachers for the Sunday school program at St. Peter's in 1926, when it was technically illegal to teach children Christianity although the government generally didn't enforce the law. The teachers were usually dedicated parishioners of St. Peter's and volunteered to teach the classes. However, the question eventually arose among the teachers: "Are we doing anything illegal by teaching the children Christianity?" Hansen replied that he understood the law to allow the teaching of religion to children in their own homes and that teaching up to at least five children could be considered legal. (His logic was that each family, independent of the number of children it had, could add yet three additional children in accordance with the law.) Whether Hansen's interpretation of the law was accurate isn't entirely clear, but in 1926 the Soviet state was in the middle of its NEP program and had previously winked at many laws that were on the books. Hansen, although he was aware of the April 8 law, thought that the risk was worth it.[9]

In the fall of 1929, there were forty-seven Sunday School teachers in total teaching under Hansen's and Muss's direction. The teachers were mostly young and recent confirmands, although all age groups were represented. Renata Schwartz, an ethnic German and sixty-one-year-old retired schoolteacher, was one of Hansen's older instructors. She had taught at the Peterschule since 1906, but like many believers was among those who was fired in 1929 when Communists took over the administration of the school. In 1928 the biblical instruction of children could be held in the church, but in 1929 Hansen informed her that due to the new April 8 law they could only be held within apartments. Following Hansen's advice, she moved the classes to her own apartment around the corner from St. Peter's at house number 10 on Zhelyabova Street. In the fall of 1929, she was teaching five students aged fourteen to sixteen.[10] Each teacher had a group of about five to eight children, and all in all the number of students most likely approached two hundred. (Hansen counted roughly 120 students in his circles.) Together, the two pastors covered the most popular languages among their parishioners. Hansen, more fluent in German, tended to use those teachers who knew German, while Muss's bilingual skills allowed him to gather Russian-speaking teachers.[11]

Helmut Hansen's boldness in challenging the limits of Soviet law was no doubt a result of his concern with the increasingly strident atheist propaganda that was virtually everywhere in Soviet Russia in 1929. He often spoke about the "unchristian spirit" present in the country and urged young people to recognize that they were engaged in a spiritual battle. Sometimes he was accused by parishioners of going a little too far in his criticism of the Soviet government in his sermons.[12] Sunday school teacher Dorothea Mai claimed that she and his wife Erna had spoken to him about the sharpness of his critique of the Soviet state. (Erna, though, said that she never criticized his sermons as anti-Soviet because they weren't.) In reply to these warnings, Mai remembered Hansen saying that he would answer for his own actions. Mai specifically noted how Hansen in his sermons would touch on the theme of the Soviet authorities being enemies of religion, and in response he would urge his parishioners to fight for their faith and be faithful to Jesus Christ.[13]

But while there were criticisms of Hansen's tact with regard to speaking about the Soviet authorities, the congregation stood by him. Bruno Biedermann, the chairman of St. Peter's *dvatsatka*, defended him and found nothing that could be considered anti-Soviet in Hansen's sermons.[14] Other dvatstaka members like the fifty-seven-year-old former caretaker of the Volkovsky Lutheran cemetery, Richard Vogel, saw nothing anti-Soviet in Hansen's sermons. On the contrary, Vogel said that they carried a "purely religious character." Biedermann, a sixty-one-year-old retiree, had served for ten years as the *dvatsatka* chairman at St. Peter's and was impressed by Hansen's serious commitment to strengthening a "religious moral spirit" within the youth of the congregation.[15]

Hansen's Sunday school teachers were employed in a variety of professions, some even working for the state, at common labor, or were university students. Whatever their vocation, Hansen emphasized that they needed to stand united in their defense of the faith and fight because this spiritual battle would only be temporary. At times the teachers asked him about how they might live faithful lives in the Soviet state. For example, someone once asked, "Should we follow

the five-day school/work week and still attend church?" One can only imagine the quandary in which young people found themselves: How should they
live as Christians in a society that was doing its utmost to stamp out religious
practice? Hansen's answer was in line with Martin Luther's understanding of
the right- and left-hand kingdoms of God. He replied that they needed to do
both: live as good citizens and Christians simultaneously. Sometimes he worried
that his critique of the state was too harsh and might confuse the youth, so he
also took care that he did not directly encourage them to become antagonistic
toward the Soviet state. They were, most importantly, to recognize the dangers
of the godless movement in the society of their day. It was a difficult balance.

Several of his youth had been taking his words to heart and a few years
before had formed a special group within St. Peter's known as the Jugendbund
("Youth League"). The group was formed initially in 1926 after a Saturday night
vigil before Easter Sunday, when confirmands received communion for the first
time. The confirmands received pins that Hansen had ordered prepared by
Kurt Muss's brother Conrad. The pins were designed by Kurt and contained
an acronym, as far as can be gathered from some photographs, taken from the
German phrase *Trau bis zum Tod Jesus dein Eigen*, or in Russian, *Veren do
smerti Iisus tvoi* ("Faithful to the grave, Jesus, thine own"), or as it was written
in most accounts, *Veren yemu do groba* ("Faithful to him to the grave"). Initially,
thirty pins were distributed, but apparently they were given in succeeding years
to those who would join this active group of youth within St. Peter's.[16] Kurt
Muss handed out his own pins to confirmands in his congregation, too.[17]

In the beginning, Hansen had hoped that the pins would be taken as a
symbol to remind the youth to be sturdy Christians. But when he noticed in
1927 that there were other youth who, though they were not yet confirmed, zeal-
ously attended Bible class and were living like real Christians, he decided to give
them the pins, too. In time he would have second thoughts, fearing that this
group could be interpreted as a distinct group within the congregation. But it

seems that the primary issue that concerned him was that the Jugendbund, as a separate entity, could then be subject to government registration. Registering the congregation was enough of a hassle without adding further complications to church life. Hansen thus encouraged the youth not to call themselves the Jugendbund and told them that they should instead understand the pins as a reminder of holy communion.

The number of participants in the Jugendbund increased to the point that it appears to have reached sixty members. The list included the Freifeldt sisters, Elsa and Marta, the Kosetti sisters, Tamara and Benita, Gustav Golde (nephew of Bishop Theophil Meier), and seminary students Conrad Gerling and Peter Mikhailov, among others. Evgeny Hoffman even managed to retain membership, although he apparently was still a member of the Communist youth group Komsomol![18] Despite misconceptions that would ultimately brand the Jugendbund as some kind of nationalistic Germanic group, the Hansens' effort to imbue the youth with a solid Christian foundation appears to have been their only goal. Erna, the mother of three young boys, especially sympathized with the youth. She desired, like her husband, to rescue them from the immoral lifestyles that they couldn't help but notice all around them. As a result, from time to time the Hansens invited the youth to their home for fun and games.

Margo Jurgens had been confirmed as a sixteen-year-old at St. Peter's in 1925 and had on her own initiative begun to teach several children the Bible in 1926. She was the type of committed Christian invited to the Hansens' apartment on these occasions. Her remembrance of these "tea evenings" was that they would begin with prayer and then the youth would play games and sing songs. These gatherings were uncovered by the newspaper *Leningradskaya Pravda* in 1928 and were described in conspiratorial terms.[19] In addition, Hansen, perhaps due to the new five-day work week and the difficulty of attending church on Sundays, offered a Bible study every Tuesday night from 7:00 to 8:30 p.m. Anywhere from twenty-five to forty youth (primarily Jugendbund members) would attend the class, a rather large number given the spirit of the times. In the fall of 1929, Hansen would teach from the Gospel of John.[20]

MEANWHILE, KURT MUSS was forming his own group of Sunday school teachers as well as crafts group instructors. Ever since his return in 1926 from the Gulag labor camp on Solovetsky Island, Muss had been assisting Hansen with children's Sunday school groups. In the three years after his release, he had been established as the pastor of the first exclusively Russian-speaking congregation in the Lutheran Church. Inspired by Hansen's example, Muss continued the practice of providing spiritual education for the children of his own parishioners. From one small Russian-speaking group led by Viktoria Seleznyova when Muss arrived in 1926, his Sunday school groups had by the fall of 1929 expanded to ten, with the addition of five groups organized around the teaching of crafts.

The crafts teachers taught skills like sewing, woodworking, and draftsmanship, for which they were paid a small fee. But as with Hansen's group, the Sunday school teachers were volunteer workers who shared the pastor's concern about the spiritual upbringing of the children. Included among the Sunday school teachers were Muss's wife Elena, Tamara Kosetti (who was studying to be a masseuse and taught sewing skills to the girls), Maria Weisberg (a retiree and former member of the Salvation Army), Mikhail Mudyugin (a student in a music school), and Dagmara Schreiber (a university student). All in all, there were about fifty to sixty kids, some participating in both the Sunday school and crafts groups.[21]

Muss gave the crafts groups the name *Pchyolki*, or "Busy Bees." Muss created them in 1927 with the idea of training children in a particular craft while at the same time emphasizing the Christian view of love for labor. Muss figured that there were about thirty children in the Busy Bees ranging in age from ten to fifteen. Funding for this project came from the freewill offerings of the believers and from the children themselves.[22] Muss even penned a hymn entitled *"Pchyolki,"* which the kids would learn and then sing. The verses went like this:

> In the name of the Lord Christ, we carry out our labor; hope and love with faithfulness we promise to Him; He who shed His blood for us. We strive so that suffering and tears would cease from the earth; so that the promise of the Father that all people should be one family would be fulfilled; that people would not be enemies to one another; that the strong would not oppress the weak; that all would become one flock and that brother would help brother when in trouble. We hold high the holy banner; may Your hand preserve us. Christ, you have promised to always be with us, send us aid in our troubled hour.

Most of the kids learned the hymn by heart.[23]

With the announcement of the April 8 law regulating religious associations, Muss had, like Hansen, decided that it was too risky to hold exclusively children's services. In response, he arranged regular worship services where the children could attend with their parents. The Sunday school classes were then moved into the apartments so that the children could better understand what was going on during the church service.

Those youth (and some adults) who taught Sunday school for Muss gathered at his apartment on Mondays to go over the lesson plans for the next Sunday. Sunday school teacher Irina Prelberg would type out Muss's notes and instructions about how to teach the lesson. One of his teachers, Viktoria Seleznyova, was a forty-eight-year-old widow of German ethnicity who worked as an accountant in a city plant nursery and had begun teaching Russian-speaking children in 1925. She noticed that with Muss's return from the Gulag in 1926, the number of children's groups increased from four to ten within a few years. Seleznyova especially admired Muss's concern that the children would not only understand the lesson but would apply it to their lives. He would reinforce the children's lesson by preaching on that topic in church, too. She herself was committed to the religious nurture of these children because she believed this would help them become useful citizens in society. Unbelievers, she felt, couldn't satisfy the demands necessary for any individual's life. But twenty-one-year-old teacher Valentina Kerman remembered that Muss articulated the goal of their teaching in religious, not moral, terms. Muss spoke of how the child, when he reached maturity, would become an idealistic Christian who could stand up in society and powerfully defend his faith in Christ.[24]

There is little doubt that Muss made a strong impression on his teachers and parishioners due to his oratorical skills and compassion. Some young women, like Irina Prelberg and Tamara Kosetti, were possessed of a religious mindset and drawn to this man of conviction by his "beautiful use of words." Kosetti recalled that Muss regularly emphasized to the ten or fifteen teachers gathered that they should stress in their lessons God's existence and responsibility for the creation of all things. Frequently, after Muss had completed giving instructions on how to teach the lesson for the coming Sunday, there would be time for conversation. The teachers would commiserate with him about how the Soviet government was persecuting religion. They felt that the mass of believers were beginning to lose their sense of religion due to the difficulty of finding employment as a self-proclaimed Christian. Muss's firm commitment to the faith was a strong influence on the youth to remain faithful to Christ as they wrestled with being Christians in an increasingly godless society. Both Prelberg and Kosetti were smitten in other ways, too, acknowledging a romantic interest in Muss before he eventually married their friend Elena Cherneshyeva in 1929.[25]

But it was primarily Muss's sincere dedication to the cause of the gospel that was the motivating factor in his popularity. On Holy Trinity Sunday in the spring of 1928, Mikhail Mudyugin, a seventeen-year-old music school student, was sent on an errand by his mother to the Leningrad House of Trade. As he exited the store, he saw the striking St. Mary's Lutheran church across the street from him. Intrigued, Mudyugin walked up to the door and read the notice: "Here on Sundays and Wednesdays at 7 p.m., an Evangelical Lutheran divine service is held in Russian." Sliding onto a bench in one of the back rows, he heard Muss pronouncing the words of the Apostle's Creed in Russian, face to face with the youth gathered there for confirmation instruction. Mudyugin noted the eyes of the pastor were inspiring and kindly, so he approached Muss afterward and asked if he could attend future sessions. He made sure to stress that it was purely for "cognitive reasons," as he had no intention of being confirmed. Mudyugin would eventually help with summer camps for children in Strelna, where he met one of the teachers and his future wife, Dagmara Schreiber. When Muss moved his congregation into St. Michael's Lutheran Church on Vasilyevsky Island in the spring of 1929, Mudyugin followed him there and was confirmed in October. Since his father was an atheist and his mother was a devout Orthodox Christian, Mudyugin hid this decision from his parents. Soon after his confirmation, he began teaching a group of six students aged thirteen to fifteen, not much younger than himself! He gathered them in the apartment of one of his students named Obram, a five-story apartment about a fifteen-minute walk from St. Michael's and across the street from a large Orthodox Church.[26]

Mudyugin noted that Muss was unorthodox in his preaching style, not standing behind the pulpit to address his listeners but standing in front of them and moving about during the preaching of the sermon.[27] Orthodox believer and attendee Elena Shukino-Bodarets was mesmerized by his sermons, explaining that Muss was "a great talent" in contrast to Hansen, whom she found somewhat ordinary. She, too, was invited to teach the children's groups, as Muss assured her that her Orthodox faith would not be a hindrance in teaching. Of course, Muss was not blindly ecumenical. He would provide his teachers guidance with the lessons, and Shukino-Bodarets remembered his words very well.[28]

Muss's fluency in Russian afforded him the opportunity to attract youth like Shukino-Bodarets and Mudyugin who were outside the traditional Lutheran family (German, Estonian, Swedish, Latvian, Finnish). Even more appealing to the youth, though, was Muss's desire to apply biblical lessons to modern life. His message spoke to the hearts of many young people who were looking for truth and not finding it in atheism or communism. Mudyugin noted how Muss would take a biblical text and apply it to the times in which they were living. He did not attribute a decisive influence to anti-religious propaganda, instead saying it would only strengthen the faith of believers. Mudyugin, who was committed to saving children from the influence of atheism, took to heart Muss's words about the necessity of not just speaking loudly about your faith but actually living your life according to the teachings of Christ.[29]

Shukino-Bodarets would hold many lengthy conversations with Muss of a theological nature. She especially remembered how he explained that the Bolshevik Revolution was guilty of dividing society into classes. A faithful Christian could not simply opt out and remain ambivalent, for there was no neutral ground in Soviet society. To paraphrase the Bible, one was either with the atheists or the Christians. But Muss assured her that God was with them, and they would ultimately win this battle of ideals.[30] In the 1920s, many Russian youth were on a serious quest for the meaning of life; the "lost generation" that F. Scott Fitzgerald and T. S. Eliot talked about in the West had its counterpart there, too. The poet Sergey Yesinin, who eventually committed suicide, characterized one approach as "a withdrawal into sensuality and mysticism."[31] The Communist newspaper *Komsomolskaya Pravda* recorded young people's fascination with Yesinin and noted that they received many letters from young people who were beginning to become genuinely interested in religion. Clearly, the Communist Party was failing to attract young people as student circles began forming religious philosophy groups for discussion.

These groups would rediscover the writings of Fyodor Dostoevsky and the Russian Orthodox philosopher Nikolai Berdyaev, who had been exiled by Lenin earlier in the decade on the "Philosophy Steamer." There also appear to have been well-organized anti-Soviet political movements within Russian universities by the late 1920s. These movements signified a certain restlessness among young people but it seems that the vast majority were apolitical, seeking solace in sex, vodka, and the foxtrot. One thing many young people had in common, though, was their opposition to the Communist ideal, which was becoming stale and sanitized.[32] While young people in the Soviet Union were searching for their path in life, spiritual mentors like Kurt Muss provided guidance and a listening ear to their problems. Mikhail Mudyugin had hoped to enter the chemistry department at Leningrad University in the fall, but since he was of a higher social class, his exams were structured to be more difficult than for proletarian youth. Mudyugin didn't succeed and when Muss returned from his honeymoon that summer, he told the pastor of his failure. Muss responded with words that Mudyugin would describe as prophetic and that would change his life. "Misha," he said, "Don't grieve! Your path is a completely different one. You have to become a pastor! To accomplish this, you will have to study a lot and above all, learn German well, because an extensive amount of theological literature is written in this language in these 'new times.'"[33] Mudyugin was encouraged, and when he later mentioned to Muss that he would enroll in the Lutheran seminary, Muss clarified for him the cost of discipleship in Stalin's USSR: "Misha, know that when you finish the seminary, not one Lutheran church will be remaining here."[34]

NOT EVERYONE IN the Lutheran Church agreed with the tactics of Hansen and Muss. Latvian Lutheran pastor Julius Zahlit thought they pushed the envelope too far when confronting the state's regulations on educating youth. In fact, Zahlit didn't operate a Sunday school at Christ the Savior Lutheran Church in Leningrad but believed that parents should educate their children as in the early days of the church. But when children were ready for confirmation, this was allowed by the state, and Zahlit said that pastors have the right to teach them since it was the entry point into the church. He himself had been subjected to a search by the OGPU, but he believed that he had complied with the law and so wasn't too concerned.

But when it came to atheist and OGPU efforts to close his church in 1929, Zahlit and his congregation fought them tooth and nail. At the beginning of the year, pressure began to be applied by a Latvian Communist club who wanted the church building for themselves. The state had been expropriating the church's property since 1918; all that remained was the smallest building, the church that was funded by Czar Nicholas I's private treasury at a cost of ten thousand rubles. The Communists understood it to be the central meeting place for believing Latvians, so they used every excuse to gain the property. At community gatherings, lectures, and after going from apartment to apartment, the Communists gathered four thousand signatures demanding that the church be closed. The Presidium of the Leningrad Soviet agreed with the Latvian Communists to close Christ the Savior Lutheran Church on October 10, accepting the logic that the church was located too close to a technological institute and Soviet Labor School Number 41, and "it doesn't correlate with the viewpoint of Soviet cultivation of educating youth."[35]

Zahlit didn't give up. He knew that according to Soviet law he could appeal the decision to the Central Executive Committee of the Communist Party in Moscow. He used every means he could to gather a thousand signatures and made the trek to the capital.[36] While there, he visited the Latvian Foreign Office on November 5 and apprised them of the situation. He took this step because he saw that the Communists had attempted similar tactics with the Leningrad German Lutheran churches, but the German consul general had taken up the matter privately with Soviet authorities and the churches had remained untouched. Zahlit said he was not wedded to the building, acknowledging that the congregation's existence was more important. But while it might be easier for the Latvian Lutheran community not to maintain a building, nevertheless they didn't want to give up their property without a fight.[37]

The Presidium of the USSR learned of the protests by the Latvian Lutherans and now considered a proposal to turn the church into the Latvian House of Enlightenment. As Zahlit met with the secretary of the Soviet Union's president, Mikhail Kalinin, he stressed that his church bothered no one and stood on its own plot of ground. Attempting to renovate it into a club would not prove successful because of the structure of the church. The secretary agreed with Zahlit and said the church as a whole (and Christ the Savior Lutheran) would continue to exist for now, but added ominously: "It's probably clear to you that we consider the church to be without rights, and in five years they will all be closed anyway." The Latvian Communists redoubled their efforts with letters to government, regional, and party organizations in Leningrad, but against all odds, on September 30, 1930, the Presidium of the USSR concluded that the church would remain with the believers. Zahlit and his parishioners had fought the Communists and won—for the time being.[38]

DESPITE THE PROBLEMS plaguing the Evangelical Lutheran Church in Russia and the seminary, John Morehead responded with a can-do spirit in regard to the mission of the church. In a November 22 letter to Bishop Malmgren, Morehead probed, "What systematic measures besides the public services of the Church, religious instruction in preparation for confirmation, and the Christian teaching within the homes of the members of the congregation have been adopted or can be adopted by the Church in Russia under present conditions?" If the Lutheran Church was to survive in the future, Morehead recognized the necessity of training a new generation of believers from which pastors could arise and continue to lead the church. This meant the seminary had to continue at all costs.

In other countries of the world, the LWC was emphasizing the preaching of the word of God, the teaching of the Bible and Luther's Small Catechism within Christian homes, and the encouraging of parishioners to witness to their faith. Although he tried to lift the spirits of the bishop with the realization that secularization was a problem encompassing the entire world, Malmgren must have wondered what more could be done in Russia.[39] After all, in response to Morehead's questions: (1) Public services in the church were about all that the April 8 law permitted. The church had been legally reduced to the bare minimum of activities within the confines of its buildings. (2) Religious instruction for confirmation was not really allowed anymore, although some pastors continued to act as if it was still legal. For example, seminary dean Friedrich Wacker continued to assist one of his students with confirmands in the village of Detskoe Selo near Leningrad, and he would reap the consequences in the coming year.[40] (3) The teaching of children in the homes of Lutheran parishioners was continuing, as we know from the actions of Hansen and Muss and their teachers. But these Sunday school classes were dangerous and were the kind of activities more wary pastors tended to avoid.

The negative reports coming from southern Russia of Lutherans wanting to leave the USSR and emigrate also worried Morehead. He knew that Sweden had already extricated some of their ethnic brethren from that region, and so with missions ever in mind he was forced to speculate: "Is God's purpose in leading Lutheran peoples centuries ago into Russia accomplished? Or has He still a great missionary purpose for the Evangelical Lutheran Church in your country?"[41] Morehead was reluctant to give up his hopes for a vibrant Lutheran Church, however unrealistic that might have been. But despite his concerns for the effect on the survival of the Lutheran Church in Russia, he bowed to reality and acknowledged that the Executive Committee of the LWC would now consider what measures needed to be taken to help Lutherans emigrate.

14

A SOMBER CHRISTMAS

Arrests and Interrogations

AS 1929 DREW to a close, Helmut Hansen wrote to his protégé, Kurt Muss, encouraging him to remain firm in the battle against atheism. "This new year in our lives will no doubt be one of the most difficult years of the struggle. Full speed ahead! A strong wind is inclined to give you strength, but constant battle will sink a person. And so, I send you my special wishes for your approaching birthday. To the coming year of battle and war to the finish!"[1] Muss and Hansen both would need to keep up their spirits. As Stalin's determination to eradicate religion could be seen in the laws of the nation and the actions of the OGPU. Seminary student Peter Mikhailov that fall displayed his Jugenbund pin from Hansen's congregation to fellow classmate Bruno Toryassan. As they looked at the pin, Mikhailov said, "If they find this on me, it's going to be bad!" He then took the pin and threw it into the furnace.[2] His fears proved prophetic because a critical moment would soon be reached in Leningrad.

On December 17, the OGPU carried out mass arrests of the pastors and Sunday school teachers of St. Peter's and Jesus Christ Lutheran Church in the dead of night. They included Hansen and his wife Erna; Muss and his wife Elena, along with his sister Luisa; Ilsa Wasserman; Evgeny Hoffman; seminary students Gotthold Sterle, Conrad Gerling, Otto Tumm, and Peter Mikhailov;

Inga Karlblum; Dorothea Mai; Maria Weisberg; Tamara Kosetti; Alexander Chaplygin; Viktoria Seleznyeva; Gustav Golde; Elsa Golubovskaya; Irina Prelberg; Ida Monakhova; Lydia Voznesenskaya; Karl Meier; Zinaida Petrova; Wilhelmina Duvan; Ksenia Rodzayenko; Ivan Grossman; Nadezhda Loran; Ksenia Bulatova; Tatyana Schaufuss; and Yekaterina Kartseva.[3]

ON DECEMBER 19, the OGPU began interrogating Muss, requesting that he first relate his history in the Lutheran Church and the reason for his activities. Muss took the occasion to explain his rationale for creating the children's Sunday school groups:

> I don't consider the groups that I formed as illegal, for freedom of religion has its place in the USSR and it allows for the religious nurture of children. And likewise, I don't consider the children's groups as an underground organization because there was no conspiracy involved. We have the signatures of the children with their attendance or non-attendance recorded, as well as the lists which were preserved by me and handed over to the representatives of the government during my arrest.[4]

Muss's protestations notwithstanding, the Soviet government did not interpret the law in the same optimistic manner that he did. They interpreted his and Hansen's actions as "attempting to get around the laws forbidding the teaching of religion to children." In their deception, the OGPU decided, Muss and Hansen were attempting to "prepare a cadre of religious-nationalist youth."[5]

The real concern of the Communists, who were advocating the idea of class struggle, was that young Lutherans were actively working against the development of class-consciousness among Soviet children. Peter Mikhailov admitted, "Working with children, we pursued the goal to plant the idea of Christianity within them, and the main thing, love to your neighbor, because we cannot carry out the basic goal of violence and class struggle."[6] One of the

most remarkable observations from a reading of the OGPU files is the honesty
and lack of fear with which the arrested Lutherans answered questions.

Since he was convinced that he was doing nothing illegal, Muss had no
qualms about answering honestly and engaging his interrogators in a discussion
of what was and was not legally permissible in the Soviet Union. For example, Muss admitted that he had moved the teaching of children to apartments
since the April 8 law had made it illegal to teach children in the church building. He acknowledged the accuracy of the list identifying his eleven Sunday
school teachers. He listed the five craft teachers and spoke of how he formed
the Busy Bees children's group. Muss confessed that he had no idea of his
teachers' political convictions. What mattered most to him was that they were
earnest and sincere Christians. Muss described in Augustinian terms that there
was a community of God existing on the earth. Soviet power only interested
him in terms of how it impacted the faith of Christian believers. "My sermons,
which you consider anti-Soviet, had the goal of revealing the sense of the times
in which we are living. I wanted the believers to understand that all of life is
under God's direction."[7]

While addressing the topic of faith and atheism, Muss acknowledged urging
his parishioners to battle atheism. Since atheism exists as a factor in Soviet society, he explained, the church could not ignore it but had to offer a response.
In fact, Muss told his parishioners that atheism was "a forethought of God,"
allowed by him in order to strengthen faith. Muss explained to the OGPU how
God was providentially controlling all events, a topic that he had reiterated
time and again to his teachers and their students.

Explaining further how he steered clear of politics in his sermons, Muss
stressed that he did not use the words "class" or "party" but addressed the issues
of faith and non-faith. Although his point went beyond the politics of the day,
by elevating the language of faith Muss was subtly belittling the role of politics.
Sunday school teacher Dagmara Schreiber, who was arrested shortly after the
new year, recalled a sermon of Muss's in which he alluded to Stalin's Five-Year

Plan: "When we see how they deface church buildings and … in fear listen to how they say in five years' time there will be no more churches, it is all futile. *All these persecutions only strengthen hearts in faith and together with all of the ruined churches, God is creating for Himself temples in the hearts of the people.*"[8]

Muss made clearer in his January 21 interrogation that atheism, not the activities of the government, was the point of his sermons. The Lutheran Church was committed to an apolitical outlook, thus the form of government in the country was of no interest to him. The fact that Luther's two kingdoms theology resonated with his Sunday school teachers came through in their own interrogations by the OGPU. For example, Zinaida Petrova described herself as "non-partisan" and elaborated further, "It doesn't matter to me which Party is in authority." A review of the typical answers given by the teachers on this topic were of the same variety: Irina Prelberg, "non-partisan"; Elsa Golubovskaya, "non-partisan"; Peter Mikhailov, "no political convictions"; Tamara Kosetti, "non-partisan"; Maria Weisberg, "none"; Luisa Muss, "I submit to any authority in power"; Otto Tumm, "no"; Ida Monakhova, "no." Not once did a Sunday school teacher express political opinions, which must have been disconcerting to Communists.[9]

The thoughtful eighteen-year-old Schreiber would give one of the most detailed answers on politics. Although she acknowledged that the teaching of the Bible to children was illegal, Schreiber nevertheless acted according to her conscience. "I am guided by my religious convictions and fulfilling the laws of the Soviet power as long as they do not contradict my convictions." If that explanation of who deserved her ultimate allegiance wasn't clear enough, Schreiber detailed the contents of one of her classes. She explained how she taught the story of Amos, God's prophet who lived in Judea in difficult times. The Assyrians had threatened Judea and because of their fear, the kings felt pressured to enter into an alliance with the empire. Amos, however, told them to rely instead on God. But the kings didn't listen to Amos, and as a result the

Assyrians conquered them. Schreiber went on to relate how the discussion points after the basic lesson would go a little deeper into critical thinking and make connections to the times in which the children were living. It was obvious that Muss, in writing the lesson, was convinced that persecutions would come to the children in the future and was in the process of preparing them for it.[10]

KURT MUSS WAS dangerous for the OGPU because he boldly preached to a new generation of believers, but Helmut Hansen was the one whose leadership they were really seeking to obstruct. Hansen was always considered Muss's mentor and the organizational mind behind what the OGPU would describe as a vast conspiracy taking place at St. Peter's. Hansen also preached strongly worded sermons against the atheists, but it was his close ties to the German consulate that the OGPU found most suspicious. Through his consulate connections, Hansen was able to put into place a system of aid for the poor in his congregation, attracting people away from the state's influence and binding them to the church.[11]

When the OGPU began questioning Hansen, they demanded concrete answers concerning the nature of his sermons and conversations with youth in his apartment. Gathering a collection of his quotes from parishioners and those who heard his sermons, the OGPU presented a picture of a man highly critical of the atheist perspective of the Soviets. For example, one listener quoted Hansen: "During the persecution of Christians [in the early church], there were few believers. But thanks to their endurance, they were able to conquer, and as a result, believers ruled the whole world. At the present time, likewise, there is a battle with atheists, and I am certain that victory will end up on the side of the believers."[12] Seminary student Otto Tumm remembered Hansen preaching the following on a confirmation day in 1929: "They may close up our mouths, but their lies won't stand. For a little time, this prattle will continue.

But truth will prevail because you can't conquer it, although you might be able to enslave the people. Today the youth have given their oath to be true to God, and they will help us fight to the end."[13]

Similar quotes painted the picture of a pastor who knew that his people were involved in a spiritual battle whether they were aware of it or not. Hansen showed clarity of thought in his interpretation of the times, comparing the church's circumstances in the Soviet Union to the persecution of the early church during the Roman Empire. In fact, he believed that the threats to the church were worse than in Roman times, and the subsequent history of the Lutheran Church in the USSR would not contradict him. In this existential battle for the life of the church, Hansen admonished his parishioners to remain faithful to Christ.[14] Despite the urgency of the times, though, Hansen was more careful in his utterances than some parishioners and OGPU agents characterized him. Sunday school teacher Inga Karlblum recalled that he never advocated for the removal of the Soviet government. Instead, his call was for a softening of its politics so that freedom of speech could exist and that aid to the poor and charitable housing for the elderly would be allowed. Another teacher, Magdalina Freifeldt, remembered that in one of the last Bible classes he held, the conversation had strayed into politics. In response to this unwanted diversion, Hansen replied, "We have gone a little too far off our topic, already straying into the realm of politics. But we aren't concerned with politics here; our only concern is religion."[15] Even Dorothea Mai, a member of the St. Peter's Lutheran *dvatsatka* who had questioned the sharpness of his sermons, also confirmed that Hansen did not consider the Soviet authorities but rather atheism as his enemy. And for that matter, he prayed that God would set the atheists on the proper path to faith. Although he could speak forthrightly at times, Mai did not see Hansen as an opponent of Soviet power and even reported him saying that Russia could not return to the past.[16]

While the OGPU did take notice of the content of Hansen's sermons, his interrogators took care not to become drawn into philosophical discussions with him as Kurt Muss's interrogators did. They were more concerned with his contacts abroad and occasional reception of money from foreigners. Hansen admitted that the LWC and the Gustav-Adolf-Verein sent money for the aid of pastors and the seminary. All this money was generally channeled through Bishop Malmgren, although he received funds on occasion. He admitted using the money he received for the poorhouse that the German government still owned and supported. In addition, Hansen received Bibles, hymnbooks, and other spiritual literature from Leipzig. In effect, Hansen's ties provided a lifeline to the Lutheran Church so that it could receive literature and continue its work among the poor. His wife Erna emphasized that one of the goals in her husband's life was to "help the poor and serve God and be faithful to Christ; this is what he wanted to leave as a testimony to his neighbors and parishioners."[17] Future parishioners and church leaders would remember his legacy of service to the Lutheran Church, but for the present, the OGPU would not understand his activities as simple Christian charity. Instead, they characterized his actions as part of a sinister conspiracy forming a cadre of willing youth who would carry out the aims of the German government.[18] The OGPU showed special interest in the spiritual musical concerts given at St. Peter's. Elena Muss told them that tickets were sold for fifty kopecks or one ruble, or simply given away free to parishioners or friends. The idea behind the concerts was to raise money to pay for the high taxes levied on the church, and also to cover heating bills and other essential repairs to the building. Registration from the authorities was not necessary, Muss claimed, because the concert was similar to a worship service in the church. Unfortunately, this is not how the OGPU would eventually interpret Hansen's actions.[19]

While all these interrogations were proceeding, the OGPU struck at another seminary professor and the pastor of St. Catherine's in Leningrad, Arnold Frischfeld. The fifty-five-year-old Frischfeld was arrested on December 18 and asked about his relationship to the children's groups formed by Kurt Muss. He denied having anything to do with them, even admitting that he thought they were illegal. He only confessed to teaching at the seminary where he taught Greek and New Testament courses. He added that the seminary existed primarily due to the funds sent by the Lutheran World Convention. Any further questions about these finances should be directed to Bishop Malmgren. The OGPU released him on the evening of December 23 but ordered him not to leave Leningrad and to be prepared to appear before them on request.[20]

AFTER THE ARRESTS of the three Lutheran pastors and scores of parishioners in Leningrad, Christmas took on a decidedly more somber tone. This was the case in all the churches in Leningrad and many cities in the USSR that winter as the Stalinist plan to deliver a deathblow to Christianity gathered steam. But word was reaching the outside world. Latvian Lutheran Pastor Mikhail Lapping appeared at the Latvian embassy in Moscow on December 23, alerting them to the fact that Muss, Hansen, and Frischfeld had been arrested (Frischfeld would be released on the day Lapping informed the Latvians of his arrest). Lapping felt that the arrests had been timed so that Christmas services would be canceled. Astonished by the brazenness of the Soviet persecution of Christians, US ambassador to Latvia F. W. B. Coleman wrote to American Secretary of State Henry Stimson, declaring that "the pastors and the congregations of the Lettish [Latvian] Lutheran churches in the Soviet Union are being subjected by the Soviet authorities to a persecution which is probably not paralleled anywhere in the world today."[21]

Other chroniclers of the times added to the evidence. A Catholic priest named G. J. MacGillivray reported the closing of 540 Orthodox churches and eleven Protestant churches in November/December alone, bringing the total number of church closures in 1929 to approximately 1,200. Between December 15, 1929, and January 15, 1930, another two thousand were supposedly slated for closure. The US State Department's legation in Riga offered a more conservative figure, citing the closure of about 579 houses of worship, including synagogues and mosques, in 1929.[22] In his report, MacGillivray mentioned the arrest of the Musses and Hansens, saying that they had simply "disappeared." Their case was thus publicized prominently in the Western press. All these attacks, including the new five-day workweek, where workers could be fired for attending church on Sundays or peasants could be expelled from their lands for doing the same, intensified the pressure against believers beyond anything that they had experienced since 1917.[23]

As Christmas drew near, an anti-Christmas campaign in the country was unleashed with ferocious intensity. In Kharkov and other cities of the Ukraine, the post office workers refused to accept or deliver Christmas mail for ministers of all Christian denominations.[24] The *Moscow Peasant Gazette* on December 20 printed a host of propagandistic anti-Christmas slogans to be promoted: "The Christmas sermon, preaching class peace, facilitates the predatory work of undermining;"; "Against Christmas—for the uninterrupted work week"; and "Struggle against the tendencies making for reconciliation with religion." Newspapers took special glee in emphasizing that with the new workweek, Christmas would be an ordinary working day, whether celebrated on December 25 or January 7 as in the Orthodox Church. Further rubbing salt in the wounds of believers, Moscow's *Pravda* announced that December 25 would be the "second day of industrialization" and workers' wages would be donated to an industrialization fund.[25] The newspaper *Rabochaya Moskva* (*Working Moscow*) in its December 24, 1929 issue reveled in the plans for Orthodox Christmas Eve. On the south banks of the Moscow River, a torchlight procession would celebrate the burial of religion, with trucks transporting models of churches, synagogues, and mosques. They would all be burned in one of the city squares, as well as any Bibles, hymnbooks, and icons that were collected along the way.

Church bells, which had often been confiscated during the civil war, were now once again removed from steeples and used for the purposes of industry. The February 1930 issue of *Bezbozhnik* produced a photomontage of bells being removed from churches entitled "Bells—For Industrialization." The

OGPU went from house to house in the villages on Christmas Eve, searching for Christmas dinners to be confiscated or destroyed. In place of the usual Christmas decorations in the stores in Moscow, now "anti-Christmas" displays were in vogue, highlighting a gigantic worker kicking the Christian, Jewish, and Muslim God down the stairs. Finally, according to a decree published by Moscow's *Izvestia* on December 18, even Christmas trees were forbidden.[26]

Regardless of the attacks directed against the church, not all of the believers were intimidated. Twenty-year-old Sunday school teachers Margo Jurgens and Benita Kosetti, who would not be arrested until February, continued gathering their Sunday school classes after the Hansens' arrest. They even formed a committee to provide aid for the arrested, with Jurgens gathering money for Hansen and his family. Jurgens stayed in his apartment and must have helped look after his sons, informing the congregation of the Hansens' arrest. The OGPU would describe them as "incorrigible followers of Hansen" who refused to give testimony, distorted facts, and exhibited "defiant behavior." One can only marvel at the incredible bravery of these young women, standing against the all-powerful secret police and defending their pastor and fellow believers.[27]

Mikhail Mudyugin described the mood of the youth of Muss's circle as "tense" due to Muss's arrest, but "our naive certainty in the justice system led us to gather signatures demanding the release of all of our innocent who were imprisoned."[28] The subject also came up during a meeting of St. Peter's *dvatsatka*. The chairman, Bruno Biederman, and another member named Lorek urged the committee to gather signatures for the release of Hansen. The majority of members, more cautious, refused to sign any document and decided to wait for actual charges to be filed against the pastor.[29]

JUST AFTER CHRISTMAS, the Leningrad Housing Administration renewed its demand from the previous summer that the seminary students move out of their dormitory rooms. Bishop Malmgren informed the Soviet authorities that he had a legitimate contract (with two-and-a-half years left on it), plus a special "protection document" (*Schutzschein*). However, all the paperwork he had accumulated was to no avail. Malmgren made calls to the state attorney and again appealed to the German consulate to intervene, as they had done so successfully in the past. But this renewed assault against religion and the church was more determined than any he had seen before.

On January 29, the official order came down. The students were to vacate their rooms within two days. In the early morning of February 1, hardened Soviet Red sailors arrived and demanded that the students remove themselves and their belongings from the premises. Gathering everything they could as quickly as they could, they fled. The local Soviet authorities informed Malmgren that they would need to move no less than twenty-five kilometers outside the city limits, so they found accommodations in the Ingrian village of Martyschkino—thirty kilometers outside Leningrad and at the end of the Leningrad regional tramline. In October, Malmgren had just ordained seminary graduate and the current pastor in Martyschkino, Paavo Haimi. Now Haimi was forced to attend to the needs of the students. Dean Wacker was forced to move with his family to Martyschkino, too. He and the students occupied the parsonage with Haimi and settled into the homes of farmers willing to take on this added responsibility.

In the long run, the situation was untenable. Four-hour round-trip travel every day was going to exhaust the students and affect their studies. Yet with good courage, the students endeavored to study hard despite the obstacles. Seminary student Johannes Lel recalled that his classmates would prepare lunch in the classroom where they studied. Malmgren pressed for solutions, though, scouting out alternative lodging that would allow the students to be able to at least reside somewhere closer to Leningrad.[30] Truth be told, the housing situation wasn't much better for Malmgren. While he was able to stay in the city, he was kicked out of the apartment he had occupied with his family since 1891. The government had been reducing the size of his apartment, allowing new residents to settle into his rooms in keeping with the policy of the communalization of housing. Finally, he was able to find a new apartment to share with his youngest daughter. Unfortunately, it lacked sufficient heat. If it became unbearable, he joked, he could always take a cold shower! Lel was impressed with how the sixty-nine-year-old bishop conducted himself despite these inconveniences. He remembered Malmgren as physically strong and possessing the gait of a younger man.[31]

In the meantime, Wacker was being questioned by the OGPU. His work with the confirmands in Detskoe Selo had come to their attention, and he was now being accused of "membership in an underground organization and having been engaged in anti-Soviet activities." It didn't help that Wacker already had a police record, having been arrested in 1925 for dissemination of Christian literature, which resulted in his being sentenced to one year's probation. But now, the OGPU had received evidence that he at one time tried to explain to confirmation students that religion does not harm a culture. Taking freedom of religion in countries like Germany, England, and America as an example, Wacker tried to illustrate that religion could lead to progress. Wacker admitted to expressing these thoughts but allowed that as he spoke Russian poorly, perhaps the students hadn't understood him properly. Although he remained free for the time being, he was now forbidden to travel beyond the Leningrad oblast.[32]

THE HANSEN-MUSS CASE now continued to accumulate even more names and addresses, as the OGPU arrested additional Sunday school teachers and brought in others for questioning. Those under arrest now included: Elsa Freifeldt, arrested on December 22, 1929; Mikhail Mudyugin and Dagmara Schreiber, arrested on January 24, 1930; Bruno Biedermann, arrested on January 21; Margo Jurgens, arrested on February 1; and Benita Kosetti, arrested on

February 7.[33] Years later, Mudyugin recalled his arrest this way: "I can't say that I took the search and arrest in any kind of tragic manner. Life was ahead of me, I was suffering for a holy cause and yes, of life in prison I had a very vague impression. In any case, the future appeared to be a novelty and promised something unusual, and for a 17-year-old youth, this was extraordinary and that was perhaps the main thing. However, during the search I was praying fervently and was completely certain of the closeness of God."[34]

Benita Kosetti, the younger sister of the already imprisoned Tamara, proved to be a thorn in the side of the OGPU. As the agents questioned her, they claimed that she was obstructing the investigation into Hansen's guilt. Not only that, but after her release she wrote them a *zayavleniya* ("declaration"). In her complaint, Kosetti charged,

> On the 13th of March I was informed that the investigation into Case No. 2195 had been concluded. Since that day, three months have passed, and I think it proper to write to you a declaration that I do not consider myself guilty according to Statute 58 (Law against Counter-Revolution). I was not a member of some counter-revolutionary organization and did not work in a counter-revolutionary group of Pastor Hansen because: (1) Such an organization did not exist; the congregation of St. Peter's was his and my place of work, to which I went only because I was a member of this congregation. While I was there, I did not support anything that was hostile towards the government. ... (2) I consider that participation in any counter-revolutionary organization is contrary to my religious convictions; as a matter of fact, I am completely apolitical and sympathetic to the idea of socialism, which I try to carry out in my own life. Concerning Statute 122 as it was explained to me, I definitely was teaching the Bible since May 1927, but I did it willingly and without pay as accepted in the Lutheran Church.[35]

As the arrests continued, Erna Hansen's physical condition was deteriorating in prison. Doctors were called in late January, and she was diagnosed with a nervous condition that was affecting her heart. She was deeply troubled about her depositions with the OGPU. She blamed herself for her husband's arrest, thinking that she had through her own naiveté convicted him by her testimony. The interrogator had falsely informed her that her husband had confessed to everything, so it would go better for all of them if she just signed a confession. Mrs. Hansen was clearly miserable and cried often that she had "hung" her husband.[36]

A historian, Natalya Stackelberg, was imprisoned with the Lutheran women for a time and provides an outside perspective on what prison life was like for them. In her published recollections, she noted that they observed an etiquette that had long since disappeared from Soviet society. For one, they addressed Mrs. Hansen with great respect as their superior, despite her forlorn condition. Such behavior was not in keeping with the class consciousness propagated by the Communists. Stackelberg would also discover in Room Number 43 her lifelong best friend, Elsa Golubovskaya. Elsa immediately helped her get settled when she arrived in the prison cell, finding her a bunk. Her gentleness and concern toward Stackelberg exhibited a Christian spirit that was mirrored by the behavior of the other Lutheran ladies imprisoned with her.[37]

Mikhail Mudyugin was also sent to the preliminary investigative OGPU prison on Shpalernaya Street known colloquially as the *Bolshoi Dom* ("Big House"). Although his cell was overcrowded, there were other Christians imprisoned with him and Mudyugin didn't feel alone. There was also an excellent library, and he read classic books like Victor Hugo's *Toilers of the Sea*. There was also a dog-eared copy of the New Testament that was passed from cellmate to cellmate. Once, Mudyugin recalled foregoing a morning walk in the courtyard and lounging on his cot, reading the New Testament, when he was approached by a limping Polish Catholic priest, Stanisław Przerembel. In a loud voice, the priest said, "It is best to read that Book on your knees, and not lounging on a cot!" Mudyugin jumped up immediately and thanked the priest for this lesson in how to revere God's word. He would remember and quote the priest's words for the rest of his life.[38] Father Stanisław had been arrested on October 10, 1929, for "systematically teaching Christianity to children," as well as running an underground seminary and conducting espionage—an accusation that would be added to any Christian who was a foreigner or had foreign contacts. The heroic Polish priest would be sent to Solovetsky Island camp on September 13, then be accused in 1932 of holding secret Masses in the labor camp and smuggling out information about the treatment of Catholics in the USSR. His activities would lead to his transfer to Butyrka Prison in Moscow. Upon his release that year in a prisoner exchange, he returned to Poland, dying in Warsaw in 1934 at the age of sixty-six.[39]

Mudyugin took ill at the end of February and found himself in the prison infirmary. One day as he looked out the window, he saw his Sunday school teaching colleague, Dagmara Schreiber, walking in the courtyard. It was only then that he learned she had been arrested, too. That was also the moment when he knew for a certainty that he loved her (they would be married a couple of years later). Once he was healthy, Mudyugin would be transferred to the Kresty Prison at the end of the spring. While there, he got to know a future archpriest of the Russian Orthodox Church, Alexander Ranne, as well as the Catholic priest, Father Boleslav Yurevich, whom he became acquainted with through the sending of secret messages that prisoners employed to communicate with those in other cells. In the prisons, it seems that an ecumenical spirit among Christians prevailed. Father Boleslav would receive a ten-year sentence just a few days before Mudyugin's release on October 21, and would eventually be among those executed during Stalin's Great Terror in 1937. Before his release from prison, Mudyugin would also see another familiar face—that of Kurt Muss.[40]

On April 19, 1930, Elena Muss's mother wrote to the authorities pleading with them to allow her daughter to be released with the promise that she would not leave the city. Elena was suffering from a condition in her lungs that would become exacerbated every spring, and being incarcerated only worsened her health.[41] Perhaps in response to this situation, Kurt Muss began to carry out acts of protest against the prison authorities. On July 3, Muss announced a hunger strike, something he had employed in 1922 when he was arrested for the first time while working with the NLC and Morehead. This time he was protesting on behalf of his wife Elena and sister Luisa, calling for their release. While his hunger strike did not free them, it apparently improved their prison conditions, because Muss called it off at 4:45 p.m. on July 7. On July 11, the OGPU announced the transfer of seventeen of the female prisoners to another building. Included among the seventeen were Elena and Luisa Muss.[42]

15

THE CHURCH IS BROKEN

The Koch Trial and the Decision in the Hansen-Muss Case

IN JANUARY 1930, Pastor Albert Koch was arrested in Grossliebenthal, Ukraine. John Morehead and his replacement from the NLC in Russia, W. L. Scheding, had visited Koch and his family often and worked closely with him in distributing food to starving villagers during the famine years. On June 19, the district court in Odessa began what would amount to a show trial in "the criminal case of the counterrevolutionary pastor A. Koch." The case was covered via radio broadcast, where Koch would be portrayed as a traitor.[1] Accumulating a plethora of paid witnesses, court prosecutor A. Mueller, a Communist from Austria, conducted a virtual kangaroo court trial against Koch. Witnesses had their one-ruble journey to the regional court in Odessa paid as long as they accused Koch of counterrevolutionary activities. Some, however, had a conscience, as in the case of one man who defended Koch. When told that he would not be reimbursed because he had lied, the man responded that he knew full well why he had been denied his money: because he had spoken the truth about Koch and exposed the lies.

The particulars of the accusation concerned an uprising that had taken place in Grossliebenthal back in 1919, when peasants rose up against the Red Army, who was forcibly confiscating food from them in accordance with "War

Communism." The revolt had been brutally suppressed by the authorities.
Now, eleven years later, the court retroactively accused Koch of belonging to
a German nationalist organization and conducting "counter-revolution" by
actively participating in a "kulak revolt" (the term "kulak" was of more recent
origin and Stalin had used it to brand affluent farmers as enemies).[2] In 1931,
Bezbozhnik journalist Lev Brandt would elaborate on the accusations against
Germans from the Ukraine by publishing a book entitled *Lutheranism and Its
Political Role*. Brandt identified Koch as a prime example of a Lutheran pastor
serving as a counter-revolutionist, providing assistance to the White armies
during the civil war of 1919–1920. Imperial German troops had intervened on
the side of the czarist-friendly White armies during the war and had even for a
time held villages like Grossliebenthal. Brandt asserted that Koch led the revolt
against the Red Army in Grossliebenthal, Alexanderhilfe, and other villages.
As a result, twenty "Communist-Spartacists" were shot on his orders.[3]

Brandt was not alone in singling out Koch. The authors of the 1931 book
Under the Wrath of Religion also painted a picture of the pastor as an active
participant in league with the officers of White Army General Denikin who
went to the front in order to bless "the kulak rebels." Koch was said to have
been part of a five-man committee leading the peasants and crying, "Beat the
communists, who want to take our land and our faith from us!" As late as 1937,
Bezbozhnik journalist Boris Kandidov returned to this episode in history and
accused Koch of being an agent and spy of the Germans.[4]

WHAT CAN ONE believe about these accusations? And why were they only
now being leveled against Koch? The fact that they had not been made against
him in 1919 and that he had continued to minister freely would lead one to
believe that Koch had nothing to do with the revolt. In fact, Lutheran pastors were simply not inclined by their theology to be advocates of violence
against the Soviet authorities. The reality was that the Red Army had shown

no magnanimity toward its White opponents at the end of the civil war.[5] If Koch had been a leader in the rebellion against Soviet power, what would have prevented his execution in 1919? Any thoughtful observer would conclude that the government in 1930 was hell-bent on eradicating the influence of active Lutheran pastors on their parishioners. His German ethnicity was just another piece of ammunition they could use against him.

Furthermore, the nebulous nature of these activities would tend to confirm such a hypothesis. While it is true that Koch was accused due to the supposed content of his sermons, he was also condemned for pastoral activities: making private visits to parishioners and instructing youth to prepare them for confirmation. What any disinterested observer would see as normal church life was portrayed in the most heinous manner.[6] Koch's activities could be twisted to fit the stereotype of the German Lutheran agitator that the authorities were promoting. He was a relic of the past that had to be done away with. Brandt seemed to let the cat out of the bag when he accused pastors like Koch of preaching to women "the old kulak-priestly ideal of 'Church, Children and Kitchen.'" Discerning the exploitation of women and children simultaneously within these ideals, Brandt claimed that Lutheran pastors were using women as "instruments" to raise children as "true wards of the church" while setting church and family against the Soviet school system. Teaching Christian values to children in a state now actively working against it with atheist indoctrination seemed to be the real issue in the accusations against Koch.[7]

Koch, for his part, denied all accusations. He had never urged anyone to rebel against the authorities, nor had he been a member of the "rebellion committee." The latter denial was important because Koch admitted to being a member of the union of colonists, but he reminded his accusers that this was merely an ethnic organization joined by all German colonists in 1917 during the interim Kerensky Government. The goal was to preserve their German heritage, nothing more. Ever since Germans began immigrating to Russia in the sixteenth century, they had taken pains to preserve their language, faith, and cultural habits. The times in which they lived, though, would no longer allow for non-political actions.

The Albert Koch case illustrates well the clash of cultures that the Stalinist assault on the Evangelical Lutheran Church in Russia and the Ukraine had initiated in 1929. All actions of Lutheran pastors would henceforth be interpreted in a conspiratorial and negative manner. If a pastor wanted to work with youth, he was subverting future generations from becoming godless, Soviet citizens. If he wanted to aid the poor, he was only doing it to keep the peasant class in thrall to its exploiters, the kulaks. If he showed any kind of pride in his ethnic heritage, he was suspected of being a German spy. Nothing he did could be seen outside the lens of politics.

The Russian Evangelical Press (REP) abroad cut through the haze of lies to remind its readers of the goal of the trial: "Pastor Koch, an active, convinced minister of the Gospel, a real religious leader of his congregation, universally loved, ... religiously deeply influencing wide circles of the German population has to be got out of the way."[8] The truth behind REP's defense of Koch was shown in the actions of his own parishioners. They boldly yet silently gathered and rallied before the courthouse in a show of support for their pastor. They knew his character and saw the accusations of anti-revolutionary propaganda for what they were: accusations made against a guiltless man.[9]

But unfortunately, the lesson of these assaults against Koch and the Lutheran church was to bring the German peasant in line with the new Soviet reality. A believer could not be a good Christian and Soviet citizen at the same time. The verdict in the case against Koch was most likely already predetermined by the Soviet government's goal of stamping out religion: "The numerous transgressions and crimes of Koch fully and entirely entitle the application of the maximum amount of the social safeguard: 'to be shot.'"[10]

While the court was concluding its deliberations, Koch's allies appealed to American President Herbert Hoover for his release. Recognizing Hoover's "humanitarian principles," Lutheran Pastor O. H. Groth of Milwaukee urged him to intervene, lamenting the fact that Koch was responsible for the care of his elderly mother, his wife, and four children. "Will the civilized world remain silent while the very foundation stones of its existence are being destroyed? Will not, cannot our government raise its voice in protest?"[11]

BUT AT THIS time President Hoover was occupied with his own troubles: the crash of the stock market in October 1929 and the rapidly advancing Great Depression. Although the US government had a legation in Riga, Latvia, monitoring religious freedom issues within Russia, its lack of diplomatic relations with the Soviet Union tied Hoover's hands. Robert Kelley, chief of Eastern European Affairs for the State Department, answered Groth on behalf of President Hoover, saying that "there would appear to be no immediate action which it would be practicable for this government to take which would be helpful."[12] John Morehead could do no less than appeal on behalf of Koch to his old friend Herbert Hoover, reminding him of the days when they worked together to save as many lives as they could from the famine in southern Russia. Morehead told the president that Koch had hosted him during the famine and had continued to be of assistance to those suffering in the Evangelical Lutheran Church in Russia in the succeeding years. Since he now served an influential role as the District President of the Regional Synod in the Odessa Region, Morehead surmised that the local Soviet authorities were singling out Koch as an example of the enemy with which concerned Soviet citizens had to be aware. Morehead supplied Hoover with secret correspondence from Lutherans on the ground in the Odessa region, apprising him of Koch's innocence and the true facts of the case.

Informing the president that he himself was trying to keep the Lutheran seminary in Leningrad alive, despite the fact that there were now only eighty pastors serving a Lutheran Church of one million people, Morehead pleaded one more time: "Mr. President, are there any measures you can kindly adopt through channels open to the Government of the United States by which a proper appeal may be made to the authorities of the Russian Government for the release of Pastor Koch? If so, the people of the Evangelical Lutheran Church in America and other countries will be profoundly grateful for your mediation."[13] Hoover had already been and would be continually deluged with letters from American organizations and interested citizens committed to defending the rights and publicizing the persecution of religious believers in the Soviet Union. Morehead's own American Committee on Religious Rights and Minorities and the "Hollywood Citizen," an organization of publishers, printers, and engravers, were among those who pleaded with the president to intervene.[14] Most likely, the president realized there was nothing he could do, even for his dear old friend, John Morehead. Hoover had effectively fought Soviet bureaucracy in the early 1920s for the right to distribute food and clothing to hungry and poor citizens, but Stalin's government of the early 1930s was in a different position. They would not be subjected to the demands of capitalists anymore. It was a new day, and Stalin was proving that Soviet power was a force with which to be reckoned.

Nevertheless, Hoover sympathetically wrote back to Morehead: "It is certainly a most distressing situation. I am asking the State Department to see if there is anything they can do, although I am afraid we have but little effect in Russia, even indirectly." Instructing him as to how to proceed further, Hoover continued, "The friends of Reverend Koch should present his situation to the German government as they, of course, have relations which we do not have."[15] Hoover's point was well taken, as the German government still held influence with the Soviet government despite the accusations of pan-Germanism leveled against Koch, Helmut Hansen, and Kurt Muss. Hoover's secretary, Laurence Richey, sought advice from the Secretary of State after receiving translations of the letters that Morehead had sent. The answer to Morehead was short and to the point: "I regret to say that there would appear to be no action which it would be practicable for this government to take which would be helpful to

Pastor Koch in the circumstances."[16] It seemed that only the German embassy had any real clout with the Soviets, and when Adolf Hitler came to power in 1933 that influence would be dramatically reduced if not completely curtailed.

However, the Soviet government was not as harsh yet toward its internal enemies as it would later be. Koch was sentenced to five years' imprisonment in the Solovetsky labor camp in the White Sea, followed by three years of exile outside of the Ukraine.[17] The German embassy could not help. Meanwhile, Albert Koch would begin the process of being shuffled between Gulag camps and exile, ultimately leading to his execution in 1937.[18]

ON SEPTEMBER 17, 1930, the courts declared that seventy-two of the accused in the Hansen-Muss case were guilty. Only thirteen of them would be allowed to walk free. According to the verdict, Pastors Hansen and Muss were the ringleaders of a "counter-revolutionary group," though their actions had not been isolated. They were part of a greater conspiracy called the "Academic Affair," which was of "monarchical, counter-revolutionary" character and supposedly led by Professor Sergey Platonov of the Academy of Science in Leningrad. (Natalya Stackelberg had been arrested as part of the "Academic Affair," too.)[19] According to the OGPU, there were several groups connected to this conspiracy, including a "German group." This is where Hansen and Muss, along with their Sunday school teachers, fit in. It also explains why Hansen was questioned about his relationship (he had none) to Orientalist academic Alexander Mervart (born in Germany as Gustav Mervart).[20] Mervart had ties to St. Catherine's in Leningrad, though, so connecting Hansen to him was a simple matter in the minds of the secret police.[21]

The Academic Affair was primarily an attempt by the OGPU to create fear among the intelligentsia of Leningrad, since Communists had been steadily losing positions of authority within the universities. The heart of the accusations leveled against Hansen and Muss concerned their religious activities in contradiction to the April 8 Law on Religious Associations. In the final verdict, seven primary accusations were made against Hansen and Muss: (1) agitation; (2) creation of the Jugendbund; (3) organization of children's Sunday school classes; (4) organization of charity work; (5) dissemination of literature; (6) relations with the German consulate; and (7) relations with foreign organizations. In the view of the court, these crimes worked against creating loyal citizens for the Soviet state. Agitation entailed a "hiding behind the religious flag of sermons and conversation" to deflect youth away from the activities of the state and the use of biblical texts to make critical parallels with the current path of the state. The Jugendbund and Busy Bees were identified as youth groups formed around the pastors with the goal of supporting their religious ideals.

The charity aid that Hansen distributed highlighted his ties to the German consulate, as he often received money from them and handed it out among the needy. However, the OGPU twisted his actions so that it would appear that the aid was given "not to everyone who is needy, as the Gospel commands a spiritual person, but patronizing instead those anti-Soviet and nationalist elements who couldn't count on the support of the Soviet authority." In doing this, Hansen used the Jugendbund to identify needy parishioners. These youth also assisted in the sale or distribution of tickets for concerts and at times themselves participated in the musical services, since they were members of the church choir.[22]

The concerts were described by *Bezbozhnik* journalist Lev Brandt as dangerous in their ability to attract not only "former people" of the czarist past but also ordinary Soviet citizens. Concerts highlighting religious themes, like those of Bach (Lutheran), Mozart, Beethoven (Catholic requiems and masses), and Orthodox Church music could lure people away from Soviet ideology. The concerts were apparently elaborate affairs, with academic choirs, the orchestra of the Soviet Philharmonic, and various artists from the State Opera, Theater, and Ballet participating. They drew large numbers of attendees and thus contributed greatly to the reduction of the church tax burden, since a freewill collection usually took place at the conclusion of the concert.[23] Although the proceeds from these concerts went to the fund of the German poor house or to those who were needy in the church and not to Hansen himself, the OGPU still painted his actions in a conspiratorial manner. "In this way Hansen not only 'scooped up' funds that were not known to the governing authorities but diverted the mass of Germans from attending culturally-enlightened state institutions all the while strengthening the German religious-patriotic feeling."[24]

The remaining charges built on this theme of Hansen and Muss developing a nationalistic spirit among Germans in Russia. The literature that Hansen assisted in distributing to Lutheran pastors came from the publishing company Rutter in Leipzig. Hansen had on occasion visited the German consulate and had workers of the consulate attending his church, with whom he often conferred. His and Muss's ties to foreign organizations clinched the sense among the OGPU that there was something of an anti-Soviet character taking place at the Lutheran churches in the city. Dr. "Marhead" (Morehead) was mentioned as one of their suspicious contacts, being the executive chairman of the LWC.

If all these charges weren't enough to convict Muss and Hansen, for good measure the OGPU added the accusation that two weeks before their arrest, they had engaged in an act of sabotage. Conspiring with the chairman of the German Reformed Church council, Ivan Hoffman, the pastors had supposedly attempted to dismantle the pipes in the church basement with the goal of poisoning the water supply with lead. This startling accusation is almost too unbelievable to consider, even for the fertile imagination of the OGPU. But it certainly fit recent government paranoia that acts of sabotage were being committed by enemies of the Soviet Union, as indicated in the famous Shakhty trial that took place in the Donbass region of the Ukraine in 1928. During Stalin's Great Terror, accusations of sabotage in league with the Germans or Japanese would become more common.[25]

As the OGPU concluded its accusations against Hansen, Muss, and their Sunday school teachers, the final statement read as follows:

All of these listed facts establish in sufficient measure that all of the activity of Hansen, his wife, Muss and the accused, were definitely directed towards the development and strengthening of Pan-Germanism for the disruption of the activities of the Soviet authorities not only regarding religious questions and the cultural-Soviet education of the mass of Germans, but in contradiction to socialist development in the interests of the foreign bourgeoisie, in which most of the efforts of Hansen and Muss were to estrange the youth from Soviet reality in order to prepare and create future anti-Soviet cadres.[26]

All that remained were the sentences. Hansen and Muss were sentenced to a Gulag labor camp for ten years; Erna Hansen and Elsa Freifeldt were sentenced to five years; most of the others (Prelberg, Selezneva, Benita Kosetti) were given three-year terms, while youth like Dagmara Schreiber and Mikhail Mudyugin were released with time served. Meanwhile, the Swedish press publicized the sentences given to Hansen and Muss and their Sunday school teachers, indicating that the foreign press was well aware of the court's decision. The Hansen-Muss case would become a major turning point in the state's relationship to those who served in the Lutheran Church. From then until the end of the Russian Lutheran Church, no pastor would again act as boldly as Hansen and Muss had.

THE PARISHIONERS IN Leningrad were especially frightened by the sentences given to the Sunday school teachers. It had a negative impact on those who might have wanted to participate in church activities, dramatically reducing the role of the laity. The Soviet authorities, assured that the battle was moving decisively in their favor, must have felt convinced that they had set the new guidelines for future activities in the church. Hence, they could afford to be magnanimous at times in individual cases because they knew that ultimately the future was with them.[27]

A good example of Stalin's ability to compromise temporarily was on display in his famous March 15, 1930 article "Dizzy with Success." In the article, he claimed that some overeager Communists had exceeded the requirements for collectivization, in the process closing churches without warrant. In hypocritical fashion, Yaroslavsky, who had shrieked loudest in the past for the closing of churches, now did an about-face. This leader of the League of the Militant Godless now criticized those atheists who had dared to obstruct Easter celebrations. The Soviet government had come to the conclusion that there was a real danger of peasants refusing to work the collective farms, so they retreated from collectivization for the time being and also called a halt to the forcible closure of churches.

It was only a tactical maneuver, however. Stalin had no intention of going back to the socially liberal NEP era of the 1920s. With regard to religious policy, he would soon begin attacking the church again after a short breathing spell.[28] For the Evangelical Lutheran Church of Russia, though, the die had already been cast. After the conclusion of the Hansen-Muss case, it was living on borrowed time.

16

SHEEP AMONG WOLVES

The Servant of the Church as Enemy of the State

FOR THE MOST PART, Lutheran parishioners had humbly acquiesced to the violent actions of the Soviet government, going to prison without starting revolts or fomenting uprisings. They might publicly protest, as Albert Koch's parishioners did. Or they might gather signatures in defense of their pastors, as Benita Kosetti and Margo Jurgens felt compelled to do. But in general, they would not resort to violence against the authorities. That is why the actions of the people of the Volga River city of Marxstadt marked a radical break in the way Lutherans responded to the Soviet authorities' lawlessness. The tension may have first surfaced when Pastor Arthur Kluck was arrested on December 1, 1929.[1]

In early 1930, Kluck, District President Nathaniel Heptner, a church elder named Schulz, and thirty-four believers were transported east toward Siberia from prison in Marxstadt. For ten days they were locked in a cattle car, allowed only a little food with no light or fresh air, mired in dirt and stink without any sanitation. After the first ten days, they arrived in Nizhny Tagil of the Ural Mountain range. As the doors to the cattle car were opened, the horrified prisoners gawked at each other's emaciated and run-down appearance.[2] In a February 25 letter, Bishop Theophil Meier related additional details of this odyssey to John Morehead. Kluck and Heptner had been sent to "an easternmost part of

Russia" where they had to travel on foot to a camp in -30 Celsius conditions. Heptner, who was sixty-seven and quite weak, couldn't manage the travel on his own, so he had to be transported via sledge. He had just served two months' imprisonment under harsh conditions in Pokrowsk (also known as Engels, on the Volga River) before being sent into exile.[3]

While Kluck was serving time in a Siberian concentration camp, his parishioners and other citizens of Marxstadt were becoming increasingly incensed by the actions of the government. All of the major churches—Lutheran, Catholic, and Russian Orthodox—had been closed, their pastors all arrested. The Lutheran church was converted into a "palace of culture" (similar to a community center). The Catholic church was turned into a theater and the Russian Orthodox church reduced to rubble. A red flag had been fastened to the iron cross high on the exterior of the Lutheran church. On the church's dome, a red star was attached that glowed at night with an electric lamp inside it.

THE LUTHERANS IN Marxstadt could not reconcile themselves to the fact that they had lost their church. At first, they protested at government gatherings, but to no avail. People then started gathering in small groups on the streets. Whenever they became too obstinate, the police would drive them away. Their numbers grew larger as the ladies gathered on the streets to meet their husbands when they finished work at the main factory, Vozrozhdeniya ("Rebirth"). Scattered groups of the irate began to linger on the streets after work. On June 5, a typical warm, summer workday, a group attempted to reclaim the church. At a signal, some men began running toward it. The crowd got larger and larger. A key was produced, but no one could open the door. However, a small window was partially open, and a young boy was lifted up to the window and slid through into the church. Other boys followed him, and soon the door was opened and people streamed into the church.

The news spread to the villages, and more people flocked to the church. Some ladies began to break up the stage that had been constructed in place of the altar, tearing it apart without hammers or axes. Others went to the kitchen to prepare food. Pictures of the members of the Politburo of the Communist Party were ripped off the walls and banners with quotations from the works of Stalin were torn down. A woman touched the keys of the organ and a familiar sound rang out and soon died away.[4] It is likely that this was none other than Kluck's wife, Bertha. She had been the church organist, and her daughter remembers her saying she wanted to see what the Communists had done to the organ.[5] Some of the children set about dismantling the red star from the church's cupola, as well as taking away the red flag from the church tower.

The building soon began to look like a church again, as the altar was restored while the objects for the palace of culture were taken away. But many began to ask each other why the horn for the factory had not sounded. They could use the help of the workers, and yet they had not come. Had they been detained? While they wondered, a group of youth came into to church, shouting, "They're coming! They're coming!" But it was not the factory workers who were coming. It was the militia on horseback, with many armed Communists behind them. The troops closed off the central square where the church was located. Soon cars came and arrested some of the men. More cars continued to stream in, this time with soldiers.

The Communist Party had its spies well placed, and apparently some had informed them of the plan to retake the church. That accounted for the troops arriving quickly as well as the fact that the factory workers were barred from leaving the plant on time. In their anger, the workers did break down the gates of the factory and push the militia guarding it aside, but when they got to the square they ran into the horsemen and armed Communists. The horsemen and Communists guarded the square all night while the Soviet authorities rounded up hundreds. Many were not guilty, but they were all imprisoned with at least a sentence of five years.

In this way, the Communists of Marxstadt broke the spirit of the people. The red star was reattached to the church's cupola. A red flag was placed on the tower. The pews were taken out and placed in the park. Within a year, the church was once again a palace of culture and the Lutherans of Marxstadt had acquiesced. The situation epitomized how the Communists attacked the Christian faith in the Soviet Union. First, those who stood up to the Soviet authorities were destroyed, their families scattered and dispersed. Meanwhile, life would go on normally, with the remaining citizens realizing the futility of challenging the Communist worldview. A new generation that didn't know the church would then be raised in a proletarian spirit. There would be no future revolts in Marxstadt because everyone knew who held political power in the city and country.[6]

DESPITE SETBACKS LIKE THESE, Morehead persevered, not willing to give up hopes for an eventual return of freedom to the church. The bishops of the Lutheran Church in the Soviet Union, however, did not share his optimism. The Hansen-Muss case in Leningrad and the difficulties surrounding housing for the seminary weighed heavily on their minds. In an emotional letter to Morehead on February 25, Bishop Meier expressed his deep concern that Christianity was dying in the Soviet Union. "The struggle against the Church, which has been ongoing for several years, is taking increasingly sharper form and the outcome has already been determined: in the course of the year 1930 the last traces of Christianity in Soviet Russia must be destroyed, for in a land like present day Russia there is no more room for the Christian faith but only for the Communist world view [*Weltanschauung*]." Meier went on, "The servant of the Christian Church is portrayed by society as an enemy of the state that must be fought against and thrust aside. Everything that is connected to the Christian faith or reminds one of it must disappear from the life of the people and its individual citizens." Anyone taking up the pastoral office was, in the biblical expression, being sent out "as a sheep among the wolves." Meier further explained to Morehead how the newly established workweek was limiting attendance at his church and how collectivization had decimated the congregations in southern Russia and the Volga region. In fact, church bells could no longer be rung legally in Moscow, and the bells had been confiscated from many churches.[7]

Meier's pessimism was usually less pronounced than Bishop Malmgren's, but given conditions in the church and the seminary, neither had an optimistic outlook. Malmgren summed up their feelings: "In this difficult time of need in which our Lutheran Church in Russia exists, only the knowledge that our brothers in the world are raising hands in prayer for us helps us maintain our perseverance."[8] Morehead took care to continually encourage the bishops to not give up hope no matter how difficult the conditions. While expressing his sympathy with Malmgren, Morehead assured him that "we are grateful that this institution for the training of pastors exists. ... Be assured of our unceasing prayers and abiding interest that God may give to the Evangelical Lutheran Church and to all the other Christian churches of Russia a great future of service that the Kingdom of God may more fully come to the millions of Russia in the future." To prove that his words were not mere rhetoric, Morehead informed Malmgren that the LWC was sending a check for $2,000 for the seminary. Furthermore, he assured him that the LWC would look favorably on funding a seminary building if Malmgren could find an appropriate place for the students. Given that it was the four hundredth anniversary of the publication of the Augsburg Confession, Morehead confessed that he had hoped they could distribute Bibles, catechisms, and tracts in Russia. But he understood that the times called for patience. Still, his enthusiasm to stand with the bishops and the Lutheran Church in Russia, even if his plans were not very realistic, gave strength to them when they were hard pressed on every side. They were not alone.[9]

In the meantime, Malmgren had been searching for better housing conditions for the seminary. After almost forty years of residence in the city, Malmgren had established many contacts, among them a German industrialist by the name of Ahrendt. Given the difficult economic conditions and his own health problems, Ahrendt had decided that it was time to return to his home in Mecklenburg, Germany. Therefore, he wanted to ensure that his two-story wooden house would have a suitable caretaker. For Malmgren, this was an answer to prayer because he knew that the students would soon wear out from the strenuous round-trip daily travel from Martyschkino to Leningrad. Even more important for Malmgren was the knowledge that the house was protected as extraterritorial property, being covered by the German-Soviet Treaty of Rapallo (1922). Ahrendt only required from Malmgren that he and his heirs receive a certain amount of rent every year. Malmgren appealed to the Gustav-Adolf-Verein for the bulk of the amount (8,000 Deutschmarks) while the LWC agreed to pay additional rental costs ($1,000 per month, albeit not with regularity).

Since the Ahrendt house was practically in the center of Leningrad, Malmgren and Dean Wacker could finally relocate back home with their families. The classes themselves would take place in the house instead of St. Anne's, as they had in the past.[10] The new house would come with a garden, another possibility for procuring food for the students and leaders of the seminary. Morehead greeted the news with thankfulness that the seminary would now be protected from the nationalization of its property. In April, Malmgren signed a five-year contract for the house, ensuring a suitable haven for the students to pursue their studies. Of course, everything would still be dependent on a state that did not mask its animosity toward religion. The foreign press seemed to indicate that the pressure had eased somewhat lately, in keeping with Stalin's "Dizzy with Success" article. But how long that lasted would soon be revealed.[11]

STALIN'S RETREAT FROM collectivization and the closing of churches appears to have been in response not only to the people's anger but also to foreign pressure. For example, a March 21 editorial in *Pravda* excoriated foreigners for their prayer meetings on behalf of persecuted believers in the Soviet Union. In apocalyptic language, the newspaper declaimed that the nations were mobilizing their masses for a crusade against the Soviet Union. In a letter dated February 8, Pope Pius XI had strongly protested Soviet persecution on behalf of the Roman Catholic Church. The archbishops of Canterbury and York chimed in, too, on behalf of believers in the Soviet Union.[12] The Christian Protest Movement in Britain likewise threatened the Soviets with recognition being removed by many nations. These actions were troubling for the Soviet Union because the success of the first Five-Year Plan was dependent on aid from foreign states. In response to the unwanted attention, the Soviets probably felt pressured to reopen some churches, although it doesn't appear that any Lutheran congregations benefited from this leniency.[13]

From the other side of the ocean, Americans also were pressing the Soviet government in support of religious believers. The American Committee on Religious Rights and Minorities (ACRRM) was formed in 1920 by a coalition of Americans of Jewish, Catholic, and Protestant backgrounds. After the letters of the pope and archbishops of Canterbury and York, the ACRRM wrote to President Hoover requesting that he not recognize the Soviet Union unless it guaranteed religious rights. One of the influential members of the committee, and chairman of a subcommittee that had drafted resolutions calling for the president and secretary of state to defend religious freedom, was none other than John Morehead.

Morehead's committee urged the United States government to go one step further and recognize the right to practice religion as a "primary human right" and communicate that principle to other nations around the world. Such language was groundbreaking, and Morehead was joined in his advocacy by influential American personalities in the sphere of religion like Henry Sloane Coffin (president of Union Theological Seminary) and Edmund Walsh (Georgetown University), as well as political figures like Henry Morgenthau (former ambassador to Turkey) and media titans like Adolph Ochs (publisher of the *New York Times*).[14] The committee's accusation that the USSR was engaging in "religious persecution on a scale unprecedented in modern times" offered a stinging rebuke. The committee professed that the actions of the Soviet government "shock the moral sense of the civilized world and ... overwhelmingly justify the protests that are being made." While sympathizing with the government's suspicion about the Orthodox Church's past ties to the czars, the committee nevertheless pleaded on behalf of the Jewish, Protestant, and Catholic minorities that had likewise suffered under the former regime. The committee was also well versed in the particulars of the April 8, 1929 Law on Religious Associations, citing several passages and recognizing in it Stalin's desire to raise children to "hate religion." Rallying the leaders of all denominations to make their voices heard in support of religious freedom, the committee reminded the Soviets that "nations, like individuals, cannot live alone and cannot defy with impunity the opinion of mankind."[15] As much as the Soviets would hate to admit it, good relations with Europe and America were essential to a state that was far from developed industrially or agriculturally. They had no desire to retreat permanently from a future where atheism reigned and religion was relegated to the scrapheap of history, but they had to move carefully and pragmatically.

AS THE STUDENTS began the sixth year of the Leningrad Lutheran Seminary, the new housing situation reflected a more hospitable atmosphere than the previous year. The rooms were spacious and airy, providing far better living arrangements for the twenty students currently enrolled. But not all was positive. Seminary costs for the previous year were above $20,000, a sharp rise from the $12,000 in the early years of the seminary. There was also now a lack of wood and coal due to the government's reluctance to supply heating material for a church institution. Furthermore, according to Malmgren the price for groceries had never been higher in the Communist era. Perhaps the above reasons contributed to the fact that a new class had not been added; and yet the fall sessions were at least beginning at St. Anne's without further governmental interference.[16]

But then the OGPU struck again. Arnold Frischfeld, who had been arrested for five days and released at the end of 1929, was re-arrested on September 20. This time the charges were graver. As the OGPU had connected Kurt Muss and Helmut Hansen to the Academic Affair and Professor Albert Mervart, Frischfeld was now accused of belonging to a "counterrevolutionary monarchical organization."[17] It was called the "Popular Union for the Fight for a Revived Free Russia" and supposedly headed by the key figure in the Academic Affair, Sergei Platonov.[18] Frischfeld was accused of being a paid informer and agent of Mervart, whom they identified as being a German secret service agent. Frischfeld was to have been providing Mervart with information from the ethnic German communities in Leningrad and the Volga and Crimean regions. Furthermore, he was creating "illegal circles and organizations of a religious and national character among the German intelligentsia, carrying out monarchical propaganda and disseminating among the members of the congregation religious and patriotic literature." Lastly, he was charged with preparing warring cadres for an anti-Soviet German youth cell called the "Steel Helmet."[19]

The activities were said to have taken place at the home of Frischfeld, where weekly gatherings were held. There, "active parishioners" held "religious conversations and anti-Soviet propaganda," all the while forming cells for the Steel Helmet. St. Catherine's Lutheran parishioner and a professor by trade, Emmanuel Furman, was said to be a leader in this group, which included youth from Hansen and Muss's circles. Large amounts of money were said to have been transferred for the support of the Lutheran congregations, including $1,500 given to Hansen for St. Anne's and the Jugendbund. (Hansen's congregation had been St. Peter's, not St. Anne's.)[20] As his case came to a close,

Frischfeld acknowledged knowing Furman (he was the chairman of the congregation's *dvatsatka*) and having met Mervart. But he categorically rejected all of the preposterous charges.[21] These charges, combined with naming the bookish Mervart a German agent, testified to the paranoia enveloping the Soviet Union. It didn't matter that Frischfeld rejected the charges. He would be sentenced on February 10, 1931 to a ten-year term in the Solovetsky Island camp.[22] His twenty-six-year-old daughter Gerda and twenty-year-old daughter Nora would share his fate, being sentenced to ten-year terms on the same day.[23] This son of a telegraph clerk who confessed to his interrogator, "I'm a religious person, I have no interest in politics," would eventually be executed at a labor camp in Archangel on November 3, 1937, at sixty-three years old.[24]

Morehead was not oblivious to the persecution. In November 1930, he earnestly conversed on this subject with a counselor in the German embassy in the United States, O. C. Kiep. Having received word about the sentences handed down to Hansen, Muss, and the large number of teachers/parishioners involved, as well as Frischfeld, he inquired of Kiep: "Do you advise world-wide publicity? Or do you advise representations to the governments of Western Europe and America?"[25] Morehead had already been pressuring the Soviet government via the ACRRM, but he must have wondered whether its efforts were having any impact. Kiep promised to write to a reliable source for advice on the situation.[26] Most likely, the Soviet Union would not publicly acknowledge the impact of world opinion, but in the future evidence would bear out that international criticism of its policy on religious freedom exerted real pressure on the government.[27]

AMID PERSECUTION, the Lutheran Church continued to seek out new ways to carry out its mission. An example of this is Pastor Ferdinand Hörschelmann Sr., who had been arrested in late 1929. On his release from prison, Hörschelmann had agreed to be sent to Siberia to uphold and serve vacant congregations. He would conduct his work among Estonians, reviving the language he had learned as a child. Morehead had always evinced a strong desire to restore the congregations populated by Latvians, Estonians, and Finns in Siberia. Hörschelmann's call intersected exactly with his wishes.[28]

Hörschelmann was one of nine pastors that Meier had mentioned to Morehead as being prepared for retirement in 1928. After his arrest, Hörschelmann rethought what he would do with the last years of his life. Since his wife was dead and he was already seventy-five years old, an age at which most pastors would have already retired to a quiet existence, his courageous decision was a bold leap of faith. Morehead's respect for Hörschelmann knew no bounds from the time he had worked closely with him during the famine in 1922. He immediately informed Meier that the NLC (through the LWC) would send $200 toward the mission expenses of Hörschelmann and his elder daughter, who would assist him. The Siberian congregations themselves would contribute to the Hörschelmann mission fund, too.[29]

Acknowledging his "deep interest" generated by the "heroic mission" of Hörschelmann, Morehead plied Meier for further information. Morehead's real concern was with the large number of Lutheran pastors now suffering in concentration camps throughout Siberia. "Will he be able also to visit and give physical and spiritual relief to our banished fellow Lutherans in Siberia in the concentration camps?" A measure of his interest in this mission could be seen by his request that Meier send copies of Hörschelmann's report to the world Lutheran press.

Hörschelmann and his daughter began their journey in mid-October, traveling first to his brother, Christian, who served a congregation in the Volga region. The plan was to eventually arrive in Omsk on October 30 and ultimately travel on to Slavgorod.[30] Hörschelmann's dedication to missions is all the more impressive given that Slavgorod's previous pastor, Friedrich Deutschmann, had fled to Zaporozhe in the Ukraine due to government persecution. Similarly,

Pastor Friedrich Merz had been banned from Omsk.[31] He would not be walking into a calm, peaceful environment.

Throughout the Soviet Union there were no longer any places where a pastor could serve without some persecution. Pastor Otto Seib, who had written a detailed letter to Morehead in 1929 about the persecutions in the Ukrainian region, took the place of Hörschelmann and the other arrested pastor in the Crimea, Arthur Hanson. Seib, like many pastors, was continuing to serve even though his financial support was dependent on whatever the foreign Lutheran organizations from Germany and America could gather for him. The High Church Council sent him to the Crimea in the hopes that they could secure for him some place of service while still supporting the church in that region.

In 1930, though, trouble found him. While making a visit as a "traveling preacher" (*Reiseprediger*) to the Ukrainian village of Neuheim, which was against the law, Seib was threatened by commissars brandishing weapons and warned to leave the village by 8:00 the next morning. After the commissars left, he asked the people to gather at 6:00 the next morning for baptisms and weddings, to be followed by a communion service. When the commissars learned that they had been tricked, they came galloping after him. Seib outmaneuvered them, just making it across the border into the Elizavetograd region where they had no jurisdiction. After he arrived in Elizovetograd, he learned that the authorities had retaliated against the Neuheim congregation, taking away their church.

Three weeks after Seib's arrival in the Crimea, the subtle and overt forms of persecution started again. He was refused permission to work in Hörschelmann's congregation in Neusatz. Meanwhile, in Hanson's parish in the village of Byten, the authorities attacked him by first arresting his landlord. Although the landlord had paid his taxes, he was charged with non-payment and sent to prison in Simferopol. Seib understood that this man had been punished for taking a pastor into his house. One month later, the landlord's entire wealth, including his home, was sold at a public auction. By applying such pressure, the Soviet authorities made it clear to Lutheran parishioners that there would be consequences for taking a pastor into their house. Seib concluded that he no longer had any opportunity to faithfully serve the people of the Crimea without endangering their own lives, so he gathered students for a last rite of confirmation on Reformation Day, October 31, 1930. In November, the defeated pastor went to the German consulate in Odessa to apply for repatriation to Germany.[32]

17

"STAND AND EAT, YOU STILL HAVE A LONG WAY TO GO"

Words and Prayers of Encouragement

AT STS. PETER and Paul in Moscow, Alexander Streck served faithfully though the church was in the shadows of the OGPU offices at Lubyanka. No church could easily acquire wood or coal, and in the enormous cathedral the temperatures rarely rose above 32 degrees Fahrenheit in the winter. Under state persecution, the number of parishioners had declined from twenty thousand before World War I to approximately two thousand by 1930. Young boys were rarely spotted in confirmation classes now.

And yet, despite atheist propaganda all around them, stringent laws on religious practice, the staggered workweek, and constant persecution, a solid remnant of believers still came to church. A faithful choir of sixty persons sang the traditional Lutheran hymns on days of worship. Streck confirmed twenty-one children that spring, including his own daughters Stella (sixteen) and Ellen (fifteen).[1] Included in the list of confirmands was Erich Franz who would go on to become a noted diplomat for West Germany.[2] The children were taught in an adjoining building of the church where evidently not all rooms had been nationalized. In the 1990s, Elsa Leventhal, who also was confirmed in 1930 with her sister Irina, recalled that Pastor Streck would often give them homework, and one of the students would always do it in school. When one teacher saw his religious books, she took them away and questioned him intensively. The boy told her everything: what the pastor taught, what books were used, who attended.

The school authorities warned Leventhal that if she continued to attend church, she would be expelled. It was not an idle threat, given that expulsion would harm her chances of attending any university or institute. Coming from an educated family (her father was a natural science professor at a Communist university), this would be a great blow to them. Despite the danger, Leventhal still had great respect for the Streck family, often visiting with Irina to play with the pastor's daughters. If they happened to stay until dinner, they were always fed. Leventhal remembered the warm manner in which the family treated its guests and also that the girls always said the prayers. However, the incident with her teacher taught Leventhal to hide her faith in God.

As for Streck and his family, the fears of Bishop Meier concerning his apartment on the church grounds came to fruition in 1930. The Strecks were forced by the state to leave their apartment, relocating to a small apartment next to the Lutheran cemetery in the northeast of Moscow (not too far from the closed church building of St. Michael's). They didn't remain long before again being obliged to move. This time, the Strecks were banished beyond the city limits to the village of Bakhovka, located west of Moscow and reached by electric train from the Belorussky train station. A generous parishioner had lent them his dacha in the village, but the journey to the city for church activities would be taxing from now on.[3]

AS THE TRYING year of 1930 drew to a close, Bishop Malmgren learned in October that the seminary's dean, Friedrich Wacker, had been arrested and deported to eastern Siberia for three years. (Earlier in the year, Wacker had been brought in for questioning and put under observation.) What Malmgren didn't know was that the OGPU had been questioning Wacker about the finances of the seminary, who received money and where it came from. Wacker admitted that since one person couldn't receive more than $500 from abroad, he once received money from the LWC in his own name. Usually, Malmgren and his son-in-law, Heinrich Behrendts, would receive $500 apiece. In this way, the LWC sent money to the seminary in the amount of $1,000 a month. There was nothing sinister in these actions except from the perspective of the OGPU, who distrusted foreigners, especially foreigners sending money to keep a "counter-revolutionary" organization alive. Fortunately, the OGPU didn't move against the seminary itself at this time, but Wacker became a victim in their struggle against religious organizations. He would never return to work at the seminary.[4]

In his despair, Malmgren gave vent to his frustration in a November letter to the director of Gustav-Adolf-Verein in Leipzig, Franz Rendtorff: "Why is God such a hidden God? Has the hour now really come, where the judgment on us will begin?" Malmgren likened his position to that of the prophet Elijah. "It's the voice of Elijah under the juniper tree that often attacks me and now which I can only resist with the exertion of my last bit of strength."[5]

While commiserating with him in all the trials he had had to undergo the past few years, Rendtorff continued with the theme of Elijah: "I am certain that the God, who has called to you out of the deep, has also called to you with a powerful, 'Stand and eat, you still have a long way to go,' and certainly will not fail to nourish you, but will give you power to go further along the troublesome desert path unto the mountain of God at Horeb."[6] Morehead likewise took time to sympathize with Malmgren and assure him of the Americans' constant prayers. As he thanked God for placing Malmgren in a position of authority for such trying times as these, Morehead emboldened him: "Be assured again, therefore, that we are thoroughly with you, with all the professors of the institution, and with the students in sympathy, the confession of our common faith, earnest prayer for their welfare, and the abiding readiness to be practically helpful as God may give us ability and opportunity."[7] Such words helped Malmgren to know that he was not alone in his struggle.

A recapitulation of his problems would explain why his level of stress had been elevated: (1) The April 8, 1929 Law on Religious Associations had drastically hampered the work of the Lutheran Church; (2) the continual hassle with housing, food, and heating for the seminary; (3) the recent spate of arrests of pastors and professors; (4) the constant need to secure funding for the seminary; (5) the travel necessary to attend High Church Council meetings in Moscow; (6) the fact that he was seventy years old and handling the responsibilities of a pastor, rector, district church supervisor, and bishop. Even Malmgren was coming to the realization that he could no longer handle all these duties. As a result, in the fall of 1930 his former student, Eugen Bachmann, was ordained as the new pastor of St. Anne's in Leningrad.[8]

As Malmgren surveyed the damage from the campaign against the churches at the end of the year, he concluded that the church had suffered its greatest blow since the early years of Bolshevik rule. Of the 183 Lutheran pastors serving Russia in 1917, by October 1930 only 83 remained.[9] By the end of 1930, at least sixteen pastors were counted as prisoners of the state, including the seventy-five-year-old Ferdinand Hörschelmann Sr., who had been arrested as a "harmful element" after his first worship service in Slavgorod. Gustav Schwalbe had been sentenced as a counterrevolutionary in Smolensk and shot on September 30. Four of the most recent seminary graduates of the class of 1928 had also suffered, one being called to martyrdom. David Kaufmann was murdered in late December in the north Caucasus; Lazhis Bluhm, who had graduated later in 1928, was threatened by the OGPU and driven from his congregation in Belarus into exile; Konstantin Rusch had been deported to Archangel; and Gotthold Störrle was arrested in the Hansen-Muss case.[10] Other pastors and professors in prison camps or exile were Helmut Hansen, Kurt Muss, Albert Koch, Johann Völl, Ferdinand Hörschelmann Jr., Arthur Kluck, Gottlob Koch, Friedrich

Merz, Arthur Hanson, Nathaniel Heptner, Konstantin Rusch, Friedrich Wacker, Arnold Frischfeld, and a Professor Saal.[11] The Lutheran Church could not survive if the number of arrests continued at this pace.

AT THE ONSET of 1931, Meier told Morehead that those pastors who remained at their posts could not satisfy the demand of the number of congregations and were themselves in serious danger of losing their freedom. "The word is out that in the course of this year the Christian church will be brought to an end, and it looks that way unless a Higher Power intervenes." Lutheran congregations no longer existed in many of the cities and had been forced to give up their church buildings. Those who remained were mostly large congregations in the more populated cities and the German colonies (Volga and Ukrainian regions).

Growing thoughtful, Meier reflected: "Often the children of God ask, 'Watchman, what time of the night?' [Isaiah 21:11]. But we also know: 'Behold, he who keeps Israel will neither slumber nor sleep' [Psalm 121:4]. This is what we believe and pray. That our brothers in the wide world do the same [pray]; that we know and that is our comfort."[12] Meier thanked the Americans for sharing their distress, a true brotherly act that had to mitigate somewhat the path of martyrdom that he saw ahead for the Lutheran Church in Russia. He knew that the GPU was constantly watching him and the other leaders in the church, so he felt compelled to warn Morehead to be careful about publicizing any of his statements abroad. Such international publicity would be dangerous for him.

With his wife suffering from rheumatism of the joints and confined to her bed for one month, as well as his own inability to travel to distant congregations, Meier could now devote time to chronicling the history of his ministry and the Evangelical Lutheran Church in Russia. Concluding that the rapidly approaching end of the church was near, he felt led to philosophize on his life's work. He told Morehead in March 1931 that he had recently completed two books, one a four-hundred-page tome entitled *Forty Years in the Service of the Evangelical Lutheran Church in Russia*. The other book was a hundred-page history of the Evangelical Lutheran Church in Russia from its founding in the sixteenth century.

Meier knew that it would be impossible to publish such books in the Soviet Union, and Germany didn't offer him much hope due to its own severe financial situation. He decided to leave the texts under lock and key at the High Church Council offices in Moscow, but did send the shorter work to Morehead personally. Perhaps, Meier wondered, someone in America might be able to publish it?[13] Morehead was intrigued by the possibilities of publishing books of this kind, and speculated about how they might make the history more interesting to Americans. He recommended tacking on an additional chapter that would focus on the historic contributions of the Lutheran Church to the nation of Russia.

He also made the bold but unrealistic suggestion that Meier add a chapter on the current persecution of the Lutheran Church. Morehead was only thinking of how an awareness of the situation of the Lutherans in the Soviet Union would awaken foreign readers to the limits on religious freedom and the nature of those adversaries who were intent on destroying it. Naturally, he knew that Meier might find this difficult, so he suggested that someone else write these chapters from information that Meier supplied.[14]

Morehead meant well, but it is astounding that he would even suggest such a project. Meier had told him how the OGPU had been watching his activities and reading his mail, so much so that he had to take special precautions in sending out any sensitive material. Even if Meier's name were omitted from an appendix to the book, the OGPU could have guessed who would be in a position to supply such information. After all, they had their informants in America, too. Meier answered Morehead's suggestions directly by reminding him that adding chapters like those he proposed would have to pass the censor. They would have little chance of seeing the light of day.[15]

YET EVEN AS the winds of persecution howled about them, Malmgren reported that the seminary students remained energetic and retained a sunny disposition. In his telling, they continued to study diligently as if they lived on an island surrounded by raging waters. But the conditions were becoming more oppressive by the month, and the voice of Christians was becoming more irritated and despondent. Children were growing up in a state that was indoctrinating them in an "atheistic-materialist *Weltanschauung*." New and arbitrary taxes were plundering the Lutheran parishioners of any money that they could scrape together. Prices for food were rising. In fact, Malmgren described his plan for the students to bake their own bread since the word on the street was that ration cards would only be given to factory workers beginning on April 1. In response to the threat, Malmgren was buying up as much flour as he could.[16] The prices for the most necessary foodstuffs were increasing throughout the country, and as "non-persons" the students and pastors/professors were not allowed to purchase food in the state consumer cooperative. Malmgren had been searching out alternatives when he discovered a newly opened market in Leningrad where groceries could be bought at a marked-down price. The catch was that he needed foreign currency to buy the goods. Malmgren asked Morehead to send $1,000 of the usual $2,000 that the LWC sent bimonthly to a special bank address where he could use foreign currency to purchase the foodstuffs at a better rate of exchange. Morehead heartily agreed, thankful that Malmgren had found a means whereby the LWC could use its resources more effectively to support the seminary.[17]

Maximizing the gifts from the LWC and other Lutherans throughout the world was imperative because the ability of the average Lutheran parishioner to support the church in Russia was becoming more and more untenable. To describe what that parishioner was up against in the countryside, Malmgren cited the typical example of a "kulak" farmer. If a farmer held more than two horses and three cows, he could be designated as a kulak and sent into forced labor. In one case, after the authorities initially overlooked one of these farmers in the Leningrad region, it soon recognized its mistake and tried to tax him retroactively for his harvest. Since the man didn't have the money they demanded, he asked to sell one of the two cows he still possessed. He received written permission from the court, but afterward the signed document was not accepted. He was asked who had given him the right to sell his cow. Why hadn't he sold his house instead? Even though he produced the document, the farmer was fined 6,000 rubles (approximately $3,000), an extraordinary amount, to be paid within three days. Since he could not come up with the money, he was sent into forced labor while his wife and three children remained behind, destitute. Actions like these were destroying Lutheran families, and with them the congregations that they had supported.[18]

Collectivization of agriculture had now resumed, despite Stalin's tactical call for a slowdown in March 1930. In response to Stalin's "Dizzy with Success" speech, eight thousand families had left the collective farms. Stalin's initial retreat from full collectivization was predicated on his desire to save the sowing of crops for that spring. But Stalin had no intention of eliminating collectivization permanently. He sent his Communist Party Committee chairman in Moscow, Lazar Kaganovich, to personally instruct local officials that collectivization of all farms was still the goal. In fall 1931, collectivization would again proceed forcefully. Malmgren made clear to Morehead that due to collectivization, congregational support of the seminary was sporadic, and he didn't expect parishioners to be in a strong position to finance the church in the future.[19] As it was, the parishioners could only cover one-fifth of the church's costs in 1931. Furthermore, the taxes that Meier was forced to pay the state as the President of the High Church Council of the Lutheran Church increased monumentally in 1931. A good example of the dramatic uptick in taxes on the Lutheran Church can be seen in the following chart:

1928	393 rubles, 92 kopecks
1929	259 rubles, 6 kopecks
1930	228 rubles, 34 kopecks
1931	3,609 rubles, 31 kopecks

The tax bill levied against the Lutheran Church in 1931 was obviously an attempt by the state to make it virtually impossible for the church to survive. Instead of direct violence (although that was always an option and used extensively), the wiser heads of state had decided on a course of indirectly strangling the church.[20]

To make matters worse, the supply of wood and coal at the Ahrendt House in Leningrad was dangerously low and the contractors who had agreed to deliver materials in February had not done so. The shortage was seriously affecting living conditions because it was difficult to keep the bedrooms and living room space reasonable temperatures. The seminary was also running a deficit of almost 5,000 rubles (approximately $2,500), despite all of Malmgren's efforts to save money. Malmgren was forced to purchase wood in lesser quantities from the farmers in the environs of Leningrad at extremely high prices.[21]

Malmgren was also coming to terms with the fact that Helmut Hansen was gone for good and would never return to the seminary. Likewise, the situation of Dean Wacker looked grave. The seminary had expended every effort to secure his release to no effect. He had been sent to a concentration camp in Bratsk (eastern Siberia) on the Angara River, and whether he would be allowed to eventually resettle in Leningrad was unclear. Furthermore, Professor Arnold Frischfeld had been held in detention since September 1930 and now had been sent north to the Solovetsky Island camp. As a result of the rapid reduction in the number of professors, Malmgren decided to take up many of the lectures himself, having been freed from his service at St. Anne's by Eugen Bachmann.

Having reached the age of seventy, Malmgren confessed that he was uncertain how much longer he could keep up with the work. In addition, he worried how long he might remain at liberty to lead the seminary. He needed to find new professors, because if something happened to him the whole operation would come crashing down.[22]

In spite of all the pressures and his realism in regard to the Lutheran Church's situation in the Soviet Union, Malmgren could at times sound surprisingly upbeat and ready for a fight. After relating to Morehead all of the problems besetting the Lutheran Church, Malmgren intoned, "Only God the Lord can help here! But He will help only if we as His co-workers stand at command and are prepared for the hour where He needs and will call us."[23] Malmgren would continue to stand at God's command, but the gale-force winds of persecution surrounding him and the seminary would not grow any calmer.

18

"STUCK DEEP IN SNOW AND ICE"

The Spiritual Life of the Church in Late 1931 and Early 1932

EARLY IN 1931, sixty-two Lutheran pastors were active; by October, that number had reportedly been reduced to forty.[1] Georg Rath, the bedraggled pastor and district president in the Ukraine that John Morehead had met during the famine years, had died. Furthermore, perhaps the most respected man in the entire Lutheran Church, Ferdinand Hörschelmann, had died on October 15 in a Siberian concentration camp at the age of seventy-six. Hörschelmann had forgone any thoughts of retirement and made the arduous journey to Siberia to serve as a pastor in extremely difficult circumstances at an advanced age. Now he was gone.

Yet as he lay dying in a concentration camp in Minusinsk, he prepared his own funeral sermon and handed it to a fellow believer. A pastor to the last, Hörschelmann hoped his words would strengthen the faith of his fellow believers in the camp. Just before he died, he was said to have received communion from the hands of an Orthodox priest. This action illustrated how denominational lines often broke down inside the camps. Persecution had the tendency to remind believers that anyone who acknowledged Jesus Christ as Lord was an enemy of the state. Now in prison, they were all brothers in Christ.[2]

When he learned of the deaths of Rath and Hörschelmann in a letter from Theophil Meier, Morehead gave vent to his emotions. Expressing his profound regret to Bishop Meier, he recalled the days when he had first become acquainted with them, traveling through the Ukraine and Crimea, feeding the hungry. In his despair, he cried out to Meier with the familiar refrain of the Old Testament prophets, "Lord, how long!" But, remembering that they suffered no longer, he comforted Meier with these words: "But what joy it must be to them to rest from their labors and to be in the presence of the Lord!" The comfort that the Lord gave to his people when contemplating the rest of the martyrs would become a more familiar theme to Morehead and the bishops in the coming years, as the Lutheran Church in Russia trod its own path to Golgotha.[3]

TOWARD THE END of 1931, the Soviet government struck a decisive blow against one of the former Russian Empire's most potent symbols. A building project that had been conceived as a memorial to the victory over Napoleon in 1812, Christ the Savior Cathedral had dominated the skyline of the Moscow River since its completion and dedication in 1883. The cathedral still had an active congregation and, standing resplendently within view of the Kremlin, was a continual reminder of the glories of "Holy Russia." The time had come to rid the Soviet Union of this powerful vestige of Christianity, once and for all. First, the cathedral was stripped of its ornaments, sculptures, and frescoes. Second, its marble was plundered, eventually being used to build a new temple to Soviet communism, the underground metro. Finally, on December 5, Stalin had the cathedral demolished. It took several tries with dynamite before the massive edifice was reduced to rubble. A planned Palace of the Soviets, topped by a stainless-steel statue of Lenin 246 feet in height, ultimately failed due to the onset of World War II and later the program of de-Stalinization carried out by Nikita Khrushchev following Stalin's death. But at least for the time being, Stalin's view of the Moscow skyline was clear.[4]

Another symbol of Russia's past was the celebration of Christmas. However, given the current state of affairs, except in large cities, Lutherans had to mark the day in private. Edith Müthel remembers that her family in the Volga village of Norka would place broken branches up their sleeves and periodically bring them home in the weeks leading up to Christmas. Out of the collection of branches they would, in conspiratorial fashion, construct a small Christmas tree.[5] Meanwhile, in Moscow, the sale of fir trees had been banned. Not so easily deterred, some believers would go into the forests just outside the city and secretly cut down their own trees. Those who wanted to challenge the law would need to cover their windows with thick curtains. Given the communal living arrangements forced on inhabitants of large cities like Moscow, few believers could effectively defy the authorities.

The Young Pioneers Communist youth group would post watch at the gates of Sts. Peter and Paul Lutheran Church in Moscow to find out which students would attend Christmas services with their parents.[6] Rumors abounded that the parishioners would be forced to register with the government, in effect forcing believers to publicly declare their allegiance to the church.[7] Believers were increasingly forced to live their lives carefully, on the outside appearing to be loyal citizens of the Soviet Union but inwardly acknowledging Christ as Lord. But there were still those who would not allow the state to drive them away from the practice of their faith, although they might be forced to worship in private.

The niece of Friedrich Wacker, Margarita Schulmeister, vividly remembers one of her last Christmases in the Volga village of Kamyschyn. While her uncle was serving time in a concentration camp in eastern Siberia, his relatives secretly celebrated Christmas. At the age of eighty-eight, Schulmeister would fondly recall old Christmas traditions from the Volga Lutheran community that had thrilled her as a six-year-old girl. Three to four weeks before Christmas, the smell of *Lebkuchen* cookies permeated the air of the village as the women prepared for the coming Christmas feast. The houses were cleaned, gifts were bought, and everything in the community shone brightly. Then, on Christmas Eve, although they could no longer go to church, the children would be dressed up and gathered in the kitchen. Someone would knock on the window, presumably the Christ Child, who would then pose the most important question: Had the children been good? If not, they would not receive any gifts. After all, the Christ Child knew everything! Then someone would play the piano while the children sang traditional Christmas carols like "Stille Nacht" and "Ihr Kinderlein Kommet." A bell was rung, the doors to the living room were opened, and there Schulmeister discovered that her father had already set up the Christmas tree. She recalled that there were no electric lights on the tree, but the gifts would be carefully placed under it while the tree would be decorated with *pfeffernuss* cookies, bon bons, and apples.[8]

In the much larger Volga village of Norka (seventeen thousand inhabitants), Edith Müthel remembered the big church being vacant that Christmas Eve because Pastor Emil Pfeiffer, her father, had gone to Saratov to celebrate Christmas in the large Lutheran cathedral of St. Mary's. The collectivization of the countryside had struck Norka hard. Many families from the church had lost fathers, sons, and brothers to the concentration camps. Naturally, Müthel mused, the families wondered where in the far north of Siberia their men were on this holy night and whether they were even among the living.

For the first time in ages, the grand old church was dark and still. No Christmas candles, no voices of children singing traditional Christmas hymns, none of the three large bells ringing out and calling the faithful to worship. Müthel remembers it being a particularly snow-laden Christmas in 1931 and that the people had not forgotten their faith, celebrating secretly within their own homes. As the believers held their own private celebration, the oldest would utter the table prayer before the Christmas Eve dinner. It would be a modest feast given the weak harvest. The Christmas stockings at the Pfeiffers' home were wrapped in white crepe paper while the oven heated the whole house, creating a warm, cozy atmosphere despite the absence of her father. However, he had not forgotten them. He had left them hazelnuts for the occasion, and modest presents were distributed in his absence. Her little brother even got ice skates.

Edith's mother recited the table prayer on this night, and the children sang old Christmas carols, such as "Von Himmel hoch, da komm ich her," "O Du Fröliche," "Stille Nacht," and "Welchen Jubel, welche Freude." The last verse of this carol was especially poignant for Edith: "Shortly such joy will soon be extinguished with the candlelight; Jesus alone can prepare a joy that will never pass away." The Christmas cactus filled with candles evoked memories that would encourage Müthel throughout the years, as she remembered it well into her nineties. In her autobiography, Müthel proclaimed, "The Christmas cactus for me today is like a glittering hope, like a beam of love, like the light of faith in Jesus Christ for one's life. Whenever possible, a Christmas cactus will stand on my windowsill."[9]

"HERE IN FARAWAY Russia, we are stuck deep in snow and ice, not only in the life of nature but also in the spiritual life." Those words from Meier to Morehead accurately described the perilous condition of the church in early 1932. The number of pastors continued to decline, sometimes because of natural causes but more often because they fell victim to the precarious existence within the concentration camps. Like his father, forty-four-year-old Ferdinand Hörschelmann Jr. had been deported to a concentration camp in Siberia. On February 12, he was working in the forest as a slave laborer when he perished after being struck by a falling tree. One of the older pastors in the Volga region, Johann Allendorf, passed away at the age of seventy-five. Mikhail Lapping, the sixty-three-year-old head of the Latvian section of the Lutheran Church in Russia, died in Moscow in March.[10]

Lapping's death would end any opportunities to hold services in Latvian or Estonian at Sts. Peter and Paul, which he had previously conducted. The last Latvian confirmation class of eleven children, five boys and six girls, would be taught by an ethnic Latvian, Pastor Julius Zahlit. Zahlit came from Leningrad to teach an accelerated course for the students, confirming them on June 12. It would be impossible to know the lifelong impact that Lutheran pastors would have on these and other students, but thankfully there are witnesses who lived to see the fall of the Soviet Union in 1991. Ethnic Latvian confirmand Olga Striks, for example, would remember her confirmation all her life and retain her faith. Wherever she lived during the days of the Soviet Union, she would carry her confirmation certificate with her. Striks remained the oldest member of Sts. Peter and Paul in Moscow until her passing in March 2017, three months before her one-hundredth birthday.[11]

As the numbers of pastors continued to plummet, Meier's confidence in the church's future dimmed even further. He was not prone to pessimistic statements about the possibilities for the continued existence of the Lutheran Church in Russia. He had written a book on the church's history, so he knew full well what it had faced various struggles since its origins in the sixteenth century. The pressure being applied to the church now, though, was greater than anything he had studied or witnessed.

For example, according to the emergency regulations of the Deutsche Bank, the High Church Council was now limited to taking only 200 Reichsmarks a month out of the bank. Given the current rates imposed by the Soviet state, they would need 1,200 Reichsmarks a month![12] Eugenie Meier, the wife of the bishop, wrote Morehead in March about the desperate condition of the church. Using the descriptive Russian word *lishenyets* ("without privileges/rights"), she explained to him that the church held no rights whatsoever in the Soviet Union. Nevertheless, she assured him of her family's sound faith, stating that they remained at their posts like soldiers in a spiritual army. God had blessed them despite these difficulties. Their youngest son, Traugott, had found work in the Austrian Embassy. The heart condition of their daughter Elizabeth was improving. She continued to work as a professor in a language institute and was editing a German-Russian dictionary. Unfortunately, Meier's twenty-two-year-old nephew, Gustav Golde, who had been instructing the children in Helmut Hansen's crafts program, had been among those arrested in the Hansen-Muss case. He had even inhabited a cell with Friedrich Wacker but was later transported to a Siberian concentration camp for a period of three years. Since Gustav was her widowed sister's sole support, his arrest was a real hardship for the family. Eugenie Meier's hope remained in "God the Lord," whose Easter blessings she wished on Morehead, who had done so much for them.[13]

AS THE SEVENTH year of the seminary wound down, Bishop Malmgren struggled to keep a positive outlook. The cost of running the seminary was once again rising. The reasons were not hard to fathom. First, the collectivization of farming had so thoroughly impoverished Lutheran parishioners that very little money could be set aside for gifts to the seminary. Parishioners who had been forced into collective farms no longer had dispensable income. They were given food from the harvest and vouchers for use in a state consumer cooperative, leaving them no currency to tithe to the church. Second, and this occurred unexpectedly, the seminary was now being charged a tax of 1,500 rubles (approximately $750) by the state for the purpose of supporting "atheist culture." And third, $2,000 that Morehead had sent in December 1931 could not be extracted from the bank.[14]

As if all these problems weren't enough, the means that Malgren had discovered for purchasing food cheaply was presenting its own difficulties. Although Morehead had successfully sent two payments through a special foreign currency bank, Malmgren now informed him to stop sending money in this manner. Citing "inner political reasons," Malmgren wrote that the sending of two drafts of money through Torgsin, one after the other had attracted the attention of the Soviet authorities.[15] Ashamed that the Lutheran Church of Russia had to make constant demands on foreign Lutherans, Malmgren thanked Morehead for their patience and charity, even though he saw no end to the seminary's needs. "We feel the public hostility against Christianity more and more. ... We see that they are continuing to close churches forcefully, or congregations are giving them up willingly because they can't pay the exorbitant taxes. And we don't know when this hate and terror will come to an end."[16] Morehead wrote back to Malmgren in February that he would send yet another gift of $2,000. Providing the encouragement the bishop so desperately needed, Morehead wrote, "We admire the heroic faith and courage with which the rector, professors, and students stand true to Christ and to the obligations of service within His church, that men may be trained for the ministry and that the Gospel may be preached to the people. The Lord God Omnipotent reigneth! And He is a God of power and love and grace!" Reminding him of their "unceasing intercessory prayers," he repeated the firm commitment of the LWC to the Lutheran Church of Russia.[17]

By the end of January, Malmgren received the $2,000 sent in December 1931, but other problems were now plaguing the seminary. Four students had been called to military service, which included the tasks of moving heavy stones and building roads. Even though as students at a seminary they were "without rights," they were still obliged to fulfill their military service. As a result, they were sent to serve at hard labor near the Finland border for three years.[18] The island of calm that had temporarily reigned at the seminary now seemed disrupted beyond repair. The students still operated under the premise that they would eventually graduate and begin serving parishes, but they were no longer oblivious to the dangers surrounding them. The fact that they could expect to become full-fledged "non-persons" on their graduation attested to their dedication to the cause of the gospel.[19]

On occasion, students could also be called into the OGPU offices for questioning. On January 29, 1932, Johannes Lel was called in for a "dialogue" with the OGPU. An officer named Tamm encouraged Lel to become an informer among the students, which Lel acknowledged would force him to become an "enemy of his friends." Tamm also asked whether he had attended St. Peter's and heard the sermons of Helmut Hansen. Lel replied in the affirmative, although most of his time had been spent at St. Anne's. Although Lel knew about the crushing of the Hansen and Muss Sunday school program a few years before, initially it didn't occur to him that this was a veiled threat. That soon changed, though, as he was handed over to Tamm's boss.

The head officer claimed that the government had educated Lel for free, but now the time had come to "pay the bill." He replied, perhaps a little too cleverly, that his father had already paid his taxes to the government. The head officer exploded, calling him a "little mutt." Lel held his ground, saying he had no other answer. The head officer shouted, "Get out of here! We have a different answer for you!" Lel was then driven in one of the infamous Black Marias (sedans used by the OGPU) to the DPZ ("House of Preparatory Incarceration"), the OGPU's holding prison for the accused in Leningrad. There he was placed in an isolated prison cell where it was hoped that loneliness would work on his psyche. Although there was little to stimulate him in the cell, Lel remembered poems that he had memorized, primarily Schiller, Heine, Pushkin, and Lermontov. Along with the singing of hymns, these helped him spiritually and psychologically in his depressed state. Afterward, he was called for two further interrogations, again with the head officer. During these the head officer finally relaxed, conversing with him on abstract themes. For example, he quizzed Lel as to whether he would choose practical over scientific materialism (Lel chose scientific). Perplexed about his ward, the officer confided that he didn't know what to do with him. But one thing was clear: he would not be allowed to finish his course work at the seminary. He was soon shipped out to a concentration camp in Kazakhstan, traveling in one of the so-called Stolypin wagons.[20]

His friend and classmate Bruno Toryassan was also brought into the OGPU offices in 1932 for questioning. Toryassan was born in 1911, the son of a Lutheran pastor of Armenian heritage and a mother who was German. His school years took place in Baku where his father, Ossip, had founded a congregation. Now a seminarian, he was approaching the end of his studies when the OGPU called. Like Lel, he was asked to spy on his fellow classmates. On refusing, he was then curtly informed that he had twenty-four hours to leave Leningrad. No doubt relieved that he had not suffered a worse fate, Toryassan took the train through the Caucasus Mountains to Vladikavkaz, where his father was serving a parish. He carried with him his Bible in which classmates had written their goodbyes. Such words would be an encouragement to him in the coming dark days, even more so because the classmates who wrote in his Bible would not survive the decade. Even though he could no longer attend classes, Toryassan's theological education was far from finished. His good friend and former roommate at the seminary, Ralph Jurgens, sent him weekly copies of his notes from the courses. Due to Jurgens's courage and diligence in mailing these documents, Toryassan was able to take his final exams in the summer of 1933.[21]

AS 1932 WENT ON, the Soviet government was more frequently acknowledging that in the next Five-Year Plan (1932–1937), the church of Christ would come to an end.[22] Naturally, Malmgren was troubled as to what the eighth year of the seminary would bring when it began operations in the fall. Sympathizing with his concerns, Morehead told him he had read in a New York newspaper about the cruel beating exacted on one of thirty Lutheran pastors languishing in a Siberian Gulag camp (the pastor had apparently refused to inform on his fellow Lutherans). "I am satisfied that the oppression of the organized institution of religion in Russia, reports of which are coming more and more into the columns of the public press of the world, will serve to isolate Russia and be of untold injury to the country along political and economic lines. ... There must be a change of policy if the present government of Russia is to have the good will of civilized mankind." But Morehead was wrong; isolation of Russia was the farthest thing from the American government's mind. While Morehead was expressing his righteous indignation against the actions of the Soviets, the American government was formulating its own plans to recognize the USSR.[23]

The American government's machinations notwithstanding, Morehead knew that he was doing right by standing with the Lutheran Church in Russia. Sounding eerily like St. Paul's recording of his persecutions in 2 Corinthians 6, Malmgren wrote to him, "It's not so much the particular rude excesses and the crude, brutal ill treatment, of which the New York papers are reporting, that we fear. Instead, it's the moral burden which daily lies more heavily on the soul. We are without rights, surrounded by hate and hostility, are continually set on with bitter humiliations and must endure it; and that which is holy to us is covered with dirt and trampled underfoot." The Lutherans had hoped that they would only have to endure for a short time, but it had now been fifteen years since the Bolshevik Revolution and the Lord had not yet shown his hand in their hoped-for liberation. Meanwhile, the atheist state continued its steady stride forward.[24]

19

A SAD AND MUDDLED AFFAIR

Conflicts in the Church as OGPU Pressure Intensifies

MEIER AND THE High Church Council were more and more of the opinion that they were fighting a losing battle, but this realization only encouraged them to rely completely on the Lord. The bishop promised that "we will not waver nor yield but will pray daily to the Lord of the church that He would lend us the strength to be faithful to His commands 'to hold on to what you have.'" To this end, he spied a "glimmer of light in the dark" in the fact that six students took their exams in early summer. Invited by Malmgren to participate in the final exams for the seminarians, Meier was duly impressed with the products of the seminary.[1] Malmgren was disappointed that only about half of the class had made it through to the end of their studies, given that six students had been forced to discontinue their preparations for the ministry. Two were taken for military service (Torrosyan and Lel) while the other four were deported to concentration camps. Two of those deported students had been connected to the Hansen-Muss case, having taught Sunday school for the pastors in Leningrad. One, Otto Tumm, was arrested and sentenced in 1930 and was currently serving his prison term. The other, twenty-two-year-old Conrad Gerling (spelled "Herling" in German), was serving time in the far north. But now the sad news had reached Malmgren that Gerling had died of spotted typhus in a concentration camp off the coast of Murmansk.

The seminary had decided to give those students completing their theological education in 1932 time to conduct practical work in local Leningrad congregations. Four German-language congregations were still active in the city (St. Peter's, St. Anne's, St. Catherine's, and St. Mary Magdalene), one Finnish (St. Mary's), one Latvian (Christ the Savior), one Swedish (St. Katherine's), one Estonian (St. John's), and the Russian-language congregation formerly led by Kurt Muss (Jesus Christ). There would be no new class in the fall, as Malmgren and his rapidly diminishing staff would be occupied with the graduating class and the remaining students at the seminary.[2] Given the knowledge that there were more than two million Lutherans who awaited some kind of pastoral service, and added to that the retirements of aging pastors and the losses to prison, labor camp, and martyrdom, it is no wonder that Malmgren could despair at times.[3] The Lutheran Church needed every student he could get placed into the pastoral office, and quickly. For Malmgren and Meier, the most difficult balance was retaining pastors but also acknowledging the realities of persecution and the desire of pastors to emigrate.

IN 1932, SOVIET Foreign Minister Maxim Litvinov agreed to allow ten pastors to leave the USSR; included in the list were Woldemar and Eduard Seib, as well as Albert Koch. The bishops, who were fighting a losing battle with the reduced numbers of pastors, now made clear the necessity of keeping them by any means possible, including refusing to sign off on their emigration papers. Their actions also affected students, because in June 1932 both bishops refused to allow Konstantin Rusch to leave for Germany, arguing that he didn't have the classical theological education to serve there. Tragically, Rusch would be arrested and eventually executed in a Gulag camp in 1941.

Woldemar Seib of Kharkov responded to these actions bitterly: "My attempts to receive German citizenship were of course refused. Malmgren is guilty. On his last trip over the border, he refused to entertain pastors' requests for emigration (besides this, he christened them with the gentle word 'deserters'). It is outrageous! The great lords sit in Petersburg, living, despite the general need, pretty well ... and have no idea at all of the awful conditions of their brothers in the provinces. And although the High Church Council ponders its own dissolution, they don't call themselves deserters!" Mikhail Baumann, a 1929 seminary graduate serving in the Ukraine, added his own disappointment, writing that the High Church Council in Moscow didn't care for the pastors but only themselves, leaving them to fight for their own existence. Only a few pastors would manage to emigrate, as the conditions for emigration were extraordinarily strict. You couldn't be the subject of a current court case or have ever been arrested in order to have your case reviewed. There were virtually no pastors in the USSR that fit those parameters. Seib, sadly, would be arrested in 1935 and perish in a labor camp in Marinsk.[4]

These complicated circumstances provide a vivid picture of the struggles that the bishops and pastors endured. While it is difficult to blame a faithful pastor like Seib for his anger, it is not accurate to say the bishops were living in luxury. Malmgren was reduced to spartan living conditions, although it is true that life in the provinces would always be worse. Still, it had to weigh on him when he knew that many of his pastors would be arrested and yet he couldn't just abandon the congregations. To that end, Malmgren counted among his blessings the five ordained Finnish/Ingrian pastors serving in the Leningrad region, apart from the emergency preachers and lay leaders. And now he could add to those numbers another ordained pastor, an elderly, mature Finn, who completed his exams in the spring of 1932.[5] So despite the rapidly advancing darkness, there was still a glimmer of light. But it was fading rapidly.

OF THE SIX graduates from the class of 1932, two were called to the South Caucasus (including Malmgren's son-in-law, Emil Hahnefeld, to Helenendorf), one to the North Caucasus, one to the Volga, one to Odessa (Karl Vögel), and two to Leningrad. One, Heinrich Maier, had requested to serve in the dangerous mission field of Siberia but died of pneumonia while Malmgren was in Germany. After his death and that of Ferdinand Hörschelmann Sr., plus the deportations of pastors Merz and Deutschmann, western Siberia could not claim one ordained pastor.[6] Writing to Morehead, Malmgren could only express the sorrow of the church with the words, "How unsearchable are His judgments and inscrutable His ways."[7]

Now, as a result of governmental pressure and the extensive daily activities required of the rector, Malmgren announced that the 1932–1933 school year would be his last, especially if help from foreign Lutherans failed. The seminary had once again finished the year in debt to the tune of 3,366 rubles and 40 kopecks (approximately $1,683). With the tax on the seminary at 5,739 rubles, the insurance for the workers at the seminary costing 1,156 rubles, and the state requiring higher salaries for the housekeepers and maids up to the sum of 5,434 rubles, Malmgren estimated that these costs alone would take up more than a third of the seminary's budget. It was difficult for him to ask for assistance when he was keenly aware of the difficulties plaguing the German and American economies, although he acknowledged that it was even worse in the USSR. Of the $13,000 budget, $9,512 came from the NLC in America alone.[8]

On October 21, Morehead wrote back, assuring him of his strong support for the seminary: "Not in the least do I waver in the conviction which has been mine from the first that this is an absolutely necessary and fundamental work for the Evangelical Lutheran Church of Russia, its preservation, perpetuation and development." With the biblical quote, "How can they hear without a preacher?" (Romans 10:14), Morehead sought to hearten the burdened rector with the knowledge that the Lutheran churches in Europe and America saw his work as "God's work," and that they viewed their support as a privilege and a duty to God. "God will not fail you. His grace will be sufficient for you."[9] In May, Franz Rendtorff of the Gustav-Adolf-Verein and Dr. Kriege of Berlin had likewise encouraged Malmgren to continue with the operation of the seminary.[10]

Morehead's assurances couldn't have come at a better time for Malmgren. "With grateful joy I have received your letter of October 21; it gives me the confidence that at the very least I will be able to finish this 8th year of the seminary and be able to place the senior students in parishes." Malmgren knew that he could not carry out his duties much longer if the pressure continued. It wasn't the economic difficulties so much as the church policy of the Soviet state that concerned him most. The seminary was a "thorn in the eye," a "foreign body" that did not fit into the ideology of Leninism.[11]

The strategy of the state was to hinder and complicate the work of the seminary as much as possible. The Soviet authorities abrogated the contract they had signed for the dormitory rooms, and the students and professors were continually being sent away into exile or labor camps under any pretext. The depletion of the ranks of professors at the seminary had placed a burden on Malmgren. Of the staff that had served at the seminary in 1929, virtually all were gone. Friedrich Wacker, Arnold Frischfeld, and Helmut Hansen were in the Gulag labor camps. Otto Wentzel, who had taken a call to serve a congregation in Helenendorf in the Transcaucasian District, had been arrested and in May 1931 transferred to an OGPU prison in Baku.[12] The bishop of the Estonians in Russia, Albert Juergenson, had died in January 1929.[13] Paul Reichert was the only professor who remained from that time, and Malmgren suspected that his longevity in service was no coincidence.

ASSISTING MALMGREN AND REICHERT with the teaching were recent graduates Eugen Bachmann of St. Anne's and Malmgren's son-in-law, Heinrich

Behrendts of St. Peter's in Leningrad, who taught Hebrew. However, in September 1932, the OGPU accused Behrendts of being involved in the theft of firewood. Apparently, Behrendts had unknowingly bought firewood for St. Peter's that had been stolen. In a show trial lasting weeks, Behrendts and several Orthodox priests accused of the same crime were placed in the prisoners' box while the public prosecutor sneered at them and insulted them.[14] Although Malmgren was not among the accused, his name was repeatedly invoked and reviled. In fact, even before the trial began, a *Leningradskaya Pravda* article entitled "Firewood Thief" had portrayed Malmgren as a deceitful racketeer.[15] Summoning up the fury of the proletariat, a Soviet journalist inveighed against Malmgren:

> The bishop of the German Lutheran Church has never received anyone in his working room. The first strange visitor was Nikolaev [one of the accused]. An extraordinarily warm handshake, a pair of warm, business words and Bishop Malmgren, rector of the Bible school, a man, who in matters of law is very knowledgeable, who knows that this concerns stolen firewood, concluded with Nikolaev a punishable arrangement to deliver firewood for his, Malmgren's, personal use, for the Bible school and for the Church. A not insubstantial role in this business was played by the pastor of St. Peter's, Behrendts, whom Nikolaev and Malmgren had been leading. ... The proletariat court will doubtless not only bring to the profiteers their deserved sentence, but also those who bought the firewood and, in this manner, have stolen from the consumers of the working classes.[16]

While all this was occurring, Malmgren was in Berlin with the vice consul of the German consulate in Leningrad, Karl Georg Pfleiderer. Pfleiderer recalled asking Malmgren if he would want to remain in Germany, given the seriousness of the charges and the calumny directed against him. His reply was bold and forthright: "I'm needed in Leningrad. The worst that could happen to me is that I could be sent to compulsory labor in the Siberian mines, but at my age, I wouldn't be able to hold out for long." He would return to the Soviet Union.[17]

In his attempt to pit the aristocratic Malmgren against the people, this Soviet journalist had underestimated him, for Malmgren was not as helpless as he had suspected. Malmgren had always been politically astute, using his connections in the German consulate to his and the church's advantage. The present situation was alleviated by his contacts with the German diplomat Johannes Kriege in Berlin and Soviet diplomat Lev Khinchuk. Kriege assured Malmgren that Khinchuk had told him Malmgren would be protected from the OGPU and his son-in-law would be let off with a fine. Khinchuk further heartened Malmgren by passing along a message through Kriege conferring the first and second general secretaries of the Leningrad Communist Party's respect and good wishes toward the seminary. At this time, German and Soviet diplomats could work together in a cordial manner, though Adolf Hitler's coming to power in Germany would soon change this relationship.

On October 5, the trial ended with twenty death sentences handed out to the main defendants, although eleven had the sentence rescinded. Behrendts was sentenced to three years in a concentration camp and the confiscation of all of his property.[18] Malmgren lodged an appeal with the highest court in Moscow, simultaneously informing the German embassy of the verdict. The appeal was successful, as Behrendts's sentence was reduced to banishment from Leningrad, which would begin on December 31, 1932. The confiscation of his property, however, would remain in force. Despite his reprieve, Behrendts was in danger of receiving additional penalties if he couldn't find a new place of employment outside Leningrad. After the death of Pastor Justus Jurgenson in Tashkent, Uzbekistan, Behrendts and his wife made the long journey east to begin serving there in March 1933.[19]

AS IF THIS situation wasn't enough for the aged Malmgren, a bitter conflict had been brewing between him and seminary professor Paul Reichert. In his letter to Morehead in November, Malmgren asserted that a "powerful intervention" was taking place in the inner life of the seminary.[20] The matter had come to a head in September at the first meeting of the seminary council for the school year when Reichert put forth a proposal to close the seminary. He saw no purpose in its further operation given the precarious situation of the church in the Soviet Union.

This was not a surprising sentiment, and it coincided with what Malmgren had privately shared with others, but such a proposal without his knowledge struck him as inappropriate. The council rejected Reichert's suggestion. On October 28, however, Reichert submitted twenty-one questions to the bishop to which he expected written replies. Malmgren refused, citing his "impertinent tone," but agreed to speak to him about these issues separately. This wasn't acceptable to Reichert, who also accused Malmgren of improprieties with the money given to him by American Lutherans. In response to these charges, Malmgren authorized a thorough auditing of his financial books by the High Church Council. In November, the council found the books to be "in blameless order," as Malmgren informed his supporters in Leipzig. Malmgren then responded in kind, accusing Reichert of close ties to the OGPU.[21] By the end of the year, Malmgren fired him, leaving the seminary with no full-time professor besides himself (Bachmann was not a regular professor).[22]

But the conflict did not end there, and took on an even sharper tone in the new year when Malmgren attempted to replace Heinrich Behrendts at St. Peter's with the recent graduate Emil Hanefeld. Hanefeld was Malmgren's other son-in-law, the husband of his daughter Adele, and placing him at one of the largest Lutheran parishes in Russia drew charges of nepotism. Then the church council of St. Peter's complicated matters even further by calling Paul

Reichert to be their next pastor. According to Malmgren, this was because the head of the church council had been called into the OGPU offices and told in no uncertain terms that if the Lutherans wanted to avoid disciplinary measures, Paul Reichert would, as an "older and experienced man," be chosen as pastor. In other words, the church would be closed if they chose Hanefeld. When Reichert was chosen as pastor on January 20, 1933, Malmgren was beside himself, not only because of what he considered the blatant interference of the OGPU, but also because Reichert had not formally resigned his call from the congregation he was serving in Novosaratovka (a suburb of Leningrad).[23]

MUCH OF THE information we possess about this controversy comes from witnesses close to Malmgren, including Malmgren himself, but not all. For example, historian Wilhelm Kahle cites the German general consul in Leningrad, Richard Sommer, who tried to understand the conflict from both sides. Sommer acknowledged that the parishioners supporting Reichert were not simply stooges of the OGPU, but that the majority truly sympathized with his predicament. While the Lutheran parishioners did acknowledge Malmgren's manifold contributions to the Church and seminary, his strict authoritative manner was not particularly well received. Sommer judged that Malmgren had ruled autocratically and acted in a high-handed manner, accepting no opinion but his own. In fact, it appears that most of the pastors in Leningrad and students at the seminary came down on the side of Reichert in this conflict.[24]

Historian Helmut Tschoerner seems to get at the crux of the problem by comparing the backgrounds of the two men. Arthur Malmgren was raised in the educated middle class (bourgeoisie) in the Baltics, afterwards spending long years as a pastor in a prominent congregation in St. Petersburg, the capital of the Russian Empire. With an aristocratic bearing and accustomed, as a high official in the Church, to having his word accepted as law, Malmgren couldn't have been happy that Reichert challenged his authority. In contrast, Reichert grew up as a son of the colonies on the Volga River. Although, he, too, had matriculated at Yuryev University in Dorpat, he spent close to twenty years serving a congregation in the village of Balzer near the Volga, and afterward in Novosaratovka, outside Leningrad.

The backgrounds of the men were representative, too, of the cultural conflict between classes in the Soviet Union. One doesn't have to accept the Marxist notion of perpetual hostility between the classes to understand that real differences existed within the Church. There were genuine differences between conservative and more liberal elements within the Church.[25] Bishops Meier and Malmgren fought against tendencies that were encouraged by the Communists due to their more "socially democratic" nature. Morehead came down on the side of the bishops, because he, too, believed that the Church needed a sound, hierarchical order.

While Reichert had also been educated in the hierarchical system of ecclesiology, he represented a different strain of pastor who did not accept the authoritative, no-questions-asked manner of the bishop. Even younger, respected pastors like Arthur Kluck were not always enamored with the old forms of leadership, although he was always respectful of the office of the bishop. While Sommer believed that neither side was free from blame in this affair, he thought the parishioners were more to blame than Malmgren because they knowingly used the OGPU to bring Malmgren down in stature. "Every means appeared right to them, if it brought them nearer to their expressed goal to throw the bishop out of the saddle and make it impossible for him to carry out any church activity." In fact, on September 19, 1934, even pastors from Leningrad would address a letter of complaint to the Gustav-Adolf-Verein about Malmgren, stating that Malmgren was operating in close association with the OGPU! Subjecting Malmgren to the devices of the OGPU by sending the letter through the ordinary postal system was an act Sommer found appalling. He feared that the OGPU censors would read the letter and it would not bode well for Malmgren's authority in religious matters.[26]

Frustrated, Malmgren now used his connections at the German consulate to have them spy on Reichert. In March 1933, vice consul Pfleiderer admitted that Reichert was conducting himself appropriately in his office at St. Peter's and no one in the congregation seemed to be complaining. Then, since Malmgren was giving bad grades to his son, Bruno, a student at the seminary, Reichert brought him to St. Peter's as the second pastor and ordained Bruno himself in April 1933. On April 26, Pfleiderer submitted a final report, echoing Sommer that Malmgren and Reichert "internally belong to different worlds." Discussing their enmity toward each other, Pfleiderer stated, "One reason is that the son-in-law of Malmgren did not receive Reichert's position. ... On the relationship of Reichert with the local Soviet authorities, which the bishop has sketched very clearly, we can only offer suspicion. ... I met with the pastor personally ... the conversation was cordial, but not open, because when the pastor spoke about how the peasants lived well on the collective farms, I thought that the opinion of the bishop was in some measure well founded."[27] It is possible that Reichert was only exercising caution with Pfleiderer, trying to appear as a respectful citizen. And yet anyone who spoke approvingly of collectivization given what it had done to parishioners would have to be looked on with some degree of skepticism.

St. Peter's would be the last congregation to be closed in Leningrad and the Reicherts would be the last pastors executed in 1938. It doesn't take an active imagination to question how they had avoided imprisonment for that long. Suspicions about Reichert could even be traced back to the Volga in 1922, when Commissar David Schultz tried to form an independent Lutheran Church under Communist control. When Friedrich Wacker blanched at his effrontery, he was kicked off the Volga region church council for insubordination to the

Communists. Council member Alexander Streck, was even threatened with prison. Wacker's place would then be taken by—Paul Reichert.[28]

But we cannot tie all of those loose threads together too tightly. Many parishioners and pastors had taken the lesson of the Hansen-Muss case to heart and tried to keep the Lutheran Church alive by not angering the authorities. The Reicherts, for their part, suffered persecution and were eventually executed for their faith. There is no evidence from the files that they appealed for clemency to the OGPU/NKVD as their former masters. It would have been easy to do so, as other spies had often made just such an appeal. The Reicherts would not, making it unlikely that they had been in league with their executors. Instead, they would keep their congregation alive, and active Lutherans would join them in worshiping the Lord, until the church was forced into extinction. Unfortunately, the bitterness between the two Lutheran professors would do little to enhance the solidarity needed to preserve the Evangelical Lutheran Church of Russia in its most difficult hour.

20

"HARVEST OF SORROW"

Seminary Struggles, Famine, and the Recognition of the Soviet Union

IT WAS DIFFICULT for an American like John Morehead to understand the nature of the Soviet Union and Stalin's cold-blooded rationale for building communism and propagating atheism in Russia. As 1932 ended, he asked Bishop Malmgren about the Communists' desire to eradicate Christianity by the end of the Second Five-Year Plan: "Is not freedom of religion guaranteed in the constitution and organic law of the present government of the USSR?" The people of the world, he said, believed seminaries and churches could function legally in the Soviet Union. It was all so confusing.[1] In February 1933, Malmgren responded, acknowledging that the Law on Religious Associations of April 1929 did allow for the registration and operation of seminaries. However, the state only reluctantly tolerated them, preferring instead to see them closed. The atheistic-materialistic worldview allowed room for only one ideology in Soviet Russia. Explaining the goal of the Communists, Malmgren admitted it would be "unspeakably difficult" to continue to operate the seminary. Soon those "without rights" would not be able to live in a large city, while at the same time a seminary was only allowed to exist in a large city. The government of the Soviet Union thrived on such contradictions.

In the meantime, the taxes levied on the seminary were becoming more burdensome. In 1931, the ground rent and building tax totaled 259 rubles together.
In 1932, the two taxes combined for a total of 2,174 rubles. Now, in 1933, the
seminary's tax would be 5,097 rubles! Malmgren lamented, "One thing is certain. As far as I can see it today, our institution will not be directly shut down
or forbidden by the government." But through chicanery and constant pressure,
the government would simply force the Lutherans to give up. So Malmgren
informed Morehead that by the summer, a decision had to be made on whether
to close the seminary.[2] At present, there were only eleven students remaining,
and six planned to graduate in the summer. There were no plans to add new
students.[3]

Despite his previous differences with Bishop Malmgren, Bishop Meier
agreed with him about the Christian church's current state, especially after
the Soviet authorities turned up the heat against the church in 1929. With
regard to the future of the Lutheran Church and seminary, he was in accord
with Malmgren. In answer to Morehead's question whether there was a plan in
Stalin's Second Five-Year-Plan to close churches, Meier, like Malmgren, offered
a nuanced perspective. The state would never publicly declare a resolution to
that effect. They were too smart for that. But in the end, there was no doubt
that they were committed to the Church's destruction. In one of the clearest
statements about the state's relationship to the Church in 1933, Meier explained
the situation to Morehead from the perspective of the state:

> We recognize no religion, in whatever form it expresses itself, and can
> only in the best case endure it and in no case give it privileges or the pos-
> sibility to contradict our ideology among the masses, or to discredit our
> economic reorganization and agitate against it. We prohibit no one from
> recognizing a religion or to observe its instructions; but we see religios-
> ity as an antiquated, backward, Enlightenment-contradicting mentality,
> holding such people as inferior and placing them in no responsible post.

The work of persons, those occupying themselves with the maintenance and dissemination of religion, the activity of spiritual persons, we hold for socially unnecessary, aiming at nothing profitable. Therefore, we treat these persons like all others who do not live from their own profitable work but who illegally enrich themselves at the expense of the working class. We will make life as difficult as possible for all of these elements, above all through higher taxes and other disadvantages in satisfying their life needs. We come from the viewpoint that generally educated people cannot be convinced of the truth of religion. We contend that those whose profession is spiritual to the greatest extent earn easy income, and we will not allow people to live this kind of easy lifestyle in our state. If this spiritual worker takes all the burdens that we place upon him and continues to serve, then he is a fanatical or fanciful martyr. If we pursue our present policies on this question to their full consequence in the course of the next five years, we will come to the important moment when the youth will not only be educated to be non-religious but anti-religious. Then we will need to take no legal measures because religion will be as good as rejected from the life of the people; because it is clear that in order to organize the life of over 100 million people on a socialist basis with the rigorous regulation of the life of each person, then the practice of religion among these people must be given a death blow. We should not deceive ourselves when we accept that on these grounds spirituality is an enemy of our socialist economic institutions. So, the necessity lies before us to remove them from their profession. For these reasons no one can reproach us that we are deviating from the prescriptions of religious freedom laid out in the Constitution. On the contrary, the law that every disruption of the practice of religion is punishable still stands. We only mean that in respect to our state's influence upon the people, religion will be deprived but without direct, violent measures.[4]

Meier's perspective was formed through his interactions and conversations with representatives of the Kremlin. He knew them well, including President Kalinin, and recognized their plan to gradually erode the religious faith of youth. Since the future was to be Communist and atheist, it was only a question of time before Christianity would be destroyed.

WITH RESPECT TO Morehead's offer to speak up on behalf of persecuted believers, Meier foresaw no help coming on this front. He quoted the prime minister of France, Eduard Herriot, as saying that whatever happened internally in the USSR was immaterial, because that nation had unlimited opportunities for commerce. Therefore, Herriot's goal was for France to try and befriend the USSR. In other words, the Soviets were good for business and companies worldwide were lining up for access to its markets.

Even though America had not recognized the Soviet Union, there were hundreds if not thousands of American engineers working in the Soviet Union. Herriot's cautious diplomacy toward the USSR was no doubt driven by the fact that Citroen and Peugeot were already in Russia.[5] In 1929, Henry Ford made his own splash into the Russian market, negotiating a $40 million contract to construct a Ford auto plant in Nizhniy Novgorod. Unemployed Detroiters by the scores would make the journey to this strange land, some never to return, swallowed up in the vast reaches of the Gulag as suspicious foreigners during Stalin's Great Terror (1937–1938). But for now, jobs were abundant and there were profits to be made. No other company in the world would conduct as much business with Stalin as would Henry Ford from 1929–1936.[6]

An African American named Robert Robinson was a good example of those who found the Soviet Union to be a beacon for unemployed workers during the Great Depression. Robinson made the journey to Russia from Detroit in the early 1930s to find work in the burgeoning factory scene. Not only did he find work, but his Soviet employers also reminded him that racial discrimination did not exist in the USSR. Further opportunities for job advancement and education were also provided to Robinson. He even became a member of the Moscow City Council. In short, it was not surprising that people throughout the world might see the USSR as the vanguard of world history while Western countries were floundering in an economic crisis that threatened to dismantle the capitalist system.

But while most workers were sympathetic or indifferent to the Soviet experiment, Robinson believed in God and was always uncomfortable with the atheist indoctrination he received. He even attended services at the Catholic Church of St. Louis, right down the street from OGPU headquarters and a few blocks from Bishop Meier's Sts. Peter and Paul Lutheran. It didn't take long for him to become disillusioned with communism, but he was trapped, being held against his will as a shining example of racial harmony in the USSR. Robinson would survive a total of forty-four years in the USSR before escaping in 1974 to Uganda. A paraphrase of Joshua 1:9 would be on his lips every day: "Never fear anymore, for the Lord was and is with me."[7]

Joseph Stalin's Soviet Union was mastering the art of propaganda among the nations while getting their companies to help him industrialize his nation. Given the changed climate regarding international business, Meier predicted that it wouldn't be long before the United States would recognize the Soviet Union. Meier was therefore in agreement with Malmgren that the Soviet state was becoming more and more powerful and there was little that the David of the Church could do in facing this Goliath-like state. As far as the future of the seminary was concerned, he, too, felt that the status quo could not continue. Malmgren was the only regular professor where previously there had been six to eight lecturers working full-time. Moreover, no help could be expected from abroad. Foreign professors would not be given visas to help a seminary that the state had consigned to death. Meier also recognized that the social position of the students was so precarious that "the few young people who announce that they will study for the pastorate are straight away considered to be martyrs." In the end, Meier also agreed with Malmgren that the seminary would not be forcibly closed but that the conditions for its further existence were as unfavorable as they could possibly be.[8] And the West, for the most part, would remain silent and do business with Stalin.

AS IF THE troubles of the seminary were not enough to concern the bishops, the Soviet Union now looked to be on the verge of another famine that could potentially dwarf the one of ten years before.[9] Malmgren straightforwardly told Morehead that hunger was prevalent in the north of the Caucasus, on the coast of Murmansk, in the forests of the Urals, on the Volga and on the coasts of the Black Sea all the way to Siberia. In other words, in virtually the entire Soviet Union! Farmers were fleeing from the villages to the cities, only to be forcibly returned to their homes where their stomachs swelled up from malnutrition. As a result, they were dying in the streets. "Guilt for this misery is not due to failure of the crops or a bad harvest. The agrarian system alone carries the guilt and its enforcement by narrow-minded communists."[10] Such words had spelled trouble for Kurt Muss during the first famine.

The "harvest of sorrow," as historian Robert Conquest has termed it, was of enormous breadth even though it struck primarily in the Ukraine. British journalist Malcolm Muggeridge, sympathetic enough to communism when he arrived in Moscow that he considered giving up his British citizenship and applying for the same in the Soviet Union, was stunned and sickened by what he saw in the Ukraine. His epiphany was all the more convincing given that his father was a noted Socialist while his wife was the niece of infamous Stalin apologists Sidney and Beatrice Webb.[11] Eluding supervision in Moscow, Muggeridge traveled throughout the north Caucasus and the Ukraine, and echoing Bishop Malmgren, witnessed a famine that "was planned and deliberate; not due to any natural catastrophe like failure of rain, or cyclone, or flooding. An administrative famine brought about by the forced collectivization of agriculture ... supported by strong-arm squads from the military and the police."[12]

Other journalists of a Socialist bent like Arthur Koestler, who would later write a classic critique of Stalinism, *Darkness at Noon*, wrote honestly about what they had seen. Koestler recalled the bodies of dead children, looking like "embryos out of alcohol bottles." Eugene Lyons, an American Communist fellow traveler, had the scales fall from his eyes when he saw what was happening in the Ukraine. Appalled by what he had witnessed and knowing that the Soviet censors would delete what he wrote, Lyons made sure his articles were smuggled out to the West.[13] The Soviets were able, though, to have the famine basically downplayed or ignored in the West due to the gullibility of those who had not seen or could not imagine the evil forces arrayed against the people and the church, especially during the past few years. Soviet propaganda was also served by journalists who valued worldly acclaim and praise above listening to one's conscience.

Walter Duranty was the most infamous of these journalists, a *New York Times* writer who labeled the famine "mostly bunk." Although he eventually had to admit there had been great loss of life, Duranty often retreated to his favorite phrase, "You can't make an omelet without breaking eggs." Of utmost importance to Duranty in 1933 was an agreement being forged between the Americans and Soviets—official recognition of the Soviet Union. His glowingly optimistic report of Stalin's Five-Year-Plan won him a Pulitzer Prize in 1932, gaining him a certain popularity among the fashionable elite in society.[14] Muggeridge and other less-famous journalists who reported the truth of the famine weren't accorded much of a hearing in contrast to those like Duranty, who were feted in the field of public opinion. Years later, when Muggeridge was asked whether his prospects had suffered on account of his reports, he expressed surprise at such a question: "*Me?* What happened to *me?* Oh yes. I couldn't get work."[15]

IN THE FALL OF 1933, as Malmgren began the academic year, the problems of higher taxes on the seminary and correspondingly smaller income would not go away. The state now gobbled up almost half of the budget through taxes (10, 622 rubles out of 25, 951). As a consequence of these demands, the seminary would begin the school year of 1933–1934 with a total of 3 rubles, 15 kopecks in its bank account.[16]

Reassuring Malmgren that the LWC would provide financial cover, Morehead asked for information as to the total of the deficit. He immediately sent out $1,500 from the LWC in early September and wrote to Dr. Ulmer of the Lutheran Gotteskasten in Erlangen. Since Ulmer's organization worked with the LWC, they could provide even more funds to make up the deficit.[17]

While Malmgren and Morehead concerned themselves with the operation of the seminary, serious negotiations leading toward official recognition were taking place between the United States and the Soviet Union. In the process of their discussions, American and Russian negotiators haggled over what kind of religious freedom agreement could be forged between the two countries. President Franklin Delano Roosevelt placed the issue of religious freedom for American citizens working in the Soviet Union high on the agenda. The Soviet's negotiator, Maxim Litvinov, was perplexed by the president's interest in religion. He was prepared to discuss repayment of former debts, the use of Soviet propaganda in America, but religious freedom? "No Americans have ever complained against religious restriction while in Russia." Litvinov concluded that Roosevelt was absorbed with a nonexistent problem to the detriment of solving the more important economic issues that were of interest to the Soviets.[18]

A shrewd politician, Roosevelt was aware that influential religious leaders in America like Morehead had been concerned with the treatment of religious believers in Russia. It seems that the president even requested that Monsignor Michael Keegan and Cardinal Patrick Hayes of New York draw up some bullet points for discussion. Roosevelt wanted not only religious rights for Americans in the Soviet Union but ultimately hoped that such rights might be secured for the Soviet people. Freedom of conscience, freedom of worship, the release of religious believers from the Gulag camps, cessation of propaganda against God in the USSR: these were issues of importance to him.[19] Given his purposeful actions directed against Christians since 1929, these requests must have occasioned a cynical guffaw from Stalin.

Whatever Stalin and Litvinov's concerns, Roosevelt knew that he would need to placate religious Americans if he was going to succeed in pushing through recognition of the USSR. The ACRRM certainly loomed large in his thoughts given the influence of its members. If an embassy were to be opened in the Soviet Union, it was important to Roosevelt that the personnel have the right to teach their children the Christian faith. Catholics of America, while divided over recognition, gave Roosevelt kudos for showing that a capitalist power was not simply focused on profit but took spiritual matters seriously. And in fairness to the president, his concern for religious freedom by all accounts appears to have been genuine.[20]

Even though the Soviet leadership remained skeptical, the Foreign Commissariat prepared a statistical memo (only one) about how many churches, cathedrals, and monasteries existed in the Soviet Union. They also listed the religious schools and to which denomination they belonged, along with how many religious groups existed before and after the Bolshevik Revolution. But had the Roosevelt administration done its homework, it would have reviewed the memos on persecution of Christians prepared by the US Legation in Riga over the past several years, as well as speak to religious leaders in the know like Fr. Edmund Walsh of Georgetown or Morehead himself. In the past, those leaders had written on just this very topic to President Hoover. Given that the president took pains to address an issue of little interest to those clamoring for recognition of the USSR, it is mystifying that he would ultimately put little pressure on Stalin, who refused to allow any interpretation of religious and civil rights that contradicted his own 1929 Law on Religious Associations.[21]

The Roosevelt administration was at least successful in securing religious rights for US citizens in the Soviet Union.[22] So on the evening of November 16, the agreement was officially signed and the United States recognized the Soviet Union. As the din from the toasts subsided and the celebration wound down in Washington, DC, that night, the undersecretary of state, William Phillips, remembered Roosevelt saying to Litvinov: "There is one other thing. You must tell Stalin that the anti-religious program is wrong; God will punish you Russians if you go on persecuting the church." Baffled to the end by Roosevelt's persistent pronouncements of religious faith, Litvinov asked if he really believed in God.[23] The Riga Legation, including a young diplomat by the name of George Kennan (who would go on to great fame as a Sovietologist), was disappointed in the final agreement. Cognizant of the lack of freedom existing in the Soviet Union, the diplomats knew that Soviet assurances regarding basic human rights were of little value.[24] Events would prove them correct in their assumptions. But for his part, Bishop Meier turned out to be a true prophet. The United States had recognized the Soviet Union by the end of 1933, just as he had said it would.

REGARDLESS OF THE American government's naiveté on matters of religion in the Soviet Union, the number of Lutheran pastors was dwindling fast by the end of 1933. Meier confided to Morehead that there were only forty-five pastors serving the Lutheran Church in Russia, including "adjuncts" (keusters), excluding the two bishops. In Leningrad and its surrounding region there were nine; in Moscow, two; in the Volga region, eight; in the Ukraine, twelve; in the Crimea, three; in the north Caucasus, six; in Tashkent, there was one pastor (Malmgren's son-in-law, Heinrich Behrendts), and in Baku and Vladivostok, also one. There were still two candidates in Leningrad who had not been ordained, and three young pastors who had been diverted into a work detail for the military (including Johannes Lel and Bruno Toryassan). Furthermore, twenty-six pastors had been deported to concentration camps where five had died and three had been released but had not yet returned to pastoral service.

The poverty of Lutheran parishioners was as bad as it had ever been. Writing to Morehead at the end of October, Meier announced that only three hundred rubles had been sent from parishioners to support the High Church Council and its officials for the year of 1933! The council's finances had been exhausted, and when the next round of state taxes would be levied at the start of 1934, Meier knew that the thousand rubles in the treasury would not cover the expected 3,800-ruble tax. As a result, Meier feared that his private property, house, and clothing would be seized and sold. While he knew that the Great Depression was impoverishing Americans, he pleaded with Morehead not to "leave us in a stitch." Not wanting to appear too demanding, though, Meier reminded Morehead that Russian Lutherans all knew his name and held it in honor because "through brotherly love you have saved us."

Meier also requested something on the order of a *Hilfsaktion* for Russian Lutherans suffering from the effects of famine, but Morehead feared that little could be done. In the famine of the early 1920s, Americans had been invited to the country by the regime-friendly Maxim Gorky and allowed a certain freedom to conduct famine relief. Those stipulations did not apply this time. First, Americans were more concerned with their own citizens suffering from hunger and want during the Great Depression; and second, the Soviet state was no longer interested in allowing foreigners the opportunity to roam freely throughout their land. Although American Lutherans remained willing to do whatever they could for their suffering brothers and sisters in the Soviet Union, conditions had changed for the worse even while politicians congratulated one another that it was a new day.[25]

"A MARTYR TO THE CAUSE"

The Tragedy of the Meiers

AS 1933 WENT ON, Bishop Meier no longer held back. He called the government the Antichrist in his sermons, warning the parishioners to be on their guard. Perhaps because of the danger to the church or the fact that he was advanced enough in age, he decided to become more direct in his criticism. Gathering together nine parishioners (four men and five women), he prepared them for the worst. One of them remembered him saying, "'Of the pastors only one remains [Alexander Streck] and soon the time will come when there will be no one, also no more church building; therefore, each of you must, like the first Christians, baptize, conduct weddings, come together for communion, teach the youth, bury the dead and do everything, so that the faith that you received from your fathers will remain.' He always said, 'What you do, do in full faith that it is just as good as if a servant of God has done it in a church building.'"[1]

Meier further instructed them that they should learn the baptismal and wedding services by heart, asking godparents whether they believed in God, and if so, that in this difficult time they would recognize God required them to take responsibility for the souls of their godchildren. Additionally, these parishioners were told to teach the children the Lord's Prayer, the Ten Commandments, and the basics of the faith. Meier predicted that soon Bibles would be thrown away and burned. His words must have rung like alarm bells in the ears of these parishioners: "Pray, pray and believe. ... It is all the same, whether man or woman, only believe in what you are doing. Soon, soon will come the time when all this will be necessary and God will demand it of you."[2]

Meier's words, echoing those of Helmut Hansen and Julius Zahlit in 1929 about returning to the days of the early church, accurately describe what was happening in the Soviet Union in the early 1930s. It was no longer easy for believers to compartmentalize their citizenship in the Soviet state and still publicly confess Christianity. Lutherans would need to be prepared for a day when the seminary and the churches would be closed. Meier and his colleague, Bishop Malmgren, both seemed to understand that the task now set before them was to fight for the preservation of the Christian faith for future generations. As such, they tried to inform as many pastors and parishioners as possible to prepare for the day when the church would be forced to go underground.

In light of his concern for the future pastoral leadership of the Lutheran Church, Meier ordained Bruno Toryassan and Ralph Jurgens in late August of 1933 at Sts. Peter and Paul in Moscow. Both would be sent to serve short-term vicarages in the northern Caucasus region under the tutelage of Bruno's father, Ossip. Despite Meier's intentions, in November Toryassan would be forcibly inducted into the army, where he would serve until 1937. This may have saved his life, since his army service coincided with the most dangerous period of persecution for servants of the church. Toryassan would live a full life and see the restoration of the Lutheran Church in the 1990s, finally being able to serve as a pastor in his old age. He passed away in Vyborg at the age of ninety-seven in 2009, a powerful witness to the hopes of bishops Meier and Malmgren for the preservation of the Church. Jurgens, however, would not survive the 1930s, dying of tuberculosis in a Gulag camp.[3]

But even with all the Church's troubles, nothing prepared Meier and his family for the heartbreaking news that would stun them that September. In an event he called "the most difficult time of my life," Meier learned that his youngest son, Traugott, had been arrested at the Austrian embassy, where he was employed. The government had seized the most valuable objects he owned along with more than $100 in cash. The family could not see or speak with him; they were only allowed to send him small sums of money from time to time. Meier's daughter Elisabeth now had to provide for the family, and her health had only just recovered. "In times like these," Meier reflected, "believing Christians can only seek their refuge with the Father in heaven, who has promised that not a hair from our head will fall without His will."[4]

WHILE THE BISHOPS were preparing for the worst, those convicted in the Hansen-Muss case were now completing their sentences. A good number of them had been forced to work on the White Sea Canal, an undertaking symbolic of the gargantuan projects associated with Stalin's plan to rapidly industrialize the Soviet Union. By all accounts, the conditions were indescribable and the cold and hunger frightful for those who had experienced it. Worse yet, the death rate (approximately 25,000 by most estimates) was horrific but justified in Stalin's mind so long as it helped him build a modern nation as quickly as possible.[5] Included among those sentenced to the far north and forced to participate in the building of the canal were the three Freifeldt sisters (Magdalina, Marta, and Elsa), Margo Jurgens (freed August 4, 1933), Erna Hansen, and Benita Kosetti.[6] Maxim Gorky, the Soviets' favorite apologist in the artistic community, lauded the canal's construction in the preface and conclusion to his book *The Canal Named for Stalin*. One of the themes trumpeted by the regime was the transformation of former enemies of the state who now saw the light through honest, hard work. The tools used to build the canal were makeshift at best. Dull pickaxes tied to wooden staves with leather or string, hammers employed instead of dynamite to break up large rocks, wheelbarrows and scaffolding made by hand were used to, as propaganda would have it, "change nature." The construction was a fabulous success but came at great human cost, completed in August 1933 after a little less than two years' time.[7]

Despite the hardships, the Sunday school teachers of Hansen and Muss all seemed to have survived their three-year stints in the Gulag camps. Some were even released early. For example, Luisa Muss is known to have begun working as a nurse as early as September 1932 in Leningrad. That year she married Otto Tumm, the seminary student who was arrested along with her and sentenced in September 1930.[8] The relationship between Luisa and Otto is illustrative of a certain bonding that occurred between many of the men and women who suffered for their faith in the Hansen-Muss case. In these trying circumstances, they found spouses of like mind and faith. For example, Elsa Freifeldt, the daughter of the late Bishop Conrad Freifeldt, married Gustav Golde, a crafts teacher for Kurt Muss's Busy Bees and a nephew of Bishop Theophil Meier.[9] Parishioners of Jesus Christ Lutheran Church, Elsa Golubovskaya (Friedenberg) and Konstantin Andrievsky, a lawyer, also married.[10] Even the youngest among them, Mikhail Mudyugin and Dagmara Schreiber, were married in August 1932 after both had been released with time served due to their youth.[11]

Upon his release, Mudyugin decided to pursue a secular education. After he married Dagmara, he completed evening classes at the Institute of Foreign Languages. Due to his prison record, he wasn't able to receive a passport (now required) to live in Leningrad, forcing him and his wife to depart for the Ural Mountains region. There he found work as a chemistry and German teacher. Mudyugin never gave up the desire to return to his beloved Leningrad, but on his homecoming he was denied residency. Again he and Dagmara moved, this time to Novgorod, where he worked as a heating technician at the factory Krasny Farforist ("Red Porcelain"). He kept trying to regain residency papers for Leningrad, but it would be many years before he was allowed to return.[12]

WHEN THE BOLSHEVIK REVOLUTION broke out in 1917, there were 183 pastors serving the Lutheran Church and eight students preparing for ordination. By January 1934, there were only seventeen left in the pastoral office, with one still being held in prison. Of the others, Malmgren wrote to Morehead that they had emigrated, retired, died, or been "corrupted" in some manner. Given the declining number of parishioners and the hardships that pastors had to face just to carry out their ministry, Malmgren was seeing less and less reason for the seminary's continuation. With the prospects for future service in the Church extremely dire, very few were applying to enter the seminary.

But Malmgren never gave up easily. He decided to send out a letter to the district presidents of the Church, asking them whether there were any prospective students for 1934–1935. Nothing less than the future of the seminary would depend on the answers he received. He was hoping that with Friedrich Wacker's and Heinrich Behrendts's potential return from concentration camp and exile, he might secure their services as professors for the seminary.[13] He apparently was in contact with Wacker, who, due to the successful intervention of the German Ministry of Foreign Affairs, had been released from his Siberian prison camp in 1933. Wacker was now living in Malaya Vishera, approximately a hundred kilometers outside of Leningrad—the distance by law he was required to live from a major city. Wacker had obtained his freedom with the stipulation that he refrain from "preaching activities," but the former dean couldn't abandon his students no matter the danger.[14] Malmgren had also come to an agreement just before Christmas with a 1929 graduate from the seminary, Woldemar Wagner, who was serving the congregation of St. Catherine's just outside Leningrad. Wagner had been one of those Volga region keusters who had coordinated relief with Pastor A. C. Ernst and the NLC back in the days of the famine. Now he would assist the seminary in the practical theology department. With Wagner on board and the potential of returning professors from internment, Malmgren forced himself to hope for an extension of the seminary's existence.[15]

But while Malmgren was in Berlin in the summer of 1934, a meeting with Soviet diplomat Lev Khinchuk discouraged him about returning Behrendts to the staff of the seminary. Khinchuk had encouraged Malmgren in 1932 when Behrendts was arrested, assuring him that his son-in-law would not be sent to a concentration camp and that his own person would be protected. But it was now 1934, and with the Nazis having come to power in Germany, German influence in the Soviet Union had been marginalized. Even though Khinchuk had told Malmgren to come to him if he had any problems, the ambassador did not think it wise to bring Behrendts back to serve at St. Peter's. In fact, in the near future Lutherans of German ethnicity would frequently be accused of serving as spies for Nazi Germany. Considering the changed environment, Behrendts remained in Tashkent, serving a Lutheran congregation of German speakers.[16]

MEANWHILE, MEIER'S SON, Traugott, had now been incarcerated in a Moscow prison for four months. His family had not been able to see or speak with him, although they were allowed to send small sums of money to him every month. Meier had received word that Traugott's trial was coming in a few weeks, and he feared that he would be sent to a labor camp far away.[17] Unbeknownst to him, though, Morehead had been accumulating more information on Traugott's situation. The old NLC employee Pastor W. L. Scheding had learned that Meier's elder son had defected many years ago from the Soviet Union. Although he had served in the White Army, the elder son eventually joined the Red Army as a pilot after the Bolshevik Revolution. This son had then escaped from the Soviet Union, flying his plane to Romania. According to Scheding's information gleaned from a Soviet official, the Soviets had always wanted to get information on the son and the Meier family had suffered as a result. Bishop Meier had been questioned on this matter many times and admitted to Scheding that his son had escaped with the plane, but he didn't know where he was hiding. Scheding speculated that Traugott was being punished for his brother's actions, but ultimately no one knew. It is just as likely that the OGPU could have been attacking the bishop by imprisoning his son.[18] In reality, there was no shortage of reasons for persecuting the family of the representative of an archaic institution that Stalin would just as soon see disappeared.

Whatever the case, Meier stood firm in his faith, proclaiming in a letter to Morehead, "Whether men can or want to help us, we don't know. But we certainly know that the Lord of the church can and will help us, when His time comes." Before that time would come, though, the Lutheran Church would suffer additional losses. In Zhitomir, Gustav Uhle had been arrested and deported for three years to Kazakhstan. Peter Withol, who had graduated from Malmgren's preachers' course with the Pfeiffer brothers in 1925, had been arrested in Lugansk. Added to these alarming events was the latest sad tiding that Heinrich Becker, who graduated from the seminary in 1929, had died of typhus on January 10 in the Volga River city of Engels. He left behind a wife and three small children. Despite these sad tidings, Meier did not forget to inquire after Morehead's health. It was a measure of the man and his character. Unfortunately, this sorrowful letter would be the last letter that Bishop Meier would ever write to Morehead.[19]

For his part, Morehead believed that the reduction in support from Americans was not solely due to the Great Depression but was occasioned by a lack of concrete information from the Lutheran Church in Russia. He mildly reprimanded Malmgren that he received "so little definite information from you about the Seminary" that it was difficult to praise the work of the seminary to American Lutherans. In Malmgren's defense, he did give information but was very cautious about what he included in a letter that would likely be subject to the prying eyes of the OGPU. Morehead did guess that censorship had to be the reason Malmgren was less forthcoming on details about the seminary, as he related in a March 1934 letter to Dr. Ralph Long, the new director of the NLC in America.[20]

As an example of how closely the OGPU kept an eye on the bishop, Morehead told Long that the last letter received from Meier in Germany had obviously been "opened, handled ruthlessly and forwarded in a wretched condition." Morehead speculated that the Soviets were trying to get some compromising information on Meier that might be used to arrest him.[21] Morehead, still endeavoring to do his utmost for the suffering Lutherans in Russia, visited the State Department in Washington, DC, with Long on April 5. There they met with E. L. Packer in the offices of the Division of Eastern European Affairs and made the bold request that the State Department instruct the US embassy in Moscow to compile information on the conditions of the Lutheran Church in Russia. Packer was disinclined to do this, suspecting that it would only cause trouble for the Lutherans. Upon reflection, Morehead and Long agreed.

Nonetheless, Morehead was still interested in the possibility of sending an American Lutheran representative to the USSR to assist the Church spiritually in its downtrodden condition. This was an issue that he had raised with Bishop Malmgren in the past, too. While Packer did not discourage Morehead from taking up the topic with the Soviet embassy, he did say that the State Department couldn't help them with it. They would have to do it on their own. To give them some insight on his position, though, he allowed Morehead and Long to peruse the correspondence between Soviet Foreign Minister Litvinov and President Roosevelt. Morehead's intentions for the representative also became apparent when he shared with Packer the hope that such a person might be able to secure the release of Lutherans exiled to the farthest reaches of Siberia. Packer, guessing the response of the Soviets, answered Morehead in the negative, thinking it "highly inadvisable for any foreigner to interfere in internal affairs in that country." Morehead's desperation in the face of the renewed persecution of Lutherans in Russia is evident in Packer's record of their conversation, as Packer informed the State Department about the Leningrad Seminary and Morehead's efforts to keep it open. Packer concluded his discussion with

Morehead and Long by agreeing that due to Morehead's participation in an international protest a few years ago (Arthur Brown's ACRRM) concerning the Soviet Union's policies on religion, it would be better for Long to go to the Soviet embassy alone and conduct exploratory discussions for a Lutheran representative to enter the USSR.[22]

WHATEVER THE SOVIET'S state's ultimate intentions were toward Bishop Meier, God in his mercy spared him from any further pain and harassment. Shortly after Easter, on Saturday, April 28, Morehead received a radiogram from Eugenie Meier that her husband had passed away earlier that day. In a memorial tribute to the bishop, Morehead reminisced, "Those who know the facts about Bishop Meier's nervous and energetic temperament and his suffering from a weak heart cannot but feel that in his care of all the churches, in his selfless gift of time and strength, and especially in his journeys for the visitation of congregations throughout Southeastern Russia as well as in the missionary journey to Central Asia, he gave his life for his Lord and Church and was really a martyr to the cause."[23]

The sorrowful news was made even more disturbing when Morehead learned from Elisabeth Meier that the Soviet government had condemned to death and executed Traugott Meier on April 19. The charge against him was the soon-to-be frequent refrain of the OGPU toward its enemies, real or imagined: "espionage for a capitalist state." Elisabeth received the report three weeks after Traugott's execution but withheld the true cause of death from her mother. Eugenie would be led to believe that Traugott had died of typhus. Elisabeth was convinced that knowledge of how Traugott had died would have driven her to the grave, and "now she is the only thing in the world I have left." Asking for prayer, Elisabeth feared that she and her mother "would not have the strength to bear these inhuman difficulties." She wrote to Morehead knowing that he was praying for them and that he would help them bear the tragedy.[24]

Traugott's sentence was a fantastic presumption, and Scheding was convinced that the bishop "only escaped the bullet by his natural death."[25] That Bishop Meier had often been protected, as had Bishop Malmgren, by his ties with the German embassy, leads to the conclusion that the changed political situation in Germany had generated nothing but ill will for the Lutheran Church hierarchy. When Adolf Hitler came to power as chancellor in 1933, and then further solidified that power through the Enabling Act, the Soviet Union's relationship toward Germany changed dramatically. The alliance that the two countries had formed to evade the Versailles Treaty restrictions on rearmament back in the 1920s had cemented relationships, giving the German embassy freedom to place the bishops under their protective care. But that protection had already been crumbling, and Traugott's death and the increased surveillance of Bishop Meier's letters probably reflected this new reality.[26]

Elisabeth was thankful to God that the news about Traugott was not given to her father before he died. Convinced that their "future was black," she began to plan their escape from the Soviet Union. Elisabeth thought that they might immigrate to their relatives in Riga or Germany, where a professor of Teutonic languages would have no trouble finding work. But to acquire a passport for foreign travel was pricy, a fee of five hundred rubles in gold! She was also concerned about a pension for her mother, for which Bishop Malmgren had promised to intercede. Fully aware of how the Soviets thought and operated, she figured it doubtful that she would retain her position as a professor after her brother's execution. The reality was that she would now be labeled by relation an "enemy of the people." She begged Morehead to offer them words of comfort, for which he was renowned. Elisabeth valued his advice, especially concerning the next steps that they should take. She even sent him the report of her father's last hours in the words of Sts. Peter and Paul's longtime Sunday school teacher, the sister of the bishop, Tilly Meier.[27]

The bishop's health had been failing since the previous summer, six years after his heart attack. For the last three years his personal secretary had eased his work burden, which he still tried to fulfill despite his fragile health. The first of several heart attacks, though, struck him on March 9. However, he did manage to sit up at a table and enjoy the Easter festival with his family on April 1. The second heart attack hit him on April 7, but he managed to get back up again and enjoy the first warm spring days, even sitting on the bench in the garden on the day before his death. Tilly found special meaning in the last family devotion he had led almost a week before his death. The text that he expounded on, John 16:22, was slated for Jubilate Sunday: "So also you have sorrow now, but I will see you again, and your hearts will rejoice." Bishop Meier was not one given to expressing his emotions, his behavior often characterized by an old traditional German stoicism. But this time, perhaps moved by this text and sensing the end was near, he gave them a glimpse into his inner feelings.

At 2:30 a.m. on April 28, the last heart attack brought about his death a half hour later, his wife at his bedside. His last work, a sermon on the text "Comfort, comfort my people," lay on his desk. Bishop Malmgren immediately boarded a train in Leningrad so that he could be there for Meier's funeral. Despite initial misgivings, these two giants of the Evangelical Lutheran Church in Russia had truly come to respect each other. Tilly treasured a comment Malmgren had made at the time of Meier's first heart attack in 1927: "Any day in the life of your brother is a very special gift of God." The almost seventy-four-year-old Malmgren arrived in time later that afternoon to lead a short prayer service at Meier's home after he was placed in the coffin. Tilly fondly remembered the comforting words that Malmgren shared with Pastor Streck and the grief-stricken family: "See, the Shepherd of Israel neither slumbers nor sleeps." These were words that parents often spoke over their children as they climbed into bed for the night. But so often in life, the parents couldn't always protect their children. Continuing with his thoughts, Malmgren said:

And our dear departed, with whom we will no longer walk and with whom we must let go, we give them over to the Shepherd of Israel—the

Shepherd of Israel who preserves the soul. The outward appearance is unimportant in contrast to the life of the soul. The evil before which the Shepherd of Israel preserves us—it's the stain, the sin that clings to all of us. He preserves us in our going out and coming in, until the time when God Himself greets us on the threshold of eternity.[28]

Tilly thought it was almost as if Malmgren was holding "a quiet, holy dialogue" with her brother.

As the coffin was brought to Sts. Peter and Paul that Saturday evening, many of the parishioners came to pay their respects. The following day, a Sunday, was a normal workday for many. Nevertheless, there was a large gathering of the faithful who came to a rare morning service with the funeral following at 1 p.m. The coffin was opened so that the parishioners and family could take their final leave from the bishop before the service. As the people bid an emotional farewell, the choir sang "Homeland, Homeland, Oh, How Lovely You Are!" (Heimatland, Heimatland, o wie schön bist du!"). Bishop Malmgren approached the pulpit and preached on the verse, "Be faithful unto death." Remembering the old Baltic homeland of Meier, from which he also descended, Malmgren looked back fondly on the long service that Meier had given to his Lord and the Lutheran Church. Pastor Alexander Streck followed him with a homily on the theme from the Epistle to the Hebrews, "Remember your teachers." The funeral service concluded, the participants took the long journey from the center of the city to the old Lutheran cemetery located in the northeast of Moscow. There all the pastors—Malmgren, Streck, and Woldemar Rüger of St. Michaels-Moscow—sprinkled bits of earth over the coffin.[29] The Lutheran Church was now forced to move on without this tireless defender of the faith.

THE TRIBUTES TO Meier continued to pour in as Morehead added his thoughts in a memorial article in honor of his friend and colleague during these turbulent years. Morehead recalled their years together during the famine, the first Lutheran Synod in Russian history, the founding of the seminary, in all of which Meier played a vital role.[30] But who would now take his place? So many of the promising young pastors had been sent to the Gulag: Kurt Muss, Helmut Hansen, and Arthur Kluck. The venerable senior pastors like Ferdinand Hörschelmann Sr. were no longer among the living. Bishop Malmgren was the only one who had the experience and trust of most of the Church, the Leningrad supporters of Paul Reichert notwithstanding.

Morehead was especially concerned about Malmgren's strong sense of duty. He feared that the last remaining bishop would take on too many responsibilities for his age, given that he remained the rector of the seminary, too. How could he add the burden of Bishop Meier's responsibilities as president of the High Church Council? Would a synod be needed in order to choose a new bishop? Despite his concerns, Morehead didn't know the other members of the High Church Council, so he temporarily sent the information about support for the pastors and the Church to Malmgren.[31] Others in the Church would soon come to the same conclusion. Who else could lead the Church but Bishop Arthur Malmgren?

According to Article 56 of the Church Constitution, in case of the death of the president of the High Church Council, the clerical member would take over the duties of the presidency until the next General Synod of the Church. Being the only clerical member on the council, that meant Bishop Malmgren would now become acting president. Furthermore, he could be expected to perform this duty for some time, as the Church had not held a General Synod since 1928 due to government intransigence. Adding to the complicated situation for Malmgren, only one district president was left in the Lutheran Church since the remainder had been arrested and banished. But that last district president still remaining free, sixty-two-year-old Woldemar Jurgens of the North Caucasus, would be arrested in a few years as well.[32] He was the father of Ralph Jurgens, who had been one of the last students ordained by Bishop Meier in 1933.[33] Ralph, too, would be arrested along with his father in 1936.[34]

Of the older pastors who had served in the time of the czars, only ten were left in office and they were widely scattered throughout the country so as to preclude anyone's participation in the High Church Council in Moscow. Malmgren himself sounded physically and emotionally tired. "How long I myself may yet be able to stick to the work is problematical. In the struggles and worries of the past 20 years I have become a lonely man, who in these days will complete his 74th year. Up to now God has kept me well in body and spirit, but in view of the daily increasing need and apparently hopeless future of the Lutheran Church in Russia, I have become weary and long for the time that God takes me to His rest."[35] However, despite his weariness the bishop wasn't through yet. Malmgren still planned on graduating seven students of the seminary in the fall. He did, however, despair of taking on other students for whom he could not find places of service and who he felt would simply be setting themselves forward as candidates for martyrdom. Malmgren's words were not an exaggeration. He admitted that there now existed no Lutheran congregation in the "entire Northwest territory of European Russia": Archangel, Olonyets, Vologda, Yaroslavl, Nizhniy Novgorod, Vyatka, Kazan, Simbirsk, Tula, Smolensk, Minsk, Orel and Kursk had no public worship life whatsoever. In the Crimea, where there had been seven pastors, only Johannes Seidlitz remained in Theodosia. The German and Estonian congregations of Ferdinand Hörschelmann's day had been closed. In Siberia, only Woldemar Reichwald continued serving in distant Vladivostok.

Despite the fact that hundreds of thousands of German, Finnish, Latvian, and Estonian Lutherans remained in Siberia, they couldn't provide housing or financial support for any pastor. Where could Malmgren send the graduating students? At the very least, though, he set Morehead's mind at ease about Eugenie Meier. After the death of the bishop, the Gustav-Adolf-Verein had agreed to give her a pension.[36] When Morehead replied in late August, he urged Malmgren to refrain from overwork, although he understood why the Church would place its trust in an experienced leader like him. He prayed that God would renew his strength "like the eagles" so that he could continue with his important service to the Church.[37]

22

"A SMALL CROWD ARMED WITH COURAGE"

More Arrests and the Closing of the Seminary in 1934

WHILE THE CHURCH was busy contemplating how it would function after the death of Bishop Meier, the toll of persecution on the families of pastors showed no signs of abating. On June 30, Arthur Kluck's wife, Bertha, wrote an appeal to John Morehead in rather clear English. She explained that after her husband's arrest and deportation, all of their property had been confiscated. She and the three children fled to Astrakhan where her father, Rev. Liborius Behning, a friend of Morehead's from the days of the famine, had lived after his release from prison until his death in March 1933. Now her mother and children were back with her in Saratov, where she taught music. She filled Morehead in on the details of Arthur's life since his arrest in 1929. From 1930, he had been held under harsh conditions in a prison cell in Samara. Later in 1931, he was transferred to a hard labor camp in the far north. Having been an academic for most of his life, physical labor had proven to be quite difficult. In 1932 he was moved yet again, this time to exile in a Siberian village where there was no work for him. At the age of forty-two, his one desire was to return to pastoral work even if it might be for only a short time. Bertha, however, was convinced that it was becoming virtually impossible to serve as a pastor in the Lutheran Church in Stalin's Soviet Union. Therefore, like so many others, she had petitioned the government in 1932 for her family to take up German citizenship. Her request refused, she was now hoping that Morehead might be able to help the family immigrate to Germany or America.[1]

As Morehead continued gathering information on the persecution of the Church from various sources, he realized that Malmgren's fears of the Church's impending demise were well founded. Some in the Swedish and Western European press were reporting that the Lutheran Church was completely destroyed. He asked Malmgren for accurate reports in order to refute these claims so that Americans and Western Europeans would still consider the urgent need to support the Church. Being an optimistic American Christian, Morehead wondered whether the LWC could cooperate with the Church in supporting young pastors who could be placed in strategic vacancies. Morehead's idea was that the local congregation could provide what support it could while the LWC temporarily assisted a pastor and his family so they could live and serve in the USSR.[2]

Malmgren appreciated his friend's determination to do whatever lay within his power to strengthen the Church, for the situation was grave. He confessed that there were many congregations in the Volga and Ukraine who desperately wanted a pastor but they could not provide housing. If any parishioners took the pastor and his family under their roof, they would be accused of harboring a counterrevolutionary. Added to this accusation, a heavy tax would be levied on them. So even if they were willing to house the pastor, the parishioners could ultimately suffer the indignity of being kicked out of their own home. These threats were the primary reason for not being able to place seminary graduates and a major reason why church life was dying. In the past year, the Crimea had seen no Lutheran worship services. Malmgren had sent one graduate there to scout out the situation and see if there was even a modest room in a large village that he could rent. The young man returned, as Malmgren said, "like the dove that Noah sent out of the ark, but he found no place to rest his foot."

In answer to a query from Morehead about a treasury fund that the Evangelical Lutheran Church had used before the revolution, Malmgren assured him that the millions that the Church had possessed had been confiscated long ago. Since the Law Separating Church and State in 1918, the Church possessed no rights as a juridical person. Due to its precarious legal situation, the Church could not develop a treasury fund again as long as the Soviets were in power. As concerned the reports in the Swedish and Western European press, Malmgren believed it was not so much exaggeration that was at fault as it was confusion. The newspaper reports claimed that forty Lutheran pastors had been arrested, but Malmgren said the forty were actually Russian Orthodox priests. Since January and February, a renewed wave of persecution had sprung up again in the land. Arrests and martyrdom were carried out against pastors and laity in all the denominations still existing in the Soviet Union.

AT THE MOMENT, the Russian Orthodox Church was suffering more grievously than other denominations.[3] After the arrest of those forty priests earlier in the year, forty additional priests were arrested in Leningrad on the church festival of Pokrovsky (meaning "patron") on October 14.[4] The Lutherans, too, had been affected earlier in the year when the OGPU carried out its latest raid. Julius Zahlit, the Latvian pastor at Christ the Savior Lutheran Church in Leningrad, had been arrested on January 20.[5] Pastor Eugen Bachmann, Malmgren's replacement at St. Anne's and sometime teacher at the seminary, had been arrested January 24. He was accused of espionage, his correspondence with Germany being cited as evidence against him.

Bachmann's case is an example of how the Soviets twisted innocuous meetings in church life to imply something sinister. As the pastor at a Lutheran church in Leningrad that German citizens attended, it was inevitable that Bachmann would interact with them. Richard Asche, a German citizen and engineer who was a relative of parishioner Maria Waldman, had been invited to Bachmann's apartment as a guest in the summer of 1931 or 1932. The Bachmanns had thrown a party for Waldman in honor of her impending departure to the south of Russia. The party lasted until midnight and included musical entertainment in which Asche apparently participated. Just before Christmas in 1933, Bachmann's wife heard that Asche wanted to play the violin for the Christmas services. Bachmann knew that such close contact with a German citizen, so shortly after Hitler had been elevated to power in Germany, would create misunderstandings with the Soviet government. But given the choir's poor preparation for the Christmas services, Bachmann agreed. At one of the choir practices, Asche commented that he had sent to Germany a letter talking about the prices of goods in Soviet stores. More than likely it was just his curiosity getting the better of him, but when German Vice Consul Velk discovered what Asche had written, he was displeased. After the New Year's Eve service, Bachmann heard from his wife that Asche had been arrested.[6]

That wasn't all. As a member of the board for the German almshouse located in the Summer Gardens in central Leningrad, Bachmann met on December 17 with fellow board members Bishop Malmgren, Paul Reichert, Woldemar Wagner, and a member of St. Anne's *dvatsatka*, Vladimir Brandt. German Consul Richard Sommer and Vice Consul Velk also attended. Supposedly, the German embassy officials asked for confirmation of the Aryan origins of some of the parishioners (opinions vary of the accuracy of this accusation, although it is possible). But more damning for Bachmann was that he handed over to the German consulate lists of needy parishioners and their relatives in the south so that they could receive aid from Germany. Unfortunately for

Bachmann, facilitating aid for Soviet citizens from abroad was no longer perceived in humanitarian terms as it was back in the days of the ARA.[7]

Bachmann was also accused of a "veiled form" of anti-Soviet propaganda in his sermons, implying that spies must have infiltrated the worship services and were writing down every word that he preached. Since Bachmann eventually appealed for rehabilitation from Nikita Khruschev on April 5, 1960, the Federal Security Bureau archives contain a description in his own words of the truth surrounding these accusations:

> In June 1934 an abstract of the protocol of the meeting of the colleagues of the OGPU was read to me. ... There was no trial because during the interrogation I only saw the interrogator. They accused me of allegedly, in veiled form, agitating against Soviet power in my sermons. But the formulaic word "veiled" speaks to the fact that the interrogator didn't find any "facts" confirming such an accusation. It was even shown to me how in one sermon I, allegedly, under the phrase "Kingdom of God," implied the "Kingdom of Hitler!" This is plainly a distortion of the truth and an arbitrary interpretation of my words and expressions!

Bachmann went on to make it clear that he had no sympathy for Hitler, who had already confined thousands to concentration camps. (Bachmann mentions by name Dietrich Bonhoeffer and other well-known pastors like Martin Niemöller and Heinrich Grüber.) Calling the interrogator's charge a "dirty accusation in the most vague form," Bachmann denied that he created in his sermons "favorable soil for espionage among the ethnic German population of Leningrad." He concluded, "I preached the Word of God and never touched on questions of politics in my sermons. Yes, and the interrogator could not find one fact in confirmation of this accusation! Because it is absolutely unfounded!"[8]

JULIUS ZAHLIT HAD likewise been a thorn in the side of the OGPU for effectively carrying out his ministry among ethnic Latvians in Russia. In 1929, when Stalin's campaign to close churches had gathered steam, there was a proposal by Latvian Communists to close Christ the Savior Lutheran Church in Leningrad. Zahlit succeeded in scuttling the plan.[9] Five years later, the OGPU would not allow mere signatures on a piece of paper to thwart its will. In fact, their ire was raised against Zahlit because he would not accept that Christ the Savior Lutheran had been closed by the local government—again—in 1933. As before, Zahlit made the journey to Moscow and met with the president of the Soviet Union, Mikhail Kalinin. Zahlit appealed to the president to allow the church to remain open, and Kalinin rescinded the ruling of the Leningrad Regional Communist Party, much to its dismay. When he was arrested in 1934, the agent informed him that because he went to Kalinin with his complaint, they would prevent him from ever seeing Moscow or Leningrad again and would disappear him without a trace. "We're fighting to close the church and for the complete liquidation of religion, and you are getting in our way!"[10]

Zahlit's interrogations began on January 24. The pastor must have been treated poorly under confinement, because he signed the OGPU document claiming that:

- Beginning in 1923 he was drinking regularly to the point of intoxication with members of his *dvatsatka*, either at his apartment or at the bar in the Znamenskaya Hotel.

- He engaged in speculation using money from the church treasury.

- He engaged in sexual relations with one (Anna, a doctor) of the late Pastor Mikhail Lapping's two daughters while drinking often with both of them.

The accusation of monetary speculation was explained by the OGPU this way: Zahlit supposedly had parishioners pay in food products for weddings and confirmations, which were then traded for money on the market. More damaging to him, the OGPU accused Zahlit of Latvian espionage since he had visited his elderly parents in 1927.[11]

From the witness of Latvian General Consul Eduard Krasts, there was little doubt that Zahlit and his parishioners' actions to save their church in 1929 had stuck in the craw of the Soviet government. As a result, Bishop Karlis Irbe in Latvia had feared sending monetary assistance to the congregation, concerned that it would harm Zahlit and the Latvian Lutherans in the eyes of the Soviet state. Yet Zahlit urged him to continue gathering religious literature as long as the Latvian Lutheran Church in Russia remained open, and since Krasts was connected to the Latvian publishing house Brekis, he attempted to do so.[12] But now on January 20 not only was Zahlit taken from his congregation, the organist and head of the youth choir, Robert Lapping, was arrested, too. Gathering with the faithful believers on January 21 and learning from Zahlit's wife, Bertha Zupan, about the pastor's arrest, a furious Anna Lapping took a hymnbook and chose hymn 580. The one-hundred-person choir must have sung these lyrics with great emotion:

> A small crowd armed with courage
> Should not be intimidated by the anger of its foes
> They seek the means to ruin you
> But do not fear their threats
> God will save us from the danger
> They won't be able to rampage for long
> For soon they will utterly perish
> And God will receive the honor and glory.[13]

But the OGPU did not fear a God they did not know, and soon other arrests followed, including Anna and Marta Lapping and Bertha Zupan. On February 7, the former secretary for the Latvian Church Council of the Novgorod region, Ivan Kandel, was added to the list of the arrested because he gathered a monetary offering for "martyrs of the Faith." The OGPU wanted to strike fear into anyone who would dare stand against the power of the government, especially if that person took any action to advocate for the rights of believers. Zahlit was sentenced to ten years, which was harsh even by the standards of the mid-1930s. Anna Lapping was sent to a labor camp, along with the pastor's wife, for three years.[14] By God's grace, though, Zahlit survived and was released into exile in 1945. Working as an accountant in exile in the Komi Republic, he wrote twice to Kliment Voroshilov, the chairman of the Presidium of the Supreme Soviet. Denying any guilt to the last, on March 27, 1956, Zahlit appealed to Voroshilov for his freedom. He was soon rehabilitated; the KGB recorded him as participating in the blessing of a restored church in the colony of Korpovas, Novgorod region, in 1957.[15] Zahlit would then manage to immigrate to Latvia and spend the remainder of his life there.[16]

AFTER BEING HELD for five months with no legal process, on June 1 Bachmann received his sentence—five years in a Gulag labor camp. The testimony in which he signed the accusations made against him includes the reason why he did so, which is rare. "Due to being held in an isolation chamber for months and in a continual state of hunger, my will was weakened, and I was prepared to sign anything in order to quickly end the interrogation." The OGPU included the additional statement that Bachmann admitted "no physical actions were taken against him during the interrogations." However, holding him incommunicado and in a condition of perpetual hunger could certainly qualify as a form of torture, even if he wasn't physically attacked. Richard Asche was simply deported from the Soviet Union.[17]

Bachmann's imprisonment included the strenuous forestry work that felled many an inmate in a Gulag labor camp. There he encountered his old seminary classmate, Konstantin Rusch, who had been in this camp for several years. Rusch interceded with his boss who, when he found that Bachmann knew Latin, moved him into the pharmacy. That work may very well have saved Bachmann's life, though he was now lost to the Lutheran Church.[18] In Malmgren's estimation, actions like these were evidence that the Church was in a catastrophic situation, as the Soviets picked off his pastors one by one.[19]

As the year drew to a close, on December 2 Pastor Emil Pfeiffer was arrested while on his way to conduct a church service at Saratov's St. Mary's Lutheran Church. His daughter, Edith, remembered that the house was turned upside down as the NKVD (the new name for the OGPU as of July 1934) searched for incriminating evidence of any kind. Word of his arrest went through the city like wildfire because those adults who had the day off work had gone to the church and realized that something had happened to their pastor. Arrests were taking place in the city all the time now, as many of Edith's friends had seen their parents taken into custody, too. In fact, her uncle, Pastor Arthur Pfeiffer, was arrested on the same day as he went to conduct a church service in the Volga River village of Yagodnaya Polyana. Emil Pfeiffer would be kept in prison until June 1935, after which he was exiled to Almaty (Kazakhstan) for five years. His daughter Gretchen was allowed to travel with him to Kazakhstan, and he soon found work in a bacteriology institute where he taught German and English. Edith would never see him again.[20]

AS HE HAD promised before the year ended, Malmgren wrote a long, detailed letter to Morehead about the situation in his country. He had delayed the letter because he had hoped to immigrate to Germany and thus speak to Morehead in person. But since the Soviet government refused to allow him to leave, he now decided to make as clear a statement as he could about the state of the Lutheran Church. "Speaking very plainly... the Lutheran Church of Russia, as a church, is very close to complete collapse." Malmgren went on to give a succinct description of the theology of the cross and how it must have appeared in a church under severe persecution: "Even an organized church has no guarantee of perpetual existence here on earth but is subject to the same law of change and decay which governs nature and history." There was a time when both bishops seemed to think that the Lutheran Church would persevere—persecuted, yes, but still continuing its existence. Morehead himself seemed to believe they just had to wait it out, doing whatever they could to keep the Church alive until a political change took place in the country.

Malmgren was now admitting that there would be no change. The Soviet Union was only becoming stronger and bolder under Stalin. Children were growing up without the opportunity to hear the gospel. Nevertheless, Malmgren assured Morehead, "The Gospel will remain, of course; it will not perish, even the gates of hell shall not prevail against it. But the organized Lutheran Church will not continue much longer; the hour of death is nigh at hand. Let there be no illusion on this point." Malmgren went on to relate the history of the Church after the Bolshevik Revolution, when there had been some hope that they might be able to carve out a form of existence within the Soviet Union. But as he related it to Morehead, "And then came the year of 1929—the crisis." Malmgren especially remembered the Christmas attack on the seminary and the Hansen-Muss case. Five professors and four students had been arrested and eventually exiled. Several professors resigned out of fear, and the number of prospective students applying to the seminary began its steady decline. It could not be denied that 1929 was a turning point in the life of the Lutheran Church, and for that matter, all Christian churches.

Malmgren had been wary about what he wrote in letters in the past, but he seemed beyond caring now. The truth had to be told to Morehead, who had expended so much blood and sweat for the Lutherans of Russia. Continuing his litany of woes, Malmgren said that after that first wave of repression in 1929, they didn't give up because they thought the persecution might abate. The Lutheran Church had never acted in a hostile manner toward the Bolsheviks, as W. L. Scheding had tried to persuade his contacts in the Kremlin in the 1920s. Yet despite their obedience to the governing authorities, the seminary students had been forced to move to Martyschkino in 1930, well beyond the borders of Leningrad. Still, the seminary survived and the students returned to Leningrad after Malmgren had found suitable housing.

But then the last of the teachers were arrested and exiled, leaving only Malmgren. Many of his students were arrested, too, or called up for military duty. Despite all this, Malmgren reiterated to Morehead that he hadn't given up. But the government held all the cards, and they could change the rules on a whim. Malmgren simply could not place any of the seven fall graduates in parishes because no one could find a place for them to serve or to provide for their physical needs. In total, fifty-seven students had completed their education since 1925 and had been ordained. But of those fifty-seven, only sixteen remained in office by the end of 1934. There were also seven more students available, the recent graduates, who couldn't find work in a parish.

Malmgren felt compelled to end this letter of his reflections with thanks to Morehead. "I must not conclude this letter—so replete with bitter reflections—without once more expressing to you my sincere gratitude for all the unwavering faithfulness which you have shown us during the past nine and one-half years, and for the love offerings which you have so unceasingly transmitted to us. May our Father in heaven bless you, my highly respected brother in Christ, and all the other members of the Executive Committee [of the LWC] and all the dear friends who have contributed toward the support of our Leningrad seminary."[21]

If Malmgren's letter was not enough indication that the seminary would no longer be in operation, then one other piece of information would have made it abundantly clear to Morehead. When former Leningrad Seminary student Johannes Lel attended a synod of the reconstituted Evangelical Lutheran Church of Russia in 1998, he sat next to an older gentleman who told him he had put in an application for the seminary—in 1934! There were not enough students for a new class, but just because this man had publicly announced his intention to enter the seminary and his name appeared on a list of prospective students, he was arrested and sent to prison for a few years—all because he intended to study theology! No, there was no longer any doubt that the doors were firmly shut on the seminary.[22]

THE PULSE OF THE CHURCH
GROWS WEAKER

The Kirov Terror and the Most Difficult Year Since 1929

IN EARLY 1935, John Morehead wrote an article introducing Bishop Malmgren to the American and European Lutheran public, desiring to share with them the facts surrounding the life of this extraordinary churchman. Ironically, Malmgren's letter of December 20 was on his desk, so he knew that Malmgren was probably preparing his exit from the Soviet Union. Still, Morehead expressed his profound gratitude to the bishop, lauding him for his work and expressing his "profound sympathy" for all that this good man of faith had endured for the cause of the gospel and the Evangelical Lutheran Church. Despite the trials of the moment, Morehead sought to assure Malmgren that their efforts had not been in vain. There had been many young students who had been educated and, despite threats to their person, would still be strong witnesses for Christ in their lives, come what may. Both men had come to a profound understanding of the theology of the cross, Morehead agreeing with Malmgren that God had promised that the gates of hell would not prevail against the church. But the promise was that the church as a whole would last into perpetuity, not necessarily individual churches.

Still, Morehead felt compelled to redouble his efforts for the persecuted pastors and parishioners, because news soon reached him through the German general consul in New York, Dr. Borchers, that death sentences had been given to a pastor, Wilhelm Lohrer (a 1928 seminary graduate) and three parishioners (Messrs. Dreier, Hoffman, and Wolter) of the Lutheran Church in Omsk, Siberia. Borchers had received this message in code from Bishop Marahrens in Germany through the German Foreign Office. Marahrens, apparently wary of publicly petitioning for German Lutherans of Russia inside a country ruled by Hitler, asked Morehead instead to intercede with Soviet Foreign Minister Maxim Litvinov.[1] Morehead dashed off a cablegram to Litvinov, copying the Russian ambassador to America, Alexander Trojanovsky: "As President of the Lutheran World Conference, I appeal to Your Excellency on ground you [sic] well known statements in Geneva to intercede in behalf of Lutheran pastor and his three church members sentenced to death in Omsk. Stop. Execution of innocent victims would cause worldwide resentment, their release, profound appreciation. Stop. During famine nineteen twenty-two was member of the ARA Moscow. John A. Morehead."[2]

The ability of the German embassy to intervene for Lutherans in Russia had indeed grown weaker since Hitler's coming to power. A Soviet diplomat to Germany, Lev Khinchuk, had alerted Malmgren to that reality one year before when the bishop had asked Khinchuk to help expedite his son-in-law's return to Leningrad from exile. Now the counselor of the Legation in the German embassy in Moscow, Gustav Hilger, apprised American charge d'affaires John Wiley as to the serious repression of the Lutherans in Russia. In Wiley's February 8 letter to US Secretary of State Cordell Hull, he quoted Hilger as saying that the past two months had been the most hostile toward the Lutheran Church since the early revolutionary period. While there had been sixty-six Lutheran pastors in the Soviet Union as of December 1, 1934, now there were only twenty-four left at liberty. Acknowledging the role of the German embassy in the past as informal "protector" of the Lutheran Church, Hilger said that the Commissariat for Foreign Affairs no longer accepted interventions for Lutherans as they had previously. As a result, the second secretary of the embassy, a Mr. Steltzer, was being transferred from Moscow. His role had been that of cultural attaché, but due to the cessation of cultural cooperation between the Soviet and German governments, this role was no longer necessary. Included in his functions had been "protection of religion."[3]

Morehead also fired off a telegram to US Ambassador William Bullitt, who was ill and currently recuperating in the States. He pleaded with Bullitt for his intervention in this case since the accused were only guilty of practicing their Christian faith.[4] Ambassador Bullitt had been a strong advocate for normalizing relations with the Soviet Union, so at first it might seem that such a request would fall on deaf ears. But Bullitt was becoming increasingly disillusioned with Soviet intransigence on the matter of debt repayment, and that wasn't his only concern.[5] In fact, within a few months, Bullitt would write to President Roosevelt about a terror that was enveloping Moscow to the extent that Russians of all stations were refusing to have any contact with foreigners.

THE TERROR HAD begun in December 1934 after the murder of Leningrad Communist party boss Sergey Kirov.[6] Although the events in Omsk were not precipitated directly by Kirov's murder, in Leningrad and throughout the country a purge was beginning to take effect in party circles and beyond. Morehead received news in March that 1,074 persons of the bourgeois class in Leningrad had been deported by the NKVD to central Asia in connection with the Kirov murder. Two hundred of the deported were of German heritage, very likely Lutheran, and had been long-time residents of Leningrad. The arrested encompassed a wide variety of people, including: (1) those who were part of the old ruling classes in czarist times; (2) those who had ethnic ties to foreign countries, especially Poland or Germany; (3) those who had received help through the

German charitable organization Brüder in Not; and (4) those Communists tied to the former opposition leaders Trotsky, Zinoviev, and Kamenev.[7] In fact, St. Anne's pastor Samuel Wohl admitted that many in his congregation were exiled, while the *dvatsatka* was practically decimated by the arrests.[8] Gustav Hilger had acknowledged as much to the American embassy in Moscow in his concern for the fate of Lutherans in the USSR.[9]

The Kirov Terror had been precipitated by the party boss's murder on December 1, 1934, at 4:30 p.m. in the hallway outside his office. Kirov's office was located in the fashionable building along the Neva River in Leningrad known as Smolny, a former educational institute for young women. All signs pointed to a lone gunman, a former Smolny office worker by the name of Leonid Nikolaev. There were a variety of motives offered for the crime, but the fact that Nikolaev had lost his job and was nearly expelled from the Communist Party were said to have made him resentful of the party hierarchy. Kirov's position as the party leader in Leningrad would have made him a natural target for Nikolaev.[10] It is after this point, though, that the reasons behind this crime become murkier. Historians have long debated whether Stalin engineered the murder, but the latest research culled from the Soviet archives by historian Matthew Lenoe seems to point in the direction of Nikolaev as a lone wolf.

Whether Nikolaev acted alone, though, historians are generally in agreement that Stalin decided to use the Kirov murder to create a martyr to the Communist cause. He launched a witch-hunt against his enemies, real or imagined. The more realistic enemies, although they were almost certainly not guilty of this murder, were the sidelined, out-of-favor Old Bolsheviks Grigory Zinoviev and Lev Kamenev. Stalin purged many party members and allies of these two (as well as allies of Trotsky) and claimed that they had been in league with foreign enemies. Not content to attack only his enemies in the party, Stalin expanded the scope to include those with suspicious ties to foreigners like Finns, Germans, and those of Baltic ancestry.[11] German Lutherans in Russia had often appealed to their fellow Lutherans in Germany for aid, and such actions now brought them under government suspicion.

IN FEBRUARY AND MARCH 1935, the NKVD conducted massive raids to arrest Leningrad residents on their list of suspected traitors. The "former people" (czarist aristocrats, merchants, and police officers) were prominent among the more than 11,000 on the list, but there were also 585 priests not serving in active churches. Mass expulsions of Orthodox clergy from Leningrad began in March, and by June Leningrad officials started to close Orthodox parishes. It is not likely that everyone on this list was Orthodox, since we know that attacks against the Lutheran Church intensified after Kirov's murder. Stalin approved the plan to conduct mass arrests in Leningrad, but told NKVD chief Genrikh Yagoda to spread them out over a few months in order to minimize the international outcry. Once the terror began, however, it would prove difficult to stop.[12]

Ethnic Germans with foreign connections were being arrested all over the country. Pastor Johannes Göhring, a 1929 Leningrad seminary graduate, was arrested in Kiev and originally sentenced to be shot, but the sentence was eventually reduced to ten years of imprisonment. He would eventually die of hunger in the Gulag labor camps.[13] A German female parishioner who had taken over services in Kiev, conducting a *Lesegottesdienst* ("reading divine service") in the absence of the pastor, was subsequently arrested. In Soviet Georgia, the ethnic German wine growers also had their wine fields collectivized, including the wine growers' cooperative known as "Concordia." The Lutheran congregation in Helenendorf, where former seminary professor Otto Wentzel served as pastor, was levied the outrageous tax of 30,000 rubles. The congregation couldn't pay the tax, thus forcing its closure. Pastor Wentzel still gathered his parishioners for worship in the local cemetery even though he and the three women remaining on his church council were publicly defamed in the basest manner imaginable in the Communist press. The pressure had already begun in December 1934 when Wentzel's former student, Emil Hanefeld, the son-in-law of Bishop Malmgren, was arrested in Tbilisi.[14]

That was not the only bad news in Georgia. Pastor Wilhelm Zimmer, a 1932 graduate of the Leningrad seminary and pastor in Alexeevka (modern-day Azerbaijan), was arrested in Baku on January 8, 1935, and thereafter exiled for five years. Five additional years would soon be added to his sentence.[15] In the German colonies located in Azerbaijan, seventy ethnic German families, comprising about three hundred parishioners in the villages of Eigenfeld, Gruenfeld, Alexevka, Annenfeld, Georgsfeld, and even Georgia's Helenendorf, were deported to the north of Russia in April 1935. No one knew the final destination of their fellow believers. The NKVD showed no regard for human weakness, even forcing women who had just given birth to make the journey.

The Lutheran Church in Tbilisi had already been reeling since it lost its sixty-three-year-old pastor, Richard Mayer, to martyrdom in 1933. Now the Soviets took what had remained: a hospital, a kindergarten, and an aid association. The worst insult was throwing twenty-eight ethnic Germans over the age of sixty-five out of a home for invalids. Because of these actions, the Lutheran heritage was rapidly disappearing from the Caucasus region.[16]

Morehead sought to inform Dr. C. C. Hein, president of the American Lutheran Church, about this persecution by sharing the contents of Bishop Malmgren's December 20 letter from the previous year. Unfortunately, he soon had additional evidence. Eugenie Meier shared with Morehead that her daughter, Dr. Elisabeth Meier, had now also been arrested. Morehead was all too aware of how powerless the Americans were in being able to secure her freedom, but he knew that Eugenie expected them to make inquiries. Of course, he would have done nothing less for the Meiers after all they had done for him when he traveled in Russia and after all they had suffered.[17]

Elisabeth was accused of heading a conspiracy of philologists and academicians through her contacts at the German embassy in Moscow. Due to her position as a professor at the Moscow Institute of New Languages (MIFL), she served as the main editor of the first edition of the *Large German-Russian Dictionary*. Moreover, her fellow academics at GAKHN (Government Academy of Arts and Sciences) often came to her apartment at the church on Starosadsky Lane to work on the project. Unfortunately for Elisabeth, the timing of the Kirov assassination played right into the hands of the NKVD, because they now "discovered" evidence that many of these academicians were involved in espionage. In all, 141 people were arrested in this case, and Elisabeth fit the profile of one that they could accuse of organizing espionage due to her associations.[18] First, her late father was a bishop of the Evangelical Lutheran Church of Russia whose congregation in Moscow was well-known as the "German embassy church." Second, her brothers had been considered enemies of the people, one escaping to Romania with a Soviet aircraft and her younger brother, Traugott, having been executed the previous year as an enemy of the people. Third, she had studied at Leipzig University in Germany. It was all too convenient for the NKVD, who was searching for enemies, and she fit their parameters precisely. One of her former students at Moscow State University, Nina Monich, had followed Meier to MIFL and had also been interrogated in Lubyanka. Monich, who died in 1994, confirmed many years later that she and others were called in and/or arrested because of their ties to the Meier family.[19]

Regarding the arrest of the philologists, it is not as if the secret police in the USSR had no experience in such matters. Back in 1930, the OGPU had acted in similar fashion when pastors Kurt Muss and Helmut Hansen were tied to the Academic Affair, supposedly headed up by famed ethnographer Alfred Mervart. This time the German ties of Elisabeth Meier proved irresistible because of Hitler's rise in Nazi Germany. She was also tied to a noted Slavic expert in Germany, Max Fasmer, to whom she had sent an etymological dictionary. This action, of course, was interpreted as Meier spying for Germany. The arrests began on the night of February 2/3, and Elisabeth was among the first to be taken. A series of arrests continued into March and May, including the academics from GAKHN, professors of German at Moscow State University, professors at MIFL, employees of the Library of Foreign Literature, the publishing house Academia, and German experts at the publishing house Soviet Encyclopedia. The last experts were accused of importing fascist terms into the new dictionary that Meier had edited. And since the meticulous Meier naturally kept accounting records of who was working with her on the dictionary and what they were paid, the NKVD took names from the accounting ledger and arrested them.[20]

Elisabeth was convicted and sentenced to ten years on August 5 and sent out on August 28 to Camp Number 3-Morsplav in Kem, located on the White Sea and just south of the infamous Solovetsky Island camp. (This was the same camp where Kurt Muss was held.) Even though the sentence was extreme, a few of her colleagues in this case were sentenced to death. Her aged mother, Eugenie, was punished for her daughter's fabricated crimes, being sent a hundred kilometers outside Moscow to the village of Kashire. Eugenie was sickly and no doubt exhausted from the events of the previous year, having lost her son and husband. And now she was all alone in a strange village with Elisabeth's banishment added to her woes.[21]

BY NOW, BISHOP MALMGREN was becoming weary of the continual drumbeat of arrests plaguing his pastors. From March through May, six pastors were arrested from Leningrad and its surrounding area. Among the six were: (1) Oktav Simon, a 1925 Bible course graduate who had replaced Eugen Bachmann at St. Anne's after he was arrested and sent to the Gulag; (2) Samuel Wohl, a 1934 seminary graduate; (3) Woldemar Assmus, an early 1930s graduate; (4) Alfred Prieb, a 1933 graduate; (5) Woldemar Wagner, a 1929 graduate and pastor of St. Catherine's who had helped teach at the seminary October 1933–May 1934.[22] The accusations leveled against the pastors concerned receiving material aid from foreign countries, in particular the funds that the

LWC and German Christian organizations (Gustav-Adolf-Verein, Martin Luther Bund) were sending to them. In the case of Alfred Prieb, he had come to the attention of the OGPU in 1931 when he wrote to his brother living in Leipzig, hoping to emigrate abroad. His subsequent application for emigration had been rejected by the Soviet government.[23]

However, the NKVD was not only interested in arresting pastors but was hoping to gather information about Bishop Malmgren's plans for the Church. They were observing Malmgren closely; Assmus was arrested on May 22, right after he visited the bishop. In his interrogation, Assmus admitted to the NKVD that Malmgren had been hoping to once again form a new class at the seminary. (Whether Malmgren had yet again changed his mind about closing the seminary is uncertain.) Although the government had not officially closed the seminary, it was not allowing students to sign up for courses.

St. Anne's pastor Oktav Simon was charged with passing along a letter to the German consulate from Malmgren, who had received it from the Mennonite preacher Heinrich Tews. The NKVD apparently majored in retroactive accusations, because the transfer of the letter occurred in 1930! Simon was arrested on May 17, 1935.[24] His interrogations began immediately. Simon was a forty-one-year-old native of Riga of Baltic German ancestry whose father had moved the family to Moscow where he held several jobs with organizations as an accountant until his death in 1919. Simon had studied at Yuriyev University in Dorpat, Estonia, from 1914–1918, but never completed requirements for his undergraduate degree. An ardent Christian, he had already been on the Cheka's radar due to his association with an evangelical Christian circle in Moscow led by the famed evangelist Vladimir Martsinovsky. In 1921, Martsinovksy was deported from the USSR and Simon, along with several others, were arrested and incarcerated for two weeks.

Undeterred by his imprisonment for the sake of the gospel, he went on to study with the Pfeiffer brothers at the Leningrad Bible School under Malmgren, graduating in 1924. He initially served as pastor in Strelna and assisted Kurt

Muss's old congregation in Leningrad after Muss's imprisonment.[25] Simon's interrogations focused on the reception of financial aid from foreign countries along with the aforementioned facilitation of information to the German consulate. Delving deeply into his past, the NKVD discovered that the ARA had provided food parcels to all of the Bible school students in Leningrad in the early 1920s. They now asked Simon to list all the students who had studied with him.

A good example of the manner in which the NKVD carried out interrogations can be ascertained from Simon's interrogation on June 25. The agent wondered, "Did you appeal to German fascists for aid?" Simon replied, "I only appealed to religious organizations" like the Martin Luther Bund. In the course of their investigation, they learned that Simon received aid via Torgsin and appealed for his parishioners' financial needs from a variety of sources, including Pastor Julius Fastena in Riga and the Red Cross.[26] Having accumulated this information, the NKVD now began to twist the evidence and present Simon as a willing accomplice with Malmgren in the service of German fascists. For example, it was noted that Simon gave Malmgren information about the German congregations in the countryside. But from what would have been something as innocuous as sharing information about the congregations' health, the NKVD spun the evidence in another direction. They claimed that Simon had given Malmgren information about German Lutheran parishes in order to receive aid from Torgsin. In other words, it was a financial transaction accompanied by the sinister undertones of espionage.

By June 29, the NKVD's relentless interrogations had worn Simon down. His NKVD photo shows an unshaven man with a tired and worn expression on his face. Simon is recorded as confessing to having received political directives of an "anti-Soviet spirit" from Bishop Malmgren. Admitting that Malmgren was a National Socialist by conviction, Simon now supposedly said that he had carried out these political directives among his parishioners and even during the divine service. The Gustav-Adolf-Verein was also said to have engaged in counterrevolutionary activity through the German consulate in the USSR. In his final interrogation on October 5 before being sent to a Gulag labor camp, though, Simon suddenly rejected all of the testimony that related to Malmgren's involvement in politics and the claims that he had been a willing collaborator. Simon could not deny, however, that he had received aid from abroad through Morehead and German sources. It was enough to convict him.[27]

St. Catherine's Woldemar Wagner, too, had been accused of extensive Germanic associations. He was arrested on March 19 while taking the train to his home in the suburbs of Leningrad in Pavlovsk. As pastor to many impoverished, elderly, and handicapped Russian Germans, he had compiled a list of twenty-four individuals in need of financial aid. Contacting Brüdershilfe and the Martin Luther Bund, Wagner secured the support for his needy parishioners. Wagner, though, also wrote articles for *Die Welt Post*, the American newspaper for Russian Germans, and probably apprised them of the situation in the USSR. Combining all these suspicious activities in the mind of the NKVD with the fact that he had worked extensively with the NLC and ARA back in the famine days was enough to bring charges against him of counterrevolutionary activities according to Statute 58. Wagner's family would not be able to see him during the half year (until September) he was kept under lock and key in the DPZ.[28]

Samuel Wohl was yet another pastor on the NKVD's list of the accused. A recent graduate of the seminary, the thirty-year-old Wohl had also been placed at St. Anne's in Leningrad and was serving there when he was arrested at Easter on April 16.[29] He was charged with praising the fascist regime in Germany and serving as an informant for Malmgren. Complicating his situation, he also was known to have received financial assistance from German organizations like the Gustav-Adolf-Verein and the Martin Luther Bund.[30] Wohl had grown up in the Odessa region in a Germany colony known as Marinovo. There he had served the local congregation as a keuster and played the organ in church, even losing his voting rights in 1926–1927 because he had been an aide for the pastor, Woldemar Seib.[31] On the recommendation of his pastor and the district president, George Schilling, he entered the seminary in the fall of 1929. Collectivization was then in full swing in his native Ukraine, and his parents would be among the many German farmers who were declared kulaks by the state and sent into exile in 1930.

Wohl's studies would be interrupted from 1930–1932 since he was one of Malmgren's students who had been called up to serve in the labor army.[32] The NKVD accused him of trying to escape across the border into Finland when he was serving in the labor army, but Wohl categorically denied the charges. In reality, it seems that one of his classmates, Georgy Fech, had successfully escaped across the border. Wohl was offered the opportunity to have his citizenship rights restored if he would just leave the seminary permanently, but he was not easily bribed. He refused and continued to study on his own while serving in the army, eventually taking his exams privately with Bishop Malmgren in May 1934.[33] But now, even though he had not completed one year in the parish, he found himself sitting across from an NKVD agent, being subjected to an intensive interrogation. During his grilling, the NKVD seized on the fact that his passport had allowed him to reside in Leningrad only for the course of his studies. Wohl admitted that he had broken the law, although given the housing shortage he couldn't have been the only one hoping to hold on to free housing. The seminary community was aware of his circumstances as well, but at first didn't force him to relocate.

Wohl must have realized that he was putting the seminary in a difficult position vis-à-vis the state, though, and the administration was eventually compelled to ask him to find alternative housing. At first, he lived with acquaintances, but not having the ability to be registered in their home, he fled to the Volodarsky region, some ten kilometers southwest of Leningrad. Since no one knew him there and he hid his identity, he was able to slip onto a collective farm and acquire a three-year passport.[34] Naturally, these actions looked suspicious in the eyes of the NKVD, all the more so since he was now a pastor at a historic Lutheran congregation in Leningrad. Given his association with the church, the agents asked him about his associations with the Finnish and German consulates.

Wohl informed them that the German consulate was keenly interested in his living conditions since St. Anne's was "one of the most privileged of the so-called aristocratic congregations" in the city. So naturally, they would want the pastor to have sufficient housing.[35] But with the ethnic cleansing of Leningrad that occurred after the murder of Kirov, a large number of ethnic German parishioners of St. Anne's had been sent into exile. The *dvatsatka* at what Wohl called this "extremely faithful German church" was virtually destroyed in the process.[36] Wohl recognized the danger to his congregation's existence but could not refrain from performing his pastoral duty. So, when it was learned that someone had been forced into exile, he boldly answered the charges of the NKVD: "When it became known to me that one or another parishioner had been exiled, during the church service I announced from the pulpit that we would be praying for this person who had to leave the city of Leningrad." When the agent responded that such an announcement from the pulpit was tantamount to an "anti-Soviet action," Wohl simply replied that he believed it was his duty to pray for them.[37]

Probing deeper into what they considered his political convictions during a later interrogation on August 15, Wohl told the NKVD that he believed there existed a planned persecution of the church in order to finish it once and for all. Throwing caution to the wind, Wohl said that the Soviets had promised freedom of conscience and religion but had broken their promise. He acknowledged that pastors were dependent on support from abroad and that without it, they could not continue their ministry.[38] Finally, on October 5, Wohl confessed that he was guilty of praying for his repressed parishioners and acknowledged that this was considered counterrevolutionary propaganda. When the NKVD investigation concluded on October 13, Wohl made certain to clear Malmgren's name: he had not received any political instructions from the bishop. He would stand on his own confession.[39]

On January 2, 1936, the sentence of six years for his honest assessment of Soviet lies would go into effect (beginning from the time of his incarceration). Oktav Simon would also be sentenced to six years' imprisonment, and Woldemar Assmus to four years.[40] Unlike Wohl, Simon, and Assmus, Alfred Prieb was not considered to be one of Malmgren's group of pastors, so while accused of counterrevolutionary activity, he was sentenced to four years' exile.[41] Woldemar Wagner would be sentenced to a five-year term in the region of Novosibirsk.[42] The courageous Samuel Wohl would eventually be re-arrested in a Siberian Gulag camp in Magadan, probably Kolyma, on March 13, 1938. Convicted of belonging to a counterrevolutionary insurgent organization, he was executed on April 13, 1938.[43]

24

THEY COULD DO NO OTHER

The Closing of Jesus Christ Lutheran Church

WHILE THE NKVD was busy plotting against Malmgren and his pastors, he wrote to Bruno Geissler (General Secretary of the Gustav-Adolf-Verein) on March 23 requesting emigration from the Soviet Union. Even the encouraging letters from John Morehead could no longer convince him that the Lutheran Church had any future in such a rigidly uncompromising atheist state. Accentuating Malmgren's fears of government snooping, the Interior Ministry intercepted his letter to Geissler, as well as many others. To this day, a report is held in the FSB Archives, chronicling all of Malmgren's visits to Germany and the cities he visited. It also has a list of those employees of the Moscow embassy and the Leningrad and Kiev consulates from the German Ministry of Foreign Affairs. The list especially cites those German officials who provided aid to ethnic German citizens of the USSR. It also contains a record of the funds expended for the upkeep of the Lutheran Church.[1]

By the middle of 1935, Malmgren's fears had finally become reality. The Lutheran Church in Leningrad was on the brink of extinction. And if the Church was facing destruction in its historic stronghold, what hope remained among the few remaining congregations scattered throughout the rest of the country?

A GOOD EXAMPLE of the pressures brought to bear against the city's congregations can be seen in the case of Jesus Christ Lutheran Church. After Kurt Muss's arrest in 1929, the congregation had borrowed pastors serving in Leningrad or the surrounding region (e.g., Oktav Simon and Paul Reichert) while continuing to meet at the church building of St. Michael's Lutheran on Vasilyevsky Island. (St. Michael's German-speaking congregation had united with Jesus Christ Lutheran's Russian-speaking congregation in the church building.)

The historical record of this congregation has been preserved by the witness of one of its parishioners, Konstantin Andrievsky. A convert from Russian Orthodoxy, Andrievsky came into the Lutheran Church on December 25, 1917, when a law was passed protecting freedom of conscience. This was the brief period of freedom before the Bolsheviks began their concerted attack on the Church. A lawyer by profession, Andrievsky spoke only Russian, so Jesus Christ Lutheran was a perfect place for him to worship.[2] He was not alone, which was evidence that Kurt Muss was correct in providing worship services for Russian speakers who were not inclined to attend Russian Orthodox church services.

Andrievsky described a welcoming yet cautious congregation in the mid-1930s. Since he taught courses not far from the church, he would stop in for services or prayer meetings in the evening, the time at which the gatherings were generally held due to the altered calendar of the workweek. He remembered that the *dvatsatka* chairman Alfred Zietnick controlled the doors so that the evening street noise would not affect the services. Andrievsky described a congregation that relied exclusively on its parishioners to pay the rent for use of the church. This they did willingly. On an evening in June of 1934, Andrievsky attended his first meeting of the *dvatsatka* at Zietnick's urging so that a lawyer would be present as discussions were held with two workers of the Cooperative of Plasterers and Painters. Along with Zietnick, *dvatsatka* member Jan Vannag and organist Evgeny Hannicke were present. (Since there was no full-time pastor, those who served the congregation, like Paul Reichert, did not attend the *dvatsatka* sessions.) Andrievsky's advice was needed because the workers had offered to paint the roof of the church for an unheard-of sum: 8,000–10,000 rubles ($4,000–5,000, approximately)! Naturally, the *dvastaka* refused what was apparently another attempt to overload the congregation with debt. In response to this impossible demand, Vannag offered to paint the roof for free.[3]

This was often how congregations like Jesus Christ Lutheran responded to the state's attempts to force them into debt or nonexistence. The parishioners would rally around the pastor and/or *dvatsatka* and do whatever they could to support their congregation. At times, the congregation would also rent the church building to Seventh Day Adventists or Eulogian Orthodox Christians in order to help with finances.[4]

In the fall of 1934, Andrievsky was asked to attend his second *dvatstaka* meeting. This time, the situation was more serious. The finance inspector had summarily increased the tax on the congregation after the state had forced it to take a loan to pay for the reconstruction of the church roof in the summer. Now the church treasury was empty. Hannicke outlined all the expenses of the past few months while Andrievsky provided a comparison between energy costs in public housing and churches. Hannicke further explained that the exorbitant state tax bill continued to escalate every year while the congregation, no doubt reflecting the effects of persecution, had dwindled to thirty-five parishioners. Thus, discussions were held to consider how the congregation could pay off its debt. If not, all were agreed, the church would be forced to close. Each member contemplated how much more he could pay in order to keep the congregation afloat. Hannicke himself had accepted very little pay for his work as organist, and now refused to accept any pay to help the congregation reduce its debt.[5]

As they all walked to the tram after the meeting, Andrievsky reminded them that he had predicted four years ago that such a situation might occur if taxes continued to rise and the congregation couldn't pay. He recommended that they not plunge parishioners into further personal debt, but simply close the church. When they gathered for his third *dvatsatka* meeting at Zietnick's apartment in April 1935, there was no longer any discussion about paying the church's bill. It was obvious that Jesus Christ Lutheran would have to close. Hannicke was told by the regional government that all the church's property would have to be transferred to them and that the last church service would be held in April.[6]

Andrievsky was not giving up without a fight, as extraordinary pressures had already been brought to bear on the parishioners and members of the *dvatsatka*.

A GOOD EXAMPLE of the complexities of being a faithful Christian in Stalin's USSR in the mid-1930s can be illustrated in the history of the Kubilius family of Jesus Christ Lutheran church. The Kubiliuses were a well-educated, intellectually curious couple in their early forties who had their own collection of rare paintings and a large library. They were conversant in at least four languages (German, Russian, Lithuanian, French, and a knowledge of English). Mikhail worked as an electrician and manager at ZHAKT (Housing and Leasing Cooperative Partnership). Before their marriage, his wife Erika had worked in the registration section of a machine production enterprise called Storer and Co. She was now busy raising their two daughters, Ilse (twelve years old) and Gertrude (eleven years old), and had been a faithful member of the St. Michael's *dvatsatka* since 1919.

On March 10, 1935, their family received a severe blow. Mikhail was arrested as a "socially dangerous element" and was now being interrogated about foreign family contacts. He told the agent he had cousins in Lithuania while his wife had four brothers in Estonia. A slew of strange questions followed: "What was his opinion on the coming to power of the fascists in Germany?" Mikhail mentioned that he had found out about it when he saw the swastika on the flag at the German consulate in Leningrad and read about the events in the newspapers. "Which Lutherans do you have connections with?" Mikhail's answer gives us some insight into the kindness of the Kubiliuses, because the daughter of the former factory owner where he worked, Lucia German, was living with them as a dependent (she was seventy-three years old). There was also a picture of the czar's family in his possession, which he explained was owned by an ethnic German named Klug, who had left for Revel (Tallinn). His fiancé had left the picture with them for safekeeping until her marriage to Klug.

The NKVD took these disparate facts and wove a case full of suspicion about the Kubiliuses' loyalties. Mikhail Kubilius was described as a fascist who systematically engaged in agitation, disseminating excerpts from the speeches of Hitler as he awaited the coming of German fascism. The NKVD had also found a Browning revolver in the apartment with six cartridges, which Mikhail said he had found in the loft of the apartment when his wife was hanging up sheets to dry. Leningrad had been a dangerous city during the years of revolution, and it is not out of the realm of possibility that a revolver had been left behind by the previous occupant. But combining this with the portrait of the czar's family and correspondence to family members beyond the borders, the NKVD agent claimed that Kubilius was avoiding questions and giving false testimony. He was ordered to be deported by March 20 with a five-year sentence at a labor camp in Yrgyz, Kazakhstan, his wife and their dependent, Lucia, being obliged to follow him into exile.

Their daughters were then taken in by an aunt who must have assisted them in writing a letter to the Soviet authorities. Shrewdly identifying themselves as

"Pioneers" (a Communist youth group), on June 16 the girls wrote a heart-rending letter to the government pleading for their parents' return:

> On March 20, 1935, our parents were sent from Leningrad to Kustanay. We beg you to please free our parents from exile and allow them to return to Leningrad or perhaps 100 kilometers from Leningrad. We are alone. We are crying a lot and are suffering without them, especially without mama, whom we love very, very much; Mama has a bad heart, and she is suffering very much without us. Once again, we beg you to please hurry this process as much as possible and return our parents to us.

One NKVD agent must have had a heart because he even wrote that their mother was not guilty of anything and should be freed. However, the girls' appeal was ultimately met with a stony response: "There is no basis to free them." In 1937, Mikhail would die in the Karaganda regional labor camp, Karlag. Lucia would die in exile in 1939 at the age of seventy-seven of complications from a hernia. Erika would eventually be freed from exile in 1954 and return to her daughters, surviving well into old age (eighty-one years) and passing away in 1973. Appealing to the Soviet authorities by letter, she succeeded in 1957 in having all three of them—herself, her husband, and Lucia German—cleared of the false charges brought against them.[7]

WHEN DISCUSSING ST. MICHAEL'S *dvatsatka*'s response to closure of the church, one has to factor in these troubling acts of the Soviet government, torturing an ordinary family whose only crime was being faithful members of the Lutheran Church. And yet despite arrests and threats against the congregation, it succeeded in delaying the church's closure for a little while. For when the regional government finally decided to close the parish on August 1, the parishioners rallied and gathered enough signatures from government officials to delay the closing until the middle of August, continuing worship services in the meantime. But the congregation was in no position to make demands for the long term. The state held all the cards, and while congregations might delay their closure, the inevitable demise of the churches was all but certain. Alfred Zietnick was forced to hand over the keys to the church on August 15, thus ending the church life of the only exclusively Russian-language Lutheran congregation in the Soviet Union.[8] Though it was composed of Czechs, Swedes, Finns, Russified Germans, and ethnic Russians like Andrievsky, they had all accepted the Lutheran Confessions while acknowledging that Russian was the operative language of their nation.[9]

Dvatsatka member and organist Hannicke was another of these unique believers who filled the pews of Jesus Christ Lutheran. A native of St. Petersburg, his family was of German Lutheran aristocratic stock. He basically grew up in the Marble Palace, a historic landmark along the banks of the Neva River located next to the Summer Gardens. There his father, a noted scholar of science, was employed as a teacher to the family of Duke Peter Oldenburg, the first cousin to the martyred Czar Alexander II.

Hannicke would spend his entire life working as a scientist at the Institute of Experimental Medicine alongside the famed scientist Ivan Pavlov. He also learned six languages, learned to play the cello and keyboard in his youth, and sometime later added the organ to his list of instruments. Hannicke was also from his youth an active and engaged Christian, involving himself in the charitable activities for which the Lutheran Church was renowned in Russia. As an adult, he would serve as a board member for the Evangelical Home of Charity on Bolshoi Samsonievsky Street.[10] He eventually became the organist for Jesus Christ Lutheran and was considered by Mikhail Mudyugin to be one of the two most accomplished organists in Leningrad, the other being St. Peter's Wolf Liss.[11] At the institute, some twelve kilometers east of Leningrad in a wooded setting very near to Koltushi's historic Lutheran church, Hannicke served as Pavlov's right hand for forty-two years, himself authoring scores of academic articles, including one on the conditional reflexes of mice during an experiment where he used the sounds of the organ pipes.[12] Given that he would seem to be a typical "former person" of the czarist regime, it seems odd that the NKVD left him alone. Whether this was due to the influence of Ivan Pavlov is uncertain.

As the *dvatsatka* members now reflected on the pressures that they had endured from the Soviet government, Andrievsky reminded them that the Lutherans were not being singled out for persecution. Orthodox parishes were also being forced to close against their will. The nearby Orthodox congregation Rozhdyestvo (meaning "Christmas," or "Nativity"), for example, had also been forced to close because of Soviet oppression. Those honest words about the perilous situation of the Christian churches in the USSR would come back to haunt him in the near future.[13]

The city of Leningrad and its oblast (region) experienced a spate of church closings in 1935, numbering seventy-nine in total. Besides Jesus Christ Lutheran, several other Lutheran churches were closed. The Estonian Lutheran congregation, St. John's, was liquidated on February 25. On August 1, St. Catherine's (Arnold Frischfeld's old congregation), along with St. Mary Magdalene and, on September 1, St. Anne's, were all closed for good.[14] Under the guise of "community needs," the government would from August until December close eight German-speaking Lutheran congregations in Leningrad and its suburbs.[15] What did "community needs" entail? When Alfred Zietnick turned the church keys over to the Soviet government in August, the government initially planned to turn the spacious building into a library. They would dither with the building for a while, before finally handing it over in 1947 to a tobacco factory for use as warehouse. In the 1950s, the church building would be remodeled from a single story into a three-story building, a factory named "Sport" occupying the premises, specializing in the manufacture of volleyballs.[16]

WITH THE MASSIVE church closings that had been occurring throughout 1935, by the fall St. Peter's was the only German-speaking Lutheran Church open in all of Leningrad.[17] Despite the dangers Alfred Zietnick had encountered, including narrowly escaping arrest in the Hansen-Muss case in 1929, this sixty-eight-year-old pharmacist would not now abandon his faith or his Lutheran Church, so he transferred his membership to St. Peter's. The remaining members of Jesus Christ Lutheran did likewise, although the repression they had experienced would eventually follow them there.[18] For Bishop Malmgren, this meant that the only church he could attend was the congregation led by Paul Reichert. Their past unresolved conflict had to weigh heavily on his mind as he contemplated how much longer he could work effectively in the Soviet Union.

Despite Christianity's weakened state by the middle of the 1930s, St. Peter's remained a center of activity for those who wanted to worship and hear the message of the gospel. The former president of the United Lutheran Synod of New York and close friend of Morehead's, Dr. Samuel Trexler, traveled to the Soviet Union in late 1934, visiting the seminary in Leningrad as well as several Lutheran congregations in Leningrad and Moscow. He especially noted his visit to St. Peter's, calling it "an oasis in the desert." When Trexler arrived, Reichert met him along with six of the younger clergy, all of them his former students at the seminary. Trexler was suitably impressed. "A nobler group of young Pastors one would not see in the church in any land. There was no defeatism in their attitude. With such men the church can hold out until conditions change in this land of brutality." Reichert told Trexler that St. Peter's had added five hundred more communicants in 1934, including increases in baptisms and marriages. Reichert even stated that the 3,500-seat church had a standing-room only crowd on Christmas Eve in 1934. Although admittedly the taxes on the congregation were very heavy, Reichert had managed to acquire a refund after one of their payments. But despite the encouraging and upbeat report Trexler gave of St. Peter's, he was not oblivious to the dangers the Lutheran Church was experiencing. "I felt that I had been in the presence of martyrs who were ready to sacrifice all that they had for the sake of the Gospel."[19] Trexler's comments would prove to be prophetic, for the six pastors whom he met at St. Peter's in late 1934 were the six who would be arrested in the spring of 1935 (including pastors Wohl and Simon). Later that year, the six would be exiled and deported to the Gulag with sentences ranging from four to six years.[20]

However, in an article written in March 1935, Trexler's prophetic skills failed him when he offered his opinion that the church had already seen the worst of the persecution, saying that "the Soviets would follow a policy of moderation from here on out."[21] He could not have been more spectacularly wrong. By the end of 1934, there were thirty-nine Lutheran pastors serving in the Soviet Union. By the end of 1935, there would only be fifteen.[22] Those fifteen pastors were Alexander Streck in Moscow; Paul and Bruno Reichert at St. Peter's in Leningrad; Ferdinand Bodungen in Peterhof, Leningrad region; Heinrich Behrendts in Tashkent, Uzbekistan; Pekka Braks in the Ingrian towns of Gubanitsa and Venjoki; Aleksanteri Korpelainen in the Ingrian villages of Haapakangas and Koltushi; Antti Jaatinen in the Ingrian village of Skouvoritsa; The Migle brothers, Alexander and Jan, who took care of the Latvian congregations in Leningrad and the Leningrad region; Leo Schulz, pastor to Estonians and serving at the oldest Ingrian congregation in Moloskovitsa (founded 1611); Selim Laurikkala, the leader of the Finnish/Ingrian congregations and pastor at St. Mary's in Leningrad; Karl Vogel at St. Paul's in Odessa, Ukraine; Ossip Toryassan in Ordzhonikidze/Vladikavkaz in the north Caucasus; Emil Reusch in Annenfeld of the Caucasus and of course, the bishop, Arthur Malmgren.[23] For these fifteen pastors and the bishop, the clock was ticking as the Second Five-Year-Plan to eradicate Christianity was well on its way toward completion by 1937.

INCLUDED IN THE list of pastors who would lose their freedom in 1935 was the independent thinker but stalwart pastor Woldemar Reichwald. While

Reichwald had at one time criticized the Lutheran Church for its hierarchical structure, in the end he remained obedient to the bishops and served faithfully in the Church until his arrest. On the night and early morning of December 27 and 28, Vladivostok's NKVD subjected Reichwald to a five-hour house search. After Reichwald's arrest, three additional raids were conducted on his apartment. Church lists (presumably of parishioners) and documents were confiscated, along with his private correspondence. The charges of espionage were being prepared, as they were now becoming the most common charge leveled against anyone with German ties in the Lutheran Church. As a matter of fact, Communist and *Bezbozhnik* journalist Boris Kandidov would posthumously accuse Reichwald of espionage in his book *Church and Espionage* (1940), one of the charges being that he had worked for the czarist police before the Bolshevik Revolution in 1917.[24] On the night and early morning of February 14 and 15 the following year, Reichwald's wife would also be arrested. Reichwald himself was held in harsh confinement, being denied gifts of food and forbidden the opportunity even to wash. He would die in exile in 1939.[25]

While news of the fate of many pastors and their last days is in short supply, occasionally surviving witnesses carried their testimonies with them into freedom. One such story concerns Simon Kludt, a fifty-four-year-old pastor who had served congregations in the Ukraine since 1908. Arrested for giving the exiled names of those villagers in need of food aid during the state-induced famine of 1932–1933, Kludt was accused of spying for Germany. His crime of spying consisted solely of writing to German aid agencies so that they would get the addresses of starving villagers. Kludt was imprisoned in Zaporozhye for forty-eight days, receiving a food package from his wife the day before he was executed. Distributing the contents to his fellow prisoners (a pastor and a parishioner), as he had a foreboding of his death, Kludt poignantly addressed them: "Tell them [his wife and eight children] that I have won the crown of life." Kludt's two cellmates suffered six more months of imprisonment and were then sent to hard labor in Siberia for ten years. They ultimately survived their ordeal and were able to tell of the great faith and witness of Pastor Simon Kludt. But unless someone lived to speak of the whereabouts of condemned pastors and parishioners, their tales went to the grave with them.[26]

As the year came to a close, it was undeniable that 1935 had turned out to be the most devastating year for Lutheran pastors in the Church's almost four-century existence in Russia. Although historians J. Arch Getty and Oleg Naumov have unearthed statistics detailing that the NKVD made fewer arrests in 1935 than in any year since 1929, that information would be cold comfort for the Lutherans of Russia. In fact, those same historians acknowledge that the percentage of arrests was increasing for those dubious categories of "anti-Soviet agitation" and "counter-revolution," charges with which Lutherans often had to contend. In the wake of the Kirov assassination, "political crimes" often defined the actions of those whose beliefs ran counter to the Zeitgeist of Stalinism.[27] Optimism, indeed, was in very short supply as Russia's Lutherans greeted the New Year of 1936.

25

"FELLOW CITIZENS WITH THE SAINTS"

The Death of John Morehead and Departure of Arthur Malmgren

IN OCTOBER 1935, Dr. John Morehead attended his last event overseas, the Third Convention of the LWC in Paris. Prior to the convention, a weary Morehead announced his intention to step down as chairman of the Executive Committee so that a younger, more vigorous man could take charge. He was now sixty-eight years old and his health had been in decline for some time. Morehead still hoped to be involved indirectly in the affairs of the worldwide Lutheran Church, but his correspondence with Lutherans in the USSR now ceased.[1] After his return to New York, he set about to "tell the story of unexampled and fruitful work of Christian love and mercy which God had enabled the Lutheran Church bodies in America to accomplish since the World War through the agency of the National Lutheran Council."[2]

Dr. Ralph Long, the new liaison to the Russian Lutheran Church at the LWC, now introduced himself to Bishop Malmgren via letter. In light of his new duties, Long asked Malmgren about the state of the Lutheran Church: How many pastors were still serving? What could the LWC do to help? Was there any change in the state's attitude toward Christianity? Can the LWC communicate with those pastors in prison or exile?[3] Long was not aware that the bishop himself had been called in to the NKVD headquarters in January and had been threatened with imprisonment and exile. Malmgren, it seemed, was now being subjected to the undivided attention of the NKVD, and interrogations of other pastors would attest to that fact. Just as Bishop Meier had been harassed in Moscow, Malmgren was now being called in for numerous chats with the NKVD in Leningrad.

His correspondence with foreigners and reception of funds from abroad appear to have been the subject of the unpleasant interrogations, as the intercepted letter from March 20, 1935, would indicate. Although they knew the answer full well, the NKVD cynically asked how this seventy-six-year-old bishop was surviving without sufficient funds from the local church.[4] Apparently, his old friend Lev Khinchuk could no longer protect him, either, because on January 19 the German ambassador to the USSR, Friedrich Werner Graf von der Schulenberg, alerted Johannes Kriege in Berlin that Malmgren was in serious danger of being arrested or sent into exile.[5] Former student Johannes Lel remembered that Malmgren once said that if the relationship of the Soviet Union to Germany ever got worse, "it would be necessary for me to buy a ticket to the next world!"[6] The pressure on him was now open and undisguised. Ralph Long would have to wait a few months before he received an answer to his questions, because plans were now set in motion to extract Malmgren from the USSR before it was too late.

The threats from the NKVD and the complications of operating the seminary were not the only reasons that decided Malmgren on this new course. Adding a further complication to his troubled life, Malmgren was now hospitalized with kidney trouble. He would be released from the hospital on March 12, but given that Morehead's health issues had led to his own retirement, it must have seemed to Malmgren that he had done all that he could possibly do for the Church.[7] Malmgren had already received assurances from Franz Rendtorff of the Gustav-Adolf-Verein (GAV) that he would be given a pension in Germany. Given the added complications from his health problems, there seemed to be little doubt that he would leave in the near future. Complicating the problem now was that the Soviets had made the rules and cost for leaving the country more difficult. While the German government worked on his exit visa, Malmgren would be forced to wait for a spell.[8]

AS BISHOP MALMGREN was waiting for his visa, Morehead's health was declining even worse than his own. Now relocated to their beloved Virginia, both he and his wife were in the last days of their lives. Surprisingly, for a man who had dedicated his life to the Church, there was apparently no real financial support for him and his wife as they neared their end. The pastor who had expended so much energy securing aid for Russia's Lutherans, spiritual and physical, hadn't had time to think about his own needs.[9] There were many, though, who couldn't forget Morehead's deeds and sought to give him some worldly acclaim for his efforts. Before his health had declined, a movement had already begun among his friends in Germany, Sweden, Finland, and Denmark to nominate him for the Nobel Peace Prize. While European friends informed the committee in Stockholm of Morehead's potential candidacy, friends in America worked through back channels to have President Roosevelt place Morehead's name into the competition.[10] Since former President Hoover was a good friend of Morehead's, his European friends also asked him to write the former president with this request. Addressing Hoover in the familiar way from days gone by as "My dear 'Chief,'" Morehead sheepishly admitted that European friends Count Carl Moltke and Dr. Alfred Jorgensen wanted him to ask for Hoover's recommendation. While Hoover was unpopular in the United States because of the Great Depression, he was still held in high regard by Europeans for so efficiently directing the feeding program for a starving continent at the end of World War I.[11]

Unfortunately, President Roosevelt and former President Hoover would not be given the pleasure of placing Morehead's name in nomination. On

May 29, after having taken care of her husband's poor health for some time, Nellie Morehead succumbed after a short illness. Relegated to his bed because of his own health problems, Morehead was unable to attend her funeral on June 1. One of his last acts was to ask his nurse to learn from the doctor how much longer until he would join Nellie. The answer was not long in coming, as Morehead passed away on the day of Nellie's funeral. On June 4 at the College Church in Salem, Virginia, his colleague Dr. Frederick Knubel, who was now the Vice President of the LWC, eulogized Morehead with the words of St. Paul in Ephesians 5:25: "Christ ... loved the Church and gave himself for it." His friend Dr. Samuel Trexler remembered the day poignantly: "It was in the late afternoon of a beautiful June day, and the peace which he had sought in vain, and to which he had been such an absolute stranger during the last score of years, now seemed to be his. After he had touched the whole world he was finally laid to rest amid simple surroundings in his own native Virginia."[12]

Tributes poured in from those whose lives he had touched. Former President Hoover declared: "Dr. Morehead was a man of great character, devotion and idealism."[13] From the Germans who had worked so closely with him to save the Lutheran Church in Russia, German ambassador to the United States, Dr. Hans Luther, expressed their gratitude: "Dr. Morehead's passing away is an irretrievable loss for the Lutheran world." The president of St. Olaf College in Minnesota, Dr. Lars W. Boe, who had served with him on the Executive Committee of the NLC, added, "The Lutherans of the world have a finer understanding of Christian love and service because Dr. Morehead has lived."[14] Speaking of his impact on institutions, Dr. Charles J. Smith reflected, "Both his seminary [Southern Theological Seminary] and his college [Roanoke] still hold much of his spirit, and through all the coming years will be grateful that a master once walked their way."[15]

The accolades could never quite capture the enormous difference that Morehead had made in the lives of Russia's Lutherans. In their most difficult hour, he had come to their rescue with aid and spiritual sustenance. Those who met him could never forget him. Trexler recollected that during his visit to the Soviet Union in 1934, he asked a pastor if he had known Dr. Morehead. "Catching his breath, he answered with deep feeling, 'No, but I once saw him!'"[16] Many Russian Lutherans were happy that they had seen him, because once they had, Morehead could never leave them without doing all in his power for them. He could not help but be deeply touched by the hardship and suffering that he had seen in the Volga region and the Ukraine during the famine of the early 1920s. This he never forgot. So, for example, when he heard in 1930 that 397 Russian German Lutherans were suffering in Siberia, he stepped in to help.[17]

The Lutherans, having been labeled kulaks, had been dispossessed of their farms in the Volga region and exiled to Siberia. The conditions were so intolerable that they had crossed the border into Harbin, Manchuria, but were unable to find any kind of work. Helpless and slated to be expelled from Manchuria, Morehead responded to their situation by coordinating a fundraising campaign that collected $56,000. The funds enabled them, with the administrative assistance of Dr. Long, to immigrate to Brazil in July 1932. There they were given land to farm, literally saving their lives. Morehead was especially pleased that worldwide Lutheranism had stepped into the breach to help. Funds came from Lutherans in Norway, Sweden, Denmark, Finland, Germany, Czechoslovakia, France, Hungary, Yugoslavia, Australia, Canada, the United States, and even from young Lutheran churches in mission fields like China.[18]

Morehead was committed to saving the people of the Lutheran Church that he loved, his efforts possessing a theological dimension that included both body and soul.[19] His fruits showed him to be a man of deep Christian conviction, compassion and love for humanity.

UNFORTUNATELY, WE HAVE no record of what Bishop Malmgren thought on hearing of the passing of his friend and colleague. The two, along with Bishop Meier, had accomplished extraordinary things in the service of

the church of their Lord Jesus Christ. By the grace of God, they had been
his instruments in keeping the Lutheran Church alive despite extraordinary
obstacles. But now, only Malmgren remained. On June 20, 1936, the lonely,
disheartened bishop finally received the exit visa for which he had long been
waiting. He departed for Berlin. Regrettably, he moved from one totalitarian
regime to another, his arrival taking place a few weeks before the infamous
Berlin Olympics where Hitler had hoped to showcase his Aryan supremacy
theories through German sport. After having his health examined, Malmgren
moved on to Mainz, where he would live with his niece for a short time. His
daughters and sons-in-law would never join him, remaining in the Soviet Union
until the end of their lives.

In his later years, the GAV provided a pension for Malmgren and partook
of his vast knowledge of the church in the Soviet Union. He was praised for
his work and received some measure of comfort for all that he had done for
the Lutheran Church over the last difficult decades. The eighty-one-year-old
Malmgren preached his last sermon in 1941 at the Castle Church in Darmstadt
on the anniversary of the one-hundred-year-old Hilfsverein that had aided poor
Protestant congregations, and naturally, also those Germans who had been
among the diaspora in the Soviet Union. Sadly, Malmgren's last years were
to provide little respite from the sorrow and troubles that he had experienced
while keeping the Lutheran church alive in the USSR. His old friends Franz
Rendtorff and Johannes Kriege died shortly after his resettlement in Mainz. In
the political realm, the 1939 Hitler-Stalin Pact was cause for concern, as were
the tragic events of the nine-hundred-day blockade of Leningrad in 1941, a city
that had been a source of joy and heartbreak for him for over forty years. In the
summer of 1944, a bomb attack on Mainz cost him his accommodations as well
as the last of his earthly possessions. The GAV arranged for him to move to the
"student home" (Studentenheim) in Leipzig, a comfortable house named after
Franz Rendtorff. There he lived with his younger sister for the last few years
of his life, occupying a small student dorm room.

Malmgren's final days proved to be not uneventful, for he witnessed the arrival of American troops in April 1945 but also the transfer of the city to Soviet troops in July 1945. He had indeed come full circle, having fled the USSR only to land in Nazi Germany, and now, at the end of his life, to fall under the occupation of the Soviets again. By all accounts, the Communists left him alone. He remained mentally fit and was able to share his vast knowledge of Russia with the famed church historian, Heinrich Bornkamm, to whose home he was frequently invited as a guest. In the middle of a very cold winter, he passed away peacefully on February 3, 1947 at the age of eighty-seven. His old friend, the former director of the GAV, Bruno Geissler, performed the funeral. Malmgren was buried in a modest grave without any special notice. Twenty years later, the GAV general secretary, Dr. Paul-Wilhelm Gennrich, removed the urn with Malmgren's ashes to the South Cemetery of Leipzig, placing a large tombstone over it with the inscribed words of Geissler's funeral text: "So then you are no longer strangers and aliens, but you are fellow citizens with the saints and members of the household of God" (Ephesians 2:19).[20]

26

"THOUSANDS OF SEEDS ... CAST TO THE WIND"

Shadows of the Great Terror

AS THE EXTRAORDINARY triumvirate of church figures, Meier, Morehead and Malmgren, passed from the scene, those pastors remaining surely had to wonder how they might continue in ministry. Nevertheless, there were men of strong faith who continued to carry on with their duties despite the danger. The redoubtable Selim Laurikkala was just such a man. He continued to defy the Soviets with his calm determination to serve the Lord in the midst of an atheist culture that would have devoured him if it could. Certainly, his Finnish citizenship still protected him to some extent, but Laurikkala conducted himself in a manner that often unnerved the Communists. In this, he was cut from the same cloth as Meier, Malmgren, and Morehead. While hardly physically imposing or aggressive in nature, Laurikkala argued for the Christian faith like a lion. It was said that he debated Communists with diplomatic skill and in such an apolitical manner that they could not pin him down. Some Communists who had infiltrated church services or his Bible classes were aware that he was speaking against them all the while, but he was so savvy in his speech that they couldn't quite make it all out.

Despite increasing persecution, in 1936 the village church Laurikkala pastored in Tuutari decided to carry on with a planned celebration of its hundredth anniversary. On such occasions, parishioners would often participate by reciting poems or special speeches. The times were such, though, that one needed special permission from the authorities to participate, and the government decided to only allow the pastor to speak. Laurikkala, like a good soldier, gave the sermon, made speeches, and even recited some poetic verses. Meanwhile, the Communists had arranged for their own holiday to counteract the church celebration, but no one came to their celebrations. The sponsors of the Communist event were ultimately forced to concede defeat and participate in the church's activities! The villages would still be a tough battle for the forces of atheism, especially in the Ingrian region. But Stalin's preparations for stronger measures to be taken against believers were already on the horizon.[1]

OTHER PASTORS WERE also resolutely remaining at their stations. In Moscow, Alexander Streck had been a particularly bold servant of the church for years. One could not have asked for a more conspicuous place to carry on ministry, yet the congregation of Sts. Peter and Paul still gathered on Sunday evenings—not in such numbers as before, but all in all it was still a functioning church. Streck had already been forced out of the church's apartment to the distant suburbs, yet he continued to make the long, uncomfortable trek to the church on crowded public transportation.[2]

The situation had certainly changed at Sts. Peter and Paul from even the early 1930s as persecution had dramatically reduced the number of churchgoers. Parishioner Olga Striks later remembered that the Christmas tree in 1935 was a small one, certainly in comparison with the old days when they would set up two large Christmas trees replete with candles. But Pastor Streck still conducted Christmas services, and Olga, an eighteen-year-old ethnic Latvian living in Moscow, attended with her family. Latvian services had mostly ceased with the death of Pastor Mikhail Lapping in 1932. No ethnic Latvian citizen would ever again be allowed to hold confirmation classes in Moscow as Pastor Julius Zahlit had in 1932.[3] Despite previous restrictions on holiday trees, though, the fir tree was actually making a comeback for the New Year's celebrations of 1936. Soviet official Pavel Postyshev had urged bringing the tree back for the sake of the children. He believed that Christians had taken a pagan symbol and used it for their purposes, so why not take this Christianized symbol, the Christmas tree, and use it for the purposes of the Communist state? It was a brilliant ploy and the Stalinist New Year celebrations, now replete with fir trees, would succeed in replacing the Christmas tree in the future. In order to make certain that the dominant Orthodox Church didn't use the fir tree's return for their own intentions, the tree had to be lit on January 1 and the sale of fir trees would not be permitted after the new year had commenced. (Whether Lutherans purchased them and secretly lit them on December 25 is unknown).[4]

Pastor Streck and the Lutherans of Sts. Peter and Paul were not the only Christians affected by the brazen measures the Soviets took against the church. Léopold Braun was an American Catholic priest called in 1934 to serve the parish of St. Louis, in the shadows of Lubyanka. Although the Roosevelt-Litvinov Agreement on religious freedom for Americans was presumably in effect, Braun thought one could hardly tell that there had been any accommodation made for believers' rights. In fact, when Braun met with Minister of Non-Orthodox Religious Affairs Ivan Poliansky in order to discuss the freedoms that Litvinov had assured Roosevelt existed, Poliansky informed Braun that no such change had occurred. On the contrary, Stalin's April 1929 Law on Religious Associations was still in effect for everyone. It was only in diplomatic circles that Litvinov sang a different tune.

St. Louis Catholic Church was being charged twenty-two times the established rate for electricity, paying five rubles and fifty kopecks per kilowatt compared to the average of fifty kopecks. Fortunately, limits on electricity were not imposed on them as they were on other churches in the city like Sts. Peter and Paul, but it was not for want of trying. The Moscow Gas and Electric Supply attempted on several occasions to get Braun to agree to certain limits, but he flatly refused. Nevertheless, the church was forced to pay the excessive rate even though it not only went against the spirit of Roosevelt-Litvinov but also against the very wording of the accord. When Braun related his situation to William Bullitt, the ambassador was indignant. He immediately offered to take the case up with Litvinov himself, but Braun and his bishop thought it best to leave it to the French embassy since St. Louis was generally considered French property.[5]

Braun described the beggarly existence of those clergy still remaining in Moscow, lamenting their inability to receive food or clothing cards. As a result, they were forced to pay higher rates for goods, as well as search for accommodations in any poor quarter since they were denied the basic right to housing. A land and building tax were also levied against St. Louis, resulting in a $377 tax bill for the year, an outrageous sum for that time. All of this in spite of the fact that Litvinov had assured President Roosevelt that religious believers in the USSR could lease buildings for worship free of charge!

Braun survived twelve years in Moscow and ultimately wrote a book on his experiences. Although he underwent threats and suffered deprivation for his ministry, Braun's American citizenship protected his person, and his fluency in French and service to French Catholics allowed him to live unharmed in the French embassy. Most importantly, though, Braun's chronicle communicates the palpable fear that enveloped the Christian clergy as they attempted to be faithful servants to the Lord. Indeed, since St. Louis Catholic Church was located only a couple of blocks from Sts. Peter and Paul, Braun's portrayal of Moscow's inhospitable climate toward Christianity gives us a very real picture of the circumstances under which Alexander Streck worked.[6]

In May 1936, the Soviet government ordered three members of Sts. Peter and Paul to take responsibility for the tax burden and other responsibilities of the church. If no one could be found, the church would be closed in August.

Naturally, many parishioners feared being sent to prison if they signed their names to this document. They needed look no further for an example of what could happen than the congregation's cantor, Ernst Hörschelmann (the son of the late Ferdinand Hörschelmann Sr.), who was already in prison. Pastor Streck ended the impasse by putting his name forth and asking three other parishioners to do likewise. An elderly female parishioner agreed to do so, as did a woman even older than her. The last name on the document was that of Harry Helms, an elderly widower who was not in the best of health. Pastor Streck recommended these three since they no longer had young children to raise. In June, Streck received the government document and answered the questions submitted to him, sending it to the regional police as well as the NKVD. Everything seemed to be in order as August passed and the church remained open for services.[7] Maybe they would survive after all?

WHILE STS. PETER and Paul was waiting to see what its future would hold, a surprising number of American tourists were still coming to the Soviet Union. These were no ordinary visitors, though; they were interested in the religious situation in the country and curious as to whether the forthcoming Stalin Constitution would bring needed relief to believers. Sherwood Eddy, a former YMCA official who had been visiting the USSR for the past several summers, assembled a large group of seventy professors, clergymen, and social workers, among others, who traveled to Moscow in August. Although Eddy himself was too ill to travel, the visitors were accorded a personal visit with Emilian Yaroslavsky, the head of the Society of the Militant Godless and a member of the Central Executive Committee of the Communist Party. They would also meet with Anna Louise Strong, a noted American Communist sympathizer, and Dr. Julius Hecker, a Russian Jew who had immigrated to America when he was young but had now returned to support the Communist government. (He would fall victim to Stalin's Great Terror in 1938, while Strong would end her days in Communist China).[8] Arriving on a separate tourist visa and not interested in a Soviet propaganda tour was a Presbyterian minister and religious radio broadcaster from Philadelphia named Donald Barnhouse.

Barnhouse's observations give us an educated outsider's view of the conditions under which Streck and other Christian pastors and priests struggled in ministering to their flocks. He initially visited the US embassy in Moscow to ask where to find open Protestant churches. The staff referred him to two experts, who would give him pertinent information about the real situation concerning religious freedom among Lutherans and Catholics in Moscow and the USSR in general. The first was described by the State Department's Loy Henderson as "a foreigner in Moscow who is in a position to be unusually well informed with regard to the experiences of the Lutheran Church."[9] The source's name is not given in Henderson's report to United States Secretary of State Cordell Hull, but it almost certainly was a German national and probably one who worked at the German embassy.

Barnhouse was not one to be taken in by Yaroslavsky's curt dismissal of any suggestion that religious believers were persecuted. He discussed with the first source the situation among Lutherans and other believers. He indicated that there were about twenty open Christian churches in Moscow, a city of four million. The government had closed most of the five hundred Christian churches that were open before the Bolshevik Revolution, and generally found three pretexts in order to close churches: (1) Due to increasing motor traffic in the city, churches had to be torn down; (2) taxes were raised to such a degree that the parishioners simply couldn't support their congregation and pastor anymore; (3) arbitrary repairs were ordered on the building to the extent that the congregation couldn't bear the cost of renovation. Since the government technically owned the church buildings, they could decide whenever they chose that repairs were needed. The closure of Jesus Christ Lutheran Church in Leningrad was a primary example of this excuse.[10]

The source lamented that only twelve Lutheran churches were left in existence:

- Two preaching in German in Leningrad (St. Peter's and St. Catherine's).

- Two preaching in Finnish in Leningrad (including St. Mary's in the city center).

- One preaching in German in Moscow (Sts. Peter and Paul).

- One preaching in Latvian in Leningrad (Christ the Savior, pastored by the Migle brothers).

- In the Ukrainian region, one in Odessa and one in Kharkov.

- One preaching in German in the Transcaucasus (Ossip Toryassan, Bruno's father, was the pastor).

- One in Tashkent (Heinrich Behrendts's congregation).

- One in Tiflis (Tbilisi), although he doubted this was still open (most likely it was closed after Pastor Richard Mayer's 1933 martyrdom).

- One other congregation is mentioned, but the State Department file does not record where it was located.

While knowledgeable of the number of the remaining Lutheran congregations, the source did not seem to be as aware of the congregations in the Ingrian countryside, but that would also lend more credence to the fact that he was probably a German. In fact, he was informed enough to tell Barnhouse that the congregation of Woldemar Reichwald in Vladivostok had been closed a few months before; his wife was arrested in February 1936 after he had been arrested near the end of the previous year. It is possible that his wife and the parishioners continued to gather the believers until her arrest. Barnhouse asked his source whether laymen were taking up leadership in the church since pastors were increasingly being arrested. The source discussed the impact of the altered workweek, explaining that only every seventh Sunday fell on a rest day. That made it virtually impossible for male parishioners to be deeply involved in church work.

The second source enlightened Barnhouse as to how the NKVD pressured the *dvatsatkas*. They would meet separately with each member and inform him or her that a meeting would be held as to whether their church would be closed. The agent would not fail to mention that in similar meetings, if a member chose to keep the church open, he or she would be sent to Siberia for ten years. So, on the day when the meeting was held, the NKVD agent would ask any member to rise if he believed his church should remain open. Most, naturally, were not ready to forfeit ten years of their life in Siberia when it was probable that they would not survive the camps. And so the churches began to close, one by one.

Despite this disheartening news about the future prospects for the church's existence, before Barnhouse left Russia he received some good news. After speaking with several members of the Eddy group, he discovered that they, too, felt that they had not been given an honest and open representation of conditions inside the churches by the Militant Godless's Yaroslavsky. At least Barnhouse was not alone in recognizing the Soviets' duplicity.[11]

THE ATMOSPHERE IN the country was becoming more fearful than ever in the summer of 1936. In the political sphere, the first of the show trials associated with Stalin's Great Terror commenced on August 19. Old Bolsheviks Grigory Zinoviev and Lev Kamenev stood in the dock as the main perpetrators of a plot to murder not only Sergey Kirov but also Stalin and other members of the Soviet Politburo. The trial had apparently been scripted, and the accused duly carried out their roles as repentant monsters who deserved nothing less

than death. But why did they submit to a sham trial? There is some debate as
to whether they believed that their lives or only the lives of their families would
be spared. What is not subject to debate is Stalin's treachery in his dealings
with them. Zinoviev and Kamenev were shot shortly after the expected August
25 guilty verdict, and most of their immediate families and those of others
accused in the plot were executed, if not immediately, then during the period
known as Stalin's Great Terror (1937–1938). Olga Kameneva, the wife of Lev
Kamenev and the government official who had bartered over food distribution
with John Morehead and W. L. Scheding in the days of the famine, had already
been imprisoned and afterward was sent into exile. She was retried in January
1938, though, and then shot in the autumn of 1941. A total of 160 persons
would be arrested and shot as a result of their connections to the accused in
the Zinoviev-Kamenev trial.[12]

On the whole, the foreign press, while uneasy about how the confessions
of the accused were obtained, still did not object too strenuously. After all,
didn't they confess to horrific crimes?[13] But Joseph Davies, the future American
ambassador who would begin his tenure in 1937, went further. Davies staunchly
defended the dictator by agreeing that the Great Purge Trials (1936–1938)
strengthened the Soviet Union by removing fifth columnists and traitors.[14]
Davies would be a poor replacement for the volatile but honest William
Bullitt, who was finally waking up to the Janus-faced nature of Stalin. The
Great Terror would affect not only Communist Party members who had run
afoul of Stalin, but also countless Christians, many of them affiliated with the
Lutheran Church.[15]

During these days of uncertainty, Sts. Peter and Paul continued holding
church services every Sunday until the evening of November 4, when several
parishioners along with Pastor Streck were arrested. That night, all three parishioners who had put their names forward as leaders of the congregation were
arrested.[16] Elza Leventhal's twenty-two-year-old sister, Irina, was also subjected
to a search on November 5 and arrested the following day. She was accused of

terrorism, a charge Elza described as "completely absurd," speculating that Irina probably didn't even know what the phrase "terrorist act" meant. Irina was sent to Butyrka Prison and within a half year shipped out to distant Kolyma. Elza tried to visit the church in the days following her younger sister's arrest, but the doors were locked.[17] The three congregational leaders were kept in prison for nine months, whereon the ladies were sent to the Gulag labor camps of Siberia. The older man, Harry Helms, apparently died shortly after the sentencing while the older woman survived being sent to the camps but died in 1943. The younger woman survived this experience, eventually being freed in 1942 but remaining in exile with all the other Russian Germans who had been deported to Siberia en masse in 1941. She worked with them in the labor army, which had been set aside for Russian citizens of German heritage. After the de-Stalinization period of Nikita Khrushchev in the mid-1950s, she would finally begin to gather together Lutheran believers and carry out the tasks for which Bishop Meier had prepared her so many years before.[18]

The American embassy in Moscow was instantly made aware of Pastor Streck's arrest since he had been ministering to those of Protestant background in the embassy community. Streck had baptized the child of an embassy employee named Johnson in May and was to have conducted the wedding ceremony of employee George Minor on November 14. Ambassador Bullitt referred to him as "the pastor of those members of our embassy of the evangelical faith."[19] He was not the first one with connections to the embassy to be arrested, as diplomat George Kennan had already noted in 1935 the arrests of doctors and dentists "who are bold enough to treat us."[20] In fact, Bullitt wrote to President Roosevelt on May 1, 1935, explaining that "the terror, always present, has risen to such a pitch that the least of the Muscovites, as well as the greatest, is in fear. Almost no one dares have any contact with foreigners and this is not unbiased fear but a proper sense of reality."[21] Kennan would echo the ambassador's thoughts in 1937, admitting that his fellow Americans rarely met or visited with Russians publicly because of the danger it posed to the Russians.[22]

To further complicate matters, Ambassador Bullitt had left the Soviet Union for good in August.[23] Fed up with a government where "the lie is normal and the truth abnormal," Bullitt had metamorphosed from enthusiastic champion of the Soviet Union to its severest critic.[24] George Kennan felt that he and fellow embassy official Charles Bohlen had convinced Bullitt of the Soviets' unreliability, although he acknowledged that the Soviet Union's actions had been the best testimony to its unscrupulous nature. For Bullitt, three years in Moscow had been an educational experience in the nature of Stalin and his regime. In March 1936, he wrote to Assistant Secretary of State R. Walton Moore, detailing the arrests and disappearances of thousands, labeling it "unbelievable."[25] Moreover, he was baffled because he knew these "persons were without question loyal to the Soviet regime."[26] In his final letter to the State Department in April, Bullitt bluntly stated that the Soviet government and all Communist parties worldwide believed in mass murder.[27]

Since ambassador-elect Davies had yet to take up his duties in Moscow, embassy charge d' affaires Loy Henderson telephoned Bullitt in Paris with the details of Streck's arrest. Although Bullitt was the ambassador-elect to France, he took it on himself to contact Moore within two hours once he heard the news. Describing the attack on Streck's character in outraged terms, Bullitt declared, "It is my profound conviction that he could not have been involved in any way in any political activities whatsoever." Showing his awareness of the NKVD's tactics, Bullitt continued, "I expressed to Henderson over the telephone for the benefit of the listeners-in of the Ogpu [the old term for the NKVD] my personal conviction that the arrest of Pastor Streck would produce a reaction of disgust on the part of the American government and the people of the United States. Streck is I believe technically a Soviet citizen. We cannot, therefore, intervene directly but I believe it would be most salutary if you should call in Troyanovsky and ask him if this means that the Soviet government is beginning a campaign against those who minister to members of the American Embassy in Moscow."[28]

Moore took up Bullitt's suggestion and met with the Soviet ambassador to America, Alexander Troyanovsky, on November 16. While working out the details for Davies's posting in Moscow, Moore touched on two cases, that of Streck and a Russian translator for the Americans named Malitsky. Moore assured Troyanovsky that the Americans weren't making a formal complaint, but simply wanted information so that they could assure Malitsky's wife as to his whereabouts. With regard to Streck, Moore said to the Soviet ambassador "he was sorry that an incident of this sort had occurred, inasmuch as both of us had always been interested in 'civilized processes.'" Troyanovsky was apparently nonplussed by Moore's questions and simply declared that since the wedding of George Minor had taken place (without Streck), no harm had been done.[29]

One of the most troubling aspects of the Streck affair is the nonchalance with which the Roosevelt administration responded to such brutal acts against Christians and those Soviet citizens who had served the American embassy. When Davies arrived on January 19, 1937, the embassy personnel were informed that he prided himself on *not* being a diplomat—that is to say, he was not like them! In fact, he reassured President Mikhail Kalinin that he had "an open mind," likely implying that Bullitt had not. Married to Marjorie Merriweather Post, one of the richest women in the world, he would live like royalty, reportedly importing two thousand pints of Birds Eye ice cream into Russia. (The ambassador liked this particular brand of ice cream, but was unaware of Soviet realities; the ice cream would spoil due to the frequent power failures).[30] When he arrived, Kennan admitted, "We doubted his seriousness. ... We saw every evidence that his motives in accepting the post were personal and political and ulterior to any sense of the solemnity of the task itself."[31] Kennan and some of the other younger officials had gathered in Loy Henderson's room at the end of Davies's first day to discuss whether they should resign en masse. They ultimately decided against it, but the State Department was so concerned that it sent a trouble-shooter to Moscow in order to sort out the difficulties. The mediator, J. Klahr Huddle, concluded that the Davies's coddled nature didn't help matters. Besides the importing of ice cream, they insisted on being transported in private trains, brought along an "entourage of sixteen aides, servants and relatives," and even found space on the Leningrad docks for Mrs. Davies's yacht, the *Sea Cloud*! Huddle also observed that Davies was unwilling to admit his lack of knowledge of the Soviet Union. To the State Department employees who prided themselves on their acquired knowledge of the Soviet regime, especially Kennan, this was a damning indictment.[32]

One incident probably best exemplified the irreconcilable differences between the ambassador and his employees. When Davies began work, an embassy electrician discovered that the ambassador's office had been bugged. The staff was appalled by the effrontery of the Soviets, but Davies hushed them like excitable schoolchildren, chuckling that it was of no account. Referring to his embassy team as "youngsters," he said they had nothing to fear and that the Soviets would soon discover that they were friends.[33]

Davies's inability to work well with embassy staff did not bode well for his tenure in office. As a matter of fact, Davies would bypass the Russia experts at the embassy and rely on reporters like the Stalinist sycophant Walter Duranty for his information and advice. When he wasn't translating during the Great Purge trials, Kennan was relegated to being Davies's sandwich gopher while Davies sanctimoniously bantered with the press. Charles Bohlen believed Davies was "sublimely ignorant of even the most elementary realities of the Soviet system and of its ideology."[34]

Davies embodied the Roosevelt administration's naiveté toward the Soviets under Stalin, and that would spell trouble for Alexander Streck. Whereas Bullitt was prepared to make inquiries for this good man who had served them at great risk to himself, in March 1937 Davies would state that religious persecution in the Soviet Union was not only exaggerated but actually diminishing (Streck was undergoing strenuous interrogations at this time). The ambassador believed Stalin was serving as a buffer between the anti-religious extremists and Christians, as evidenced by the Stalin Constitution of 1936 that allowed for freedom of worship and anti-religious propaganda.[35] Indeed, Davies quoted the wording if not the intent of the constitution accurately.

President Roosevelt would not be as precise. While trying to convince Americans of the necessity of the Lend-Lease Agreement with the Soviet Union in 1941, he had cause to cite Article 124 of the Stalin Constitution of 1936 in defense of religious freedom. Confessing that he couldn't quote it exactly, he continued, "but anyway: freedom of conscience ... freedom of religion. Freedom equally to use propaganda against religion, which is essentially what the rule is in this country; only, we don't put it quite the same way."[36]

Americans didn't put it quite the same way because it wasn't the same. Roosevelt assumed that believers and unbelievers had the same right to express their faith or lack of faith. But that interpretation was accurate only in the days of Lenin. Under the April 8, 1929, Law on Religious Associations, a subtle but important change had been made. From that time forward, religious believers were only allowed the right to worship while atheists could exercise the right to anti-religious propaganda. That was what the Stalin Constitution would reiterate in 1936. In other words, nothing had changed since 1929.

Had the president and ambassador to the USSR bothered to look at the translation that their own embassy personnel had provided of a *Bezbozhnik* article in July 1936, they would have discovered the nuances of the Stalinist use of language. The article admits that people can "profess" whatever religion they choose but only anti-religious people have the right to engage in propaganda. Article 124 stated, "In order to guarantee to citizens freedom of conscience, the church in the U.S.S.R. is separated from the State and the schools from the church. The freedom to perform religious rites and the freedom of anti-religious propaganda are secured for all citizens." Again, that is an important distinction because it meant that Christians could not express their religious convictions in public. With the excessive tax rates on churches, the staggered workweek, and the persecution, arrest, and execution of pastors, the right to worship inside a church building would soon become moot because eventually there would be none left. *Bezbozhnik* confirmed that the Soviet Union would continue to struggle against "all kinds of reactionary ideas, against religion, and for a scientific, materialistic world conception. ... In a country of socialism, the overcoming of religion will proceed at a still more rapid, and hitherto unattained, rate."[37] While oftentimes he left the sharp statements about destroying religion to his subordinates, at other times Joseph Stalin could be quite blunt and leave nothing to the imagination. While speaking to an American delegation in 1936 about the role of the clergy, Stalin admitted, "The Party cannot remain neutral when regarding the propagators of religious prejudices, with regard to reactionary clergy poisoning the minds of laboring masses. Have we annihilated the clergy? Yes, we have annihilated it. The trouble is that it is not yet completely liquidated."[38] Any relaxing of measures against Christians was only a temporary retreat, just as in the early days of collectivization. Stalin remained committed to Christianity's destruction.

After the turmoil in the USSR and troubles within the embassy, it is no wonder that George Kennan was ready for reassignment. Davies was eager to oblige him.[39] However, unbeknownst to him, Soviet ambassador Troyanovsky had somehow purloined an internal memorandum of Kennan's and presented it to Stalin. Troyanovsky characterized Kennan's attacks on Ambassador Davies as an attempt to turn President Roosevelt against the Soviets. Troyanovsky satisfactorily concluded, though, that he had failed in turning Roosevelt against them. In fact, Kennan admitted that he "could never forgive F.D.R." for so summarily dismissing the embassy team's analysis of the USSR.[40] When writing down his thoughts about the effects of the Bolshevik Revolution, Kennan poignantly confided to his diary that its "victims are no more to it than the thousands of seeds which are cast to the wind, in order that one tree may grow."[41]

As for Davies, he would only spend nine months of his eighteen-month term in Moscow, but would perform more effective work for Soviet propaganda in the future. He would pen a book, *Mission to Moscow*, that would eventually be turned into a Hollywood movie portraying Joseph Stalin as a genial uncle and stalwart ally of the United States. The popular actor Walter Huston would play the role of Davies in the film.[42] Kennan and his colleagues may well have wondered what would have happened if only Streck had received an equal measure of Davies's respect and concern.

THE NKVD BIG LIE

Linking the Russian Lutheran Church to Hitler

ON THE SAME night that Alexander Streck was arrested (November 4, 1936), a layman from the defunct Jesus Christ Lutheran, Konstantin Andrievsky, was subjected to the unwanted attention of the NKVD and placed under arrest. The fifty-seven-year-old Andrievsky worked as a lawyer at the Leningrad Bureau of Communal Apartments in the Kirov region of Leningrad, and the NKVD described him as possessing a "sharp, counter-revolutionary temperament."[1] Even though Jesus Christ Lutheran had closed in 1935, the NKVD had only now decided to accuse him of being a member of an illegal Lutheran congregation. Andrievsky was accused of carrying out anti-Soviet agitation among his circle of believers with the goal of discrediting the activities of the party and government.[2]

But as his interrogation continued, it seemed more likely that the real target of the NKVD was Pastor Paul Reichert and his son, Bruno. In Andrievsky's NKVD file of December 28, the agent admits, "Pastor Reichert has still not been arrested." In fact, the agent links Bishop Malmgren to Reichert's "counter-rev-olutionary Fascist activities," which would have no doubt amused the pastors, who were not on the best of terms. (The agent must have been unaware of cur-rent events in the Lutheran church, too, since Bishop Malmgren had already left the USSR for good in the summer.)[3]

Coupled with the arrest of Streck, the NKVD's preparations to build a case against the pastors of the largest Lutheran congregation in Leningrad signaled that it was now going after the mother churches of its two largest cities, Moscow and Leningrad. But this experienced lawyer was not giving them the evidence they wanted, because during the questioning on December 16 the NKVD agent lost patience and commanded Andrievsky to stop with his denials and name the members of his counterrevolutionary group. Paul Reichert was named, along with Alfred Zietnick and the organist Evgeny Hannicke. (Reichert had substituted from time to time at Jesus Christ Lutheran after Kurt Muss's arrest.) Parishioner Woldemar Schmidt was also mentioned. Andrievsky was quoted as saying that they had worked undercover for some time at St. Michael's (where Jesus Christ Lutheran had worshiped) and then began gathering at Zietnick's apartment in 1935 when the church was closed. There they had spread slanderous rumors about the Soviet government's persecution of religion and oppression of believers. Andrievsky's previous statements that the Orthodox were undergoing even greater persecution than the Lutherans now came to light.[4]

In July 1935, Andrievsky was said to have claimed that a Lutheran pastor from a fascist organization had come from Munich to initiate conversations with Reichert about forming fascist cadres in the Lutheran congregation. Reichert supposedly told Andrievsky what the pastor from Munich had told him—Hitler had great authority among the people and the Lutheran pastors were members of the Fascist Party. The Church was transforming its confession into a "weapon of the government in the hands of Hitler." Hitler was being presented as the leader of the German people who would save the country from communism. It is not at all impossible that a Nazi-sympathizing German pastor could have attempted to engage in espionage within the USSR, although the risks would seem to far outweigh any gains. At any rate, Reichert supposedly refused to organize the group for fear of being discovered. Andrievsky would not say what counterrevolutionary activities Reichert had performed. He did not know.[5]

From Andrievsky's interrogation of April 23, 1937, though, a clearer picture of the incident between Reichert and the fascist pastor from Munich emerges. It seems that this story was accurate to some degree, but Andrievsky explained that Reichert recognized immediately that this German pastor guest, if he was that, was a Nazi spy. He quickly told the German pastor to leave his apartment and was quite agitated by the incident. Far from conspiring with the Nazi pastor, Reichert was appalled by his insolence.[6] Why had he said something different in his previous testimony? Well, Andrievsky now rejected the testimonies he gave to the NKVD on November 15 and December 16, 1936. Speaking boldly, he asserted: "The confession presented to me by the investigating organs of the political charges to what I consider strange crimes and likewise, the fictitious details in the protocols of the investigation, were signed by me under conditions of horrible torture of a psychologically violent manner (although I was not beaten physically)."[7] Concerning the incident with the Munich pastor and Paul Reichert in July 1935 and his supposed testimony, Andrievsky noticed that the phrase "refused to sign" had been erased from the document. Instead, a signature of his somewhat lower on the document was used as if he had confirmed the previous testimony. Furthermore, this signature was only given, he confessed, to "save his mind from madness in an instinctive quest to save his own life." Apparently, this evidence was taken from the December 1936 inquiry because Andrievsky related that after his interrogation he was put into solitary confinement with another agent from midnight until 1 p.m. December 16. "I categorically deny all of these protocols from December 16, rejecting it to be of no value. I reject the order of the material of the inquiry written as not being taken from my words, but rather imposed on me by the agent [whose name is written here] in the absence of the protocols from November 15 and December 16 which were signed by me under similar pressure from this agent."[8]

This preserved testimony gives us an extraordinary glimpse into the fact that not all of the arrested simply gave in to NKVD pressure, however violent. An astute lawyer like Andrievsky was not one to be overwhelmed by the

charges against him. Instead, he recognized how the NKVD was fabricating
evidence and called them on it. This son of a Russian Orthodox priest may
have already had one strike against him due to his ecclesiastical origins, but
he knew his rights under Soviet law better than the NKVD agents who were
interrogating him. The NKVD, however, was not finished with him. They now
sought to incriminate Andrievsky primarily through the testimony of two of
his acquaintances, Ivan Gusev (an apartment building manager) and Sergey
Borisov, a lawyer working on Vasilyevsky Island in the city.[9]

Borisov would never appear before their tribunal to be confronted by
Andrievsky, always seemingly traveling on a business trip of some kind.[10] When
he did give his private testimony to the NKVD, though, he accused Andrievsky
of saying that "slavery flourishes everywhere in the USSR, the peasants are
enslaved in the collective farms and amidst the population of the USSR are
many unsatisfied people." Regarding the new Stalin Constitution, Borisov
denounced Andrievsky for claiming that the rights it espoused existed solely on
paper. For added measure, he also accused Andrievsky of being an anti-Semite.[11]
Although Andrievsky would not be given the opportunity to confront Borisov
directly, he called it a lie. He never said the constitution was just "dust"— on
the contrary, he thought it would raise the prestige of "our Soviet Union."
Indeed, many Christians praised the Stalin Constitution for expanded rights.
But Andrievsky also cleverly pointed out the absurdities in the statements of
both of his accusers. For example, Andrievsky noted that Gusev must have
hurriedly signed "yes" to one testimony because it actually contradicted his
previous testimony! If these witnesses knew him to have been a counterrevolutionary, Andrievsky wondered why they continued to interact and work
with him as a legal advisor.[12]

But it seems that deep down Andrievsky knew Gusev and Borisov had
not been searching for a pretext to incriminate him. He had pity on these
men because he had also served as their spiritual adviser. For example, Borisov
was not happy with his Orthodox faith and sought to engage Andrievsky in

conversation about the Evangelical Lutheran confessions, repeatedly visiting him in his apartment to discuss religion. Since he was experiencing difficulties in his family life, Borisov was thankful for Andrievsky's cheerfulness and moral support. The frustrated Andrievsky queried the NKVD agent, "What kind of witnesses are these—Gusev and Borisov, who overlooked my counterrevolution in the course of two-plus years, when both of them took so much moral and domestic advice from me? Why did they both so insistently seek out my counterrevolutionary company when they were surrounded by millions in Leningrad?" ... It's obvious that I became a counterrevolutionary in their evaluation much later, perhaps at 11:30 P.M., November 3rd, 1936, when Borisov left my apartment and I was arrested one hour later!" Despite the accusation of counterrevolutionary activity, Andrievsky affirmed that both men were orderly and honest men in their affairs, not guilty of counter-revolution.[13] But Andrievsky would stew in prison until the middle of 1937 when he would receive his sentence.[14]

ON DECEMBER 5, 1936, the Stalin Constitution was ratified to great acclaim. The Party felt comfortable enough in its unquestioned authority to write such a generous constitution, but atheists worried that they might lose ground to the forces of religion, which they considered by no means to be dead. As if confirming their fears, clergy and believers received the news with glee, many writing to Stalin with congratulations for his magnanimity.[15] Priests in the Vyazma diocese praised Stalin, calling his constitution "the immortal historical document" while five hundred believers in the Mordovan region of central Russia came together to pray and thank God for Article 124. Other priests suggested that they could rally support for the constitution from their pulpits![16] Joseph Davies, ever inclined to give Stalin the benefit of the doubt, informed embassy employees that he had heard Stalin was defending the more liberal clauses regarding religious practice in the constitution. Stalin was reported as saying if there was a danger to the Communist Party in this new constitutional language, it would have to overcome it.[17]

What did Article 124 say? Loy Henderson spelled it out for US Secretary of State Hull: "In order to guarantee to citizens freedom of conscience, the church in the U.S.S.R. is separated from the State and the schools from the church. The freedom to perform religious rites and the freedom of anti-religious propaganda are secured for all citizens."[18] Clergy who formerly could not own property were now allowed the right to vote again, the right to work, as well as the opportunity to run for public office.[19] It was reported by the journal *Socialist Agriculture* that in the western Russian regions, people who had hidden their faith were now more open about being believers. The people in that region wanted to nominate a priest named Araviski, described as an eloquent, well-read citizen who knew Soviet law well.[20] In essence, on paper everyone but lunatics and convicted criminals were given the right to vote.[21] Likewise, the children of believers and pastors could once again attend schools, join collective farms, and even receive food ration cards.[22]

But the real battle for the constitution's interpretation was going to take place in the villages between local officials and the newly encouraged believers. Orthodox Christians began to request worship processions or for the local village soviet to reopen their church. In one instance, the parishioners would not go to work on the collective farm after local authorities refused to reopen their church.[23] In the Kuibyshev region, a citizen interpreted the constitution as denying the village soviet the right to manage the church. Another citizen, a bookkeeper in Zel'man area, said that priests could now assemble believers freely without the village soviet's approval. In the Muslim region of Dagestan, even bolder readings of the constitution would threaten the forces of atheism. Citizens mistranslated the "freedom of anti-religious propaganda" spelled out in the text to proclaim instead "freedom of religious propaganda!"[24] Atheists had reason to fear the opening of this Pandora's box.

In March/April 1937 articles, *Pravda* and *Komsomolskaya Pravda* worriedly discussed the propensity for young people to return to the church and participate in its activities. Students were once again joining church choirs. In the Nizhniy Novgorod region, 182 youth of Komsomol age (eighteen to twenty-five years old) were serving as members of church boards. Even Communist youth were being married according to religious rites, as well as observing church holidays and serving as godparents at baptisms.[25] Nikolai Ustraliov, a noted émigré who kept an extensive diary on his return to the Soviet Union, praised Stalin and the Party for restoring pride in the nation through the constitution: "People are proud—I am a Soviet citizen. ... Long live the USSR! Long live the Soviet state!"[26]

As usual with Stalin, though, the devil was in the details. When a concerned Communist expressed his fear that priests would exercise their right to vote according to the constitution, a village soviet chairman in the Voronezh region assured him: "They will be deprived of the vote on Election Day."[27] Despite such reassurances, with representative seats to the Supreme Soviet scheduled for late 1937, other leaders of the USSR were in full panic mode. As the February-March plenum of the Central Committee of the Communist Party discussed the upcoming elections, Stalin gave them a hint of things to come when he launched into an attack on enemies of the regime.[28] Nikolai Yezhov, the NKVD chief since September 29, 1936, was similarly unequivocal in declaring that adoption of the constitution only sharpened the struggle against counterrevolutionary elements.[29] The reassuring message from the regime was that anti-Soviet elements would be dealt with before they could exercise their new freedoms. "Anti-Soviet elements" was a term that marked anyone considered dangerous by the state, which certainly included religious believers, especially those of dubious ethnicity (e.g., Finns, Germans, Latvians). Nikolai Ustraliov's pride in the constitution would be short-lived, for he soon discovered that Stalin and Yezhov did not issue idle threats. 1937 would see the height of Stalin's Great Terror, and he would be numbered among its victims.[30]

BUT WHILE THE finishing touches were being put on the Stalin Constitution, Alexander Streck was experiencing the reality of Stalin's intentions with regard to religious freedom. While Ambassador William Bullitt was angrily responding to the news that Streck had been arrested, the pastor was undergoing the first of his interrogations by the NKVD. On November 15, the NKVD initiated the process by asking him about the 1924 Synod of the Evangelical Lutheran Church in Moscow. The transcript of the interrogation from the recently opened KGB archive leads the reader to believe that the NKVD was interested in portraying Bishops Meier, Malmgren, and the High Church Council as tools of the German government, engaged in "a counterrevolutionary, nationalist and pan-Germanic work."[31]

Streck's responses have to be understood, for the most part, as fabricated. During Stalin's Great Terror, the NKVD made up allegations of spying, usually for Japan or Nazi Germany, out of whole cloth. We have to read between the lines and be careful about jumping to conclusions. In this case, Streck's refutation of virtually all the words attributed to him by the end of the interrogation process in July 1937 must be given greater weight (and it is rare that such files would even preserve such a refutation). These records give us a window into the mindset of the NKVD and how it attempted to brand Soviet citizens and religious figures like Streck as saboteurs in the pay of Nazi Germany.

One way the NKVD accomplished this was to speak about Streck's connections to foreign organizations. Surprisingly, since he was ministering to Protestants at the US embassy, his ties to Americans are not mentioned in any of the open files. (However, not all of the files related to Streck are available for viewing.) His connection to the German embassy was of primary interest. Since Sts. Peter and Paul was often considered the "German embassy personnel's church," and given the toxic relationship between Nazi Germany and the USSR, Streck's ties to those in the German embassy were highlighted in the interrogations and cast in the most damning light. German Christian organizations like the Gustav-Adolf-Verein and the Union of Germans Beyond the Borders were considered to be the paymasters, sending cash not only for the Lutheran Church and its parishioners but also for enabling the bishops and pastors to engage in subterfuge.

What were the accusations that the NKVD was developing against Streck? Besides carrying out the counterrevolutionary work of the German government among Soviet citizens of German descent, he was accused of being involved in a grand plot to assassinate the leaders of the Politburo, including Stalin himself! These fantastic charges echo the Communist Party line taken after the assassination of Sergey Kirov, the NKVD claiming that the Kirov murder was only the beginning of the enemy's diabolical action to undermine the Soviet Union.

German embassy employees Messrs. Gerhardt and Schwindt were said to have been Streck's contacts, the NKVD claiming that their plans were developed with the pastor in the sacristy of Sts. Peter and Paul.[32] Most likely Gerhardt and Schwindt were embassy employees who happened to attend a Lutheran church whose services were in German. They may also have been links for financial support to the church that was funneled through the embassy, but the NKVD interpreted any contact that Streck had with them in the worst manner. As the interrogations dragged on through November 23, Streck was called in at whatever hour suited the NKVD and kept for hours on end, including one interrogation that began at 9 p.m. on November 25 and continued until 1 a.m. on November 26, only to start up again the next day at 11 a.m.[33]

SHOWING THAT IT had done its homework on the divisions within the Lutheran Church, the NKVD also portrayed bishops Meier and Malmgren as proponents of a hierarchical form of church government that strove to sideline those who advocated a more synodical, democratic form of government. In the mid to late 1920s, Jakob Fritzler and Eduard Luft had sought to entice Lutherans to adopt this kind of church structure. Luft had, according to ELCR Kharkov District President Gustav Birth, even seen himself as filling the role of a second Luther. Fritzler was the president of the Free Lutheran-Reformed Church of a Congressional Position (FELRCCP), which had been used by Soviet authorities as a wedge against the more organized, hierarchical form of church government employed by the Evangelical Lutheran Church of Russia. Both these men, though, were no longer useful to the Soviets, since they were never interested in any form of church government. Fritzler was arrested on April 23, 1933, and sentenced to ten years in a labor camp. His congregation in Fischer was closed within a year on December 5, 1934. Luft was arrested in 1934 and died shortly thereafter.[34]

The NKVD, though, sought to recast the contacts of Meier and Malmgren with German nationalists as allying with those who could not countenance a more flexible church structure. The bishops were said to prefer to keep power within the hands of their more malleable puppets. The High Church Council was called "the fulfilling entity" of the bishops' plans. The NKVD even put words in the mouth of Streck that the bishops' actions were against the "spirit of the Lutheran Church. ... Nowhere, not in any country but the USSR, had such a situation existed, where everywhere the principle of synodical government was preserved."[35]

Meier and Malmgren were said to have plotted since 1924, along with High Church Council members Paul Althausen and Robert Derringer, to preserve the hierarchical system in the interests of developing "nationalistic, counterrevolutionary work" among German parishioners of Soviet citizenship. Ironically, and quite probably missed by the NKVD, the system of church government had not changed appreciably since the days of the former Bishop Freifeldt in the early years of the Soviet Union. In fact, having two bishops instead of one was evidence against the concentration of power within the hands of a potential führer. Among the accused, Malmgren was safely ensconced in Germany, while Meier, Derringer, and Althausen were already dead. In fact, Althausen (a member of St. Michael's in Moscow) had been executed by the Soviet government in 1935 in the Elizabeth Meier affair. Perhaps this is why Streck mentioned their names (if indeed the NKVD did not twist his words).[36]

Whatever the case, in further interrogations on November 25, several Lutheran pastors were named as cohorts of Streck in counterrevolutionary activities: Gustav Birth, Johannes Seidlitz, Helmut Hansen, Kurt Muss, Arthur Kluck, Eugen Bachmann, and Alexander Wolfius of the Peterschule, among others. When Streck was accused of not naming all his fellow counter-revolutionists, the NKVD added the names of Arnold Frischfeld and Woldemar Rüger. Rüger had served St. Michael's in Moscow and had already been placed under arrest in 1935, but the NKVD has Streck saying he was from Leningrad. Streck would have known better than this, since St. Michael's congregation had met a few blocks from Sts. Peter and Paul after its own church was closed in 1928 (and was now closed down completely). For good measure, the NKVD continued adding names of other so-called conspirators, like pastors Wilhelm Lohrer of Omsk and Friedrich Mertz, with whom Streck was not intimately acquainted. The interrogations that we possess end on November 26 and do not continue again until January 10, 1937.[37] It appears that the NKVD was preparing a major case against Streck, perhaps intending to close the last Lutheran church in Moscow. We don't know what happened with the parishioners after his arrest, although there is evidence to indicate that Streck's wife, Veronika, bravely continued to conduct the worship services among the faithful in the church building, which had not yet been taken over by the Soviet government.[38] As for the Evangelical Lutheran Church of Russia as a whole, only eleven pastors remained in office by the end of 1936. Its physical extinction was imminent.[39]

28

"BLESSED ARE THEY THAT SUFFER PERSECUTION FOR JUSTICE'S SAKE"

The Great Terror and the Destruction of the Lutheran Pastorate in the USSR

BY THE END of the Second Five-Year Plan, the Soviets had expected that Christianity would be on its deathbed. And yet despite the pressure, arrests, and torture, the euphoria of believers in response to the new Stalin Constitution was evidence that Christianity's obituary had been premature. Further proof of its vibrancy would be found in the results of a census conducted by the Soviet government at the beginning of 1937. On January 6/7, the eve of Orthodox Christmas celebrations, the government asked this question: "Do you believe in God?" The results were expected to show the victory that atheism had achieved over Christianity, but it turned out to be a debacle. To its great alarm, the government discovered that more than half of Soviet adults still considered themselves believers and were bold enough to acknowledge their faith to the census takers! The Communist Party was flabbergasted. In Leningrad, the League of the Militant Godless had for all intents and purposes collapsed.[1]

Stalin had himself formulated the question about religion, making clear that pollsters measure the current convictions of the citizen as opposed to religion

340

passed down by one's parents. Despite this more adequate measure of religion in the country, 55.3 million claimed to believe in God (56.7 percent), 42.2 million (43.3 percent) stated that they were unbelievers, and 900,000 said they didn't know.[2] This revelation was enough to spoil the celebratory mood of the Communist Party as it prepared to commemorate the twentieth anniversary of the Bolshevik Revolution.

But it's not as if Soviet citizens weren't frightened by the implications of acknowledging belief in God in an avowedly atheist state. The violent closure of churches during collectivization was still etched in recent memory, while rumors abounded that a pogrom along the lines of the St. Bartholomew's Day Massacre was being planned against believers. Others expected the imminent arrival of the Antichrist. The apocalyptic rumors of the end times that had marked the period of forced collectivization now returned with a vengeance. Some prophesied the return of Czar Mikhail, who would rule Russia at the time of the final resurrection. One Orthodox believer claimed, "The prophecies of the sacred writings say that when the time of the Antichrist comes people will destroy each other; Zinoviev and the others were *vozhdi* [leaders] not long ago, judged and shot people themselves and today they are being judged and shot; it's God's punishment for the fact that people have forgotten God and the church."[3]

LUTHERANS WERE FOR the most part not as mystically inclined as the Orthodox, but the late Bishop Meier's identification of the regime as the Antichrist resonated strongly with many in the Church. After all, state pressure on religion had been steadily increasing even in the Lutheran stronghold of Ingria. In 1935, churches in the Ingrian villages of Tuutari, Ropsu, Haapankangas, and Skuoritsa had their church bells taken away. Prayer houses in Hajaka and Konnu were closed. The finances of the congregation in Spankkova had been expropriated. In 1936, the traditional and well-attended church festivals in Tuutari, Venjoki, and Kolppana were prohibited. The Toksovo congregation saw its bells thrown down from the church tower and cut up with a welding torch. The cross was also thrown down as the altar was taken from the church and reduced to rubble.[4] It is no wonder that interpretations of the Antichrist's appearance would not be far from the mark in any part of the Soviet Union.

Koltushi parishioner Katri Kukkhonen remembered that many villagers were placed in a quandary by the census: how should they answer this question about their faith? They could be fired, especially if they worked for the government. Students and teachers could easily be dismissed from an institute for an answer in the affirmative, too. Kukkhonen considered the situation of her close friend, Amalia Laskinen, who was the daughter of a keuster from the Petrozavodsk church. Amalia studied at a pedagogical institute and didn't even think of the potential unpleasantness when she answered the question about her faith in the affirmative. Her primary fear was that of denying her Lord and Savior. The following day she was expelled from the institute.

But when the census came to Koltushi in January and February, Kukkhonen said that everyone in the village said yes, he or she believed in God! For the youth, however, it was a decisive moment. If they said yes, the doors to higher education would be closed. And indeed, they were closed, but the youth remained firm in their Christian faith. The faith of the Lutherans in Koltushi was even more remarkable because their pastor, Juhana Varonen, had been forced to return to Finland at the end of 1935. Despite his departure, parishioners and servants of the church conducted services in the pastor's absence in the wooden church up on the hill. Finally, in February 1937, Aleksanteri Korpelainen came to shepherd the congregation while continuing his service nearby at the congregation in Haapankangas.[5] Korpelainen had been a lay minister in the early 1920s in the Leningrad region village of Gubanitsa. He was considered to have been one of the most energetic pastors of a period that came to be known as "The Time of Awakening in Ingria." Even though conditions for Korpelainen and Koltushi were far different in 1937, the bold stands taken by the villagers and the character of their pastor would challenge the Soviets' plans to eradicate religion in the Ingrian regions.[6]

According to Soviet archives, 15,000 Christian believers still celebrated Western Christmas in 1935 despite the many closures of key Lutheran churches in Leningrad. On Easter Sunday, May 1, 1937, a total of 81,500 people attended Orthodox services.[7] Even in Moscow, Catholic priest Léopold Braun was amazed at the courage of his Soviet parishioners. Hundreds of them would disappear never to be heard from again. But while they were at worship, they listened in rapt attention to the reading of the Scriptures, especially when they heard the consoling words, "Blessed are they that suffer persecution for justice'[s] sake: for theirs is the kingdom of heaven."[8] In short, belief in God was far from extinct and the government knew it. It had stirred up a hornet's nest when it approved the new constitution, for it was being interpreted as permission for believers to act on their faith. The Soviets had to act swiftly before religious believers took their constitutional rights too seriously.

In response to this upsurge in religious activity, the last half of 1937 would be marked by a new wave of persecution aimed primarily at the remaining pastors/priests and believers who were active in the church. The churches would be closed on a massive scale so that believers would understand unequivocally that anti-Soviet elements would have no rights. The 1937 census was annulled, and when a new census was taken in 1939, the government carefully avoided posing any question about religion.[9]

BUT OUTSIDE OF the Ingrian region, the Lutheran Church in Russia began the year 1937 virtually rudderless when it came to pastoral leadership. There were only eleven actively serving the Evangelical Lutheran Church of Russia at the beginning of 1937. They were: (1 & 2) Paul and Bruno Reichert at St. Peter's in Leningrad; (3 & 4) Alexander Migle and his brother, Jan, serving the

Latvians at Christ the Savior Lutheran Church in Leningrad; (5) Ferdinand Bodungen, who primarily served in Peterhof but also at Christ the Savior, Leningrad; (6) Aleksanteri Korpelainen, who served at Haapakangas and Koltushi, Leningrad region; (7) Leo Schultz, serving Estonians at Moloskovitsa in Karelia; (8) Heinrich Behrendts, serving Germans in Tashkent, Uzbekistan; (9) Pekka Braks, in the Ingrian villages of Venjoki and Gubanitsa; (10) Karl Vogel in Odessa (Ukraine); and (11) Selim Laurikkala, serving Finns and Ingrians at St. Mary's in Leningrad proper and other Finnish-speaking congregations in the Leningrad region.[10]

Vast regions like Siberia, the Volga, and the Ukraine were bereft of spiritual leaders, not to mention the capital city of Moscow. While these few remaining pastors were holding firm, many of their friends and colleagues were suffering and dying in the Gulag labor camps. Arthur Kluck had been arrested in 1929 and somehow had survived the backbreaking labor of felling and transporting trees all day. An academic unused to such labor, Kluck had been working at slave labor for at least five years.[11] Historian Anne Applebaum, in her comprehensive work *Gulag*, discovered that work in the forests could be the most taxing form of prison labor, especially in the winter. When the winter storms known as *burany* (or *purgai*) raged, the workers were so blinded by the swirling snow that they could only walk back to the camps attached to each other by a rope. Some were left behind when they fell to the ground from exhaustion and their corpses would not be discovered until the spring thaw.[12]

While the Lord was preserving Kluck under impossible circumstances, his family was visited by the NKVD one night in 1937. The officers searched the apartment thoroughly and found nothing but Christian books. The senior NKVD officer informed his colleagues, "We'll send the kids to an orphanage. Prepare the paperwork!" Kluck's mother-in-law's legs were swollen, and she couldn't stand up or get out of bed, which she made clear to the officers. If they wanted her to move, she said, "Then you'll have to carry me out, bed and all." The senior officer summoned his own doctor, who confirmed a diagnosis of rheumatism and a weak heart. The NKVD officers ultimately left the family untouched. This was a miracle in a year when there were few stories of hope, but the paralyzing fear of that encounter would remain with Gisela Kluck all of her life.[13]

Unfortunately, Kluck would not receive any such reprieve from the NKVD. Several years after his death, Kluck's family was visited by a fellow prisoner who spoke reverently of the pastor's faith. After an exhausting workday, the man recalled that the prisoners would devour the little bits of bread they had scraped together for supper and then collapse onto their wooden plank bunks, grasping the few hours of precious sleep they would need in order to survive until the next day. But Arthur Kluck would sit up and pray—for a long time. The man noticed the pastor praying often and urged him, "Arthur, why are you praying so long? You better get some sleep!" Arthur looked up at him and replied, "It's the one thing that I can still do for my family." And he would go on praying.

Gisela Kluck remembered that she and her brothers would pray with their mother every night for him. She is convinced that God answered her father's prayers and helped her and her younger brother, Arthur Jr., survive and eventually immigrate to Germany after the fall of communism in the USSR in 1991. With tears of joy, on arrival she would address her late mother (who did not survive World War II), "Mama, we finally made it to the promised land—Germany!" On October 28, 1937, the NKVD in the Novosibirsk region sentenced Kluck to death on the charge that he was a participant in an organization called "The Union for the Salvation of Russia." The Union was said to be disseminating counterrevolutionary rumors, making defamatory statements against the Communist Party and Soviet government, and consistently praising life in Germany while preparing for an armed insurrection against the Soviet Union.

After the fall of the Soviet Union in the 1990s, children from Marxstadt like Gerhard Fink remembered the pastor with the sonorous voice who enthralled them in church with his recitation of familiar Bible stories—Daniel in the lions' den or David and Goliath. Friedrich Fischer remembered Kluck for the selfless and bold act he performed, marrying his uncle Andrei and aunt Olga in an apartment when the church in Katharinenstadt had been closed in 1927. The unbelievable nature of the charges against Kluck would eventually be refuted publicly by the Soviet state on his rehabilitation in 1989, but this was 1937 and no respite was in sight. Despite his wife's pleas, Arthur Kluck would not be freed. On November 9, he was executed.[14]

BACK IN MOSCOW, the NKVD restarted the interrogation of Alexander Streck in January 1937, addressing the questions more sharply because they believed Streck was not answering them directly. On March 2, they brought Harry Helms face-to-face with his pastor in order to force them to refute one another. The NKVD records Streck as saying that Helms promised to lead a reformation in the Church, seeing himself in the role of an ecclesiastical Hitler. Helms was portrayed as the one who led Streck into this fascist circle within the church. This conversation between the two supposedly (and conveniently) took place in March or April 1933, shortly after Hitler's Enabling Act secured his power base in Germany. Streck claimed to have no memory of such a meeting. They then tried to twist the words of Helms so that it appeared as if he was accusing Streck of sinister ties with embassy personnel. Streck admitted to conversing with them, but only about church matters. The NKVD interrogators either couldn't imagine that it was logical for Streck to seek assistance for the operation of the church from the German embassy, or were simply looking for any connection between Streck and foreigners so they could be rid of him.

On March 4, the NKVD concluded that Streck was a member of a counter-revolutionary terrorist group carrying out Fascist spying for the German embassy. Several of his acquaintances had been arrested because, they claimed, Streck had drawn them into his circle. By April 25, the NKVD completed its inquiry into Streck and passed his case along to the *troika*, a special committee of three judges generally consisting of the regional NKVD chief, the chief party secretary of the region, and a representative of the prosecutor's office or the local government. Their task was to speed up the process of convictions, condemning a prisoner in absentia without even the pretense of judge, jury, and trial. In this manner, troikas decided the fate of millions of individuals in the Soviet Union during Stalin's Great Terror.[15] Thus at 11:51 a.m., July 3, General Vasily Ulrich presided over a closed session of the troika in the case of Pastor Alexander Streck.[16] Usually in these cases the victim would confess his guilt and profess his undying love for Stalin or the Soviet state. But Streck was not allowed to speak publicly to Ulrich and the troika, and in any case he had already laid waste their plans for a compliant witness. Previous to the final session, Streck rejected *all* the charges brought against him from the time he was arrested in November 1936. "I have never been a Fascist," he declaimed. When asked why he had previously confessed to these crimes, Streck indicated that he had been imprisoned for a long period and this had affected his nervous condition. Plus, he acknowledged that he had been subjected to "rude methods," probably indicating some kind of torture.[17]

In the end, Streck was a faithful witness, boldly refuting the lies that the Soviets had so painstakingly concocted. It didn't matter to them, but it is important that his refutation was preserved for the sake of his honor and that of the church. Streck was sentenced to death, and the fifty-four-year-old pastor was executed on July 27, probably in Butyrka Prison in Moscow where he had been held. His family was thereafter exiled to Kazakhstan, never to return to Moscow.[18] Recalling the heroism of Pastor Streck, a church council member arrested in his case declared: "I was blessed to once know such great men!"[19]

29

HEROES OF FAITH IN THE GULAG

Re-Arrests and Deaths in the Camps

IN THE LATTER half of 1937, NKVD Commissar Nikolai Yezhov ordered that on August 5 "all republics and regions launch a campaign of punitive measures against former kulaks, active anti-Soviet elements, and criminals." Included in that definition were "sectarian activists" and "church officials" currently held in the prisons and labor camps who were carrying out what was identified as "active anti-Soviet espionage." Approximately 936,000 people would be arrested in the USSR in 1937.[1]

Pastor Helmut Hansen was one of those who fell under the scope of Yezhov's decree. Hansen had been laboring in Gulag labor camps after receiving his ten-year sentence in September 1930. His health had declined over the years as he suffered from inflammation of the heart muscle (myocarditis), a form of diabetes, and anemia. Furthermore, he had apparently not been a model prisoner in the eyes of the Gulag camp administration and had suffered for it. In early 1937, he sent the letter of another prisoner (presumably he had not been allowed the privilege) to the city of Segezha and also used the right for official correspondence to send his own private letters, no doubt to his wife Erna, who had been freed and was working as a nurse in Petrograd District of Leningrad. For this offense, he was put in the camp prison for five days without having those days deducted from his sentence.[2] In 1937, Erna and the boys succeeded in traveling to visit him in his Gulag labor camp in the Karelian village of Medvezhegorsk, an unimaginable journey at that time and a true testament to the love that they had for each other.[3]

As the year proceeded, though, the NKVD continued to gather evidence from his fellow prisoners within the camps, portraying Hansen as an enemy of the Soviet state. One claimed, perhaps accurately, that Hansen didn't believe the Soviet evidence of espionage against Marshal Tukhachevsky and the other military leaders executed by Stalin in June 1937. Hansen supposedly exclaimed, "I can't understand how they harmed their own government since they [the government] were protected by them." Indeed, if Hansen did say this, he saw through the case that Stalin had manufactured against the popular marshal.[4] Evidence years later would confirm that Nazi Germany had planted false evidence of Tukachevsky's betrayal, and in the accusatory spirit of the times when the purges were in full operation, he wouldn't have had a chance to counter Stalin's paranoia.[5] Nor, ultimately, would smaller fish in their eyes, like Helmut Hansen.

Another witness claimed that with respect to the coming twentieth anniversary of the Bolshevik Revolution in 1937, Hansen had said, "We can't expect an amnesty for the twentieth anniversary of the revolution because there are still classes and camps, but when we reach the fiftieth anniversary of Soviet power then we can expect amnesty because there will be no camps or classes." This statement, the witness said, was accompanied by a knowing smile, meaning that Hansen considered it all nonsense. The witness prefaced his comments about Hansen with the statement "as a former servant of the cult, he was inclined in an anti-Soviet direction against all the activities of Soviet power and politics carried out by the Communist Party." With regard to Statute 58, which allowed for the sending of prisoners to other camps (usually with a stricter regime), Hansen allegedly stated that they all had to be prepared to be sent to Solovetsky Island, as the Soviet government would fabricate evidence against someone who held to "older views."[6]

A final witness in the files recorded a conversation from August 16, 1937, where Hansen was accused of saying that he argued with other prisoners about how a Soviet citizen should believe and act. Hansen supposedly said that to be a Soviet citizen, you had to act like Stalin, but it was impossible for everyone to follow on the Stalinist path because millions of citizens simply can't do it. Each person was subject to his own opinions and inevitably contradictions would arise in the political sphere.[7] Whether Hansen actually made these statements cannot be determined with any degree of certainty, but given his bold nature they do not seem to be out of character. Hansen never shied away from confronting the Soviet atheistic perspective, although he had simultaneously advocated submission to the government in all things not pertaining to religion. It is not likely, either, that he had grown less cynical toward the Soviet's destruction of Christianity in his homeland. He was never fooled by the lies being perpetrated in the name of communism and atheism.

Accused now for a second time of anti-Soviet agitation, this time among prisoners in the Gulag camps, Hansen was sentenced to death on September 2. In the official death sentence, it was noted again that Hansen had organized underground children's groups for the purpose of religious education. This was described as "counterrevolutionary agitation against the Communist Party and Soviet power." At 1:15 a.m., September 22, in the Karelian Republic of the USSR, a Soviet government that could no longer countenance a hero of the faith who spoke freely from his conscience, carried out the execution of Pastor Helmut Hansen in the forests of Medvezhegorsk.[8] Years later, after the fall of the Soviet Union, evidence of mass graves would be uncovered there.[9]

STALIN'S PROMISE TO annihilate the clergy picked up steam in the late summer and autumn of 1937. John Morehead's dear friend from Grossliebenthal, Pastor Albert Koch, had originally been arrested in 1930, was released in 1932, and then worked as an accountant in the Kursk region. On August 31, 1937, though, he was arrested and imprisoned in Butyrka Prison in Moscow. There is information that he was shot afterward, although no date is given.[10]

Several connected to the Hansen-Muss case or seminary were also re-arrested. Gustav Golde, the nephew of Bishop Meier and husband of Elsa Freifeldt, had been working as a teacher at Middle School Number 2 in Leningrad when he was arrested on August 6. On September 20, he was sentenced to death and shot on September 24.[11] Heinrich Behrendts, seminary professor and son-in-law of Bishop Malmgren, who had been falsely accused of the firewood theft in 1932 and given reprieve by being exiled to Uzbekistan, was now arrested in September. This time, he would die in a Gulag labor camp.[12] Former pastor of St. Catherine's in Leningrad (and seminary professor for a brief spell) Woldemar Wagner had been arrested in Leningrad in 1935 with several of his other pastoral colleagues in the city. Like many others, he would be re-arrested, too, in his case on September 10 inside a labor camp in the Novosibirsk region. His wife, Paulina, had last heard from him via post in August. But shortly afterward, she and their three children were exiled to Kazakhstan, like so many of German Lutheran background in 1937. Having heard nothing from her husband for quite a long time, she wrote to the NKVD when Woldemar's five-year sentence was set to conclude in 1940. She received no answer until 1957, when she and the family learned that he had died of a kidney disease (acute renal failure) in 1942. Only it wasn't true. After the fall of the Soviet Union in 1990, Woldemar Wagner's great-grandson learned that he had been executed on September 24, 1937.[13]

Likewise, Ossip Toryassan had been languishing in a Soviet prison cell in Vladikavkaz since 1936, having been arrested for his work as a pastor. Since November 1933, his son Bruno had been serving a detachment of the labor army in the distant taiga of Khabarovsk but apparently had come back to Vladikavkaz.[14] Bruno managed to visit his father in prison, cherishing the last moments they would spend together on earth. Before his execution on October 23, Ossip gave his son his most prized possession—his Bible. Bruno would attempt to decipher his father's notes in Gothic German script until the end of his life, treasuring the wisdom and honoring the courage of this man who had given his life for the Lord.[15]

THE NKVD ALSO finally dealt with the Lutheran pastor who had caused them the most grief, Kurt Muss. Since December 28, 1935, Muss had been laboring in Camp Number 14 in Mai-Guba, located in the general vicinity of Kem and offshore from the Solovetsky Island camp in northern Russia. His wife had long since left him and married another. He had been allowed to write once a month while in the camps, and in this way his mother, Alexandra, was able to keep in touch with him. A confirmand from his last class in May 1929, Dagmara Zeksel, had also been corresponding with him. After giving her own blood for money, she was able to purchase a train ticket to visit him in the far north. Muss was working as a clerk in the administrative management office of the camp, evidently due to his academic capabilities. Because he was not an ordinary inmate, he was given the privilege of visitors. Dagmara, who according to her own account was in love with him, arrived at the camp and stayed with people nearby for six days. Muss would come to her after work and she would feed him. As she left, Muss asked her to send him books on becoming a paramedic. Since she herself had been studying to become a doctor, she easily found and sent him the books.

Muss informed Zeksel that all the books she sent had made it to him, but in August 1937 he stopped answering her letters. Zeksel was certain that something had happened, and her hunch was not incorrect.[16] Muss had been watched for his actions in the camp, especially for his penchant to continue to speak unabashedly about his faith in Christ. The NKVD had been steadily accumulating evidence from fellow prisoners in order to incriminate him. One man claimed that in front of all the prisoners, Muss had spoken negatively about how the Communists were educating youth in the Soviet Union. Muss, he complained, was gathering fellow Russian Germans and urging the prisoners to be disobedient to Soviet power. He accused Muss of saying that the Soviet Union had imprisoned the entire country and placed its citizens on hunger rations, and if someone expressed this opinion publicly, he would subject himself to the highest measure of punishment. Contradicting himself in his own testimony, this man further stated that Muss was one of those "hidden, anti-Soviet characters."[17]

Another witness who claimed to have known and observed Muss for close to ten months may have been closer to the truth. In his bitter recriminations against Muss, he characterized him as a man "impregnated to the core with anti-Soviet religious aspirations, clearly expressing his open hatred to the current system and with everything in his power and means to plant his religious teachings into the mass of prisoners." One imagines that Muss was not inclined to hatred, but to Communists and atheists his ideas were indeed dangerous. That is why he was arrested in the first place. Dramatic plays would often be staged in the Gulag camps as a means to take the prisoners' minds off their hardships. They had become a popular means of entertainment for those subjected to the mind-numbing, repetitive labor of the camps. This witness claimed that Muss had directed a well-known nineteenth-century play by Alexander Ostrovsky, "The Guilty without Fault." Muss used the opportunity to address the prisoners with his own thoughts, the witness continued, engaging them in a "deeply religious sermon," continually urging the prisoners to put their hope in God. This individual described Muss as an "enemy of the Soviet people," accusing him of calling the Constitution of the USSR "a collection of pretty words and nothing else," all the while admonishing prisoners to change their lives through religion.[18] Who knows how many prisoners gathered hope in their dire circumstances by Muss's reminder to put everything in the Lord's hands?

A hand-drawn picture of Kurt near the end of his life, sketched by a fellow inmate named Lukin, survived the camps. His family preserved the portrait, and it was eventually passed along to interested parishioners of St. Michael's

Lutheran in St. Petersburg. In the drawing, Muss's forehead is creased with lines, having aged prematurely. A close look at his face also shows signs of his having been beaten. His had not been an easy path. Zeksel said that Muss had always known that he would be obliged to carry his own cross of suffering, perhaps even to his death.[19] Now that moment had come. Excoriating him as a fascist who praised Hitler, the NKVD brought out all of its verbal ammunition to calumniate Muss when its troika in Karelia took up his case on September 13. After placing him in a special cell, it didn't take long for them to formally proclaim that he would be shot. Shortly before midnight on October 4 (11:50 p.m.) in the far north region of Mai-Guba near the White Sea, Kurt Alexandrovich Muss joined the ranks of the martyrs of the Evangelical Lutheran Church of Russia. There would be many more before 1937 concluded.[20]

AMONG THEM WOULD be Dr. Elisabeth Meier, who was imprisoned in virtually the same region and perhaps the same camp as Muss, the White Sea region near the city of Kem. We know that her mother had begged John Morehead and the LWC to do whatever it could to help her when she was arrested in 1935. But the letters that the Evangelical Lutheran Church in America archives preserve between Ralph Long and Eugenie Meier cease around this time. From Russian state archives, though, we know that Eugenie was exiled to a village called Kashire (a hundred kilometers outside Moscow) shortly after her daughter's sentencing. A friend of Elisabeth's named Anita Weinberg appealed to Pompolit, the one human rights organization existing in the Soviet Union. (Pompolit is a Russian acronym standing for "Political Help for Prisoners," and was often called the "Political Red Cross.") Anita was most likely a fellow member of Sts. Peter and Paul in Moscow and apparently also worked for Pompolit and knew the director, Yekaterina Peshkova. Peshkova was the ex-wife of the famous Stalinist apologist and author Maxim Gorky. Peshkova was renowned for managing to get politicals out of prison, earning the gratitude of the prisoners' families and apparently some grudging respect from the NKVD.

Addressing Peshkova, Weinberg begged her to find some way to get Elisabeth released so that she could assist her aged mother in her later years. In the two years since she had been arrested, this talented academician had been working as a heavy laborer in the forests, then as an accountant, and finally was reduced to sewing mittens for the slave laborers. "For what and to whom is it necessary that these two people should suffer?," Weinberg cried. Giving her phone number and work hours, Weinberg begged Peshkova to call her. But even if Peshkova had moved heaven and earth in her attempts to help free Elisabeth Meier, sympathy from the government was in very short supply in 1937. Through the preservation of history undertaken by the Russian human rights organization Memorial, we now know that on August 1, 1937, Dr. Meier was re-arrested inside the camp, as Kurt Muss and Helmut Hansen had been. On September 2, a troika of the Karelian Soviet Republic declared her guilty of treason, applying Article 58 probably due to her German ethnicity, Lutheran faith, and work as a professor of German on the dictionary that had landed her in the Gulag in the first place. She was executed on September 20, the same day Kurt Muss was sentenced to death. Many years later, in 1989, she would be rehabilitated when Mikhail Gorbachev's program of glasnost shed light on the terror created by Stalin.[21]

30

LAST CHRISTMAS IN LENINGRAD

Erasing Three Centuries of Lutheran Presence

IN LENINGRAD, PAUL REICHERT and his son Bruno could not have been oblivious to the arrests of pastors taking place all around them. In fact, Bruno's sudden resignation from the pastoral ministry on October 18 gives us a hint that the family knew something was afoot. Perhaps Elza Golubovskaya had discussed the questions posed about them in her husband Konstantin Andrievsky's interrogations, and the threats that he had received while in NKVD custody. Or perhaps Andrievsky's friend and St. Peter's parishioner Alfred Zietnick had alerted his pastor. It's also possible that since Golubovskaya was in contact with them, the Reicherts learned that Andrievsky was sentenced on July 7 to eight years in a labor camp, his appeals to poor health rejected after a month of tests at the Haas Hospital in Leningrad.[1]

Whatever the case, Bruno's resignation from the ministry, which was accepted by the inspector of cults for the Kuibyshev region of Leningrad on October 29, meant that only his father remained at St. Peter's. Now Paul Reichert stood alone—the last Lutheran pastor remaining in Leningrad.[2] But both father and son would not remain free for long. Grabbing the keys from the doorkeeper, Ivan Ilyin, NKVD agents trundled up the stairs of house number 16, Sophia Perovskaya Street (now Malaya Konyushennaya Street), on the night of

November 16/17.[3] The twenty-nine-year-old Bruno had served with his father at St. Peter's since 1932 and still lived in the family apartment located just off Leningrad's busiest thoroughfare. Twin daughters aged twenty-five (Gertrude and Irmgard) as well as a twenty-three-year-old son (Wolfren) were also registered at the apartment with Paul Reichert and his sixty-year-old wife, Ida.[4] The NKVD documents charged the Reicherts with being members of a fascist spy ring carrying out activities for a foreign government. As such, they were charged under the notorious Statute 58.[5]

In their search of the five-room apartment that evening, the NKVD sealed off two rooms and left the key with the doorkeeper.[6] Interrogations began that night at the NKVD's notorious Bolshoi Dom ("Big House"), Bruno being asked for the names of his closest acquaintances. It continued a few days later as his questioner took him back in time, asking when he began on the path of fighting Soviet power. Bruno supposedly answered that it all started at his "reactionary German school," the Peterschule, and continued under Bishop Malmgren's direction at the seminary. The Peterschule had been recognized as anti-Soviet back in 1928, having been reorganized under Communist leadership when the Lutheran teachers and administrators were removed. His counter-revolutionary convictions were said to have been strengthened in conversations with the *dvatsatka* at St. Peter's and interaction with a German embassy employee by the name of Wilhelm Buchholz. Buchholz was a member of the *dvatsatka* with whom Bruno had become acquainted in 1934. Their meetings allegedly took place primarily at the church until Buchholz's departure from Leningrad in the spring of 1937. Bruno's testimony claimed that Buchholz and another embassy employee, Albert Aurich, were often at Malmgren's apartment where conversations of a counterrevolutionary nature occurred.[7]

As always, a historian can never be certain of the accuracy of NKVD transcripts, especially in the latter 1930s. While most of the material is clearly fabricated, it is not impossible that the conversations Bruno is alleged to have described took place at Bishop Malmgren's apartment. The NKVD could easily have interpreted as anti-Soviet any discussions between the bishop and his German embassy guests dealing with the dangers threatening the Church.

The idea supposedly proposed by Buchholz was for Bruno to indoctrinate the youth groups in a more fascist orientation. In 1935, Buchholz also allegedly asked him to recommend possible spies for Germany. Bruno, under duress from Malmgren and Buchholz, was said to have agreed.[8] Included in the list of youth he connected to the German consulate were two German teachers, Erik and Lilya Martinson. Lilya happened to be the sister of Bruno Toryassan. In the summer of 1936, Bruno Reichert was said to have turned them over to Buchholz for work as spies.[9]

THE NKVD'S ACCUSATIONS of spying for Germany were often leveled against high-ranking Communists during the Terror, but as we can see, they were also lodged against ordinary citizens of German ethnicity. The ground for such concerns had been laid on December 3, 1936, when NKVD Commissar Nikolai Yezhov warned, "Each year we draw nearer and nearer to a war. Foreign intelligence services get more active, develop a feverish activity on our territory."[10] An April 2, 1937, directive ordered surveillance of German embassy personnel and anyone connected with them. By autumn of that year, the NKVD went a step further. Soviet citizens of German nationality were now subject to arrest as well as German citizens living in the Soviet Union. In this "German operation," 42,000 ethnic Germans would ultimately be given the death penalty, two-thirds of them being Soviet citizens.[11]

Such fevered statements like Yezhov's did not bode well for the Reicherts. Just as with Kurt Muss and Helmut Hansen eight years before, the NKVD now cast a wide net of suspicion on the Reicherts' close acquaintances. It didn't matter that the elderly pharmacist Alfred Zietnick didn't speak any German. On November 22, he, too, was arrested as part of the alleged Nazi German spy ring.[12] Zietnick's interrogations began on November 25. He was accused of having joined Kurt Muss's counterrevolutionary German nationalist group in 1929, the NKVD claiming that the German government had been using Muss at that time. This revisionist history does not quite fit because the German and Soviet governments had a more-or-less cordial and working relationship at the time. However, the language used does fit the year 1937, when Hitler's National Socialists were the Communist state's bitterest enemy. The confession attributed to the seventy-year-old man whom Konstantin Andrievsky described as a "strong believer" simply does not ring true.[13]

In fact, Zietnick had been one of the foundational members of Jesus Christ Lutheran in 1923. It was he who noted that many of the historic Lutheran ethnic groups no longer knew the languages of their heritage, and thus it was essential to form a Russian-speaking Lutheran congregation. It was also Zietnick who recommended and convinced members that the congregation be named Jesus Christ Lutheran rather than St. Paul's. He furthermore urged the parishioners to emulate the early Christian church and provide aid to the poorer members of the congregation. This was no cultural Christian and accusations that he was a secret German fascist sympathizer were ludicrous.[14]

In 1929, Zietnick had avoided arrest due to his age. The irony that he was now eight years older seems not to have made any impression on his jailers. Nevertheless, after Zietnick dodged a prison sentence in 1929, the NKVD claimed that he continued his counterrevolutionary activities at St. Michael's Lutheran until 1935 when it was closed. He then transferred his membership over to the Reicherts' St. Peter's, where the pastor supposedly informed Zietnick of his continuation of the espionage activities that had begun under Helmut Hansen. With the complicity of parishioners Woldemar Schmidt and Sergey Berner (who had been arrested with Zietnick), German consulate personnel Messrs. Aurich and Buchholz were said to have been cultivating the parishioners in a fascist spirit of animosity toward Soviet power. Their propaganda resulted in the Russian parishioners gathering secrets of an economic-military nature that were then passed on to the Reicherts, who would in turn forward them on to the German consulate personnel. It all fit together quite nicely, or so the NKVD wanted the Soviet people to believe.

Zietnick was pressed for more names during his interrogations but told them he could give no more because he wasn't privy to all the details. After being accused of lying, Zietnick was recorded as telling the NKVD agent, "I confirm that I have spoken the truth of my criminal activities directed against Soviet power."[15] Alfred Zietnick did not run from danger in 1929 or 1935. A weaker Christian might have slipped out the back door of the church and blended into the crowds, but the faithful Zietnick continued his active engagement in the church despite the danger. When one Lutheran congregation was closed, he simply moved over to another worshiping community.

PAUL REICHERT'S INTERROGATIONS now began on November 20, three days after his arrest. The NKVD agents traced Reichert's connections with the German consulate back to their origins and began quizzing him about his visits there. Reichert made it clear that he went to the consulate strictly to carry out a religious function, possibly conducting a service of some kind but more likely discussing church matters. The NKVD was also suspicious that several employees (Aurich, Buchholz) and General Consul Sommer not only met Reichert at the consulate but also attended St. Peter's on occasion. What's more, Aurich and Buchholz were even added to the *dvatsatka* at St. Peter's, ostensibly at Sommer's request, so that the consulate might be able to provide material aid and remain aware of the church's needs.[16]

Reichert's ties to Sommer were traced back to 1933, no doubt providing ammunition for the NKVD since that was the year in which Hitler came to power in Germany. Initially, Reichert said that Sommer had cautiously approached him. But by 1934 he was already becoming bolder, urging him to unite the Russian-Germans in the Lutheran Church and lead them in a more fascist direction. The idea was that German Lutherans in the USSR, being persecuted for their faith (yes, the NKVD spoke about their persecution!), would be ripe for developing a cadre of agents who would help Nazi Germany in a future war with the USSR. Reichert was said to have acknowledged his guilt, accepting Sommer's recommendations to form a fascist spy ring within St. Peter's under Aurich and a German consulate employee named Lippert. Several parishioners from St. Peter's were said to have joined the Reicherts. They were Woldemar Schmidt, Alfred Zietnick, Sergey Berner, Erwin Deters, Josef Beech, Erwin and Lilya Martenson, Ernst Essifer, Konstantin Kem, Fyodor Stroh, Christian Ulrich, Heinrich Ulrich, Yakov Kern, and Georgy Dauwalter. One of the most baffling participants said to have joined this conspiracy was an ethnic Armenian named Tigran Kegomyants. Showing that their imagination knew no limits, the NKVD decided that the seventy-three-year-old caretaker of the German Lutheran cemetery was a reasonable recruit to promulgate fascist propaganda among visitors to the cemetery.[17]

Perhaps in an attempt to protect younger parishioners (as with Sts. Peter and Paul in Moscow), the *dvatsatka* at St. Peter's was by now basically composed of the elderly. The names of the members indicate German ethnicity: Emilia Must (sixty years old), Elsa Weinberg (fifty-five), Anna Schultz (sixty-five), Konrad Ulrich (sixty), Evgeniya Martens (seventy-two and a retired German teacher). The treasurer was the seventy-one-year-old August Kort.[18] In keeping with the strict reporting of their activities required of congregations, the *dvatsatka* now informed the inspector of religious cults that in the absence of a pastor, they could not hold divine worship services on November 21.[19] The state had expropriated so much of its wealth through confiscatory tax policies and in the past year had demanded expensive repairs to the church façade and roof. The bill from August 22 totaled about 7,500 rubles, even though the financial records of the church at the beginning of July registered only 3,542 rubles in the treasury. On October 24, only 1,942 rubles remained. And now the NKVD had taken away its pastors. The situation of St. Peter's is a perfect illustration of how the state, by applying financial pressure and terror tactics against the congregation, left the *dvatsatka* with little choice but to submit to its will.[20] On December 17, at the council meeting of the Presidium of the Kuibyshev region, a request was received from the St. Peter's *dvatsatka* to close the church and hand it over to the government.[21] One week later, on Christmas Eve, this request was made official in a written letter signed by all the members of the *dvatsatka*.

Apparently unaware of the letter, though, parishioners arrived at the church that evening to celebrate Christmas Eve. There was nothing to indicate that the church had been closed. The doors were simply locked. Some parishioners gave up and went home, but others filtered over to Zagorodnii Avenue and the Latvian Lutheran Church, Christ the Savior, which had not yet been closed.[22] Its pastors, Alexander and Jan Migle, had just been executed on December 15 along with the chairman of the *dvatsatka*, Jakov Smigla, and eight other parishioners. The pastors and parishioners were said to have been part of a counterrevolutionary Latvian nationalist group, an accusation that had been leveled against approximately two hundred Leningrad Latvians in 1937, the vast majority of whom were members of Christ the Savior.[23]

Despite the devastation wrought against the Latvian Lutherans, there was a large crowd of people gathered that Christmas Eve, some traveling from the very fringes of the city, composed of many ethnic groups. The attendance was astonishing because Christmas Eve, like Christmas Day, was a normal working day in Soviet Russia in 1937. Inside the church that night there was no pastor conducting a service. There was no organist, either, and thus no worship service. To gather under these conditions was a strong testament to the faith of these remarkable believers, because they would not allow the Soviet government to keep them from celebrating the Lord's birth. Soon, each group started to sing Christmas hymns in its own language. Most likely, Estonian, Finnish, Latvian, German and Russian voices were among those heard that evening. Kurt Muss's young protégé, Mikhail Mudyugin, was a witness to the proceedings, and although he described the singing as disorderly compared to historic Christmas services, he believed that the songs had never sounded sweeter in the Lord's ears. In the grip of persecution and at the height of Stalin's Great Terror, the church proved that it was alive even while it was dying. It would be the last Christmas celebrated in a Lutheran church in the city until the end of the twentieth century.[24]

ON JANUARY 2, the troika reached its decision on the individuals involved in the Reichert case. All were sentenced to be shot, except for the Martinson couple (Ervin and Liliya) and Konstantin Kem.[25] It is possible that the accused were shot in the basement of the Bolshoi Dom, or they may have been shot in the fields of Levashovo.[26] If they were shot in the Bolshoi Dom on Liteyny Avenue in the center of Leningrad, they would then have been transported to Levashovo on the outskirts of the city where mass graves would have been dug and the bodies deposited, awaiting the resurrection of the dead on the last day. Soviet officials long denied that Levashovo was used as a burial ground for victims of the Great Terror, but when interest in Stalin's repressions was at its height during Mikhail Gorbachev's glasnost period (late 1980s), the government capitulated and a memorial complex at Levashovo cemetery was dedicated.

In this tragic affair of the destruction of the Lutheran Church in Leningrad, there is no doubt of the innocence of the Reicherts and the St. Peter's *dvatsatka* members arrested with them. In 1939, the NKVD officer, I. M. Lobov, who had interrogated Paul Reichert, was himself arrested and accused of "corrupting Soviet legality." He explained during his own interrogation how the NKVD operated during the Great Terror in Leningrad: "In the first section of the Third Department of the Leningrad Regional NKVD, the case against the members of the church *dvatsatka* of the German Lutheran churches in Leningrad was falsified. The falsification ... occurred in that the protocols of the arrested were not taken from their own words but were created by the officers themselves and then they had the accused sign the protocols." The Reicherts and the eleven other *dvatstaka* members would be fully rehabilitated by the state in 1957.[27]

31

UNDER THE WATCHFUL EYE
OF THE NKVD

Being German Proves Fatal

WITH ALMOST ALL the churches shut down, native Lutheran pastors conducting worship services were a thing of the past. The last Soviet citizen and ordained pastor remaining free in the Soviet Union, Ferdinand Bodungen, had been arrested on November 27, 1937. Bodungen had faithfully shepherded the congregation of Sts. Peter and Paul in the Leningrad suburb of Peterhof since 1901. All the NKVD could accuse him of was receiving some money and a parcel from Germany and Latvia. Out of this evidence, they concocted the threat of espionage. Working quickly, the NKVD convicted him on January 10 and executed him five days later. Like his fellow Lutheran pastors, the Reicherts, his body was then disposed of in the fields of Levashovo.[1]

Other Lutheran pastors may have still been alive but were imprisoned, so the few congregations struggling on at the beginning of 1938 were being kept alive solely by their parishioners. Those who attempted to step up and serve, like the peasant laborer Abraham Koskelainen, now attracted the attention of the ever-vigilant NKVD. When the persecution had begun to escalate in 1937, the Finnish consistory appointed Koskelainen to fulfill the duties of a pastor, first in Koltushi (January 26, 1937), then in other Ingrian village churches like Hietamäki and Jarvirsarii (May 25), and finally in Duderhof (August 31). The Soviet government, however, would not recognize Koskelainen as a pastor or register him, leaving him in limbo. Given Stalin's call to "annihilate the clergy," they developed plans to arrest him. Due to a serious illness, however, he was allowed to remain under house arrest. He would die of natural causes in 1938.[2]

Journalist Boris Kandidov celebrated the work of the NKVD in a February 5 article in the newspaper *Izvestia*. "During the last year, the valiant agents of the People's Commissariat for Internal Affairs detected and annihilated a number of gangs of wreckers, diversionists, terrorists and spies which had been organized by the agents of foreign intelligence services with the assistance of the Orthodox, the Catholic, the Lutheran and the Mohamedan [*sic*] clergy, and of sectarian missionaries." Elaborating on how these religious people had established a fifth column within the country in league with Nazi Germany and Japan, Kandidov sounded the alarm on the danger posed by these theists: "Every honest Soviet citizen must help the Soviet intelligence service reveal and destroy the spies and diversionists in clerical garments. Often the religion mask serves to disguise spies of the enemy. This is completely proved by the undermining activities of the clericals."[3]

ALTHOUGH KANDIDOV RAILED against the clergy, he and his atheist allies were aware that many believers remained faithful to the Church after their pastors were gone, in spite of the danger. The Soviet government had been stunned by the evidence of its failed census in early 1937, recording the public affirmation of a large number of believers who had not turned to atheism after years of state-sponsored propaganda. A good example of the trials and tribulations of those parishioners can be seen in the life of Tamara Kosetti, who had been arrested in the Hansen-Muss case in 1929. She had been sent to a camp in

Irkutsk after the guilty verdicts were delivered in 1930, but in spite of her tragic situation, Tamara's life had taken a romantic turn. Her former Peterschule classmate in Leningrad, Reinhold Mai, undertook the arduous journey to Siberia and proposed marriage. Tamara accepted, and after her release she would give birth to three children as they moved from place to place due to her criminal record. (Her sister, Benita, would marry Reinhold's brother, Arnold. They had also known each other as students at the Peterschule.)

The Mai's nomadic existence began in 1933 as they returned to Leningrad only to be denied residency. Not one to be dissuaded by circumstances, as evidenced by his long-distance courting of Tamara, Reinhold sought and found work as an agronomist in the city. They then moved to one of the islands on the outskirts of the city. The following year they moved again, this time to Koltushi (about twenty kilometers east of Leningrad), when Reinhold was hired by the village commune's machine-tractor station. Tamara was able to find work as an accountant at the commune while raising her children.

At the beginning of 1936, the Mais left Koltushi. Tamara went back to school and found employment as a kindergarten teacher in September 1937, working in the Moskovsky region of Leningrad at the school "Proletarian Victory." But life was hard. Her husband switched jobs, finding work in suburban Pavlovsk where he and their three children took up residence.[4] Tamara seems to have stayed at her parents' apartment on Rubinstein Street in Leningrad during the week since they couldn't find a place for the family in the city, again probably due to her police record. Her granddaughter says that she would visit with her children and husband whenever possible, probably on weekends, as a daily trek would be exhausting. Or perhaps they met in Leningrad, since St. Peter's organist, Wolf Liss, described Reinhold as a longtime member of St. Peter's. It is possible that he resumed attending the church until its closure. After all, his cousin, Marta, was an organist on staff at the church.[5]

One day at school in early 1938, however, Tamara found herself unable to avoid her past. The children were building a replica of the Kremlin with blocks, and someone attached a portrait of Stalin to its walls. The children then commenced to parade around the blocks, but one child inadvertently knocked the portrait of Stalin to the floor. Tamara quickly restored it to its proper place, but these were not ordinary times. Suspicion and fear ruled the day. Someone reported the incident and made an accusation against the former Gulag camp prisoner. As a result, in the late evening/early morning of February 2/3, Tamara once again found herself under arrest.[6]

Tamara's family had already received a shock when her stepfather, Paul Neiman, captain of an icebreaker in the Leningrad ports and a faithful member of St. Peter's, was arrested on the night of December 9, 1937. As the NKVD rudely escorted him out of his own apartment, Neiman looked back at his wife, Emilia, and cried out, "Mila, I'm not guilty of anything!" The following morning, Emilia went looking for him at the DPZ on Shpalernaya Street, the former czarist prison.[7]

The poet Anna Akhmatova, a native of Leningrad who herself spent seventeen months waiting for information about her son, would vividly describe the long lines that Emilia was subjected to that morning in her classic poem "Requiem." The poem depicts a woman waiting in line for word on her loved one, lips blue from the cold, asking Akhmatova: "Can you describe this?" Akhmatova's response: "Yes, I can." At this response, "something like the shadow of a smile crossed what had once been her face."[8] Now Emilia, too, stood for hours in the long, gloomy line. When she reached the window, a voice asked, "Who are you?" After she identified herself, the voice said, "Wait!" When the window reopened, she was ordered to leave Leningrad in twenty-four hours and report to Birsk (in the republic of Bashkortostan, central Russia), her new settlement in exile. Tamara's sister Benita and their mother had to think quickly and take stock of the family predicament, concluding that it was only a matter of time before they were all in trouble. After all, the Reicherts were under arrest along with many other members of St. Peter's at that time. They opted to take Tamara's three children (Reinhold, Valentin, and Renata) and

Benita's son, Pavel, with them to Birsk. Arnold Mai, Benita's husband, planned to join them later. Tamara was subsequently arrested on the night of February 2/3 while her stepfather, Paul Neiman, was executed the following day.[9]

RUSSIANS OF GERMAN descent or perceived German links like Tamara Kosetti's family would constitute the first wave of arrests in a series that would focus on Leningrad's Lutherans, especially those who had ties to St. Peter's or the Peterschule. Such arrests were no longer limited to suspected enemies within the Communist Party, or even pastors. They were also targeting ordinary citizens as Nikolai Yezhov's thirst to provide even more victims for Stalin grew. The NKVD's prepared documents from January 31 show that they were planning to accuse Kosetti of belonging to a "German Fascist youth counter-revolutionary organization" carrying out espionage.[10] That organization was apparently the Jugendbund to which many of Helmut Hansen's confirmands had belonged back in the 1920s. The arrests at Christmas in 1929 had broken the back of Hansen's youth group, but the NKVD either refused to believe it had ceased activities or, more likely, decided to use this Germanic-sounding organization to increase the number of arrests to please Yezhov and Stalin.[11]

Tamara Kosetti's interrogation began on February 7, with the NKVD agents attempting to link the kindergarten teacher to a German consulate-inspired, anti-Soviet conspiracy involving a host of past acquaintances at the Peterschule. One of those prominently mentioned in her case was Margo Jurgens, the young woman who had been in the Jugendbund with Tamara and who along with Tamara's sister, Benita, had tried to raise money to support Hansen's family after his arrest in 1929. Tamara's interrogation records her identifying her sister Benita and Jurgens as part of this revived Jugenbund conspiracy, headed up by Wilhelm Derringer (a musician and organist) and Franz Müller (a former classmate of Tamara's at the Peterschule). In a chance meeting with Jurgens at a health club on January 20, Jurgens is said to have told her she was helping to regather the Jugendbund's former members and collecting funds for its directors. The plot recorded in NKVD files was an attempt to fight Soviet power through this Germanic organization, but the language attributed to Tamara is awkward at best, making it evident that these were not her own words.[12]

For example, after some initial questions, Tamara is recorded as saying, "I'm tired of hiding the truth from the inquiry, so I will be open with you. I beg you to accept my testimony." Besides this stilted language, the facts attributed to her are wrong. She allegedly states that Jurgens is a former Peterschule student along with Derringer and Müller, but Jurgens went to a Soviet school, and Tamara would have known that. In addition, in her testimony she mentions that Erna Hansen corresponded with her brothers in Germany. She knew Erna well enough to know that her brothers lived in Finland. But of course, the NKVD preferred for this plot to have Germanic roots. They would only use Finnish contacts when attempting to tar Ingrian Lutherans with being traitors. The logical explanation is that Tamara's alleged testimony was being prepared to fit this German spy plot spun by the NKVD.[13]

Despite what appear to be fabrications, the historian can glean some truths from the NKVD's record of Tamara's testimony. She took pains to mention in her interrogations that her husband, Reinhold, had no knowledge of any conversations with Jurgens about the Jugendbund.[14] Before her second interrogation began on April 4, the ever-courageous Reinhold came to the prison (March 7) to see if he could help her, but in the process was himself arrested.[15] In fact, unbeknownst to him, Reinhold would be linked to yet another fabricated German fascist plot, this one led by the former Lutheran pastor Woldemar Wagner. Wagner had been sentenced in 1935 to a five-year Gulag term in the Novosibirsk region and had already been re-arrested and executed in September 1937.[16] But since Wagner had served in Leningrad, he was said to have gathered twenty-eight Leningrad Lutherans of German ethnicity to conduct counterrevolutionary activities during 1930–1935. Reinhold Mai was considered to have been one of those.

Another of the key figures in the conspiracy working in close association with Wagner was said to be the talented musician and former organist of Leningrad's St. Peter's, Wolf Liss. Liss had already been arrested on February 19, and on February 28, these additional twenty-eight parishioners were rounded up.[17] Liss had been under investigation in April 1935 in conjunction with the case tied to pastors Wagner, Samuel Wohl, and Alfred Prib, accused of receiving aid from the German humanitarian organization Brüdershilfe.[18] After three months Liss was exonerated, but since his passport was not returned to him, he was forced to move 101 kilometers outside Leningrad to Malaya Vishera (where Friedrich Wacker had been exiled years before and still remained). He must have eventually received permission to work in Leningrad again, because on January 7, 1937, Liss moved to Detskoe Selo and found work as an organ technician for the Muzkomedii Theater in Leningrad at 200 rubles a month, as well as at the State Conservatory for 365 rubles a month. Given his talents as an organist, virtually all churches in Leningrad, not just Lutheran, requested him to do repair work on their organs. Theaters and conservatories in Leningrad also took advantage of his skills.[19]

With this latest arrest, Liss's German ties came to the forefront of the investigation. This time, those relationships would not be taken as lightly as in 1935. He was asked to list the musicians in Germany with whom he had contacts, and the list was extensive.[20] Since Wagner had already been executed, the NKVD focused on Liss and made him responsible for the counterrevolutionary activity of the Russian-German Lutherans in Leningrad. Most of the accused were young to middle-aged parishioners of St. Peter's. Among those listed were Ernst and Waldemar Zeidel (the uncles of the Mai brothers), Axel Unbegaum, Herbert Hesse, Walter Tiedemann, Georgy Eichfuss, Herman Bergholdt, Woldemar Kem, Heinrich Schlipper, Eduard Glokov, Wilhelm

Shoch, Benjamin Yanchurov, Ferdinand Autzen, Elfrieda Ber, Reinhold Mai and his cousin, Marta, and eventually Arnold Mai. The interrogations would last for close to four months.[21]

AS ARRESTS WERE being made of influential parishioners now that pastors were mostly out of the way, the Soviet government also turned its sights on the spacious church buildings that had housed congregations for years. The buildings were being fought over by interested parties grappling for real estate, especially as the larger churches were located right in the center of Leningrad. Not only were St. Mary's and St. Peter's in a central location but they also contained valuable art that was of interest to curators. Although the *dvatsatka* of St. Peter's had signed over the church to the authorities in December, apparently it still was required to handle matters pertaining to the building because on January 13 it gave its seventy-one-year old treasurer, August Kort, the authority to take 1,542 rubles from the church bank account to pay those workers who had been making repairs. Normally, they would have requested funds from the chairman, Sergey Berner, but he had been arrested.[22] In fact, we now know that Berner had already been executed. Evidently the Leningrad Soviet greedily eyed the church where Helmut Hansen had held concerts in the past, because on January 24 it was decided by their Department for the Preservation of Monuments that St. Peter's would be turned into a concert hall known as Lengosestrada—Leningrad Government Hall. The department chairman for this institution, Comrade Borisov, noted in a letter to the Leningrad Soviet secretary, Comrade Ziminoy, that the building constructed in 1838 was in good condition and needed very little repair. But then, the government had already confiscated money from St. Peter's parishioners for that purpose.[23]

But not only were the buildings immediately confiscated, the objects within them were also removed. On February 20, the administrative inspector for the Regional Soviet of the Kuibyshev region of Leningrad, a Comrade Leibovich, acknowledged that August Kort and Emilia Must of the *dvatsatka* had turned over all of the church inventory, minus a keyboard and glass-plated bookshelf that had been loaned to Pastor Reichert. (Kort and Must couldn't turn over these goods since they were under the control of the local NKVD agents, who had already sealed the rooms of the Reichert apartment.)[24] The world-famous Hermitage Museum and the Russian Museum received chalices, crosses, Bibles, and other churchware. Perhaps most desired by their curators, though, was the famed Karl Bryullov painting of the crucifixion that had hung above the altar for almost a century, as well as a Hans Holbein masterpiece of Jesus with Thomas and the other disciples and a copy of an Albrecht Dürer wood print.[25] The Museum of the History of Atheism, housed in the former Kazan Cathedral (kitty-corner from St. Peter's across 25 October Avenue), gobbled up items, too, including Martin Luther's *Church Postils*.[26] The famed organ produced by the Walcker firm in Germany and played by Wolf Liss, Marta Mai, and previously a young Peter Tchaikovsky, who had learned to play organ on this instrument, was sent on to Moscow—ironically, to the Tchaikovsky Concert Hall.[27]

The sculpture on the roof of an angel holding a cross, though, was an eyesore to the Soviets. An obvious Christian symbol in an officially atheist country was an embarrassment to the authorities, and its presence was unavoidable to the pedestrians strolling in the city center. While debate was raging over whether the building should be remodeled as a concert hall for the city, a photo from 1938 shows the angel with the cross in plain sight with a sign on the church facade displaying a temporary exhibition entitled "Panorama."[28] On September 17, the chairman of the Leningrad Soviet (equivalent to a mayor), Alexey Kosygin, who would rise to fame as the Premier of the Soviet Union (1964–1980), called for the immediate reconstruction of St. Peter's. On October 8, Kosygin reiterated his demand that the angel with the cross needed to be removed from St. Peter's. The inspector for religious cults in Leningrad, Comrade Gavrilov, finally reported to Kosygin on October 28 that the angel with the cross had been removed from the church. In addition, he informed Kosygin that a commission of Soviet artists (sculptors, architects, etc.) affirmed that the cross could even be effectively removed from the angel without distorting its artistic appearance, since the cross "isn't an artistic object," anyway.[29]

Just around the corner from St. Peter's at St. Mary's, where Mikhail Mudyugin had first heard Kurt Muss preach a sermon that would change his life, interested parties were fighting over the building now that the *dvatsatka* had acknowledged on March 20 that it had no pastor to serve the congregation and could no longer pay its expenses.[30] (Pastor Pekka Braks had been executed at the end of 1937.) A Mr. Abolimov put in one of the first requests on March 25, asking for the building to house his typewriter factory. He offered to give back two of his five properties scattered throughout the city so that his firm (Soyuzorgchyot) could reconstruct the considerably larger area of the church into a factory.[31] In April, the requests for the building came fast and furious: a Comrade Smirnov of the Construction Department for Living Quarters of the Leningrad Soviet hoped to reconstruct it into separate apartments for workers; a company named START wanted to use it for a sports club; another entity named Rossnabfilm wanted to turn it into a film and music studio. The most influential might have been the request by the director of the State Hermitage Museum, an I. Obreli, who requested the building to serve as a warehouse for special items from the museum.[32] It seemed that the Leningrad Soviet was leaning toward giving the building to the Hermitage, but at the last minute, on May 13, it decided to transfer the property to its Construction Department for Living Quarters. Socialist class consciousness in the person of the proletariat would win the battle for the longtime church building.[33] Unlike with St. Peter's, the Hermitage also lost out on St. Mary's churchware. The items compiled over centuries—clocks, elaborate wooden chairs with figures carved on them, vases, curtains, a painting of Jesus' ascension, and a painting of the evangelists in a wooden frame—were transferred to the Museum of the History of Religion in the former Kazan Cathedral. At least the Lutheran churches were providing Soviet citizens with an education of what had once been a vital part of their history.[34]

In Moscow, Sts. Peter and Paul struggled on without their martyred pastor, Alexander Streck, his wife Veronika boldly leading the flock every Sunday in services within the church. Mostly elderly women and men remained faithful, but it was only a matter of time before their building was confiscated, for it was difficult to hide the large Lutheran church a fifteen-minute walk from the Kremlin. On the Sunday of August 7, the parishioners found the doors locked as they came to church. The Soviet authorities had finally closed the church for good, inviting the Arktika Theater to become its new occupant.[35] According to the *Frankfurter Zeitung*, the spot in front of the church formerly occupied by statues of Saints Peter and Paul was replaced by a large picture of Stalin holding a young girl in his arms with the caption, "We thank Comrade Stalin for our happy youth!"[36] With the Strecks exiled to Kazakhstan and with the Meier family gone, too, the lights of Sts. Peter and Paul would not come back on until the 1990s.

WHILE THE SOVIETS set about occupying churches and counting the wealth stolen from the congregations, believers like Tamara Kosetti continued to be threatened with imprisonment. In her second interrogation on April 4, Tamara was forced to acknowledge her participation in the Jugendbund from 1925–1930. Names reemerged from her past as the NVKD attempted to tar Tamara with guilt by association: Professor Alexander Wolfius from the Peterschule, Pastor Helmut Hanson, Arvid Ballod (the son of St. Peter's caretaker), and the supposed masterminds of this plot, Wilhelm Derringer and Franz Müller. She acknowledged having known Müller since her childhood but had heard Derringer's name for the first time from the NKVD agent. It didn't matter.

In her file, Tamara is recorded as saying that she met with Müller shortly after her release from the Siberian Gulag in 1932. He is then said to have used her apartment to gather ten co-conspirators as he proposed that she join the Jugendbund organized by Derringer in order to spy and commit terrorist acts against the leaders of the party and government. Included among those meeting in Tamara's apartment was said to have been Erna Hansen.[37] The NKVD arrested her on March 4 as another key figure in this conspiracy. This was now Erna's second arrest. She had struggled in the years since her husband's 1929 arrest to provide for her family of three boys, Ralf, Gerhardt, and Meinhardt (ages nineteen, sixteen, and fourteen, respectively). She no longer had the pastor's apartment on 25 October Avenue (Nevsky Avenue); her family was now housed in her brother's apartment on Geslerovsky Avenue in the Petrograd District of Leningrad.[38]

Erna was forty-eight and had worked as a nurse at the emergency ward of a health institute since her release from the Gulag in 1933. She had no property to speak of and was recorded as having satisfactory health. Still, the NKVD took away from Erna the few items she possessed in this world, including a five-gram wedding ring. Her husband, Helmut, was listed as being in the camps, as was her brother Otto (in Chita, Siberia), but we know that Helmut had already been executed in September 1937.[39] In fact, her brother, a noted engineer and the technical director of the Leningrad factory, Progress, had been arrested on December 16, 1937, and was also no longer alive, having been shot on January 15, 1938. He was only forty-four years old.[40] Probably due to such potential danger, her sister, Irina, who had married Kurt Muss's brother, had avoided any contact with those in the church. Her son, Erik, remembered his mother saying they should not stir up trouble by having any connection with the church. It was simply too dangerous.[41]

As Erna's interrogations began, the NKVD expressed an interest in her acquaintances who had studied at the Annenschule or the Peterschule, since they were in the process of arresting influential persons associated with those institutions. Furthermore, she was asked if she had any relatives living outside the USSR (she had two brothers in Helsinki).[42] The next question was a command: Erna was to list her counterrevolutionary activities before this most recent arrest. But apparently, Erna was no longer the timid soul whom Natalya Stackelberg described in 1930 as weeping continually and needing comfort from her fellow Lutheran cellmates. She had survived forced labor on the White Sea Canal in one of the worst of the Gulag camps. In no uncertain terms, Erna answered, "I have not carried out any counterrevolutionary activities since 1930. Before 1930 I was part of a counterrevolutionary group in the Lutheran Church for which I was sent to Karelia [the location of her camp] where I remained until 1933." The agent countered, "You're not telling the truth. Give us your testimony with details!" Erna again insisted, "I will tell you once again, that I have not carried out any counterrevolutionary activities from 1930 until the day of my arrest!"[43] It took great courage in 1938 to stand up to the NKVD and tell them they were wrong to accuse her of political activities.

On April 5, when the interrogation continued, the topic of the Jugendbund was again raised, and she admitted to having imbued German youth in a "nationalist spirit" along with her husband. Perhaps she felt that she couldn't contradict what she had been convicted of many years ago, and "nationalist" or "Pan-Germanic" was the phrase that Soviet authorities used in those days to describe suspect Russian Germans. But since Hitler's rise to power, the NKVD now frequently used the term "fascist" to describe them. Erna did not give them the satisfaction of that reply. When the agent demanded that she speak about her further criminal activities, she again refused to play their game. "Since 1930 I stopped my counterrevolutionary activity." The agent must have been furious, because he says, "You are not telling the truth. Our investigation has uncovered the exact details. ... We demand that you stop with your denials and tell the truth!" It is heartbreaking to imagine what they did next to change her mind, but the record has her say, "I acknowledge that I have really tried to hide the evidence. ... I've decided to tell the whole truth."[44] Did she break down under physical pressure or torture? Were threats made against her three boys? Did the agent tell her that her husband had been executed the previous year and that the same could happen to her? It is also conceivable that they just made up her confession. There is nothing in the record to let us know, but the text changes dramatically and has her confessing to being a spy for Germany. (These are virtually the same words Tamara Kosetti is recorded as speaking in her April 4 testimony, a strong hint that their replies were standard, fabricated NKVD fare).

In response to the question of what her concrete actions were, a stream of information came pouring out: "I gathered and transferred to German intelligence the following data: (1) On the preparation of weapons of varying calibers for Factory Number 7 (guns, mortars and howitzers); (2) On the preparation of radio equipment at the Kulakov Factory for the Red Army; (3) On the location for the preparations for mobilization of Factory Number 7 and the Kulakov Factory." When asked how she gathered this material, Hansen said that she compiled this information through the personal observations of factory workers and then passed it on to Wilhelm Derringer. These are the last words she is recorded as speaking.[45]

In the Mai family alone, Reinhold, his brother Arnold, the Mai boys' uncles, Ernst (a music specialist at a Leningrad radio station) and Woldemar Zeidel, and their cousin, Marta Mai (an organist at St. Peter's), would all be executed in 1938. Emilia Niemana, Tamara and Benita's mother, would die in exile in 1943. Tamara was eventually released in 1948 but only saw her children a few times afterward, as she was forced to conclude her prison sentence in exile in the Novosibirsk region on a collective farm. She died twelve days before Benita, on July 22, 1952.[46]

KONRAD MUSS WAS also among those accused of belonging to this web of conspirators. The brother of the late pastor, Kurt, Konrad was the engraver who had made the pins for confirmation students in the 1920s. On March 10, he joined the ever-growing list of the arrested.[47] Just as Konstantin Andrievsky's words were twisted to blacken the image of the Reicherts, Muss appears to have been used to indict the former teachers of the Peterschule, principal Erich Kleinenberg and teacher Alexander Wolfius. The NKVD agent asked him about the German cultural organization "Bildungsverein," which had been active in the 1920s. Kleinenberg and Wolfius, as scholars and linguists, were associated with this entity. In fact, practically all the employees of the German consulate were said to have attended its sessions. Muss himself confessed to being a participant, but he informed them that it had been closed on the arrest of most of its members.[48] At this point, the NKVD agent asked him to speak about his counterrevolutionary activities, and Muss initially answered that he had not engaged in counterrevolutionary activities. The agent accused him of lying, because Kleinenberg was said to have counted him among the counterrevolutionaries. Immediately, the recorded answer changed. Now, he not only said that Kleinenberg had recruited him for counterrevolutionary work, but he had done so as far back as 1925! Kleinenberg brought him into the Bildungsverein and cultivated a "German nationalist spirit" within him while he was a student at the Peterschule.[49]

Kleinenberg allegedly complained about the poverty of the citizens of the USSR, praised Germany, and argued for perpetrating terrorist acts in order to combat Soviet power. Recorded in the unnatural language in which the NKVD was so proficient, Kleinenberg declared to Muss in August 1937: "I've known you for a long time. I trust you. ... Therefore, in the name of German intelligence, I am commissioning you to select people for the violent removal of the leaders of the Party and Soviet government." Muss was said to claim that he and the group he formed had been commissioned to carry out terrorist acts against Leningrad's Communist party boss, Andrey Zhdanov, but until their arrest had done practically nothing. Near the end of 1937, Kleinenberg supposedly sent Muss to Novgorod to gather info on air bases, warehouses, and the like.[50]

It was open season on Soviet citizens of German heritage, and other German Lutherans outside the immediate Peterschule/St. Peter's circles would also be

subjected to arrest. Former seminary student Otto Tumm, who had married
Luisa Muss after serving prison time for his conviction in the Hansen-Muss
case of 1929, was re-arrested in July 1937. He was soon released, but then arrested
again on February 28, 1938. Tumm was convicted of anti-Soviet activity and
sentenced to ten years. He was sent to Tashkent, eventually ending up in the
dreaded Gulag camp of Kolyma, where he died in 1942. Luisa herself was in the
camps at the time of his arrest, and a haunting photo exists of her, emaciated,
after her release from the camps in 1939. Subsequently, Luisa would be exiled
to Kazakhstan with her two boys and live a full life, serving as a nurse. She died
in 1983, retaining her Christian faith but keeping it concealed. Still, her strong
moral character had an impact on her coworkers. After the fall of the Soviet
Union, her daughter-in-law spoke of the faith that she had never lost despite
the persecution she had undergone.[51]

The Wagner/Liss case reached its conclusion in late June with all the alleged
participants declared guilty. The situation of Herman Bergholdt provides a
good example of how the NKVD took initial evidence and manipulated it
to its own benefit. Bergholdt was originally from Assureti, just outside modern-day Tbilisi (known as Tiflis to Russian-Germans at that time). It was one
of those cities to which German Lutherans had migrated in the early nineteenth century when they believed the world was coming to an end. As a young
man, Herman's father had encouraged him to obtain a quality education in
Leningrad. So, in 1929, he traveled to Leningrad to attend a language institute that trained future teachers of the German language. While in Leningrad,
he befriended other Russian Germans who studied at the institute and also
attended the concerts arranged by Helmut Hansen at St. Peter's. After his
studies, he returned to Georgia to teach German, but his hunger for deeper
learning in the field of technology led him to enroll at an institute where he
graduated with a degree in engineering. He returned to Leningrad with his
wife, Nadezhda, and young daughter and found work as a radio engineer at
an institute and rented an apartment in the Petrograd region of Leningrad.

The family had not even lived there for a year before they heard a knock on the door one evening and opened it to find two pleasant young men standing there, who asked Herman to come with them to clarify some matter. It was February 27, 1938, the day twenty-eight people connected to Wolf Liss and St. Peter's Lutheran were arrested. When his wife asked when her husband would return and whether he should take something along with him, the young men replied, "What do you mean? What do you mean? No, your husband will be back home tomorrow!"

The NKVD repeatedly questioned Herman about his connections in Leningrad, but he only replied that he had gone to Wagner's church and heard the organ. Thus they concocted a terrorist act pulled off by him on the Leningrad railroad system. When he objected that he was living in Georgia at that time, they changed the accusation to a terrorist act against the rail system in Tiflis. Herman had actually taught in a village where was no railroad, but it didn't matter to the NKVD.[52] Just as Emilia Neimana searched for her husband in the prisons, Nadezhda Bergholdt now did the same, but she would never see her husband again. When Herman's daughter, Elena, read her father's file years later after the fall of the Soviet Union, she spied a frightful yet ambiguous phrase on his document: "Ten years without the right of correspondence."

The Bergholdts' world was coming to an end in a way unimaginable to their millennialist ancestors from the nineteenth century. Now, instead of the Lord's second coming, those Germans from Georgia and Russia were coming to terms with the arrival of the Antichrist in Soviet atheism. Everyone accused of being part of the Wagner/Liss conspiracy, including Herman Bergholdt, was executed on June 28.

THE THEATER OF the absurd reigned in NKVD headquarters as enemies, some real but most imagined, went to their graves in order to fill prescribed quotas.[53] Konrad Muss and Erna Hansen were sentenced to death as participants in a plot to kill Leningrad Party head Sergey Kirov and party member and successor to Kirov, Andrey Zhdanov. Their executions were carried out on October 22.[54] It did not matter that Leonid Nikolaev and several suspected accomplices had already been convicted shortly after he killed Kirov back in 1934, or that Grigory Zinoviev and Lev Kamenev had been convicted and executed along with 160 others in 1936.[55] Various ethnic groups were now accused of conducting espionage for some foreign power, and for Lutherans, it was generally supposed that those ties were to Nazi Germany or Fascist Finland. These victims were fed to the Moloch-like death machine whose appetite was strong in 1938.

The truth of what happened to all these people would remain hidden in most cases until the de-Stalinization period under Nikita Khrushchev or until Mikhail Gorbachev initiated his glasnost period in the late 1980s.[56] But as early as February 4, 1939, an agent of the Third Department of the Leningrad NKVD, K. P. Tikhomirov, confessed to the spuriousness of the charges against the Lutherans of German heritage and how false evidence was obtained:

In June or July of 1938, an order came down from the former head of the NKVD, Litvin, of the immediate detainment and arrest of all former members of the *dvatsatkas* of the German Lutheran churches. In the course of a few days, we worked day and night to detain and arrest the suspects, but the administration of the department complained about us and suggested that we fulfill the orders of the commissar— arrest even more. ... Therefore, we arrested 25 persons. Of these individuals, 75% were senior citizens. We, seeing before us people who might be anti-Soviet on the strength of their conversations with Lutheran pastors, and likewise due to their religious convictions and ethnicity as Germans, began to obtain proof of their anti-Soviet inclinations and with oversimplified methods we wrote down accusations of the "second category." Khatenever, the substitute for the boss of the NKVD, threw [Agent] Sisoyev out of the room because he couldn't fabricate an organized counterrevolutionary group. So, the agents found new proof. In sum, the investigating organs "created" four of the groups that were demanded from "congregations" which included 32 persons. All were repressed.[57]

Tikhomirov may have felt emboldened to make such an honest statement since the national NKVD commissar, Nikolai Yezhov, had stepped down from his position on November 23, 1938.[58]

Ultimately, the terror would only end with Yezhov's fall from power and execution. On April 10, 1939, the noose that had been tightening around him resulted in his arrest. Stalin let his faithful minion linger in prison until February 2, 1940, when he was shot in a cell of his own making not far from Lubyanka headquarters.[59] Pavel Postyshev, one of Stalin's henchmen who also fell afoul of the dictator, waxed prophetic in a Butyrka Prison cell in Moscow in 1938. Describing Yezhov as Stalin's faithful hunting dog, Postyshev predicted that as soon as the hunt was over, Stalin would declare the dog mad and destroy it.[60] The tragedy of Russia and its dedicated Lutherans was that so many faithful witnesses to the gospel of Jesus Christ were destroyed in the process of a satanic bloodlust that closed the decade of the 1930s.

BY THE END OF 1938, the organized Evangelical Lutheran Church in the Soviet Union was dead, except for one last holdout. The village congregation in Koltushi had always been one of the strongest in Russian Lutheranism. The pastors may have been gone, but in 1939 the people still filled the wooden church on the hill on Sundays. Faithful parishioners like Katri Kukkhonen made sure the assembled heard the word of God. She felt as if "God had let loose all the powers of hell and pushed the angel of death towards the earth in order to punish mankind for sin." It wasn't uncommon for the preacher to take the text straight from the book of Revelation because, as Kukkhonen recalled, the stark reality of events led all to believe the time of the beast of Revelation had come. They prayed and prayed, fervently and often, expecting that the Lord's second coming was as near as the early church had thought. "But God's plans," Kukkhonen declared, "were different from men. God's time clock went more slowly, but correctly." The Lord was not coming yet, and so they remained faithful. Someone would always play the organ in the church and the youth had not dispersed or given in to the tenor of the times. They remained faithful despite the hardships that were brought on those who clung to what was considered an outmoded form of thinking by the enlightened atheists. Even though local Communists purposely arranged all-night dances for the youth before church holidays, especially on the eve of Christmas or Easter, the Koltushi youth did not abandon their faith in Christ. They formed a church choir that sang songs from the hymnal, recited poetry, and retained the Lutheran teaching from the confessions. Youth even began to lead the services, and others from congregations now closed throughout Ingria offered to share the word of God. In fact, people from all over the region began to show up on Sundays since the only remaining services were taking place in Koltushi.

But in August 1939, the last holdout among Russia's Lutheran congregations held its last service. The youth prepared a festive church program that lasted the entire day and Kukkhonen addressed the youth with words from John 1:45–46: "Can anything good come from Nazareth?" She then repeated the apostle Philip's words to Nathaniel: "Come and see!" The regime looked in horror at these activities and decided to lock the church for good, forbidding any further church services. It would later be burned to the ground. But the people still gathered in the cemetery surrounding the church, so the authorities banned them from the church grounds entirely. The parishioners silently responded by moving two kilometers further down the hill amid the enormous birch and pine trees, close by some old rusty, ancient crosses. There outdoor services were held and people from around Ingria kept coming, until arrests began in October of 1940. Kukkhonen and other important parishioners were taken into custody and sent to Siberia. Although a few churches in Ingria would open briefly during World War II, Lutheran public worship now ceased with the closing of the Koltushi parish. People would have to practice their faith in secrecy during the remaining years of darkness.[61]

THE GATES OF HELL SHALL NOT PREVAIL AGAINST THE CHURCH

THE YEARS BETWEEN 1939 and the fall of the Soviet Union in 1991 were bleak for Christians. World War II in particular enacted a severe toll on the nation as well as Christians, whether underground or open about their faith. Former dean of the Leningrad seminary Friedrich Wacker had survived the Great Terror and the closing of the churches, but when Nazi Germany invaded the USSR on June 22, 1941, he knew his family would suffer and he deemed it best that they suffer together. Previously, he would illegally take the local night train from Malaya Vishera to visit his wife and children in Leningrad, assuming that under the cover of dark he could slip in and out of their apartment more easily. But with the coming of war to Russia, he decided to risk it and take the day train. The caretaker at the apartment recognized him and informed the NKVD. He was arrested on June 28, 1941. When his wife heard about his arrest, she went looking for him. She, too, was arrested. Wacker was shot on July 10, the last professor of the Leningrad Lutheran seminary who had been left alive. His wife suffered the same fate.[1]

After Stalin's death, Nikita Khrushchev's de-Stalinization program led to some liberalization, but no long-lasting improvements in religious freedom were forthcoming. Eventually, two Lutheran churches were allowed to quietly open their doors in the 1970s (Pushkin and Petrozavodsk), and in the late 1980s Mikhail Gorbachev's glasnost experiment gave new life to free speech in the Soviet Union.[2] It was the beginning of the end for communism in the Soviet Union, because when the USSR disintegrated in 1991, churches suddenly began to reopen throughout the former Soviet territory. In St. Petersburg (Leningrad returned to its former name in 1991), Lutheran congregations struggled to regain their property. St. Peter's, being in the city center, was at the center of this debate, and now a spirited argument arose within the neighborhood as to whether the "swimming pool" should be returned to what remained of the old congregation. The Baltic Sea Steamship Company was reluctant to part with this valuable property since it rented out the church and operated the swimming pool, allowing as many as 128 organizations to use the premises. The city government was certainly not inclined to take into account the opinions of this small band of Lutherans, but the glasnost period had unleashed the long-stilled voices of the Russian public. In a 1991 article, even the newspaper *Evening Leningrad* took the side of the Lutherans: "When the judiciary in our country operates in contradiction to the moral law, it stands to reason that we should consistently observe the latter."[3]

As the reassembled church council of St. Peter's appealed for the return of its building, though, some parents in St. Petersburg complained about losing their swimming pool. Where would their children go? These Lutherans could find other churches, couldn't they? Initiating a letter-writing campaign, they even received support from employees of the Russian National Library! But the days when atheism ruled as the arbiter over public opinion were fast receding. Most Russians in the 1990s were now ashamed of the Communist past and its destruction of the church. More representative and influential was the opinion voiced by one reader of the newspaper, "Smena" (appropriately, the Russian word means "Change"): "When I walk past the Evangelical German

Lutheran church, it seems to me that the mournful figures of Sts. Peter and Paul appeal to our conscience. How can you take children to a swimming pool church?! It is the purest form of blasphemy!"

The city government eventually relented, and St. Peter's succeeded in regaining its sanctuary. On Reformation Day 1992, the first divine service was held within the walls since Paul and Bruno Reichert had conducted services in 1937.[4] Lyudmila Shmidrina, the granddaughter and niece of the martyred pastors, became the choir director for the congregation. She had observed the resolute quest of her mother, Irina, to clear the names of her father and brother from the stain of being labeled an "enemy of the people." In the 1960s, Irina obtained a document dated November 22, 1957, rehabilitating her father and brother and establishing their innocence. This led her to search for and finally read the actual case file of the pastors, learning of their last days and burial in Levashovo. The lifelong pain of her mother combined with the memory of her grandfather and uncle exercised a powerful effect on her and pulled her back to the church.[5] Today she serves as the choir director for St. Mary's Lutheran church, just around the corner from St. Peter's.

Former members of St. Peter's, too, came streaming back to the church on its reopening. Irma von Löwenich's family had been a part of St. Peter's since the days of her grandparents in the late nineteenth century. She was baptized there in 1913, had studied at the PeterSchule, and was among those who were in Pastor Helmut Hansen's last confirmation class of May 1929. On the day the church reopened, she wore a white dress and carried flowers in her hand. She captivated a new generation of believers with stories of the grand old church and the "coffee evenings" at the Hansens' apartment that *Leningradskaya Pravda* had found so outrageous. She remembered with joy and tears the concerts and the services, but especially her spiritual leaders, Helmut and Erna Hansen and the Reicherts. They had given their lives so that a new generation of believers could be born and nurtured. Irma passed away in 2000 at the age of eighty-seven, a powerful witness that God's promise that the church would endure is not mere words.[6]

As far as records can determine, Elsa Freifeldt (Golde) lived until 1995 and might well have seen the church of her youth returned to the congregation.[7] She was buried in Smolenskoe Cemetery in St. Petersburg, along with her parents. Meanwhile, at St. Michael's on Vasilyevsky Island, Kurt Muss's old sanctuary saw some of his surviving confirmands also return to the reopened church. They remembered with fondness their old mentor, a picture of him and the 1929 confirmation class being hung on a wall of the church. How many of them might have recalled the lyrics of that hymn they sang on their Confirmation Day in May 1929?

> By our own strength in the hour of trial
> Through adversity we would not stand
> But standing to fight for us
> Is the Chosen One of God's kingdom[8]

Dagmara Schreiber died of tuberculosis in 1963, but her sister, Elena, survived to see St. Michael's doors open and the volleyball factory that occupied the premises expelled. She died in 1993, but her brother-in-law, Mikhail Mudyugin, returned, albeit in a different garb.[9] Mudyugin had taken note of Kurt Muss's counsel about the churches being closed by the time he left the seminary, so he gave up a theological education for a secular one, becoming a noted academic in the years after Muss's martyrdom. However, he never lost his hope to serve one day in the church. In 1958, he caused a public sensation when he left his position at a linguistic institute and became an Orthodox priest. Rising through the ranks of the Church, the elderly Mudyugin was eventually elevated to the rank of archbishop. But with the fall of communism, he was often seen frequenting the reopened Lutheran church of his spiritual father, Pastor Kurt Muss. Mudyugin was invited from time to time by the pastor of

St. Michael's, Sergey Preiman, to address the congregants during the service in his Orthodox garb.[10]

It may have seemed farfetched after that last Christmas Eve in 1937 that he would one day be asked to preach in German at St. Peter's, but that is just what happened as worship services were renewed in the early 1990s. Mudyugin also had the opportunity to share his extensive experience of God's faithfulness to believers, lecturing at the newly reopened seminary located in the Lutheran church in Novosaratovka, the former parish of Paul Reichert.[11] He provided an important dimension to an ecumenical relationship between Orthodox and Lutherans. He even penned a preface in 1994 to a new book on the selected works of Martin Luther, urging Russian Orthodox to read this influential theologian. Mudyugin died in 2000 and was mourned by many in Orthodox and Lutheran circles.[12]

In 1992 in the village of Koltushi, a new church was built on a hill not far from the old one, the place where the church from centuries past had stood and new church leaders from the 1980s like Aari Kugappi had continued to lead services in the fields despite pressure from KGB agents. Katri Kukkhonen was ninety-two years old, but after all she had endured, she wouldn't miss the dedication of the new church for all the world. The new seminary for what would become the Evangelical Lutheran Church of Ingria was situated just down the hill from the church. It would be named in honor of the pastor whom the Communists could never stifle or rattle, Selim Laurikkala. Kukkhonen died in January of 2001 at the age of 100, knowing that God had preserved her all those years and allowed her to see a new generation enter the Lutheran Church in her home village.[13]

At St. Anne's in St. Petersburg, where the Leningrad Lutheran Seminary had conducted classes under Bishop Malmgren's leadership, a remnant of believing Lutherans gathered to rent the church on Sundays for divine worship. In the intervening years, it had been turned into the Spartak Theater, but after the fall of communism the sounds of disco pulsated throughout its halls until the wee hours of the morning. Now, as a Lutheran pastor from Germany, Heinz Klitzka, prepared students for confirmation, he heard the story of one of his seventy-seven-year-old students, Edith Müthel. Her father, Emil Pfeiffer, had been ordained in this very church on a warm, July Sunday back in 1925 when she was just five years old. All her life the pastor's daughter never forgot the vivid images from that solemn occasion: the sun flooding through the stained-glass windows, the aroma of the flowers permeating the church, and the rising crescendo of the music as her father knelt before the altar to be ordained by Bishop Arthur Malmgren. Unable to be confirmed in 1935 due to her father's arrest, she quietly took classes in 1997 to prepare for her long-delayed confirmation. As her tears flowed freely, the elderly woman took her place at the altar amidst teenage and middle-aged believers. She had come home—at long last.[14]

While most of those who had experienced the days of persecution were dying out at the dawn of the new century, there were survivors who could tell a new generation that despite the long years of suffering under communism, God had never abandoned his people. The rising of this phoenix-like Church from the ashes of the Communist experiment was proof that the gates of hell had not prevailed, although, as St. John might attest, they did have their "little season." After Johannes Lel's arrest and expulsion from the Leningrad seminary in 1932, he had been sent to Semipalatinsk in Kazakstan, where he worked as an economist. Mobilized for the Soviet labor army in 1942 (as a "religious person" and ethnic German), he survived the war and landed a bureaucratic position in Solikamsk as a manager of labor. In the 1990s, at the age of eighty, Lel was called to serve as a pastor for the Evangelical Lutheran congregation in Solikamsk.

Meanwhile, his former classmate Bruno Toryassan had also been preserved by God in the intervening years in many ways. Two days before the Soviet Union's entry into World War II (dated from the June 22, 1941 Nazi Germany attack on Russia), Toryassan was called up for military service. Since his ancestry was half German, he should have been sent from Baku to the so-called Azerbaijani Gulag with the many other Germans who were feared to be potential supporters of Hitler. But the commander of the resettlement brigade looked at his last name and declared, "What kind of German is this? You're Armenian!" So, while hundreds of other Germans were sent to the Gulag, Toryassan remained free and served in the military until the end of World War II. After demobilization, he married and worked as the main accountant for a machine building factory for thirty-eight years until his retirement. When the Soviet Union disintegrated in 1991 and an outbreak of violence against Armenians in Azerbaijan erupted, his family resettled in the St. Petersburg region.

It was there that he began to assist the pastor at Sts. Peter and Paul in Vyborg by leading a seniors' Bible study class and helping with church services. Finally, the time had come for him to perform the pastoral duties for which he had been ordained by Bishop Meier in 1933! At a Lutheran Church synod in Moscow in 1999, the two former classmates, Bruno Toryassan and Johannes Lel, met once again. They had last seen each other sixty-seven years before. Lel was now eighty-nine; Torosyan, eighty-seven. Of the fifteen students who had entered the Leningrad seminary in 1929, the first year of Stalin's brutal assault on the church, only five had made it to graduation. Of those five, only these two lived to see the dawn of the twenty-first century.

These two witnesses were the Caleb and Joshua to Lutherans in Russia. Like those Israeli scouts from the Old Testament, it was given to them to glimpse the promised land that great prophets like Moses would not see. They were among those for whom Dr. John Morehead and bishops Arthur Malmgren and Theophil Meier had fought to preserve the Evangelical Lutheran Church of Russia. Lel would continue to serve the congregation in Solikamsk, passing away in 2001 at the age of ninety-one. Torosyan would live until the age of ninety-seven, his memory intact and his desire to preserve the history of his Lutheran Church strong. This living testimony to God's faithfulness was mourned by both re-established Lutheran churches at his funeral in 2009.[15]

No doubt pastors Lel and Toryassan had heard of, if not seen, that extraordinary American Lutheran, John Morehead. After witnessing the devastation of the Volga region famine in the early 1920s and raising funds to feed the hungry, Morehead could not look the other way. Like the good Samaritan, he had seen his brother in peril and was compelled to help the Lutheran Church fortify itself after the Bolshevik Revolution. He had gathered funds, raised up supporters, and worked tirelessly until the point of exhaustion so that a historic church could breathe again. He had truly been his brother's keeper. Morehead was always impressed by the courage of those who read the times and prepared their parishioners for the inevitable persecution. Kurt Muss was one of his protégés, a young man who risked his life to feed the hungry in body and soul. Bishops Meier and Malmgren, likewise, drove themselves to physical and spiritual exhaustion for the good of their Lutheran Church. They all seemed to know that the persecution would be severe, but that in the end, the man-made sandcastles of Soviet utopianism would not withstand the timelessness of God's word. These remarkable men and so many others, named and unnamed in this chronicle, were used by God to sustain the church in times of spiritual famine for the day when it would be revived with the living waters of his word. That day is now at hand.

ACKNOWLEDGMENTS

AS THE GRANDSON of Germans from Russia, the topic of Soviet persecution of Lutherans was always in the back of my mind as I served on the mission field in Russia (1994–1996, 2001–2014). But in 2012, I spoke to the congregation of St. Michael's Lutheran in St. Petersburg about a martyred pastor who served in their church in the 1920s, the Rev. Kurt Muss. After the service, a St. Michael's parishioner, Olga Ryumina, asked me what I knew about Muss. It soon became clear that, compared to her and her daughter Tanya, I did not know much. The Ryuminas began helping me research the topic, connecting me to literature and the archives of the Muss-Tumm family, which they possessed.

So I am grateful to the Ryumina family, first and foremost. I am also grateful to Bishop Aari Kugappi of the Evangelical Lutheran Church of Ingria in Russia for taking my research seriously and wanting to uncover the lost history of martyrs and heroes of the faith who retained their faith in our Lord Jesus Christ against incalculable odds. I also want to thank Pastor Dmitry Lotov, who researched in Moscow's FSB (formerly KGB) archives to learn the fate of his predecessor at Sts. Peter and Paul Lutheran, the Rev. Alexander Streck. Raisa Mikhalovna was very kind to direct this foreigner to books related to my topic in the Russian State Library in Moscow (the former Lenin Library). Nadezhda Cherepenina opened the doors of the Russian State Archives in St. Petersburg for me, and fellow archivist Larissa went out of her way to grant me access to church documents. Mikhail Shkarovsky directed me to find the means to get access to the FSB Archives. Joel Thoreson, the archivist at the Evangelical

Lutheran Church in America archives, went above and beyond in narrowing my search so that I could explore the vast amount of material available there.

I have also been served by several families who shared with me their photo and letter collections related to the persecution of the Evangelical Lutheran Church of Russia in the 1920s and 1930s. The Ryumina family has allowed me use of the Muss-Tumm family photo and letter collection as well as the library of the Lutheran museum inside St. Peter's Lutheran Church in St. Petersburg. Pastor Dmitry Lotov has shared from his collection of photos at Sts. Peter and Paul Lutheran Church in Moscow. I have also received photos from Gisela Kluck-Deterrer, who holds documents from her father (Rev. Arthur Kluck) and mother (Bertha). Similarly, Alexandra Nikolaev allowed me access to photos and letters pertaining to her grandfather, Ernst Hörschelmann, the organist of Sts. Peter and Paul Lutheran, as well as her great-grandfather, the Rev. Ferdinand Hörschelmann. Joel Thoreson has shared photos from the extensive Russian German Lutheran collection in the Evangelical Lutheran Church of America archives. All archives where I did research are acknowledged in the notes.

I am grateful to Dr. Robert Kolb for advising me on the book-writing process. I am likewise grateful to Dr. Robert Rosin for shepherding me through the process of writing and submitting a dissertation, patiently answering my questions no matter where he happened to be on the globe. Many thanks to Elliot Ritzema and Lexham's team of editors, who expertly arranged, shaped, and fit my thoughts into a coherent story. I am very grateful to them!

My family has always been supportive of me. Thanks to my brother Andy and sisters Jenny and Julie. My father, son of Russian German immigrants, always has been a rock and faithful counselor to me. And I simply couldn't have soldiered on without the love and support of my late mother, Betty. Lastly, and most importantly, my thanks go to my wife, Raziyeh, my Russian-speaking companion and life partner whom I love whom with all my heart and every fiber of my being. To all of these, my sincere thanks are extended.

PHOTO GALLERY

LENINGRAD LUTHERAN SEMINARY PHOTO, 1929.

Seminary staff in the front row, left to right: Prof. Brock, Rev. Paul Reichardt, Rev. Helmut Hansen, Prof. Arnold Frischfeld, Seminary Dean Friedrich Wacker, Bishop Arthur Malmgren, Maria and Johannes Waldmann (caretakers), and Rev. Heinrich Behrendts.

KURT MUSS in the Gulag—
most likely a last portrait before
his execution on October 4, 1937.
Years later, a fellow inmate gave
his sketch to the Muss family.

KURT MUSS, family photo, circa
1920s.

KURT AND YELENA MUSS at the piano in their Leningrad
apartment, autumn 1929.

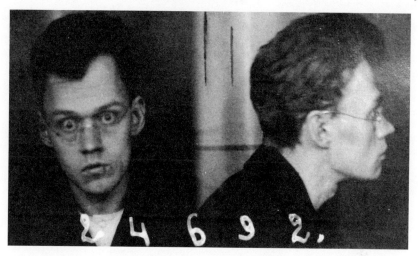

PASTOR KURT MUSS, upon his arrest on December 17, 1929.

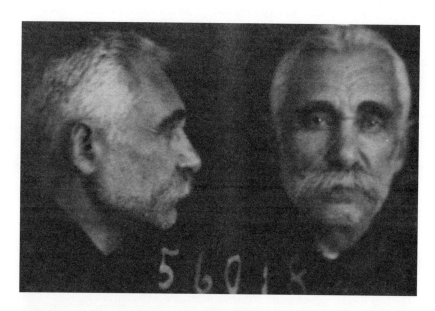

FIFTY-SEVEN-YEAR-OLD LAWYER and Lutheran parishioner, Konstantin Andrievsky, upon his arrest on November 4, 1936. He was sentenced on July 7, 1937, to eight years imprisonment. His ultimate fate is unknown.

SUNDAY SCHOOL TEACHER, LUISA MUSS, upon her arrest on December 17, 1929. Luisa was released in 1932, whereupon she married seminary student, Otto Tumm. She would serve an additional stint in the Gulag before being released again. Her husband Otto died in a Siberian Gulag camp in 1942. Luisa would live a full life with her two sons in Kazakhstan, passing away in 1983.

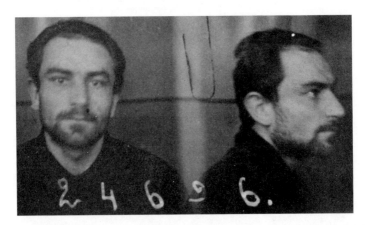

OTTO TUMM, a seminary student arrested on December 17, 1929. Tumm was released with the other Sunday school teachers in 1932 and married Luisa Muss the same year. He was re-arrested in July 1937, promptly released and then arrested yet again on February 28, 1938, whereupon he was convicted of "anti-Soviet activity" and sentenced to ten years imprisonment. He died in a Siberian Gulag camp in 1942.

LUISA MUSS WITH HER SONS, Ulrich (born 1938) and Lothar (born 1936), after her release from a Gulag prison camp in 1939. Her emaciated condition gives evidence of the effects from imprisonment.

THE EFFECTS OF THE FAMINE are shown in these contrasting photos of Bishop Johannes Gruenberg, pastor of a Latvian-speaking church in Petrograd. He would die in 1923 of a heart attack, no doubt brought about by conditions of famine.

SUNDAY SCHOOL TEACHER and seminary student, Peter Mikhailov, upon his arrest on December 17, 1929. Released in 1932, he would continue to attend church while it was open. During World War II, he served heroically as a medic.

PASTOR ALEXANDER STRECK of Sts. Peter and Paul Lutheran-Moscow, upon his arrest on November 4, 1936. Despite the strenuous appeals of the American ambassador to Moscow, William Bullitt, whose embassy community Streck also served, he was executed on July 27, 1937.

EIGHTEEN-YEAR-OLD SUNDAY SCHOOL TEACHER, Dagmara Schreiber, upon her arrest on January, 24, 1930.

EIGHTEEN-YEAR-OLD SUNDAY SCHOOL TEACHER and future Russian Orthodox Church archbishop, Mikhail Mudyugin, upon his arrest on January 24, 1930.

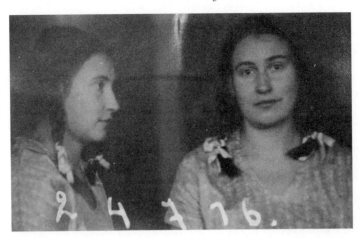

TWENTY-TWO-YEAR-OLD SUNDAY SCHOOL TEACHER, Tamara Kosetti, upon her arrest on December 17, 1929. She was released in 1932, re-arrested in 1938 and died in Siberian exile in 1952.

STRELNA SUMMER CAMPS, 1929. In the center sits Seminary student Konrad Gerling (in black suit and tie) and his fellow classmate next to him, Peter Mikhailov. Standing in the foreground on the far left is Dagmara Schrieber and seminary student Otto Tumm next to her. Mikhail Mudyugin is in the upper corner on the far right.

STRELNA SUMMER CAMPS, 1929. In the center with a black tie and suit is Pastor Helmut Hansen, the creator of the summer children's camps. Seminary student Peter Mikhailov stands in the right foreground.

Strelna was a famous Baltic Sea resort area. Hansen hoped to provide some spiritual and educational opportunities in a pleasant setting for children in poverty. The year 1929 would be the last year that the camp was held due to Hansen's arrest during the Christmas season of 1929. He would never be released and was executed in the fall of 1937.

PASTOR JULIUS ZAHLIT, arrested on January 20, 1934, was sentenced in 1935 to ten years imprisonment, eventually being released in 1945 and sent into exile. The archival record indicates that as late as 1956 during the Khrushchev Thaw, he appealed to Kliment Voroshilov of the Presidium of the Supreme Soviet for release from exile. By all accounts, he would emigrate to Latvia (still part of the USSR) and spend the remaining years of his life there.

FUTURE PRESIDENT OF the United States, Herbert Hoover, when he served as director of ARA. NLC representative, Pastor W. L. Scheding, is photographed alongside (circa 1922–1923).

THE ATHEIST MAGAZINE

Bezbozhnik (Godless)— Christian, Jewish, and Islamic images of God are confronted by a Soviet worker, scaling the heavens.

BEZBOZHNIK MAGAZINE

from December 1936. The caption to the left, displaying a Communist New Year's tree says, "Ours"; the caption on the right, showing a Christian Christmas tree in gloomy surroundings is entitled, "Theirs."

THE FUNERAL OF Latvian-speaking pastor, Mikhail Lapping, held at Sts. Peter and Paul Lutheran church in Moscow in March 1932. Pastors Woldemar Rueger, Alexander Streck, and Julius Zahlit can be seen on the left side of the casket in pastoral garb. Evgeniya Meier, Bishop Theophil Meier's wife, stands in the foreground of the casket on the right.

METROPOLITAN VENIAMIN (BENJAMIN) at his trial in Petrograd. He was executed on July 31, 1922.

JOHN A. MOREHEAD

(1867–1936), in National Lutheran Council offices, ca. 1930s. Executive Secretary of the National Lutheran Council and first president of the Lutheran World Convention. John A. Morehead biographical photo file.

ELCA Archives image. http://www.elca.org/archives.

VOLGA FAMINE RELIF JOURNEY, 1922.

Left to right: John Morehead with Pastor Georg Rath of Alexandrovsk and Moscow Pastor Theophil Meier during their Volga train journey. Morehead visited Russia through the auspices of ARA, distributing food and clothing donated by the NLC.

LUTHERAN WORLD CONVENTION Executive Committee members meeting with Baron Albert Radvansky of Hungary.

Left to right: John A. Morehead, Executive Secretary of the National Lutheran Council and president of the Lutheran World Convention; Ludwig H. Ihmlels, Bishop of Saxony; General Inspector Albert Radvansky; Per Pehrsson of Gotenborg, Sweden; Prof. Alfred T. Jorgensen, Denmark. Meeting possibly at the Lutheran World Convention in Copenhagen, Denmark, June 26 to July 4, 1929.

Photo by Pobuda Alfred, Budapest, Hungary. National Lutheran Council photo files - f. Russia 1922–1923. ELCA Archives image. http://www.elca .org/archives.

LUTHERAN WORLD CONVENTION Executive Committee, likely meeting in Oslo, Norway, September 1930.

Left to right: Per Pehrsson of Gotenborg, Sweden; John A. Morehead, European Director National Lutheran Council; Ludwig H. Ihmlels, Bishop of Saxony; August Marahrens, Bishop of Hanover; Prof. Alfred T. Jorgensen, Denmark.

National Lutheran Council photo files. Russia 1922-1923. ELCA Archives image. http://www.elca.org/archives.

NOTES

CHAPTER 1

1. Frederick K. Wentz, *Lutherans in Concert: The Story of the National Lutheran Council (1918–1966)* (Minneapolis: Augsburg, 1968), 9.

2. Robert Kolb and Timothy J. Wengert, eds., *The Book of Concord: The Confessions of the Evangelical Lutheran Church* (Minneapolis: Fortress, 2000), vii–viii.

3. William Herman Theodore Dau, ed., *Four Hundred Years: Commemorative Essays on the Reformation of Dr. Martin Luther and Its Blessed Results, in the Year of the Four-Hundredth Anniversary of the Reformation* (St. Louis: Concordia, 1916).

4. Theophil Meier, Наследие Лютера в России: К 400-летному Юбилейю Реформацию Отмечатому Евангелическо-Лютеранскоми Обшинами в России [*Luther's Heritage in Russia: On the Occasion of the Celebration of the 400th Anniversary of the Reformation in the Evangelical-Lutheran Community in Russia*] (Moscow: Gotika, 2003), 91–92, 221–23.

5. Daniel H. Johnson, *Loyalty: A Biography of Richard Gustavovich Reusch* (St. Cloud, MN: SunRay Printing, 2008), 88.

6. Michael Burleigh, *Sacred Causes: The Clash of Religion and Politics, from the Great War to the War on Terror* (New York: Harper Perennial, 2008), 1–2, 9–11.

7. Wentz, *Lutherans in Concert*, 9–11.

8. Wentz, *Lutherans in Concert*, 11–12. Knubel was a pastor serving in Manhattan and a representative of the General Synod. In 1918 he would be elected the first president of the United Lutheran Church in America, where he would serve for the next twenty-six years.

9. Samuel Trexler, *John A. Morehead: Who Created World Lutheranism* (Whitefish, MT: Kessinger, 2010), 63–64.

10. Lauritz Larsen to Frank L. Polk, April 15, 1919, NLC Papers, Archives of ELCA.

11. Lauritz Larsen to Frank L. Polk, April 15, 1919, NLC Papers, Archives of ELCA.

12. William Philip to NLC, April 22, 1919, NLC Papers, Archives of ELCA; NLC Meeting, April 22, 1919, NLC Papers, Archives of ELCA; Trexler, 65.

13. NLC Meeting, April 26, 1919, NLC Papers, Archives of ELCA.

14. NLC Meeting, April 26, 1919 and March 13, 1920, NLC Papers, Archives of ELCA.

15. Trexler, *John A. Morehead*, 43, 146.

16. Trexler, *John A. Morehead*, 30, 34, 51.

CHAPTER 2

1. Olga A. Litzenberger, *Evangelical Lutheran Church in Russian History: 16th-20th C.* (Moscow: Lutheran Heritage Foundation, 2003), 33–35.

2. Litzenberger, *Evangelical Lutheran Church in Russian History: 16th–20th C.*, 39-40.

3. Timothy J. Wengert, ed., *Dictionary of Luther and the Lutheran Traditions* (Grand Rapids: Baker Academic, 2017), 650–51, 733.

4. Maxim Ivanov, *Lutheran Quarter of Petersburg* (Saint Petersburg: Russia, European House, 2004), 59, 61.

5. Wengert, *Dictionary of Luther and the Lutheran Traditions*, 193–94.

6. Wengert, *Dictionary of Luther and the Lutheran Traditions*, 651.

7. Johannes Schleuning, Heinrich Roemmich, and Eugen Bachmann, *Und siehe, wir leben!: Der Weg der evangelisch-luthersichen Kirche Russlands in vier Jahrhunderten* (Erlangen, Germany: Martin Luther-Verlag, 1977), 105.

8. Victor Dönninghaus, *Die Deutschen in der Moskauer Gesellschaft: Symbiose und Konflikte (1494–1941)* (Munich: R. Oldenbourg Verlag, 2002), 373–74.

9. Richard Walter Report, July 18, 1919, NLC Papers, Archives of ELCA.

10. Litzenberger, Olga. Евангелическо-Лютеранская Церковь в Российской Истории (XVI–XX vv.) [*The Evangelical Lutheran Church in Russian History (16th–20th c.)*] (Moscow: The Lutheran Heritage Foundation of Education and Culture, 2003), 227–32. The synod would not be allowed for yet another six years (1924).

11. Schleuning et al., *Und siehe, wir leben*, 106.

12. William B. Husband, *Godless Communists: Atheism and Society in Soviet Russia, 1917–1932* (Dekalb, IL.: Northern Illinois University Press, 2000), 48. "Soviet society would be nonreligious rather than anti-religious in the immediate future."

13. Richard Walter Report, July 18, 1919, NLC Papers, Archives of ELCA.

14. Richard Pipes, *Russia under the Bolshevik Regime* (New York: Vintage Books, 1995.), Kindle edtion, loc. 8454 of 14900.

15. Archimandrite Augustine, "Annenschule," in Karev, V. Editor, Немции в России: Энциклопедия Том 1, А-И [Germans of Russia: Encyclopedia. Volume 1, А-И] (Moscow: ERN, 1999), 43.

16. Richard Walter Report, Archives of ELCA. Sts. Peter and Paul in Moscow had built a boys' school during the war for 650,000 rubles, the equivalent of $325,000. That school now became state property.

17. N. P. Ulyanov, "Судбы Учителей Петришуле, 20–30 г." ["Fate of the Teachers at the Peterschule, 1920–30s"], in Немции в России: Люди и Сулбы [*Germans in Russia: People and Fates*] (St. Petersburg, Russia: 1998), 203.

18. March 21 Report, NLC, 1919, NLC Papers, Archives of ELCA.

19. Husband, *Godless Communists*, 45–46.

20. Robert Conquest, *Religion in the USSR* (London: Bodley Head, 1968), 14.

21. Edward E. Roslof, *Red Priests: Renovationism, Russian Orthodoxy, and Revolution, 1905–1946* (Bloomington, IN: Indiana University, 2002), 23.

22. Husband, *Godless Communists*, 47, 184.

23. N. S. Timasheff, *Religion in Soviet Russia: 1917–1942* (New York: Sheed and Ward, 1942), 22.

24. Richard Walter Report, Archives of ELCA; *Germans in Russia, Volume 1*, 754.

25. Glennys Young, *Power and the Sacred in Revolutionary Russia: Religious Activists in the Village* (University Park, PA: Pennsylvania State University, 1997), 61. The state bakeries would not sell to clergy, and since there were no private bakeries, pastors would have to rely upon the good will of their parishioners.

26. March 21 Report, NLC, 1919, NLC Papers, Archives of ELCA; Theophil Meier to Carl Paul, January 10, 1921, NLC Papers, Archives of ELCA.

27. Schleuning et al., *Und siehe, wir leben*, 108; Heinrich Roemmich, *The Rose and the Sickle: Survival of the Lutheran Church in Russia* ed. Oscar Sommerfeld, trans. Frederick Lenz (Saskatoon, SK: Division of Communication: Evangelical Lutheran Church of Canada, 1984), 12.

28. Roemmich, *The Rose and the Sickle*, 13.

29. Oscar Mees to Johannes Schleuning, November 4, 1920, NLC Papers, Archives of ELCA. A good guess as to the identity of the pastor would be Wilhelm Kentmann.

30. John Mueller to H. G. Stub, May 20, 1919, NLC Papers, Archives of ELCA.

31. Litzenberger, *The Evangelical Lutheran Church in Russian History (16th–20th c.)*, 256–57.

32. Pipes, *Russia under the Bolshevik Regime*, Kindle loc. 8469 of 14900.

33. Pipes, *Russia under the Bolshevik Regime*, Kindle loc. 8471.

34. Roslof, *Red Priests*, 23–24; Richard Pipes, *The Russian Revolution* (New York: Vintage Books, 1991), Kindle edition, loc. 21101.

35. Litzenberger, *The Evangelical Lutheran Church in Russian History (16th–20th c.)*, 256–57. By the middle of 1922, Freifeldt would update that statement and acknowledge that while the attention of the government was initially upon the Orthodox Church, it would soon be turned against the Lutherans, too. See Kahle, Willaim, *Geschichte der Evangelisch-Lutherischen Gemeinden in der Sovetunion, 1917–1938* (Leiden, Germany: E. J. Brill, 1974), 61.

36. Litzenberger, *The Evangelical Lutheran Church in Russian History (16th–20th c.)*, 256–58.

37. Pipes, *Russia under the Bolshevik Regime*, Kindle loc. 315, 370.

38. Wentz, *Lutherans in Concert*, 43.

39. Finnish Pastors to George Rygh, March 17, 1920, NLC Papers, Archives of ELCA; Pipes, *Russia under the Bolshevik Regime*, Kindle loc. 2377.

40. "The Appeal of the Finnish Pastors in Russia," 1922?, NLC Papers, Archives of ELCA.

41. NLC Meeting, March 13, 1920, NLC Papers, Archives of ELCA; "The Appeal of the Finnish Pastors in Russia," 1922, NLC Papers, Archives of ELCA.

42. John Morehead to Lauritz Larsen, December 1920 and Oscar Mees to Johannes Schleuning, December 17, 1920, NLC Papers, Archives of ELCA.

43. NLC Report, March 1921, NLC Papers, Archives of the ELCA.

44. Pipes, *Russia under the Bolshevik Regime*, Kindle loc. 2435.

45. NLC Report, March 1921. These actions would later be used in false accusations of anti-Communist activity against pastors like Albert Koch of Grossliebenthal, a village 30–40 kilometers from the Black Sea port city of Odessa. See Russian Evangelical Press, no.8, 1930, LWC Papers, Archives of the ELCA.

46. NLC Report, March 1921, NLC Papers, Archives of ELCA.

47. NLC Report, March 1921. Fastena would announce his departure from Russia by April 1921. See Theophil Meier to Carl Paul, April 23, 1921, NLC Papers, Archives of ELCA.

48. NLC Report, March 1921,

49. NLC Report, March 1921.

50. Pipes, *Russia under the Bolshevik Regime*, Kindle loc. 3269, 3359, 3377.

51. NLC Report, March 1921.

CHAPTER 3

1. Theophil Meier to Carl Paul, April 23, 1921; Viktor Krieger, translated by Alex Herzog, *Volga German Intellectuals as Victims of Political Persecution* (Lincoln, NE: American Historical Society of Germans from Russia, 2009), 17.

2. Theophil Meier to Carl Paul, January 10, 1921, NLC Papers, Archives of ELCA.

3. Theophil Meier to Carl Paul, April 23, 1921, NLC, March 13, 1921; and Theophil Meier to Carl Paul, January 10, 1921, NLC Papers, Archives of ELCA.

4. Theophil Meier to Fritdjof Nansen, August 29, 1921, NLC Papers, Archives of ELCA. There is even a statue of Nansen on the street near the Primorskaya metro station in St. Petersburg.

5. Fritdjof Nansen to Lauritz Larsen, April 1, 1921, NLC Papers, Archives of ELCA.

6. Lauritz Larsen to Fritdjof Nansen, March 16 and April 25, 1921, NLC Papers, Archives of ELCA.

7. Lauritz Larsen to Conrad Freifeldt and Theophil Meier, May 13, 1921, NLC Papers, Archives of ELCA.

8. John Morehead to Fritz Tömmler, August 1, 1921, NLC Papers, Archives of ELCA.

9. Conrad Freifeldt to Carl Paul, August 1921, NLC Papers, Archives of ELCA; Litzenberger, *The Evangelical Lutheran Church in Russian History (16th–20th c.)*, 385.

10. Conrad Freifeldt to Lauritz Larsen, August 9, 1921, NLC Papers, Archives of ELCA.

11. Bertrand M. Patenaude, *The Big Show in Bololand: The American Relief Expedition to Soviet Russia in the Famine of 1921* (Stanford, CA: Stanford University Press, 2002), 26–27.

12. Patenaude, *The Big Show*, 28–30, 45.

13. Lauritz Larsen to George Borell, September 6, 1921, NLC Papers, Archives of ELCA.

14. Lauritz Larsen to Reinhold Birk, November 21, 1921, NLC Papers, Archives of ELCA.

15. Trexler, *John A. Morehead*, 89; Patenaude, *The Big Show*, 53, 60–61, 71.

16. Trexler, *John A. Morehead*, 89–91. Ransome was actually a secret agent for the British government. However, due to his sympathy for the Bolsheviks, they had to proceed carefully with him. They feared that he might share secret information detrimental to other Russians or British officials with the Bolsheviks. As one British intelligent agent summed up his positives and negatives succinctly:

'He will report what he sees, but he does not see quite straight.' See Robert Service, *Spies and Commissars* (Public Affairs, 2012), Kindle edition, loc. 4554, 4570, 4589.

17. NLC Meeting, January 18, 1923, NLC Papers, Archives of ELCA.

18. Lauritz Larsen to Theodore Benze, December 29, 1922, NLC Papers, Archives of ELCA.

19. NLC Meeting, January 18, 1923.

20. Patenaude, *The Big Show*, 91–95; Lauritz Larsen to L. Hopp, December 17, 1921.

21. Arthur Kluck to A. C. Ernst, May 10, 1922, NLC Papers, Archives of ELCA.

22. Lauritz Larsen to Editor of *Skandinaven,* April 13, 1922, NLC Papers, Archives of ELCA.

23. Lauritz Larsen to Editor of *Skandinaven*, April 13, 1922.

24. Memorandum upon the Russian Red Cross, 1922, NLC Papers, Archives of ELCA.

25. Memorandum upon the Russian Red Cross, 1922. With the fall of the Soviet Union in 1991, classified documents made their way into the public sphere. Historians Harvey Klehr and John Haynes worked with Russian archivists to publish the information in several books. For example, they write that the aforementioned David Dubrowsky broke with the CPUSA in 1935, eventually testifying before the House Special Committee on Un-American Activities. There he admitted that the CPUSA received money from the Bolsheviks through their front groups. In a secret document, it appears that the CPUSA planned to steal as much as 40 percent of the funds raised for famine relief. This display of impudence was actually too much for the Comintern, who refused. It leads one to wonder how many funds raised by these Communist front groups went to famine relief. See Harvey Klehr and John Haynes, *The Soviet World of American Communism* (New Haven, CT: Yale University Press, 1998), 109–114.

26. Litzenberger, *The Evangelical Lutheran Church and the Soviet Government, 1917–1938*, 123; John Morehead, "In Memory of Bishop Meier," 1934, LWC Papers, Archives of ELCA.

27. Trexler, *John A. Morehead*, 91; A. A. German, Немецкая Автономия на Волге 1918–1941 [*German Autonomy on the Volga 1918–1941*] (Moscow: MSNK Press, 2007), 121–22.

28. Trexler, *John A. Morehead*, 92

29. Trexler, *John A. Morehead*, 91–95; Litzenberger, *The Evangelical Lutheran Church and the Soviet Government, 1917–1938*, 390.

30. Theophil Meier to John Morehead, February 17, 1922, NLC Papers, Archives of ELCA.

31. NLC Meeting, January 18, 1923.

32. NLC Meeting, January 18, 1923, and John Morehead to Theophil Meier, February 14, 1929, NLC and LWC Papers, Archives of ELCA.

33. Lauritz Larsen to Jacob Gruebele, April 5, 1922, NLC Papers, Archives of ELCA.

34. John Morehead to President Herbert Hoover, July 10, 1930, LWC Papers, Archives of ELCA.

35. Albert Koch to W. L. Scheding, July 17, 1923, NLC Papers, Archives of ELCA.

36. Kahle, *Geschichte*, 332.

37. Private Document Collection of Ferdinand Hörschelmann Family; Johannes Völl, "Zum Gedenken an Pastor Ferdinand Hörschelmann," *Heimatbuch der Deutschen aus Russland* (Stuttgart: Die Landsmannschaft der Deutschen aus Russland, 1964), 139–141; O. Kubitskaya, Немцы России:Энциклопедия,Том 3, П-Я (*Germans of Russia: Encyclopedia. Volume 3, Р-Я*), (Moscow: ERN, 2006), 708.

38. *Germans of Russia, Volume 3*, 549.

39. Alexander Streck to A. C. Ernst, 6 May 1922, LWC Papers, Archives of ELCA.

40. Lauritz Larsen to NLC, January 16, 1922, NLC Papers, Archives of ELCA.

41. Lauritz Larsen to P. C. Galprin, January 6, 1922; Gustav Beschorner to Lauritz Larsen, January 4, 1922; Lauritz Larsen to Frank Page, February 28, 1922, NLC Papers, Archives of ELCA.

42. John Morehead to Theophil Meier, August 1, 1922, NLC Papers, Archives of ELCA.

43. Frank Page to Lauritz Larsen, June 15, 1922, NLC Papers, Archives of ELCA.

44. June 7, 1922 report from ARA, NLC Papers, Archives of ELCA. Unfortunately, due to a heat wave, many of the crops were damaged, rendering Ernst's optimism a bit premature. Furthermore, the people farmers really did need draught animals to help with the harvest. The food aid would thus continue to be of importance. See Oscar Mees to A.C. Ernst, August 4, 1922, NLC Papers, Archives of ELCA.

CHAPTER 4

1. Trexler, *John A. Morehead*, 96.

2. NLC Meeting, January 18, 1923; Theophil Meier to John Morehead, June 12, 1922, NLC Papers, Archives of ELCA.

3. Private Document Collection of Kurt Muss Family; Germans of Russia, Volume 2, 577; Mikhail Shkarovsky, "Пастор Курт Мусс и Общиа Русских

Лютеран в Петрограде-Ленинграде" [Pastor Kurt Muss and the Congregation of Russian Lutherans in Petrograd-Leningrad], April 27, 2011, http://spbda.ru/publications/professor-mihail-shkarovskiy-pastor-kurt-muss-i-obschina-russkih-lyuteran-v-petrograde-leningrade/.

4.   Theophil Meier to John Morehead, June 12, 1922, NLC Papers, Archives of ELCA.

5.   W. L. Scheding to John Morehead, March 1, 1924, NLC Papers, Archives of ELCA.

6.   Lauritz Larsen to Theophil Meier, August 16, 1922, NLC Papers, Archives of ELCA.

7.   NLC Meeting, January 18, 1923.

8.   NLC Meeting, January 18, 1923.

9.   Lesley Chamberlain, *Lenin's Private War: The Voyage of the Philosophy Steamer and the Exile of the Intelligentsia* (New York: St. Martin's Press, 2007), 34, 100, 305–12.

10. John Shelton Curtiss, *The Russian Church and the Soviet State, 1917–1950* (New York: Little, Brown, 1953), 121–23.

11. Timasheff, *Religion in Soviet Russia,* 28–29.

12. Roslof, *Red Priests,* 35.

13. Pipes, *Russia under the Bolshevik Regime,* Kindle loc. 8568, 8577.

14. Roslof, *Red Priests,* 44–45; Timasheff, *Religion in Soviet Russia,* 29.

15. Pipes, *Russia under the Bolshevik Regime,* Kindle loc. 8665 of 14900.

16. Pipes, *Russia under the Bolshevik Regime,* Kindle loc. 8575, 8596, 8623, 8644, 8670, 8677.

17. John Morehead, "In Memory of Bishop Meyer," 1934, LWC Papers, Archives of ELCA.

18. John Morehead, "In Memory of Bishop Meyer," 1934; Litzenberger, *Evangelical Lutheran Church in Russian History (16th–20th c.),* 137.

19. Roslof, *Red Priests,* 66–67. Lauritz Larsen must have acquired a copy of this picture, since it exists in the NLC files of the ELCA Archives in Chicago.

20. Pipes, *Russia under the Bolshevik Regime,* Kindle loc. 8748.

21. Patenaude, *The Big Show,* 662.

22. Roslof, *Red Priests,* 71–73.

23. Patenaude, *The Big Show,* 400.

24. Patenaude, *The Big Show,* 398–408.

25. John Morehead to Theophil Meier, July 8, 1922, NLC Papers, Archives of ELCA.

26. John Morehead to Theophil Meier, August 2, 1922; Lauritz Larsen to Kurt Muss, September 11, 1922, NLC Papers, Archives of ELCA.

27. John Morehead to Robert Withington, February 8, 1935, LWC Papers, Archives of ELCA; Lauritz Larsen to W. L. Scheding, September 24, 1922, NLC Papers, Archives of ELCA.

28. W. L. Scheding to John Morehead, March 1, 1924.

29. Shkarovskii, "Pastor Kurt Muss."

30. W. L. Scheding to Lauritz Larsen, January 6, 1923, NLC Papers, Archives of ELCA.; W. L. Scheding to John Morehead, March 1, 1924.

31. Patenaude, *The Big Show*, 109, 181, 676–83.

32. Superintendent Meier would send sensitive reports almost yearly on the condition of the Church labeled "Confidential." The information gleaned could be very useful even for publicity purposes. But NLC officials would take extraordinary care that no one would publish the name of the author or contents. If it was known that they were writing such reports, the danger to Meier and other Lutheran pastors in Russia would be very real. See Lauritz Larsen to Oscar Mees, Sept 24, 1922, NLC Papers, Archives of ELCA.

33. W. L. Scheding to John Morehead, March 1, 1924. Russian historian Mikhail Shkarovsky says that Muss found himself under arrest on December 23, not November, like Scheding. But Shkarovsky mentions that Muss was in Butyrka Prison on the 23, so that was likely the date when he was transferred to the prison in Moscow. See "Pastor Kurt Muss and the Congregation of Russian Lutherans in Petrograd."

34. John Morehead to Robert Withington, 8 February 1935; John Morehead to O. T. Benze and W. L. Scheding, April 9, 1923, NLC Papers, Archives of ELCA.

35. W. L. Scheding to John Morehead, April 11, 1923, NLC Papers, Archives of ELCA. Shkarovsky indicates that Muss was sentenced on April 13. See "Pastor Kurt Muss and the Congregation of Russian Lutherans in Petrograd."

36. Pokrovskaya to Philip Matthews, May 18, 1923, NLC Papers, Archives of ELCA—author's translation from Russian.

37. Shkarovsky, "Pastor Kurt Muss."

38. Shkarovsky, "Pastor Kurt Muss"; W. L. Scheding to John Morehead, March 1, 1924.

39. John Morehead to Robert Withington, February 8, 1935.

40. Theodore Benze to John Morehead, June 17, 1923, NLC Papers, Archives of ELCA. This would actually change in 1924, as Superintendent Meier noted in a sermon on June 17.

41. W. L. Scheding to John Morehead, January 6, 1923, and Lauritz Larsen, September 4, 1922, NLC Papers, Archives of ELCA; Pipes, *Russia under the Bolshevik Regime*, Kindle loc. 8780, 8796, 8815.

CHAPTER 5

1. Patenaude, *The Big Show*, 190.

2. John Morehead to Oscar Mees, February 1, 1923, NLC Papers, Archives of ELCA.

3. W. L. Scheding to Lauritz Larsen, December 21, 1922, NLC Papers, Archives of ELCA.

4. W. L. Scheding to John Morehead, January 6, 1923; W. L. Scheding to John Morehead, "Confidential," 1923, NLC Papers, Archives of ELCA.

5. Theodore Benze to director of administrative office for foreign affairs of the Soviet Union, February 27, 1923, NLC Papers, Archives of ELCA.

6. W. L. Scheding to John Morehead, March 30, 1923, NLC papers, Archives of ELCA.

7. Patenaude, *The Big Show*, 196–98.

8. Theodore Benze to John Morehead, July 5, 1923, NLC Papers, Archives of ELCA.

9. Charles Glöckler, "What the National Lutheran Council has done for Russia," December 1, 1922, LWC Papers, Archives of ELCA.

10. Conrad Freifeldt to Benze, April 29, 1923, and Theodore Benze, "Freifeldt Funeral," June 3, 1923, NLC Papers, Archives of ELCA.

11. W. L. Scheding to John Morehead, May 2, 1923, NLC Papers, Archives of ELCA.

12. Lauritz Larsen to L. Hopp, January 6, 1923, and W. L. Scheding to John Morehead, May 2, 1923, NLC Papers, Archives of ELCA.

13. W. L. Scheding, to Lauritz Larsen, February 16, 1923, NLC Papers, Archives of ELCA.

14. W. L. Scheding, February 16, 1923, and W. L. Scheding to Lauritz Larsen, December 21, 1922, and W. L. Scheding, "Life at Ebb Tide," July 11, 1923, NLC Papers, Archives of ELCA.

15. Patenaude, *The Big Show*, 186.

16. John Morehead to Lauritz Larsen, August 9, 1922, NLC Papers, Archives of ELCA.

17. Theodore Benze to John Morehead, May 2, 1923, and Don Haskell to Theodore Benze, June 5, 1923, NLC Papers, Archives of ELCA.

18. W. L. Scheding to Oscar Mees, February 1, 1923, NLC Papers, Archives of ELCA.

19. Theodore Benze to John Morehead, April 3, 1923, and John Morehead to Lauritz Larsen, August 9, 1922, NLC Papers, Archives of ELCA.

20. John Morehead to Theodore Benze and W. L. Scheding, April 9, 1923, NLC Papers, Archives of ELCA.

21. John Morehead to Theodore Benze and W. L. Scheding, April 9, 1923, NLC Papers, Archives of ELCA.

22. Theodore Benze to John Morehead, April 23, 1923, NLC Papers, Archives of ELCA.

23. Karl Lander, June 27, 1923, NLC Papers, Archives of ELCA.

24. Trexler, *John A. Morehead*, 101; Wentz, *Lutherans in Concert*, 39; Theodore Benze to John Morehead, February 6, 1923, and Oscar Mees to Theodore Benze, February 21, 1923, NLC Papers, Archives of ELCA.

25. Theodore Benze, "Freifeldt Funeral," June 3, 1923, LWC Papers, Archives of ELCA; Kahle, *Geschichte*, 65.

26. Timasheff, *Religion in Soviet Russia*, 31.

27. Theodore Benze, "The Church Year in Russia," June 17, 1923, NLC Papers, Archives of ELCA.

28. Timasheff, *Religion in Soviet Russia*, 33.

29. Roslof, *Red Priests*, 112–17.

30. Curtiss, *Russian Church and the Soviet State*, 162.

31. Pipes, *Russia under the Bolshevik Regime*, Kindle loc. 9108, 9142; Roslof, *Red Priests*, 110.

32. Roemmich, *The Rose and the Sickle*, 21–22.

33. Schleuning et al., *Und siehe, wir leben*, 110.

34. W. L. Scheding to John Morehead, "Confidential," 1923.

35. Trexler, *John A. Morehead*, 105–6, 116.

36. Superintendent Malmgren had also received an invitation but was forced to refuse. His wife had become sick and died on July 4, leaving him a widow with three unmarried daughters. See Helmut Tschoerner, *Arthur Malmgren— Theologe, Pfarrer, Bischof in Russland und der Sowjetunion* (Erlangen, Germany: Martin Luther Verlag, 2012), 60.

37. Trexler, *John A. Morehead*, 109–11; Theophil Meier to John Morehead, October 16, 1923, NLC Papers, Archives of ELCA; Kahle, *Geschichte*, 70–71.

38. Theophil Meier to John Morehead, October 16, 1923, and W. L. Scheding to Theodore Benze, October 19, 1923, NLC Papers, Archives of ELCA; Kahle, *Geschichte*, 71–72.

39. W. L. Scheding to John Morehead, October 9, 1923, NLC Papers, Archives of ELCA.

40. W. L. Scheding cablegram, November 2, 1923, W. L. Scheding to John Morehead, October 5, 1923, and W.L Scheding to John Morehead, October 9, 1923, NLC Papers, Archives of ELCA.

41. Dmitri Volkogonov, *Trotsky: The Eternal Revolutionary*, trans. and ed. Harold Shukman (New York: The Free Press, 1996), 7; Robert Conquest, *The Great Terror: A Reassessment* (New York: Oxford University Press, 2007), 7.

42. W. L. Scheding to Oscar Mees, December 20, 1923, NLC Papers, Archives of ELCA.

43. W. L. Scheding to John Morehead, October 16, 1923, and Olga Kameneva to Oscar Mees, February 26, 1925, NLC Papers, Archives of ELCA.

CHAPTER 6

1. Kahle, *Geschichte*, 472–73. It should be taken into account, though, that over two million parishioners had become citizens of the new countries Estonia and Latvia.

2. Schleuning et al., *Und siehe, wir leben*, 112.

3. Theophil Meier to Friends of the Lutheran Church, February 1, 1924, NLC Papers, Archives of ELCA.

4. Schleuning et al., *Und siehe, wir leben*, 112.

5. Theophil Meier to John Morehead, July 21, 1924, NLC Papers, Archives of ELCA; Kahle, *Geschichte*, 526.

6. Official Report of First Ev. Lutheran Synod, June 21–26, 1924, NLC Papers, Archives of ELCA.

7. Kahle, *Geschichte*, 72, 74.

8. John Morehead, "Report on First Evangelical Lutheran Synod," August 20, 1924, NLC papers, Archives of ELCA. The Lutheran Church's commitment to serving in the military would be illustrated in the case of Vladimir Romanov. The seventeen-year-old Romanov left the Orthodox Church in 1924 due to the schism initiated by the Living Church. He joined Jesus Christ Lutheran in Leningrad and then entered the Leningrad seminary. In 1927, however, he was called up for military duty but refused on the grounds of his religious

convictions. Either Bishop Malmgren feared that Romanov's decision would complicate the relationship with the authorities or he simply did not accept Romanov's reasoning. In any case, he was expelled from the seminary in 1927. Fortunately for him, the judge only fined him and assigned him to a work detail with the comment, "What do we need a bastard like that in the army for anyway?" In a sad twist of irony, Romanov actually did serve in World War II but perished at the front in 1943. See Shkarovsky, "Pastor Kurt Muss."

9.   Historian Olga Litzenberger simply states that Hansen refused to sign the resolution and spoke out against it. Historian Wilhelm Kahle traces the charge to the *Leningradskaya Pravda* article and concludes that the accusation against Hansen was unverifiable. See Litzenberger, *The Evangelical Lutheran Church and the Soviet Government, 1917–1938*, 157; and Kahle, *Geschichte*, 79.

10. Kahle, *Geschichte*, 80–81, 528–29.

11. Völl, *Heimatbuch*, 140. Wilhelm Kahle speculates as to whether the Soviet government influenced the selection in any way. Although there is no proof, it would certainly want to be able to keep an eye on the Church and that would be easier to do if its main office was based in Moscow. See Kahle, *Geschichte*, 90.

12. Kahle, *Geschichte*, 90–91.

13. John Morehead, "Report on First Evangelical Lutheran Synod," August 20, 1924.

14. Kahle, *Geschichte*, 403; Theophil Meier to Friends of the Lutheran Church, February 1, 1924.

15. John Morehead, "Report on First Evangelical Lutheran Synod," August 20, 1924.

16. Kahle, *Geschichte*, 98–99.

17. John Morehead, "Report on First Evangelical Lutheran Synod," August 20, 1924; Kahle, *Geschichte*, 35.

18. John Morehead, "Report on First Evangelical Lutheran Synod," August 20, 1924; John Morehead to Reu, Aug 20, 1924; NLC Papers, Archives of ELCA.

19. Georg Schilling to W. L. Scheding, March 18, 1924, NLC Papers, Archives of ELCA. Morehead sent the report of the convention to Dr. Reu of the Iowa Synod. He noted that he had to edit the final report because there were Soviet spies in America, and he wanted to present the relationship of the Lutheran Church in Russia to the government in the best possible light. Yet he regretted that he could not publicly disseminate the information about the persecution of the church, including Bishop Meier's inquisition at the Cheka headquarters. See John Morehead to Reu, August 20, 1924.

20. Robert Derringer, "Church Report to Lutheran World Convention," August 19, 1927, Lutheran World Convention Papers, Archives of ELCA.

21. P-34994, List 4, FSB Archives of St. Petersburg Region.

22. Fond 1001, Opis 8, Delo 52, List 10, Russian State Archives of St. Petersburg.

23. Theophil Meier to John Morehead, December 1924, LWC Papers, Archives of ELCA.

24. John Morehead to Olga Kameneva, December 12, 1924, LWC Papers, Archives of ELCA.

25. Schmieden to Oscar Mees, January 27, 1925, LWC Papers, Archives of ELCA.

26. The decision had actually been made on January 27, the day that Schmieden wrote to him that he would soon receive his visa! See NKVD to Oscar Mees, February 5, 1925, LWC Papers, Archives of ELCA.

27. Schmieden to Mees, February 16, 1925, LWC Papers, Archives of ELCA.

28. Oscar Mees to Olga Kameneva, February 19, 1925, LWC Papers, Archives of ELCA.

29. Olga Kameneva to Oscar Mees, February 26, 1925, LWC papers, Archives of ELCA.

30. Schmieden to Oscar Mees, February 28, 1925, LWC Papers, Archives of ELCA.

31. Olga Kameneva to Oscar Mees, February 26, 1925; Schmieden to Oscar Mees, February 28, 1925; Schmieden to Oscar Mees, February 24, 1925; John Morehead, "LWC Meeting Notes in Gothenburg," November 15–19, 1925; Theophil Meier to Oscar Mees, March 17, 1925, LWC Papers, Archives of ELCA.

CHAPTER 7

1. Theophil Meier to John Morehead, May 12, 1925, LWC Papers, Archives of ELCA; Litzenberger, *The Evangelical Lutheran Church and the Soviet Government, 1917–1938*, 343, 349, 384. Deutschmann would go on to serve in Slavgorod (1925–1928) in the Altai region of Siberia after this trip. Alexander Siegfried would never serve in Siberia, immigrating to Germany and dying in Helsinki in 1957. See Litzenberger, *The Evangelical Lutheran Church and the Soviet Government, 1917–1938*, 349, 357.

2. Theophil Meyer to Ernst Holzmeyer, July 1925, and Theophil Meier to Tilly Meier, July 21, 1925, LWC Papers, Archives of ELCA.

3. John Morehead, November 15–19, 1925, "LWC Meeting Notes in Gothenburg."

4. Theophil Meier to John Morehead, November 13, 1922, NLC Papers, Archives of ELCA.

5. John Morehead to Theophil Meier, March 24, 1924, LWC Papers, Archives of the ELCA.

6. John Morehead to Lutherisches Oberkirchenrat, November 26, 1924; Theophil Meyer to Theodore Benze, July 21, 1924; and Arthur Malmgren to John Morehead, May 5, 1925, LWC Papers, Archives of ELCA.

7.   John Morehead to Arthur Malmgren, May 12 and June 17, 1925, LWC Papers, Archives of ELCA.

8.   Arthur Malmgren to John Morehead, April 17, 1925; and John Morehead to Arthur Malmgren, May 12 and June 17, 1925, LWC Papers, Archives of ELCA.

9.   Arthur Malmgren to John Morehead, June 17, 1925; and Lutherisches Oberkirchenrat to John Morehead, May 5, 1925, LWC Papers, Archives of ELCA; Johannes Lel, "Как Нас Уничтожали, Но не Уничтожили" ["How They Were Trying to Destroy Us, but Didn't Succeed"], Наша Церковь [*Our Church*] (September 2001): 15; "Будьте Богом храними..." ["May God Preserve You..."], unpublished article by Tanya Ryumina, 2011.

10. John Morehead to Arthur Malmgren, May 12, 1925, LWC papers, Archives of ELCA; Oscar Mees to W. L. Scheding, October 18, 1922; and Lauritz Larsen to John Morehead, October 24, 1919, NLC Papers, Archives of ELCA.

11. Arthur Malmgren to John Morehead, June 17, 1925; and John Morehead to Arthur Malmgren, July 7, 1925, LWC Papers, Archives of ELCA.

12. I will use the designation "seminary" from now on, as the Bible school operated as a seminary and was perceived as such in the eyes of Lutherans in Russia and America.

13. Arthur Malmgren to John Morehead, September 7, 1925, LWC Papers, Archives of ELCA.

14. Arthur Malmgren to John Morehead, September 7, 1925; and Friedrich Wacker, "Church Calendar 1927," LWC Papers, Archives of ELCA.

15. Müthel, *An Gottes Hand*, 19.

CHAPTER 8

1.   Theophil Meier, "Church Report: 1926," LWC Papers, Archives of ELCA.

2.   Litzenberger, *The Evangelical Lutheran Church and the Soviet Government, 1917–1938*, 116–17, 328, 344; Theophil Meyer to John Morehead, August 21, 1924, LWC Papers, Archives of ELCA.

3.   John Morehead to Theophil Meier, March 25, 1924, LWC Papers, Archives of ELCA.

4.   Theophil Meier to John Morehead, August 21, 1924, and John Morehead to Robert Withington, February 8, 1935, LWC Papers, Archives of the ELCA.

5.   Shkarovsky, "Pastor Kurt Muss;" Muss-Tumm Family Letter Collection; Arthur Malmgren to John Morehead, February 5, 1927, LWC Papers, Archives of ELCA.

6.   *Unsere Kirche, October-November 1927*, LWC Papers, Archives of ELCA.

7.   Arthur Malmgren to John Morehead, June 22, 1926, John Morehead to Arthur Malmgren, October 29, 1926, and Friedrich Wacker to John Morehead, Decem-

ber 28, 1926, LWC Papers, Archives of ELCA. Bishop Meier estimated more than half of the Lutherans in the USSR lived in the Volga region, approximately 520,000.

8.   Theophil Meier, "General Report of the Church: 1926," LWC Papers, Archives of ELCA.

9.   The fact that the Lutheran Church stood in no close relationship with the state was beside the point. It and its pastors were symbolic of the old manner of life and were supposed to die out in atheist Russia. See Theophil Meier, "Confidential Church Report: 1925," LWC Papers, Archives of ELCA.

10. Arthur Malmgren to John Morehead, September 20, 1926, LWC Papers, Archives of the ELCA; Litzenberger, *The Evangelical Lutheran Church and the Soviet Government, 1917–1938*, 114.

11. Arthur Malmgren to John Morehead, September 20, 1926; *Unsere Kirche, October–November 1927*, LWC Papers, Archives of ELCA.

12. John Morehead to Arthur Malmgren, December 3, 1926, LWC Papers, Archives of the ELCA. Mrs. Schultz would be relocated to Dresden where she would receive some regular assistance. As late as 1935, Morehead was requesting funds to help her and her two children. See John Morehead to LWC, February 27, 1935, LWC Papers, Archives of ELCA.

13. Kahle, *Geschichte*, 573. Seminary professor Albert Juergensonn would replace Palsa as bishop until his own death in 1929.

14. *Unsere Kirche, October–November 1927*.

15. Kahle, *Geschichte*, 571; John Morehead to Arthur Malmgren, December 3, 1926.

16. Kahle, *Geschichte*, 572–78; John Morehead to Arthur Malmgren, December 3, 1926.

17. Kahle, *Geschichte*, 577.

CHAPTER 9

1.   Theophil Meier to John Morehead, February 11, 1927, LWC Papers, Archives of ELCA.

2.   Theophil Meier to John Morehead, May 12, 1927, LWC Papers, Archives of ELCA; Litzenberger, *The Evangelical Lutheran Church and the Soviet Government, 1917–1938*, 369. The called pastor was none other than Arthur Kluck. In a letter to Morehead on February 17, 1925, Meier described him thus: "Pastor Kluck is without a doubt the most able of the younger pastors. He is not the kind of man that catches your attention [shines] at first glance, but he is a devout believer, a good Lutheran pastor, an excellent speaker, very amiable in personal communication, moreover energetic and consistently and thoroughly

reliable." Meier's defense of Kluck was all the more courageous given that he had been condemned to one year's probation (1925) by the government for storing forbidden religious literature (e.g., Bibles, hymnals). Kluck replaced Meier at Sts. Peter and Paul for two months in 1926, but ultimately decided that he should remain in Marxstadt. See Theophil Meier to John Morehead, February 17, 1925; Bertha Kluck to John Morehead, June 30, 1934, and Kluck Family Documents.

3.   Lutherisches Oberkirchenrat to Morehead, March 18, 1927, and Theophil Meier to John Morehead, August 19, 1927, LWC Papers, Archives of ELCA.

4.   Theophil Meier to John Morehead, May 12 and August 4, 1927; Litzenberger, *The Evangelical Lutheran Church and the Soviet Government, 1917–1938*, 348. Pastor Hörschelmann's youngest son, Ernst, had become the organist at Sts. Peter and Paul in 1926. See "Прервание Мелодие" ["Interrupted Melody"], in *Neues Leben, Number 21, 2001.*

5.   Theophil Meier to John Morehead, Carl Paul, and Ludwig Ihmels, August 4, 1927, Theophil Meier to John Morehead, March 18, 1927, August 21, 1924, and John Morehead to C. C. Hein, May 1, 1935, LWC Papers, Archives of ELCA.

6.   Theophil Meier to John Morehead, Carl Paul, and Ludwig Ihmels, August 4, 1927.

7.   John Morehead to Theophil Meier, September 1, 1927, John Morehead to High Church Council, April 6, 1927, Arthur Malmgren to John Morehead, July 27, 1926, and October 12, 1927, LWC Papers, Archives of ELCA.

8.   Paul Althausen to John Morehead, August 5, 1927, LWC Papers, Archives of ELCA.

9.   John Morehead to Arthur Malmgren, April 1, 1926, LWC Papers, Archives of ELCA.

10. John Morehead to Theophil Meier, November 30, 1927, LWC Papers, Archives of ELCA.

11. "High Church Council Report: 1926–1927," August 19, 1927, LWC Papers, Archives of ELCA.

12. Arthur Malmgren to Morehead, February 5 and March 13, 1927, LWC Papers, Archives of ELCA.

13. John Morehead to Arthur Malmgren, April 6, 1927, LWC Papers, Archives of ELCA.

14. John Morehead to Arthur Malmgren, May 9, July 2, September 20, and December 23, 1927, LWC Papers, Archives of ELCA.

15. Kurt Muss to John Morehead, fall 1928, LWC Papers, Archives of ELCA.

16. John Morehead to Arthur Malmgren, March 3, 1927, LWC Papers, Archives of ELCA.

17. Kurt Muss to John Morehead, fall 1928.

18. John Morehead to Arthur Malmgren, December 11, 1928, LWC Papers, Archives of ELCA.

19. Fond 1001, Opis 8, Delo 52, Lists 15, 53, 91, 104, 129 and 181, Russian State Archives of St. Petersburg.

20. Arthur Malmgren, "Report on the Lutheran Seminary in Leningrad: 1927–1928," Arthur Malmgren to John Morehead, February 5, 1927, and John Morehead to Arthur Malmgren, August 2, 1927, LWC Papers, Archives of ELCA.

21. Arthur Malmgren to John Morehead, September 15, 1928, LWC Papers, Archives of the ELCA; Санкт-Петербургский мартиролог духовенства и мирян: Евангелическо- лютеранская Церковь [St. Petersburg Martyrology of Clergy and Laity: Evangelical Lutheran Church], December 14, 2004, http://www.petergen.com/bovkalo/mar/luthd.html; Litzenberger, *The Evangelical Lutheran Church and the Soviet Government, 1917–1938*, 391.

22. John Morehead to Theophil Meier, December 11, 1928, LWC Papers, Archives of ELCA; *Osteuropa, 1928*.

23. John Morehead to Arthur Malmgren, August 2, 1927, LWC Papers, Archives of ELCA.

24. Theophil Meier to John Morehead, January 9, 1929, LWC Papers, Archives of ELCA.

25. Litzenberger, *The Evangelical Lutheran Church and the Soviet Government, 1917–1938*, 333, 334, 337, 342, 357, 363, 373, 380–382, 384, 388, 389. Johannes Schlundt would actually immigrate to West Germany in 1973 and die in 1993 at the age of ninety-three, having lived to see the revival of the Lutheran Church in post-Communist Russia. See Litzenberger, *The Evangelical Lutheran Church and the Soviet Government, 1917–1938*, 389.

26. Fehler and Rusch would be freed through the intervention of the High Church Council by New Year's 1929. See Theophil Meier to John Morehead, January 9, 1929.

27. Theophil Meier to John Morehead, January 21, March 30, and February 3, 1928, LWC Papers, Archives of ELCA.

28. Theophil Meier to John Morehead, October 14, 1927, and John Morehead to Theophil Meier, May 13, 1927, LWC Papers, Archives of ELCA.

29. Theophil Meier to John Morehead, February 3, 1928, LWC Papers, Archives of ELCA.

30. Theophil Meier to John Morehead, March 2, 1928, LWC Papers, Archives of ELCA.

CHAPTER 10

1. Theophil Meier to John Morehead, February 3, 1928.

2. Theophil Meier to John Morehead, March 30, 1928, LWC Papers, Archives of ELCA.

3. Theophil Meier to John Morehead, March 30, 1928, LWC Papers, Archives of ELCA.

4. Theophil Meier to John Morehead, November 23, 1928, LWC Papers, Archives of ELCA.

5. Robert Derringer to John Morehead, September 11, 1928, and Report on the General Synod 1928 to John Morehead, LWC Papers, Archives of ELCA; Litzenberger, *The Evangelical Lutheran Church and the Soviet Government, 1917–1938*, 381. The Transcaucasian region included cities in the northern Caucasus as well as the modern-day countries of Georgia and Azerbaijan.

6. Peter Haigis and Gert Hummel, *Schwäbische Spuren im Kaukasus: Auswanderergeschichten* (Metzingen, Germany: Verlag Ernst Franz, 2002), 10–11.

7. Haigis and Hummel, *Schwäbische Spuren im Kaukasus*, 101–23.

8. Haigis and Hummel, *Schwäbische Spuren im Kaukasus*, 127–53; 169–70.

9. Haigis and Hummel, *Schwäbische Spuren im Kaukasus*, 153, 244.

10. Kurt Muss to John Morehead, "Report on General Synod 1928 to Morehead, September 2–5, 1928, LWC Papers, Archives of ELCA.

11. Timasheff, *Religion in Soviet Russia,* 27–28.

12. Kurt Muss to John Morehead, "Report on General Synod 1928 to Morehead, September 2–5, 1928" and Robert Derringer Report to LWC, August 19, 1927, LWC Papers, Archives of ELCA.

13. Timasheff, *Religion in Soviet Russia,* 27.

14. Johann Völl, "Bilder aus der Geschichte einer Kirche unter dem Kreuz," in *Heimatbuch der Deutschen aus Russland 1958* (Stuttgart: Die Landsmannschaft der Deutschen aus Russland, 1958), 105; Litzenberger, *The Evangelical Lutheran Church and the Soviet Government, 1917–1938*, 384.

15. Johann Völl, "Bilder aus der Geschichte einer Kirche unter dem Kreuz," 106.

16. Johann Völl, "Bilder aus der Geschichte einer Kirche unter dem Kreuz," 106–7.

17. Kurt Muss to John Morehead, "Report on General Synod 1928 to Morehead, September 2–5, 1928."

18. *Heimatbuch der Deutschen aus Russland 1958,* Johann Völl, 112.

19. Schleuning et al., *Und siehe, wir leben,* 128.

20. Robert Derringer to John Morehead, September 11, 1928, LWC Papers, Archives of ELCA.

21. Schleuning et al., *Und siehe, wir leben*, 118–21. I can attest to the large size of the cathedral, having visited Privalnoye (Warenburg's Russian name) in 2001. The church was still standing in an abandoned field, its roof long since shorn off by local Communists. See Kahle, *Geschichte*, 104.

22. John Morehead to Johannes Grasmück, June 8, 1936, and John Morehead to Woldemar Reichwald, February 10, 1927, LWC Papers, Archives of ELCA.

23. Schleuning et al., *Und siehe, wir leben*, 120

24. Schleuning et al., *Und siehe, wir leben*, 118–21, 156.

CHAPTER 11

1. Kahle, *Geschichte*, 78, 106, 144, 153.

2. J. Arch Getty and Oleg V. Naumov, *The Road to Terror: Stalin and the Self-Destruction of the Bolsheviks, 1932–1939* (New Haven, CT: Yale University Press, 1999), 36–37, 39.

3. Getty and Naumov, *Road to Terror*, 41.

4. Robert Tucker, *Stalin in Power: The Revolution from Above, 1928–1941* (New York: W. W. Norton, 1990), 92.

5. Getty and Naumov, *Road to Terror*, 42.

6. Tucker, *Stalin in Power*, 94.

7. Tucker, *Stalin in Power*, 93.

8. Gabel, *And God Created Lenin*, 323.

9. Kahle, *Geschichte*, 376.

10. Tschoerner, *Arthur Malmgren*, 80–81.

11. Dönninghaus, *Die Deutschen*, 140–41.

12. Kahle, *Geschichte*, 104.

13. Olga Kurilo, Лютеране в России: XVI–XX VV. [Lutherans in Russia: 16th–20th c.] (Sterling Heights, MI: Lutheran Heritage Foundation, 2002), 146–47.

14. Theophil Meier to John Morehead, February 3, 1928, LWC Papers, Archives of ELCA. Current pastor of Sts. Peter and Paul in Moscow Dmitry Lotov recalls that his grandfather worked in the aerodynamics factory and could still make out the basic outlines of the church building (Dmitry Lotov to Matthew Heise, October 2013).

15. Dmitry Lotov to Matthew Heise, October 2013.

16. Litzenberger, *The Evangelical Lutheran Church and the Soviet Government, 1917–1938*, 227.

17. Theophil Meier to John Morehead, March 30, 1928, LWC Papers, Archives of ELCA.

18. Litzenberger, *The Evangelical Lutheran Church and the Soviet Government, 1917–1938*, 227.

19. Maxim Ivanov, Лютеранский Квартал в Петербурге [*The Lutheran Quarter in Petersburg*] (Saint Petersburg, Russia: Yevropeiskiy Dom, 2004), 39.

20. P-87890, Volume 1, List 605, FSB Archives of St. Petersburg Region; Litzenberger, *The Evangelical Lutheran Church and the Soviet Government, 1917–1938*, 227. Kurt Muss is often accused of spying for Great Britain, but in reality his contact was with Morehead of the NLC in America. He distributed aid in 1922 for the American Lutherans in the Rostov and the Don River region in southern Russia and sent a report on his activities, as Morehead required. This report was used as an excuse for the charge of espionage. The report contained only information about distribution of aid to suffering Lutherans, but Muss was critical of the Soviet government, claiming that it was to blame for the famine. Morehead was convinced that this was the reason for Muss's arrest. See John Morehead to Robert Withington, February 8, 1935, LWC Papers, Archives of ELCA.

21. P-87890, Volume 1, List 113–14, FSB Archives of St. Petersburg Region.

22. P-87890, Volume 1, List 235–36, FSB Archives of St. Petersburg Region.

23. P-87890, Volume 1, List 23, 119, FSB Archives of St. Petersburg Region.

24. P-87890, Volume 1, List 236, FSB Archives of St. Petersburg Region; P-87890, Volume 2, List 612, FSB Archives of St. Petersburg Region.

25. P-87890, Volume 2, List 612, FSB Archives of St. Petersburg Region.

26. Ulyanov, "Fate of the Teachers at the Peterschule," 196; "Petrischule" ["Peterschule"], *Wikipedia.ru*, last modified December 25, 2013, http://ru.wikipedia .org/wiki/Petrishcule.

27. P-87890, Volume 2, List 619, FSB Archives of St. Petersburg Region.

28. Ulyanov, "Fate of the Teachers at the Peterschule," 197–99, 201. Wolfius was a particularly well-respected teacher, having taught from 1903–1928 at the Peterschule. In 1920 he led the noted British science fiction writer H. G. Wells on a tour of the school, and it made a favorable impression on him. Wells wrote of the Peterschule in his book *Russia in the Shadows* (1921) and spoke of how the Russian school system was not completely broken, this after having been given a Potemkin-style tour of a school in Petrograd that had not impressed him in the least. Wells admired the Peterschule's geometry and geography classes, remarking on the teaching and the materials that were available to the students.

In addition, apparently the Peterschule's students were not aware of Wells as a writer, convincing him that he was in a normal school. The indication that the students were genuinely unaware of Wells's status as a writer was in contrast to the previous school, where they had obviously been coached to speak of him as the most famous writer in English literature! See H. G. Wells, *Russia in the Shadows* (New York: George H. Doran, 1921), 119–21.

29. Ulyanov, "Fate of the Teachers at the Peterschule," 202.

30. Ulyanov, "Fate of the Teachers at the Peterschule," 199, 202–4.

31. Timasheff, *Religion in Soviet Russia*, 43–44.

32. Ulyanov, "Fate of the Teachers at the Peterschule," 227.

33. Ulyanov, "Fate of the Teachers at the Peterschule," 227.

34. Litzenberger, *The Evangelical Lutheran Church and the Soviet Government, 1917–1938*, 230.

35. Litzenberger, *The Evangelical Lutheran Church and the Soviet Government, 1917–1938*, 242; Mikhail Shkarovsky and Nadezhda Cherepenina, История Евангелическо-Лютеранской Церкви на Северо-Западе России, 1917–1945 [*The History of the Evangelical Lutheran Church in Northwest Russia, 1917–1945*] (Saint Petersburg, Russia: Dmitry Bulanin, 2004), 133.

36. Theophil Meier to John Morehead, January 9, and John Morehead to Theophil Meier, February 15, 1929, LWC Papers, Archives of ELCA.

37. Arthur Malmgren to John Morehead, January 9, 1929, LWC Papers, Archives of ELCA.

38. Arthur Malmgren to John Morehead, February 15 and March 24, 1929, LWC Papers, Archives of ELCA.

39. Trexler, *John A. Morehead*, 109–11.

40. John Morehead to Arthur Malmgren, March 15, 1929, LWC Papers, Archives of the ELCA.

41. Litzenberger, *The Evangelical Lutheran Church and the Soviet Government, 1917–1938*, 233; One of the primary calls of the religious dissidents during Mikhail Gorbachev's glasnost period of the late 1980s was for the repeal of the 1929 Law on Religious Associations, a testament to its endurance and harmful impact on Christian communities in Russia. See Koenraad de Wolf, *Dissident for Life: Alexander Ogorodnikov and the Struggle for Religious Freedom in Russia* (Grand Rapids, MI: Eerdmans, 2013), Kindle edtion, loc. 3815, 3861.

42. "Translation of Law on Religious Associations in USSR 1929," LWC Papers, Archives of ELCA.

43. "Decree of the All-Russian Central Executive Committee and the Council of People's Commissars Respecting Religious Associations: April 8, 1929,"

Department of State Records-Decimal File 1930–1939, 361.6121, RG 59, National Archives II. Translation mine.

44. Kahle, *Geschichte*, 275.

45. Timasheff, *Religion in Soviet Russia*, 41–42.

46. Tschoerner, *Arthur Malmgren*, 81.

47. Kahle, *Geschichte*, 278.

48. Decree of the All-Russian Central Executive Committee and the Council of People's Commissars Respecting Religious Associations: April 8, 1929;" P-87890, Volume 3, List 34, FSB Archives of St. Petersburg Region.

49. Decree of the All-Russian Central Executive Committee and the Council of People's Commissars Respecting Religious Associations: April 8, 1929;" Theophil Meier to John Morehead, August 4, 1927, LWC Papers, Archives of ELCA.

50. Tschoerner, *Arthur Malmgren*, 90–91.

51. Louis Sussdorff Jr. to Henry Stimson, January 15, 1930, 861.404/283, RG 59, National Archives II.

52. Johann Völl, "Bilder aus der Geschichte einer Kirche unter dem Kreuz," iii.

53. Arthur Malmgren to John Morehead, October 12, 1929, LWC Papers, Archives of ELCA.

54. John Morehead to Theophil Meier, March 8, 1928, and Arthur Malmgren to John Morehead, April 5, 1928, Archives of ELCA. In 1928 Morehead had offered to ship biblical tracts to Russia for use in evangelization. Both Meier and Malmgren dissuaded him from doing this, explaining that as anti-religious propaganda flourished, tolerance towards religious literature of any kind was increasingly limited.

55. Louis Sussdorff Jr. to Henry Stimson, January 15, 1930; Kahle, *Geschichte*, 276.

56. Litzenberger, *The Evangelical Lutheran Church and the Soviet Government, 1917–1938*, 234.

57. Litzenberger, *The Evangelical Lutheran Church and the Soviet Government, 1917–1938*, 234.

58. *Bezbozhnik [Godless]* 8 (April 1929).

59. *Bezbozhnik 12* (June 1929).

60. Marina Mikhailova, "Семейная Фотография [Family Photograph]," in Дорога Вместе [*The Road Together*] no. 1, 2009, http://www.doroga-vmeste .ru/2009/2009_1_semejnaja_fotografia.shtml.

61. P-87890, Volume 2, List 496, 532, FSB Archives of St. Petersburg Region.

62. P-87890, Volume 2, List 614, FSB Archives of St. Petersburg Region.

63. P-87890, Volume 2, List 506, FSB Archives of St. Petersburg Region.

64. Kahle, *Geschichte*, 278.

65. P-87890, Volume 3, List 562-563, FSB Archives of St. Petersburg Region.

66. P-87890, Volume 3, List 562–63, FSB Archives of St. Petersburg Region.

67. Kurilo, *Lutherans in Russia*, 20.

68. Kahle, *Geschichte*, 274–75.

69. Tschoerner, *Arthur Malmgren*, 82.

70. P-87890, Volume 2, List 489, FSB Archives of St. Petersburg Region.

71. P-87890, Volume 2, List 620, FSB Archives of St. Petersburg Region; P-87890, Volume 3, List 40, FSB Archives of St. Petersburg Region; Muss-Tumm Family Photo Collection.

72. Vladimir Brovkin, *Russia after Lenin: Politics, Culture and Society, 1921–1929* (London: Taylor & Francis e-Library, 2005), Kindle edition, 217.

73. Frederick S. Starr, *Red and Hot: The Fate of Jazz in the Soviet Union 1917–1991*, 2nd ed (New York: Limelight Editions, 1994), 89–93.

74. Brovkin, *Russia after Lenin*, 117.

75. Brovkin, *Russia after Lenin*, 120.

76. Sheila Fitzpatrick, *Stalin's Peasants: Resistance and Survival in the Russian Village after Collectivization* (New York: Oxford University Press, 1994), Kindle edtion, loc. 36; Lynne Viola, "The Peasant Nightmare: Visions of Apocalypse in the Soviet Countryside," *The Journal of Modern History* 62, No. 4 (December 1990), 753.

77. Abortion numbers declined precipitously after the imposition of a ban in 1936. See *"Abortii v Rossii"* ["Abortion in Russia"], Wikipedia.ru, last modified December 24, 2013, http://ru.Wikipedia.org/wiki/Abortii_v_Rossii.

78. P-87890, Volume 2, List 316, FSB Archives of St. Petersburg Region.

79. P-87890, Volume 3, List 136, FSB Archives of St. Petersburg Region.

80. Kahle, *Geschichte*, 276.

CHAPTER 12

1. Timasheff, *Religion in Soviet Russia*, 40; Tucker, *Stalin in Power*, 93; Efraim Briem, *Kommunismus und Religion in der Sowjetunion: Ein Ideenkampf*, trans. Edzard Schaper (Basel, Switzerland: Verlag Friedrich Reinhardt AG, 1948), 326.

2. German von Schmidt to LWC, October 31, 1929, LWC Papers, Archives of ELCA; Theophil Meyer to John Morehead, February 25, 1930, LWC Papers, Archives of ELCA.

3. Tucker, *Stalin in Power*, 93.

4. Theophil Meyer to John Morehead, February 25, 1930.

5. P-87890, Volume 3, List 22, FSB Archives of St. Petersburg Region.

6. P-87890, Volume 3, List 22, FSB Archives of St. Petersburg Region.

7. Arthur Malmgren to John Morehead, October 24, 1929, LWC Papers, Archives of ELCA.

8. Fitzpatrick, *Stalin's Peasants*, 43.

9. Fitzpatrick, *Stalin's Peasants*, 39–40.

10. Otto Seib to John Morehead, November 29, 1929, LWC Papers, Archives of ELCA.

11. German von Schmidt to LWC, October 31, 1929. For a translation of goods to pounds, see "Pood," Wikipedia, last modified January 4, 2017, https://en .wikipedia.org/wiki/Pood.

12. John Morehead to Theophil Meier, November 16, 1931, LWC Papers, Archives of ELCA.

13. A. Reinmarus and G. Friesen, Под Гнётом Религии: Немцы Колонисти СССР и Их Религиозные Организации [*Under the Wrath of Religion: German Colonists of the USSR and Their Religion*] (Moscow: Government Publishing Co., 1931), 102.

14. "Pastorenverfolgung in der Krim," *Der Sonntagsbote,* August 17, 1930; Obituary of Ferdinand Hörschelmann Sr. from the private collection of his great-grand-daughter, Alexandra Nikolaev.

15. Theophil Meier to John Morehead, October 4,1929, LWC Papers, Archives of ELCA.

16. Fitzpatrick, *Stalin's Peasants*, 39–40.

17. Viola, "The Peasant Nightmare," 762–65, 767.

18. Karoline Glöckler to Charles Glöckler, December 1, 1929, LWC Papers, Archives of ELCA.

19. Edith Müthel to Matthew Heise. The NKVD would arrest Rev. Pfeiffer and eventually execute him in 1939 in Butyrka Prison in Moscow.

20. Edgar Charles Duin, *Lutheranism under the Tsars and the Soviets* (Ann Arbor, MI: Xerox University Microfilms, 1975), 747–49.

21. Heinrich Friesen, "Анти-Советская Кампания в связи с Емиграцой Меннонит из СССР" ["Anti-Soviet Campaign in Connection with the Emigration of Mennonites from the USSR"], *Bezbozhnik* 24 (December 1929).

22. German von Schmidt to LWC, October 31, 1929.

23. Theophil Meier to John Morehead, February 25, 1930.

24. *Die Evangelische Diaspora*, 12 Jahrgang (1930), 18–20.

25. Duin, *Lutheranism under the Tsars and the Soviets*, 750.

26. Kahle, *Geschichte*, 376.

27. S. Glyazera, "Солидная Коллективизация" ["Solid Collectivization"], *Bez-bozhnik* 19 (September 1929).

28. V. Sarabyanov, "Пятилетний План на Религии" ["Five Year Plan on Reli-gion"], *Bezbozhnik* 21 (November 1929).

29. Duin, *Lutheranism under the Tsars and the Soviets*, 749–50.

30. Otto Seib to John Morehead, November 29, 1929.

31. Otto Seib to John Morehead, November 29, 1929.

32. Otto Seib to John Morehead, November 29, 1929.

CHAPTER 13

1. Arthur Malmgren to John Morehead, October 12, 1929, LWC Papers, Archives of ELCA.

2. John Morehead to Arthur Malmgren, September 27, 1929, LWC Papers, Archives of ELCA.

3. Arthur Malmgren to John Morehead, October 24, 1929, LWC Papers, Archives of ELCA.

4. Lel, "How They Were Trying to Destroy Us," 14.

5. P-87890, Volume 1, List 116–17, Volume 2, List 610, FSB Archives of St. Peters-burg Region.

6. P-87890, Volume 1, List 109, FSB Archives of St. Petersburg Region.

7. P-87890, Volume 1, List 229–30, FSB Archives of St. Petersburg Region.

8. P-87890, Volume 1, List 213, 235, FSB Archives of St. Petersburg Region.

9. P-87890, Volume 1, List 116–17, 279, FSB Archives of St. Petersburg Region; P-87890, Volume 2, List 616, FSB Archives of St. Petersburg Region.

10. P-87890, Volume 1, List 236–37, 410, 413, FSB Archives of St. Petersburg Region; P-87890, Volume 2, List 648, FSB Archives of St. Petersburg Region.

11. P-87890, Volume 1, List 116–17, FSB Archives of St. Petersburg Region.

12. P-87890, Volume 2, List 614–16, FSB Archives of St. Petersburg Region; P-87890, Volume 1, List 236, 267, FSB Archives of St. Petersburg Region; P-87890, Volume 3, List 146, FSB Archives of St. Petersburg Region.

13. P-87890, Volume 1, List 215, 316, FSB Archives of St. Petersburg Region.

14. P-87890, Volume 1, List 180–81, 335, FSB Archives of St. Petersburg Region.

15. P-87890, Volume 1, List 333–35, 444, FSB Archives of St. Petersburg Region. Biedermann also remarked that the Lutheran World Federation's unsolicited financial assistance to St. Peter's was of great benefit in receiving the increasingly burdensome state tax placed upon the congregation.

16. P-87890, Volume 2, List 611–12, FSB Archives of St. Petersburg Region.

17. P-87890, Volume 2, List 337, 614, FSB Archives of St. Petersburg Region. It seems that the phrase that the OGPU copied as *Trau bis zum Tod Jesus dein Eigen* may actually come from a German Lutheran hymn written by Johann Ludwig Konrad Allendorf:

> *Bis in den Tod sind wir, Jesus, Dein eigen,*
>
> *bis in den Tod bleibt uns, Herr, Deine Treu;*
>
> *und vor der Welt wolln wir freudig bezeugen,*
>
> *daß unser Leben durch Dich ward ganz neu,*
>
> *da Du für uns.*

See "Songs by Johann Ludwig Konrad Allendorf," Songselect by CCLI, accessed December 31, 2013, https://us.songselect.com/search/author?Authors=4294890360.

18. P-87890, Volume 2, List 611–12, FSB Archives of St. Petersburg Region. Erna Hansen was a little suspicious of Hoffman. By 1930 she said that she hadn't seen him in two years and was not at all certain that he had received the Jugendbund pin or been a member. When she tried to give him ten tickets to invite friends to the church's musical services in 1928 or 1929, he returned them to her saying that he was avoiding their "community" as he was trying to find other work. She didn't recall seeing him after that. See P-87890, Volume 2; List 315, FSB Archives of St. Petersburg Region.

19. P-87890, Volume 1, List 113–114, 243, FSB Archives of St. Petersburg Region.

20. P-87890, Volume 1, List 121, FSB Archives of St. Petersburg Region.

21. P-87890, Volume 3, List 9, 13–14, FSB Archives of St. Petersburg Region.

22. P-87890, Volume 3, List 13–14, 45, FSB Archives of St. Petersburg Region.

23. P-87890, Volume 3, List 41, FSB Archives of St. Petersburg Region.

24. P-87890, Volume 3, List 146–47, 151–52, 549, FSB Archives of St. Petersburg Region.

25. P-87890, Volume 3, List 86–87, 188, FSB Archives of St. Petersburg Region.

26. P-87890, Volume 3, List 528–29, FSB Archives of St. Petersburg Region; July 22, 2017; Konstantin Kostromin, "Богослов и Исповедник: Избранные Главы из Книги 'Михаил Мудьюгин: Музыкант, Полиглот, Инженер и Богослов' ["Theologian and Confessor: Selected Chapters from the Book *'Mikhail Mud-*

yugin: Musician, Polyglot, Engineer and Theologian"], http://russophile
.ru/2017/07/22/богослов-и-исповедник/.

27. Oleg Sevastyanov to Matthew Heise, November 2012.

28. Shkarovsky and Cherepenina, *History*, 131.

29. P-87890, Volume 3, List 530, FSB Archives of St. Petersburg Region.

30. Shkarovsky and Cherepenina, *History*, 131–32.

31. Brovkin, *Russia after Lenin*, 127.

32. Brovkin, *Russia after Lenin*, 127–28, 131–32; Chamberlin, 1.

33. Konstantin Kostromin, "Theologian and Confessor."

34. Oleg Sevastyanov to Matthew Heise, September 2017.

35. P-35162, List 55, 63–74, FSB Archives of St. Petersburg Region; Shkarovsky and
Cherepenina, *History*, 117.

36. Shkarovsky and Cherepenina, *History*, 115.

37. F. W. B. Coleman to Henry Stimson, January 18, 1930, 861.404/284, RG 59,
National Archives II.

38. Shkarovsky and Cherepenina, *History*, 117.

39. John Morehead to Arthur Malmgren, November 22, 1929, LWC Papers,
Archives of ELCA.

40. P-87890, Volume 3, List 371, FSB Archives of St. Petersburg Region.

41. John Morehead to Arthur Malmgren, November 22, 1929, LWC Papers,
Archives of ELCA.

CHAPTER 14

1.   P-87890, Volume 2, List 610, FSB Archives of St. Petersburg Region.

2.   "Этот день в Истории Прихода Святого Михаила" ["This Day in the
History of the Congregation of St. Michael's"], accessed May 9, 2017, https://
vk.com/spbstmihail?w=wall-89023090_651.

3.   P-87890, Volume 2, List 642, FSB Archives of St. Petersburg Region.

4.   P-87890, Volume 3, List 9, FSB Archives of St. Petersburg Region.

5.   P-87890, Volume 2, List 614, FSB Archives of St. Petersburg Region.

6.   P-87890, Volume 2, List 617, FSB Archives of St. Petersburg Region.

7.   P-87890, Volume 3, List 13–14, FSB Archives of St. Petersburg Region.

8.   P-87890, Volume 3, List 563, FSB Archives of St. Petersburg Region (emphasis
mine).

9.   P-87890, Volume 3, List 22, 438, 188, 119, 86, 66, 49, 104, 222, FSB Archives of St. Petersburg Region.

10.   P-87890, Volume 3, List 651–52, FSB Archives of St. Petersburg Region.

11.   P-87890, Volume 2, List 604 and P-87890, Volume 1, List 277, FSB Archives of St. Petersburg Region.

12.   P-87890, Volume 2, List 606-7, FSB Archives of St. Petersburg Region.

13.   P-87890, Volume 2, List 606-7, FSB Archives of St. Petersburg Region.

14.   P-87890, Volume 2, List 606–7, FSB Archives of St. Petersburg Region.

15.   P-87890, Volume 1, List 222, 237 and P-87890, Volume 2, List 495, FSB Archives of St. Petersburg Region.

16.   P-87890, Volume 1, List 312 and P-87890, Volume 2, List 349, FSB Archives of St. Petersburg Region.

17.   P-87890, Volume 3, List 41 of FSB Archives of St. Petersburg Region.

18.   P-87890, Volume 1, List 267–68, 270, 232 and P-87890, Volume 2, List 622, FSB Archives of St. Petersburg Region.

19.   P-87890, Volume 3, List 41–42 and P-87890, Volume 2, List 622, FSB Archives of St. Petersburg Region.

20.   P-87890, Volume 3, List 454–56, 458, 461, FSB Archives of St. Petersburg Region.

21.   F. W. B. Coleman to Henry Stimson, January 18, 1930.

22.   Rev. G. J. MacGillivray, *The Anti-God Front of Bolshevism: A Statement of Facts* (London: Catholic Truth Society, 1933), 21; Louis Sussdorff Jr. to Henry Stimson, January 15, 1930.

23.   MacGillivray, *Anti-God Front of Bolshevism*, 22.

24.   Kahle, *Geschichte*, 292.

25.   Louis Sussdorff Jr. to Henry Stimson, January 15, 1930.

26.   *Bezbozhnik* 4 (February 1930); P-87890, Volume 1, List 313, FSB Archives of St. Petersburg Region; MacGillivray, 24–27.

27.   P-87890, Volume 2, List 613, 630, FSB Archives of St. Petersburg Region.

28.   Konstantin Kostromin, "Theologian and Confessor."

29.   P-87890, Volume 2, List 499, FSB Archives of St. Petersburg Region; P-87890, Volume 1, List 383, FSB Archives of St. Petersburg Region.

30.   Arthur Malmgren to John Morehead, February 9, 1930, LWC Papers, Archives of ELCA; Lel, "How They Were Trying to Destroy Us," 16.

31.   Lel, "How They Were Trying to Destroy Us," 16; Tschoerner, *Arthur Malmgren*, 84, 86.

32. P-87890, Volume 3, List 368–71, 375–77, FSB Archives of St. Petersburg Region; Margarita Schulmeister to Matthew Heise, October 2013. An oblast would be similar to a county.

33. P-87890, Volume 1, List 153, Volume 2, List 362, 418, 455, and Volume 3, List 528, 566, FSB Archives of St. Petersburg Region.

34. Konstantin Kostromin, "Theologian and Confessor."

35. P-87890, Volume 2, List 613, 210, 579, FSB Archives of St. Petersburg Region.

36. P-87890, Volume 2, List 503–5, FSB Archives of St. Petersburg Region; Natalya Stackelberg, "Кружок Молодых Историков и 'Академическое Дело'" ["Circle of Young Historians and the 'Academic Affair'"], in *In Memoriam: Исторический Сборник Памяти Ф. Ф. Перченка* [*In Memoriam: Historic Collection of Memories of F. F. Perchenka*] (St. Petersburg, Russia: Feniks, 1995), 19, 25.

37. Stackelberg, "Circle of Young Historians," 24–25.

38. Kostromin, "Theologian and Confessor."

39. "Book of Remembrance—Biographies of Catholic Clergy and Laity Repressed in the Soviet Union (USSR) from 1918 to 1953: Biography of Monsignor Stanisław Przerembel," January 20, 2016, https://biographies.library.nd.edu/catalog/biography-1354.

40. Konstantin Kostromin, "Theologian and Confessor."

41. P-87890, Volume 2, List 542, FSB Archives of St. Petersburg Region.

42. P-87890, Volume 2, List 583–85, FSB Archives of St. Petersburg Region.

CHAPTER 15

1. Heinrich Roemmich, "Die Ev. Luth. Kirche in Russland unter der Sowjetherrschaft," in *Heimatbuch der Deutschen aus Russland 1961* (Stuttgart: Die Landsmannschaft der Deutschen aus Russland, 1961), 92–93.

2. Russian Evangelical Press, No. 8, 1930, LWC Papers, Archives of ELCA.

3. Lev Brandt, Лютеранство и его Политическая Роль [*Lutheranism and Its Political Role*] (Leningrad: OGIZ Priboi, 1931), 87–88.

4. Reinmarus and Friesen, *Under the Wrath of Religion*, 89–90; Boris Kandidov, Церковь и Шпионаж [*Church and Espionage*] (Moscow: Government Anti-Religious Publishing Co., 1937), 17.

5. Richard Pipes, *Russia under the Bolshevik Regime*, Kindle loc. 3172, 3184, 3196.

6. Russian Evangelical Press, No. 8, 1930.

7. Brandt, *Lutheranism and Its Political Role*, 94–95. Brandt used the phrase "Kirche, Kinder und Küche." He would go on in the following pages of his

book to accuse Kurt Muss of using philosophy to engage youth in counterrevolutionary activities.

8.   Heinrich Roemmich, "Die Ev. Luth. Kirche in Russland unter der Sowjetherrschaft."

9.   Heinrich Roemmich, "Die Ev. Luth. Kirche in Russland unter der Sowjetherrschaft."

10. Russian Evangelical Press, No. 8, 1930.

11. O. H. Groth to Herbert Hoover, March 24, 1930, 861.404/306, RG 59, National Archives II.

12. Robert Kelley to O. H. Groth, April 1, 1930, 861.404/306, RG 59, National Archives II.

13. John Morehead to Herbert Hoover, July 10, 1930, LWC Papers, Archives of ELCA.

14. Arthur J. Brown to Herbert Hoover, February 17, 1930, 861.404/288, *Hollywood Citizen* to Herbert Hoover, February 10, 1930, 861.404/287 and Edlef Sell to Herbert Hoover, January 13, 1932, 861.404/344, RG 59, National Archives II.

15. Herbert Hoover to John Morehead, July 15, 1930, LWC Papers, Archives of ELCA.

16. W. R. Castle to Laurence Richey, August 5, 1930, LWC Papers, Archives of ELCA.

17. Russian Evangelical Press, No. 8, 1930.

18. Жертвы политического террора в СССР [Victims of Political Terror in the USSR], "Albert Koch," last modified December 13, 2016, http://lists.memo.ru/index11.htm; Litzenberger, *The Evangelical Lutheran Church and Soviet Government, 1917–1938*, 360.

19. P-87890, Volume 2, List 627–41, FSB Archives of St. Petersburg Region.

20. Natalya Stackelberg, "Circle of Young Historians," P-87890, Volume 2, List 581–82, FSB Archives of St. Petersburg Region.

21. Alexander Bovkalo, "St. Petersburg Martyrology of Clergy and Laity," http://www.peter-gen.com/bovkalo/mar/luthm.html.

22. P-87890, Volume 2, List 627–41, FSB Archives of St. Petersburg Region.

23. Brandt, *Lutheranism and Its Political Role*, 93.

24. P-87890, Volume 2, List 635, FSB Archives of St. Petersburg Region.

25. P-87890, Volume 2, List 627–641, FSB Archives of St. Petersburg Region; Robert Conquest, *The Great Terror*, 150.

26. P-87890, Volume 2, List 640-641, FSB Archives of St. Petersburg Region.

27. P-87890, Volume 2, List 627–41, FSB Archives of St. Petersburg Region; Tschoerner, *Arthur Malmgren*, 83.

28. Timasheff, *Religion in Soviet Russia*, 45.

CHAPTER 16

1. Litzenberger, *The Evangelical Lutheran Church and the Soviet Government, 1917–1938*, 360. Actually, there is some debate as to just when Kluck was arrested. Historian Olga Litzenberger, who had access to his diaries in the local Volga region archives, dates the arrest to December 1, 1929. On the other hand, the records of human rights societies in Russia, such as the website "Victims of Political Terror in the USSR" date his arrest to June 20, 1930 (Жертвы политического террора в СССР [Victims of Political Terror]), last modified December 13, 2016, http://lists.memo.ru/index11.htm; Arthur Kluck Family Documents). The latter date is almost certainly incorrect, though.

2. Schleuning et al., *Und siehe, wir leben*, 144–45.

3. Theophil Meier to John Morehead, February 25, 1930, LWC Papers, Archives of ELCA.

4. Arvid Liebert, "Unruhe in Marxstadt," *Der Bote 2/1995* and *3–4/1995*.

5. Gisela Kluck-Detterer to Matthew Heise, April 2014.

6. Liebert, "Unruhe in Marxstadt."

7. Theophil Meier to John Morehead, February 25, 1930.

8. Arthur Malmgren to John Morehead, February 9, 1930, LWC Papers, Archives of ELCA.

9. John Morehead to Arthur Malmgren, April 2 and April 29, 1930, LWC Papers, Archives of ELCA. Morehead had expressed the hope that the Christian churches and the Soviet authorities could reach a "modus vivendi" in order that "the Churches and their institutions may have freedom to worship, to work and develop in their congregational and institutional life." Of course, the Soviets under Stalin's leadership had no intention to allow the Church to develop any kind of institutional life. See Morehead to Malmgren, April 29, 1930.

10. Tschoerner, *Arthur Malmgren*, 86–87, 93; John Morehead to Arthur Malmgren, June 23, 1930, LWC Papers, Ar-chives of ELCA.

11. John Morehead to Arthur Malmgren, May 26, 1930, LWC papers, Archives of ELCA.

12. Luukkanen, 90–92, 100.

13. Timasheff, *Religion in Soviet Russia*, 45.

14. Arthur J. Brown to President Hoover, February 17, 1930, LWC Papers, Archives of ELCA.

15. "Warn Soviet It Kills Hope of Recognition," March 24, 1930, *New York Times*.

16. Arthur Malmgren to John Morehead, September 24, 1930, Theophil Meier to John Morehead, Nov 4, 1930, Arthur Malmgren to John Morehead, September 10, 1930, LWC Papers, Archives of ELCA. It had been decided not to hold the classes in the new student dormitory. Since St. Anne's was located on the same street, the distance wasn't too far for the students to travel.

17. P-74581, List 76–77, Archives of the FSB of the St. Petersburg Region.

18. P-82833, Volume 8, List 18, Archives of the FSB of the St. Petersburg Region.

19. P-74581, List 76–77, FSB Archives of St. Petersburg Region.

20. P-82833, Volume 8, List 71, 73, FSB Archives of St. Petersburg Region.

21. P-82833, Volume 6, List 327–31, FSB Archives of St. Petersburg Region.

22. P-82833, Volume 7, List 300, FSB Archives of St. Petersburg Region; "St. Petersburg Martyrology of Clergy and Laity: Evangelical Lutheran Church."

23. P-82833, Volume 9, List 169, FSB Archives of St. Petersburg Region.

24. Жертвы политического террора в СССР [Victims of Political Terror in the USSR], http://lists.memo.ru/index21.htm; P-82333, Volume 8, List 328–29.

25. John Morehead to O. C. Kiep, November 12, 1930, LWC Papers, Archives of ELCA.

26. O. C. Kiep to John Morehead, November 18, 1930, LWC Papers, Archives of ELCA.

27. John Morehead to O. C. Kiep, December 5, 1930 and John Morehead to Rev. Henry Bagger, November 14, 1935, LWC Papers, Archives of ELCA.

28. Alexandra Nikolaeva (great-granddaughter of Hörschelmann) to Matthew Heise, October 2013.

29. John Morehead to Theophil Meier, October 14, 1930 and December 11, 1928, LWC Papers, Archives of ELCA.

30. John Morehead to Theophil Meier, December 10, 1930 and Theophil Meier to John Morehead, November 4, 1930, LWC Papers, Archives of ELCA.

31. Arthur Malmgren to Professor Bruhn, December 24, 1930, LWC Papers, Archives of ELCA.

32. Schleuning et al., *Und siehe, wir leben*, 136–38.

CHAPTER 17

1. Dönninghaus, *Die Deutschen*, 518, 525–27; P-45647, List 7, 29, FSB Archives of Moscow Region.

2. Erich Sommer, *Geboren in Moskau: Errinerungen eines Baltendeutschen Diplomaten 1912–1955* (Munich: Langen Müller, 1997), 12.

3. Elza Georgiyevskaya, "Церковная Жизнь Москвы в 20–30-е Годы" ["Church Life in Moscow in the Years 1920–30"], Наша Церковь [*Our Church*] 3–5 (1996): 60–63.

4. Tschoerner, *Arthur Malmgren*, 87; P-87890, List 553–54, 692, FSB Archives of St. Petersburg Region.

5. Tschoerner, *Arthur Malmgren*, 95.

6. Tschoerner, *Arthur Malmgren*, 87–88, 95; Arthur Malmgren to John Morehead, November 3, 1930, LWC Papers, Archives of ELCA.

7. John Morehead to Arthur Malmgren, December 10, 1930, LWC Papers, Archives of ELCA.

8. Schleuning et al., *Und siehe, wir leben*, 215.

9. Kahle, *Geschichte*, 326.

10. Arthur Malmgren to Prof. Bruhn, December 24, 1930; Theophil Meier to John Morehead, August 19, 1930, LWC Papers, Archives of ELCA.

11. Theophil Meier to John Morehead, August 19, 1930; Arthur Malmgren to John Morehead, November 3, 1930, LWC Papers, Archives of ELCA; Schleuning et al., *Und siehe, wir leben*, 128–29.

12. Theophil Meier to John Morehead, March 10, 1931, LWC Papers, Archives of ELCA.

13. Theophil Meier to John Morehead, March 10, 1931; Arthur Malmgren to John Morehead, April 10, 1931, LWC Papers, Archives of ELCA.

14. John Morehead to Theophil Meier, May 19, 1931 and November 16, 1931, LWC Papers, Archives of ELCA.

15. Theophil Meier to John Morehead, December 19, 1931, LWC Papers, Archives of ELCA.

16. Arthur Malmgren to John Morehead, January 31 and March 28, 1931, LWC Papers, Archives of ELCA.

17. Arthur Malmgren to John Morehead, August 30, 1931, John Morehead to Arthur Malmgren, November 16, 1931, LWC Papers, Archives of ELCA.

18. Arthur Malmgren to John Morehead, January 31, 1931, LWC Papers, Archives of ELCA.

19. Arthur Malmgren to John Morehead, April 10, 1931, LWC Papers, Archives of ELCA.

20. Kahle, *Geschichte*, 125–26; Tucker, 186–88.

21. Arthur Malmgren to John Morehead, February 12, May 20 and August 30, 1931, LWC Papers, Archives of ELCA.

22. Arthur Malmgren to John Morehead, February 12, 1931, LWC Papers, Archives of ELCA.

23. Arthur Malmgren to John Morehead, January 31, 1931, LWC Papers, Archives of ELCA.

CHAPTER 18

1. Theophil Meier to John Morehead, October 19, 1931, LWC Papers, Archives of ELCA. Wilhelm Kahle still numbered fifty-three pastors as active in 1932. See Kahle, *Geschichte*, 326.

2. Theophil Meier to John Morehead, October 19, 1931. Alexandra Nikolaeva to Matthew Heise, October 2013.

3. John Morehead to Theophil Meier, November 16, 1931, LWC Papers, Archives of ELCA.

4. Karl Schlögel, *Moscow, 1937*, trans. Rodney Livingstone (Cambridge, England: Polity Press, 2012), 546–48, 553, 556.

5. Edith Müthel to Matthew Heise, October 2013.

6. Sommer, *Geboren in Moskau*, 37.

7. Dönninghaus, *Die Deutschen*, 526.

8. Margarita Schulmeister to Matthew Heise, October 2013.

9. Müthel, *An Gottes Hand*, 47–50.

10. Theophil Meier to John Morehead, March 17, 1932, LWC Papers, Archives of ELCA.

11. Olga Striks, "Последняя Конфирмация в Московской Общине Святого Петра" ["The Last Confirmation in the Moscow Congregation of St. Peters"], Наша Церковь [*Our Church*] 3–5 (1996): 70–71; Dmitri Lotov to Matthew Heise, March 2014.

12. Theophil Meier to John Morehead, February 7, 1932, LWC Papers, Archives of ELCA.

13. Eugenie Meier to John Morehead, March 19, 1932, LWC Papers, Archives of ELCA.

14. Arthur Malmgren to John Morehead, January 8, 1932 and May 15, 1932, LWC Papers, Archives of ELCA.

15. Torgsin were state-run hard currency stores that operated in the USSR from 1931–1936. See "Torgsin," wikipedia.us, last modified October 18, 2017, https://en.wikipedia.org/wiki/Torgsin.

16. Arthur Malmgren to John Morehead, January 8 and 30, 1932, LWC Papers, Archives of ELCA.

17. John Morehead to Arthur Malmgren, February 2, 1932, LWC Papers, Archives of ELCA.

18. Arthur Malmgren to John Morehead, March 19, 1932, LWC Papers, Archives of ELCA; Lel, "How They Were Trying to Destroy Us," 17.

19. John Morehead to Arthur Malmgren, December 5, 1931, LWC Papers, Archives of ELCA.

20. Lel, "How They Were Trying to Destroy Us," 18.

21. Tanya Ryumina, "May God Preserve You...," unpublished transcript, 2011; Tamara Tatsenko, Alexander Pastor and Hans Schwan, "Bruder Bruno," *Der Bote 4*, [*2002*].

22. Arthur Malmgren to John Morehead, March 19, 1932, LWC Papers, Archives of ELCA.

23. John Morehead to Arthur Malmgren, April 8, 1932, LWC Papers, Archives of ELCA.

24. Arthur Malmgren to John Morehead, May 15, 1932, LWC Papers, Archives of ELCA.

CHAPTER 19

1. Theophil Meier to John Morehead, July 13, 1932, LWC papers, Archives of ELCA.

2. Arthur Malmgren to John Morehead, Jan 30, March 19 and May 15, 1932, LWC Papers, Archives of ELCA.

3. Arthur Malmgren to John Morehead, April 14, 1932, LWC Papers, Archives of ELCA; P-87890, Volume 2, List 609, Archives of the FSB-St. Petersburg Region.

4. Litzenberger, *The Evangelical Lutheran Church and the Soviet Government, 1917–1938*, 265–67, 350.

5. Arthur Malmgren to John Morehead, March 19, 1932, LWC Papers, Archives of ELCA.

6. Litzenberger, *The Evangelical Lutheran Church and the Soviet Government, 1917–1938*, 342, 384.

7. Arthur Malmgren to John Morehead, September 27, 1932, LWC Papers, Archives of ELCA.

8. Arthur Malmgren to John Morehead, October 10, 1932, LWC Papers, Archives of ELCA.

9. John Morehead to Arthur Malmgren, October 21, 1932, LWC Papers, Archives of ELCA.

10. Tschoerner, *Arthur Malmgren*, 105.

11. Arthur Malmgren to John Morehead, November 26, 1932, LWC Papers, Archives of ELCA.

12. Litzenberger, *The Evangelical Lutheran Church and the Soviet Government, 1917–1938*, 263; Tschoerner, *Arthur Malmgren*, 96.

13. Arthur Malmgren to John Morehead, January 9, 1929, LWC Papers, Archives of ELCA.

14. Litzenberger,*The Evangelical Lutheran Church and the Soviet Government, 1917–1938*, 267; Tschoerner, *Arthur Malmgren*, 97. Tschoener says the seminary was accused of buying six cubic meters.

15. Georg Kretschmar and Heinrich Ratke, *The Evangelical Lutheran Church in Russia, the Ukraine, Kazakhstan and Central Asia* (St. Petersburg, Russia: AO Satis, Der Bote, 1996), 42.

16. Kahle, *Geschichte*, 354.

17. Litzenberger, *The Evangelical Lutheran Church and the Soviet Government, 1917–1938*, 267.

18. Litzenberger, *The Evangelical Lutheran Church and the Soviet Government, 1917–1938*, 267–268; Tschoerner, *Arthur Malmgren*, 97.

19. Kretschmar, 42.

20. Arthur Malmgren to John Morehead, November 26, 1932, LWC Papers, Archives of ELCA.

21. Tschoerner, *Arthur Malmgren*, 99.

22. Kahle, *Geschichte*, 135–36.

23. Kahle, *Geschichte*, 136; Tschoerner, *Arthur Malmgren*, 98.

24. Kahle, *Geschichte*, 136–37; Tschoerner, *Arthur Malmgren*, 100.

25. *Unsere Kirche, No. 3, 1928*. In a 1926/27 article entitled, "The Heritage of Luther," Pastor Eduard Luft attacked the leadership of the Lutheran Church in the German Communist journal, *Das Neue Dorf*. See Heinrich Roemmich, "Die Ev. Luth. Kirche in Russland unter der Sowjetherrschaft."

26. Kahle, *Geschichte*, 136–37; Litzenberger, *The Evangelical Lutheran Church and the Soviet Government, 1917–1938*, 272.

27. Litzenberger, *The Evangelical Lutheran Church and the Soviet Government, 1917–1938*, 272.

28. Alexander Streck to A. C. Ernst, May 6, 1922, NLC Papers, Archives of ELCA.

CHAPTER 20

1.   John Morehead to Arthur Malmgren, December 30, 1932, LWC Papers, Archives of ELCA.

2.   Arthur Malmgren to John Morehead, February 17, 1933, LWC Papers, Archives of ELCA.

3.   Arthur Malmgren to John Morehead, January 7, 1933, LWC Papers, Archives of ELCA.

4.   Theophil Meier to John Morehead, February 3, 1933, LWC Papers, Archives of ELCA.

5.   Theophil Meier to John Morehead, February 3, 1933, LWC Papers, Archives of ELCA.

6.   Tim Tzouliadis, *The Forsaken: An American Tragedy in Stalin's Russia* (London: The Penguin Press, 2008), 30–34.

7.   Robert Robinson, with Jonathan Slevin, *Black on Red: My 44 Years inside the Soviet Union* (Washington, D.C: Acropolis Books, 1988), 73–79, 107–108.

8.   Theophil Meier to John Morehead, February 3, 1933.

9.   John Morehead to Theophil Meier and Arthur Malmgren, March 23, 1933, LWC Papers, Archives of ELCA.

10.   Arthur Malmgren to John Morehead, April 30, 1933, LWC Papers, Archives of ELCA.

11.   S. J. Taylor, *Stalin's Apologist: Walter Duranty, The New York Time's Man in Moscow* (Oxford: Oxford University Press, 1990), 200.

12.   Malcolm Muggeridge, *Winter in Moscow* (Grand Rapids: Eerdmans, 1987), xx–xxi.

13.   Taylor, *Stalin's Apologist,* 168, 202.

14.   Taylor, *Stalin's Apologist,* 155, 182, 210, 218–19, 222–23.

15.   Taylor, *Stalin's Apologist,* 206.

16.   Arthur Malmgren to John Morehead, November 1, 1933, LWC Papers, Archives of ELCA.

17.   John Morehead to Arthur Malmgren, Sept 5, 1933.

18.   John Richman, *The United States and the Soviet Union: The Decision to Recognize* (Raleigh, NC: Camberleigh and Hall, 1980), 134, 160.

19.   Michael Cassella-Blackburn, *The Donkey, the Carrot, and the Club: William C. Bullitt and Soviet-American Relations, 1917–1948* (Westport, Conn: Praeger, 2004), 97.

20. Richman, *The United States and the Soviet Union*, 156, 159–61.

21. Cassella-Blackburn, *The Donkey*, 100, 102.

22. Richman, *The United States and the Soviet Union*, 163.

23. Richman, *The United States and the Soviet Union*, 152.

24. Richman, *The United States and the Soviet Union*, 158–59.

25. John Morehead to Theophil Meier, December 5, 1933, LWC Papers, Archives of ELCA.

CHAPTER 21

1. Schleuning et al., *Und siehe, wir leben*, 149.

2. Schleuning et al., *Und siehe, wir leben*, 147–49.

3. "May God Preserve You…," Tanya Ryumina, 2011.

4. Theophil Meier to John Morehead, October 29, 1933, LWC Papers, Archives of ELCA.

5. Anne Applebaum, *Gulag: A History* (New York: Doubleday, 2003), 63–65.

6. Shkarovsky and Cherepenina, *History*, 361–62; P-6790, List 13, FSB Archives of St. Petersburg Region; Bovkalo, "St. Petersburg Martyrology of Clergy and Laity"; Marina Mikhailovna, "Family Photograph."

7. Applebaum, *Gulag*, 64, 67–71.

8. Muss-Tumm Family Photo and Letter Collection.

9. "St. Petersburg Martyrology of Clergy and Laity: Evangelical Lutheran Church."

10. P-34994, List 4, FSB Archives of St. Petersburg Region.

11. Евангелическо-Лютеранский Приход Святого Михаила (г. Санкт-Петербург) [Evangelical Lutheran Church of St. Michael's (City of St. Petersburg)] Музей-Прихожане-Женщины [Museum-Female Parishioners], https://spbstmihail.jimdo.com/музей/прихожане/женщины/#schreiber.

12. НГ-Религии [NG Religion], "Крутой маршрут архиепископа: Михаил Мудьюгин прошел путь от инженера до архиерея" ["Cool Journey of the Archbishop: Mikhail Mudyugin Path from Engineer to Bishop"], by Архимандрит Августин (Никитин) [Archimandrite Augustine (Nikitin)], March 2, 2005, https://rusk.ru/st.php?idar=10377.

13. Arthur Malmgren to John Morehead, January 20, 1934, LWC Papers, Archives of ELCA.

14. Mikhail Shkarovsky, "Новомученик Пропст Фридрих Ваккер," ["New Martyr, District President Friedrich Wacker], April 8, 2016, http://sdsmp.ru/ns/item.php?ELEMENT_ID=6852.

15. Arthur Malmgren to John Morehead, January 20, 1934; Litzenberger, *The Evangelical Lutheran Church and the Soviet Government, 1917–1938*, 338; "Открытый список": Вольдемар Богданович Вагнер [Open List: Woldemar Bogdanovich Wagner], https://ru.openlist.wiki/Вагнер_Вольдемар _Богданович_(1898).

16. Mikhail Shkarovsky, "Епископ Артур Малмыгрен" ["Bishop Arthur Malmgren"], accessed April 15, 2013, http://spbda.ru/publications/mihail -shkarovskiy-episkop-artur-malmgren/.

17. Theophil Meier to John Morehead, Jan 26, 1934.

18. W. L. Scheding to John Morehead, March 25, 1934, LWC Papers, Archives of ELCA.

19. Theophil Meier to John Morehead, Jan 26, 1934; Litzenberger, *The Evangelical Lutheran Church and the Soviet Government, 1917–1938*, 333, 341, 384.

20. John Morehead to Arthur Malmgren, February 14, 1934, LWC Papers, Archives of ELCA.

21. John Morehead, "In Memory of Bishop Meyer of Moscow, Russia," 1934, LWC Papers, Archives of ELCA.

22. E. L. Packer, April 6, 1934, RG 59, 861.404/380, National Archives II.

23. John Morehead, "In Memory of Bishop Meier of Moscow, Russia," 1934.

24. Elisabeth Meyer to John Morehead, May 1934, LWC Papers, Archives of ELCA.

25. W. L. Scheding to Ralph Long, August 7, 1934, LWC Papers, Archives of ELCA.

26. Stephan Lorant, *Sieg Heil: An Illustrated History of Germany from Bismarck to Hitler* (New York: Bonanza Books, 1979), 104–5, 211–12, 220–21.

27. Elisabeth Meyer to John Morehead, May 1934.

28. "Tilly Meier's Report on Her Brother's Death," May 1934, LWC Papers, Archives of ELCA.

29. "Tilly Meier's Report on Her Brother's Death," May 1934, LWC Papers, Archives of ELCA.

30. John Morehead, "In Memory of Bishop Meyer of Moscow, Russia," May 1934.

31. John Morehead to Arthur Malmgren, May 28, 1934, LWC Papers, Archives of ELCA.

32. Arthur Malmgren to John Morehead, July 3, 1934, LWC Papers, Archives of ELCA; Litzenberger, *The Evangelical Lutheran Church and the Soviet Gov-*

ernment, 1917–1938, 392. The church needed government permission to hold a church convention and perhaps now sensing the disarray among Lutherans after Bishop Meier's death, the government refused to allow a convention to elect a new bishop. See Arthur Bliss Lane to Secretary of State Cordell Hull, May 13, 1937, RG 59, 861.404/414, National Archives II.

33.　Lel, "How They Were Trying to Destroy Us," 19.

34.　"May God Preserve You," Tanya Ryumina.

35.　Arthur Malmgren to John Morehead, July 3, 1934, LWC Papers, Archives of ELCA.

36.　Arthur Malmgren to John Morehead, July 3, 1934, LWC Papers, Archives of ELCA; Kahle, *Geschichte*, 600.

37.　John Morehead to Arthur Malmgren, August 22, 1934, LWC Papers, Archives of ELCA.

CHAPTER 22

1.　Bertha Kluck to John Morehead, June 30, 1934, LWC Papers, Archives of ELCA; Gisela Kluck-Detterer to Matthew Heise, July 2015.

2.　John Morehead to Arthur Malmgren, August 22, 1934, LWC Papers, Archives of ELCA.

3.　Arthur Malmgren to John Morehead, September 25, 1934, LWC Papers, Archives of ELCA.

4.　Arthur Malmgren to John Morehead, October 18, 1934, LWC Papers, Archives of ELCA.

5.　P-35162, Volume 2, List 3, FSB Archives of St. Petersburg Region.

6.　P-92125, Volume 2, List 70–71, 74, FSB Archives of St. Petersburg Region.

7.　P-92125, Volume 2, List 74–75, FSB Archives of St. Petersburg Region.

8.　P-92125, Volume 3, List 68–69, FSB Archives of St. Petersburg Region.

9.　P-35162, Volume 1, List 55, 63–74, FSB Archives of St. Petersburg Region.

10.　P-35162-Volume 2, List 340, FSB Archives of St. Petersburg Region.

11.　P-13562, Volume 1, List 10–12, 15, 39–45, FSB Archives of St. Petersburg Region.

12.　P-35162, Volume 1, List 4, 17, FSB Archives of St. Petersburg Region.

13.　Shkarovsky and Cherepenina, *History*, 118.

14.　Shkarovsky and Cherepenina, *History*, 118.

15.　P-35162, Volume 2, 341, 435, FSB Archives of St. Petersburg Region.

16.　Shkarovsky and Cherepenina, *History*, 119.

17. P-92125, Volume 3, List 105–6, and Volume 1, List 129, FSB Archives of St. Petersburg Region.

18. Schleuning et al., *Und siehe, wir leben*, 216.

19. Arthur Malmgren to John Morehead, September 25, 1934, LWC Papers, Archives of ELCA.

20. Edith Müthel, *An Gottes Hand*, 55; Edith Müthel, *I Remember*, 105–6.

21. Arthur Malmgren to John Morehead, December 20, 1934, LWC Papers, Archives of ELCA.

22. Lel, "How They Were Trying to Destroy Us," 19.

CHAPTER 23

1. John Morehead to C. C. Hein, May 1, 1935, LWC Papers, Archives of ELCA; Martin Luther Bund to John Morehead, 1935? LWC Papers, Archives of ELCA; Litzenberger, *The Evangelical Lutheran Church and the Soviet Government, 1917–1938*, 328. Marahrens initially greeted Hitler's accession to power with approval. However, he eventually became alarmed by Hitler's attempt to merge all churches into one state church. Ultimately, his thinking was informed by theological considerations, not political. As a confessional Lutheran, he could not acquiesce in allowing state power to usurp the Lutheran Confessions that had guided his regional church in Hannover. As a result of his stand, the Third Reich's bishop, Ludwig Müller, led a concerted effort in the fall of 1934 to remove him from office. Not only did the Hannoverian land's court refuse to remove Marahrens, but on March 5, 1935, the legality of his position in the church was reaffirmed by the Superior Court in Celle. Hitler had lost this battle, and Marahrens would remain in office until the end of the Nazi regime. Unfortunately, that did not mean his position was strong enough to thumb his nose at Hitler and the state church. His decision to go through Borchers in New York to convey the message about the Russian Lutherans to Morehead may have reflected his caution. See Lowell C. Green, *Lutherans against Hitler: The Untold Story* (St. Louis: Concordia, 2007), 300–308.

2. John Morehead to Maxim Litvinov, February 18, 1935, LWC Papers, Archives of ELCA. Later, these sentences were reduced to banishment in Siberia.

3. John Wiley to Cordell Hull, February 8, 1935, RG 59, 861.404/389, National Archives II.

4. John Morehead to William Bullitt, February 18, 1935, LWC Papers, Archives of ELCA.

5. Will Brownell and Richard N. Billings, *So Close to Greatness: A Biography of William C. Bullitt* (New York: Macmillan, 1987), 146.

6. Dennis J. Dunn, *Caught between Roosevelt & Stalin: America's Ambassadors to Moscow* (Lexington, KY: The University Press of Kentucky, 1998), 47.

7. Kirov Terror Document, April 1935?, LWC Papers, Archives of ELCA.

8. P-80626, Volume 1, List 83, FSB Archives of St. Petersburg Region.

9. Other historians cite a total numbering between 60,000 and 100,000 individuals being deported from Leningrad for having some vague connection to the Kirov assassination. See Gary Kern, *A Death in Washington: Walter G. Krivitsky and the Stalin Terror* (New York, Enigma Books, 2004), 83.

10. Matthew Lenoe, *The Kirov Murder and Soviet History,* Annals of Communism Series (New Haven and London: Yale University Press, 2010), Kindle edition, loc. 3275, 3292, 3737.

11. Lenoe, *Kirov Murder*, Kindle loc. 5455, 5535, 5679, 5695, 5760, 5776, 5829, 5893,5986, 6308.

12. Lenoe, *Kirov Murder*, Kindle loc. 9586, 9618, 9633; Roslof, *Red Priests*, 188.

13. Litzenberger, *The Evangelical Lutheran Church and the Soviet Government, 1917–1938*, 345.

14. Kirov Terror Document, April 1935?

15. Litzenberger, *The Evangelical Lutheran Church and the Soviet Government, 1917–1938*, 387.

16. Kirov Terror Document, April 1935?; Litzenberger, *The Evangelical Lutheran Church and the Soviet Government, 1917–1938*, 365–66. Mayer's death was shrouded in mystery as the German embassy had arranged for him to immigrate to Germany and join his seven children, who had lived there since 1924 thanks to the intervention of the Association of Aid to Germans Beyond Borders. The Soviet government, though, revealed that he had signed a document refusing to leave the USSR. His children believed that he had been forced to sign such a declaration against his own will. The Soviets claimed that Pastor Mayer died of old age in February 1933. See Litzenberger, *The Evangelical Lutheran Church and the Soviet Government, 1917–1938*, 366.

17. John Morehead to C. C. Hein, May 1, 1935.

18. Международный Мемориал: Проект "Уроки истории" [International Memorial: Project "Lessons in History"]; "Ученые ГАХН дома и на следствии / Доклад Марины Акимовой на семинаре 'Москва. Места памяти'" ["Academics of the GAKHN House and Its Investigation / The Paper of Marina Akhimova at the Seminar 'Moscow: A Place of Memory.'"], April 1, 2015, http://urokiistorii.ru/article/52560.

19. «Воспоминания о ГУЛАГе и их авторы" [Memory of the Gulag and Its Authors], Andrey Sakharov Center, Второе рождение: 1941–1952 // Воля: журнал узников тоталитарных систем [*Second Birth: 1941–1952 // Will:*

Journal of Prisoners in a Totalitarian System], 1995; "Нина Дмитриевна Монич" [Nina Dmitriyevna Monich], http://www.sakharov-center.ru/asfcd/auth/?t=page&num=4183.

20. Международный Мемориал: Проект "Уроки истории" [International Memorial: Project "Lessons in History"], "Ученые ГАХН дома и на следствии / Доклад Марины Акимовой на семинаре 'Москва. Места памяти'" ["Academics of the GAKHN House and Its Investigation/ The Paper of Marina Akhimova at the Seminar 'Moscow: A Place of Memory.'"], April 1, 2015, http://urokiistorii.ru/article/52560.

21. Жертвы политического террора в СССР [Victims of Political Terror in the USSR], compact disk, 3rd ed. (Moscow: Звенья [Zvenya], 2004), http://bezogr.ru/o-mejerah-e-a-i-e-g--peshkovoj-e-p.html; "Academics of the GAKHN House."

22. Litzenberger, *The Evangelical Lutheran Church and the Soviet Government, 1917–1938*, 331, 376, 382, 338, 341.

23. Shkarovsky and Cherepenina, *History*, 55; "'Open List': Woldemar Bogdanovich Wagner."

24. Shkarovsky, "Bishop Arthur Malmgren"; P-80626, Volume 1, List 4, FSB Archives of St. Petersburg Region.

25. P-80626, Volume 1, List 12–13, 17–19, FSB Archives of St. Petersburg Region.

26. P-80626, Volume 1, List 20, FSB Archives of St. Petersburg Region. The seventy-year-old Fastena had served in Astrakhan, Voronezh, and Moscow until approximately 1922, when he immigrated to Latvia. He had not forgotten his fellow Lutherans in Russia, still doing his best to provide aid in difficult times. See Litzenberger, *The Evangelical Lutheran Church and the Soviet Government, 1917–1938*, 384.

27. P-80626, Volume 1, List 7, 13, 21, 27, 31–34, FSB Archives of St. Petersburg Region.

28. "'Open List': Woldemar Bogdanovich Wagner."

29. Litzenberger, *The Evangelical Lutheran Church and the Soviet Government, 1917–1938*, 341.

30. P-80626, Volume 1, List 83, FSB Archives of St. Petersburg Region.

31. P-80626, Volume 1, List 81–82, 95–96, 116–18, FSB Archives of St. Petersburg Region.

32. P-80626, Volume 1, List 81–82, FSB Archives of St. Petersburg Region.

33. P-80626, Volume 1, List 82, 103–4, FSB Archives of St. Petersburg Region.

34. P-80626, Volume 1, List 82, FSB Archives of St. Petersburg Region.

35. P-80626, Volume 1, List 83, FSB Archives of St. Petersburg Region.

36. P-80626, Volume 1, List 83, 107–9, FSB Archives of St. Petersburg Region.

37. P-80626, Volume 1, List 87–88, FSB Archives of St. Petersburg Region.

38. P-80626, Volume 1, List 105–6, FSB Archives of St. Petersburg Region.

39. P-80626, Volume 1, List 116–18, 119, FSB Archives of St. Petersburg Region.

40. P-80626, Volume 1, List 162–72, FSB Archives of St. Petersburg Region.

41. P-80626, Volume 1, List 138–39, FSB Archives of St. Petersburg Region; Skarovsky and Cherepenina, *History*, 56.

42. "'Open List': Woldemar Bogdanovich Wagner."

43. Жертвы политического террора в СССР [Victims of Political Repression in the USSR], 2007; http://lists.memo.ru/index.htm.

CHAPTER 24

1. P-30561, List 244, FSB Archives of the St. Petersburg Region.

2. P-34994, List 72, FSB Archives of the St. Petersburg Region. There was an initial congregation worshiping in Russian before Muss took over the services, led by the father-son pastoral team, Albert and Johannes Masing. They gathered in whatever building they could find. See Litzenberger, *The Evangelical Lutheran Church and the Soviet Government, 1917–1938*, 365.

3. P-34994, List 72–74, FSB Archives of St. Petersburg Region.

4. Shkarovsky, "Pastor Kurt Muss." Eulogius was a Russian Orthodox bishop based in Paris, who had fled the Soviet Union. His followers managed to worship separately from the official Russian Orthodox Church in the USSR. See "Eulogius," Wikipedia, last modified September 20, 2017, https://en.wikipedia.org/wiki/Eulogius_(Georgiyevsky).

5. Fond 1002, Delo 52, List 163, Russian State Archives of St. Petersburg.

6. P-34994, List, 73, FSB Archives of St. Petersburg Region.

7. "Этот день в Истории Прихода Святого Михаила [This Day in the History of the Congregation of St. Michael's], accessed September 18, 2017, https://vk.com/spbstmihail?w=wall-89023090_763; P-21636, List 1–4, 9–12, 14, 23–24, 27, 40, 48, FSB Archives of St. Petersburg Region.

8. Shkarovsky, "Pastor Kurt Muss."

9. P-34994, Lists, 73, FSB Archives of St. Petersburg Region.

10. "Этот день в Истории Прихода Святого Михаила" [This Day in the History of the Congregation of St. Michael's], accessed August 6, 2016, https://vk.com/spbstmihail?w=wall-89023090_365. See also "Duke Peter Georgievich of Oldenburg," *Wikipedia*, last modified October 24, 2017, https://vk.com/spbstmihail; https://en.wikipedia.org/wiki/Duke_Peter_Georgievich_of_Oldenburg.

11. Shkarovsky, "Pastor Kurt Muss."

12. "This Day in the History of the Congregation of St. Michael's," https://vk.com/spbstmihail?w=wall-89023090_365.

13. P-34994, List 73–74, FSB Archives of St. Petersburg Region.

14. Fond 7384, Opis 33, Delo 51, Lists 2, 7, 9, 16, 17, Russian State Archives of St. Petersburg.

15. Shkarovsky and Cherepenina, *History*, 56.

16. Прогулки по Санкт-Петербургу ["Walks around St. Petersburg"], last modified October 26, 2017, http://walkspb.ru/zd/sv_mih.html. Vladimir Putin grew up right around the corner from St. Michael's. He would have only known the Gothic structure as a sports equipment factory. The diabolical nature of the Communists was on full display as they placed each new floor right in the middle of the stained-glass windows, ensuring the building's demise if someone ever reconverted it into its original church design. See Sergey Tatarenko to Matthew Heise, November 2010.

17. Kahle, *Geschichte*, 140.

18. P-37251, List 37, 147–48, FSB Archives of St. Petersburg Region; Shkarovsky and Cherepenina, *History*, 134.

19. Samuel Trexler, "What of the Church in Russia?" March 1935, LWC Papers, Archives of ELCA; John Morehead to P. O. Schallert, August 23, 1935, LWC Papers, Archives of ELCA; Trexler, *John A. Morehead*, 98–99.

20. Litzenberger, *The Evangelical Lutheran Church and the Soviet Government, 1917–1938*, 331, 338, 341, 376, 382.

21. Trexler, "What of the Church in Russia?"

22. Kahle, *Geschichte*, 326–27. By my count, there were fifteen pastors serving at the end of the year. Wilhelm Kahle says fourteen and for some reason does not include Alexander Streck in Moscow.

23. Kahle, *Geschichte*, 327, 597–601.

24. Martin Luther Bund to John Morehead, April 2, 1936, LWC Papers, Archives of ELCA; Kahle, *Geschichte*, 298; Walter Kolarz, *Religion in the Soviet Union* (New York: St. Martin, 1961), 255.

25. Schleuning et al., *Und siehe, wir leben*, 141.

26. Litzenberger, *The Evangelical Lutheran Church and the Soviet Government, 1917–1938*, 358; Schleuning et al., *Und siehe, wir leben*, 152–53; Heinrich Roemmich, "Die ev.-luth. Kirche in Russland in Vergangenheit und Gegenwart," *Volk auf dem Weg, January 1954*, 263; Martin Luther Bund to John Morehead, March 1, 1936.

27. Getty and Naumov, *Road to Terror*, 156.

CHAPTER 25

1. John Morehead to Rev. Henry Bagger, Nov 14, 1935.

2. Trexler, *John A. Morehead*, 158.

3. Ralph Long to Arthur Malmgren, May 1, 1936, LWC Papers, Archives of ELCA.

4. Shkarovsky, "Bishop Arthur Malmgren."

5. Kahle, *Geschichte*, 140.

6. Lel, "How They Were Trying to Destroy Us," 19.

7. Kahle, *Geschichte*, 140.

8. Tschoerner, *Arthur Malmgren*, 105.

9. Trexler, *John A. Morehead*, 160.

10. Trexler, *John A. Morehead*, 151.

11. John Morehead to Herbert Hoover, July 23, 1935, LWC Papers, Archives of ELCA.

12. Trexler, *John A. Morehead*, 160–62.

13. Trexler, *John A. Morehead*, 149.

14. Chas. A. Fegley, "Tributes to Dr. Morehead: Lutheran Leaders Lay Laurel Wreaths on His Grave," June 20, 1936, *Lutheran Companion*, 778–79, 783.

15. Trexler, *John A. Morehead*, 164.

16. Trexler, *John A. Morehead*, 99.

17. Wentz, *Lutherans in Concert*, 67–68.

18. Trexler, *John A. Morehead*, 142–43.

19. John Morehead to O. C. Kiep, December 5, 1930, LWC Papers, Archives of ELCA.

20. Tschoerner, *Arthur Malmgren*, 106–9.

CHAPTER 26

1. *The Path of Faith*, 78.

2. Georgiyevskaya, "Church Life in Moscow," 62–63.

3. Olga Striks to Dmitry Lotov, March 2014.

4. Karen Petrone, *Life Has Become More Joyous, Comrades: Celebrations in the Time of Stalin* (Bloomington, IN: Indiana University Press, 2000), 86–87, 93.

5. Leopold L. S. Braun, *In Lubianka's Shadow: The Memoirs of an American Priest in Stalin's Moscow, 1934–1945* (South Bend, IN: University of Notre Dame Press, 2006), 57–60, 62. The temperatures in Sts. Peter and Paul

Lutheran, only a few blocks from St. Louis Catholic Church, were often no
higher than 32 degrees Fahrenheit due to Soviet malice. See Dönninghaus, *Die Deutschen,* 518.

6. Braun, *In Lubianka's Shadow,* 60–61, 64–65. Braun admitted that he and the Living Church's Bishop Vvedenskii were the only clergy with cars. The other priests and pastors, like Alexander Streck, were forced to spend hours traveling back and forth on public transportation to their suburban lodgings. See Braun, *In Lubianka's Shadow,* 65.

7. Schleuning et al., *Und siehe, wir leben,* 149–50.

8. Loy Henderson to Cordell Hull, September 18, 1936, 861.404/404, RG 59, National Archives II; Alan Cullison for the Associated Press "Stalin-Era Secret Police Documents Detail Arrest, Execution of Americans," *LATimes.com,* November 9, 1997, http://articles.latimes.com/1997/nov/09/news/mn-51910/4; "Anna Louise Strong," *Wikipedia,* last modified November 2, 2017, https://en.wikipedia.org/wiki/Anna_Louise_Strong.

9. Loy Henderson to Cordell Hull, September 18, 1936.

10. Loy Henderson to Cordell Hull, September 18, 1936.

11. Loy Henderson to Cordell Hull, September 18, 1936; Schleuning et al., *Und siehe, wir leben,* 141. For a discussion of the Tbilisi congregation, see Litzenberger, *The Evangelical Lutheran Church and the Soviet Government, 1917–1938,* 597–601.

12. Conquest, *The Great Terror,* 91–105; Getty and Naumov, *Road to Terror,* 265–67.

13. Conquest, *The Great Terror,* 105.

14. Dunn, *Caught between Roosevelt & Stalin,* 79.

15. Conquest, *The Great Terror,* 41.

16. Schleuning et al., *Und siehe, wir leben,* 150.

17. Georgiyevskaya, "Church Life in Moscow," 63.

18. Schleuning et al., *Und siehe, wir leben,* 150–51.

19. William Bullitt to R. Walton Moore, November 14, 1936.

20. John Lewis Gaddis, *George F. Kennan: An American Life* (New York: The Penguin Press, 2011), 95.

21. Dunn, *Caught between Roosevelt & Stalin,* 47.

22. Gaddis, *George F. Kennan,* 102.

23. Dunn, *Caught between Roosevelt & Stalin,* 57.

24. Gaddis, *George F. Kennan,* 104.

25. Tzouliadis, *The Forsaken,* 72.

26. Dunn, *Caught between Roosevelt & Stalin*, 47.

27. Tzouliadis, *The Forsaken*, 72. W. H. Chamberlain, sympathetic to the Bolshevik experiment when he arrived in Russia, was stunned by what he had observed when he, like Bullitt, left Russia in the summer of 1936. "I went to Russia believing that the Soviet system might represent the most hopeful answer to the problems raised by the World War and the subsequent economic crisis. I left convinced that the absolutist Soviet state ... is a power of darkness and evil with few parallels in history." See Tzouliadis, *The Forsaken*, 73.

28. Brownell and Billings, *So Close to Greatness*, 189–90; William Bullitt to R. Walton Moore, Nov 14, 1936.

29. R. Walton Moore, Nov 16, 1936, 124.61/108, RG 59, National Archives II.

30. Gaddis, *George F. Kennan*, 103; Dunn, *Caught between Roosevelt & Stalin*, 73.

31. Gaddis, *George F. Kennan*, 104.

32. Gaddis, *George F. Kennan*, 104–5.

33. Dunn, *Caught between Roosevelt & Stalin*, 75. Regarding the listening devices, in 1939 Bullitt would learn indirectly (through Loy Henderson) from a Soviet military intelligence defector, General Walter Krivitsky, that a member of Bullitt's staff had been working for the Soviets and that the Soviets knew everything of interest occurring in the embassy. According to Krivitsky, every Soviet citizen working inside the embassy was expected to give a periodic report to the NKVD. As a matter of fact, in those early years the Americans had been sending messages uncoded through the Soviet telegraph agency. During World War II, an American named Tyler Gatewood Kent was accused of spying for the Nazis and imprisoned for seven years. Since he had also served in the American embassy in Moscow from 1933 until 1939, historian Gary Kern speculates that he may have been Krivitsky's spy. Most likely, his spying for the Soviets was related to an OGPU mistress he had at the time in Moscow. Observing Soviet behavior firsthand, he afterward turned towards the Nazis as a counterweight to the Soviets. Krivitsky was said to have committed suicide in Washington, D.C. but the suspicious circumstances of his death point toward murder. See Kern, *A Death in Washington*, 159–60, 175, 285.

34. Dunn, *Caught between Roosevelt & Stalin*, 73–75.

35. Dunn, *Caught between Roosevelt & Stalin*, 77.

36. Tzouliadis, *The Forsaken*, 203–4.

37. Loy Henderson to Cordell Hull, Sept 28, 1936, RG 59, 861.404/403, National Archives II. In May 1937, Arthur Bliss Lane of the State Department would forward translated articles from the Russian bureau to Secretary of State Hull. The October 1936 issue of a German-language journal *Osteuropa* spelled out the situation quite clearly. Ninety-nine percent of collectivization was said to have been completed in the Volga region, destroying the Lutheran Church

in the process. Older folks were said to still gather in their homes for religious meetings. In the absence of the clergy, lay preachers and members of the *dvatstaka* conducted prayer meetings. In the Ingrian region, forced deportations to Siberia devastated the Lutheran Church while church buildings were turned into Communist clubs or theaters. With collectivization mostly accomplished, it was felt that now the new Stalin Constitution could be revealed at the end of 1936. See Arthur Bliss Lane to Cordell Hull, May 13, 1937, 861.404/414, RG 59, National Archives II.

38. Tzouliadis, *The Forsaken*, 205.

39. Gaddis, *George F. Kennan*, 106.

40. Gaddis, *George F. Kennan*, 107, 110–11.

41. Gaddis, *George F. Kennan*, 88.

42. Dunn, *Caught between Roosevelt & Stalin*, 87.

CHAPTER 27

1. P-34994, List 4, FSB Archives of St. Petersburg Region.

2. P -34994, List 1, FSB Archives of St. Petersburg Region.

3. P -34994, List 29, 30–32, FSB Archives of St. Petersburg Region.

4. P -34994, List 12–13, FSB Archives of St. Petersburg Region.

5. P -34994, List 14, FSB Archives of St. Petersburg Region.

6. P -34994, List 74, FSB Archives of St. Petersburg Region.

7. P -34994, List 47, 69, FSB Archives of St. Petersburg Region.

8. P-34994, List 11, FSB Archives of St. Petersburg Region.

9. P -34994, List 11, FSB Archives of St. Petersburg Region.

10. P -34994, List 54, 65, 78, FSB Archives of St. Petersburg Region.

11. P -34994, List 20, FSB Archives of St. Petersburg Region.

12. P -34994, List 70, 79, FSB Archives of St. Petersburg Region.

13. P -34994, List 70, 71, FSB Archives of St. Petersburg Region.

14. P -34994, List 80, FSB Archives of St. Petersburg Region.

15. Schlögel, *Moscow, 1937*, 187.

16. Petrone, *Life Has Become More Joyous, Comrades*, 186.

17. Joseph Davies to Cordell Hull, March 17, 1937, 861.404/412, RG 59, National Archives II.

18. Loy Henderson to Cordell Hull, September 28, 1936.

19. Sheila Fitzpatrick, *Everyday Stalinism: Ordinary Life in Extraordinary Times: Soviet Russia in the 1930s* (New York: Oxford University Press, 1999), 179; Duin, *Lutheranism under the Tsars and the Soviets* 761.

20. Joseph Davies to Cordell Hull, March 17, 1937.

21. Marc Jansen and Nikita Petrov, *Stalin's Loyal Executioner: People's Commissar Nikolaiy Ezhov, 1895–1940* (Palo Alto, CA: Hoover Institution Press, 2002), 107.

22. Schlögel, *Moscow, 1937*, 341.

23. Sarah Davies, *Popular Opinion in Stalin's Russia: Terror, Propaganda and Dissent, 1934–1941* (Cambridge, England: Cambridge University Press, 1997), 78–79.

24. Petrone, *Life Has Become More Joyous, Comrades*, 186–87.

25. Joseph Davies to Cordell Hull, March 17, 1937.

26. Schlögel, *Moscow, 1937*, 342.

27. Petrone, *Life Has Become More Joyous, Comrades*, 180.

28. David R. Shearer, *Policing Stalin's Socialism: Repression and Social Order in the Soviet Union, 1924–1953* (New Haven, CT: Yale University Press, 2009), 297–98.

29. Jansen and Petrov, *Stalin's Loyal Executioner*, 54, 106.

30. Schlögel, *Moscow, 1937*, 342.

31. P-45647, List 7, FSB Archives of the Moscow Region.

32. P-45647, List 9–11, 20, 25, FSB Archives of the Moscow Region.

33. P-45647, List 27, 30, FSB Archives of the Moscow Region. Again, this is probably some form of the conveyor method. The accused would be kept under interrogation without break, sometimes for eighteen hours in a row. The NKVD would exchange officers while the accused would not be given a break. See Robert Conquest, The Great Terror, 123–24.

34. Kahle, *Geschichte*, 420–22; Litzenberger, *The Evangelical Lutheran Church and the Soviet Government, 1917–1938*, 201–205, 365, 386–387; "Victims of Political Terror," last modified, December 13, 2016, http://lists.memo.ru/index21.htm.

35. P-45647, List 24, FSB Archives of the Moscow Region.

36. P-45647, List 24–25, FSB Archives of the Moscow Region; "Lessons of History in the 20th Century," accessed April 1, 2015, http://urokiistorii.ru/article/52560.

37. P-45647, List 27–30, 40, FSB Archives of the Moscow Region; Litzenberger, *The Evangelical Lutheran Church and the Soviet Government, 1917–1938*, 382.

38. Schleuning et al., *Und siehe, wir leben*, 151.

39. Eugenie Meier to LWC, December 21, 1936, LWC Papers, Archives of ELCA; Litzenberger, *The Evangelical Lutheran Church and the Soviet Government, 1917–1938*, 277.

CHAPTER 28

1. Sarah Davies, *Popular Opinion in Stalin's Russia*, 74.

2. Schlögel, *Moscow, 1937*, 113, 118.

3. Sarah Davies, *Popular Opinion in Stalin's Russia*, 79–81. The author recalls such predictions when Mikhail Gorbachev came to power in 1985 and the USSR disintegrated in 1991. Gorbachev was considered to be "Czar Mikhail."

4. Junker and Arkkila, *Nacht und Neuer Morgen*, 23.

5. *The Path of Faith*, 81, 84.

6. Junker and Arkkila, *Nacht und Neuer Morgen*, 20–21.

7. Sarah Davies, *Popular Opinion in Stalin's Russia*, 74–75.

8. Braun, *In Lubianka's Shadow*, 99.

9. Sarah Davies, *Popular Opinion in Stalin's Russia*, 80–81. By Easter of 1938, only five of the thirty-three open churches in 1937 in Leningrad would remain open. See Davies, 81.

10. Kahle, *Geschichte*, 597–601.

11. Gisela Kluck-Detterer to Matthew Heise, March 2014.

12. Applebaum, *Gulag*, 224–25, 228.

13. Arthur Kluck Family Documents.

14. Gisela Kluck-Detterer to Matthew Heise, March 2014, N. N. Ablazhei, "Stalinism in the Provinces: 1937–1938," Yakov Krotov Biblioteka, http://krotov.info/libr_min/18_s/ta/stalinism_08.htm; Arthur Kluck Family Documents.

15. Applebaum, *Gulag*, 107.

16. P-45647, List 147, FSB Archives of the Moscow Region.

17. P-45647, List 143, 145, FSB Archives of the Moscow Region.

18. P-45647, List 147, FSB Archives of the Moscow Region.

19. Schleuning et al., *Und siehe, wir leben*, 150. American Catholic priest Father Léopold Braun writes in his book that a "Lutheran bishop" in Moscow was "savagely shot." Since his church was only a few blocks from Streck's, he undoubtedly knew him and heard what happened. Braun even claimed that after his execution by firing squad, Streck's clothes had been sent back to his wife. See Braun, *In Lubianka's Shadow*, 64. That almost assuredly is incorrect, though. Current Sts. Peter and Paul Lutheran pastor, Dmitry Lotov, corresponded with the relatives of Streck and learned that they had waited for him in exile in Kazakhstan, but he never came (Dmitry Lotov to Matthew Heise, October 2013). From the NKVD file on Streck, we now know that his daughter, Stella Leipus, wrote to Nikita Khrushchev on January 31, 1956, inquiring as

to the whereabouts of her father. Writing in exile from a collective farm in the Karaganda region of Kazakhstan, she informed Khrushchev that she was the only family member still alive and that her family had never learned whether her father had survived the Stalinist years or not. It was already nine-and-a-half years after his "ten-year sentence without the right to correspondence" was to have expired. Surely, if he was still alive, he should be freed so that his daughter could provide comfort to him in his old age. (What Leipus didn't know, and we know today, is that the phrase "ten years without the right of correspondence" was code language indicating that the prisoner had been executed.) On November 20, 1957, the courts declined Leipus's plea and refused to rehabilitate Streck. His innocence and the spurious nature of all charges against him would only be admitted in 1996, when he was formally rehabilitated by the Russian Republic. See P-45647, List 129, 308–12, FSB Archives of the Moscow Region.

CHAPTER 29

1. Getty and Naumov, *Road to Terror*, 474–75, 492.
2. P-17014, List 1, 4, FSB Archives of St. Petersburg Region.
3. Olga Ryumina to Erik Muss, 2006.
4. P-17014, List 9, FSB Archives of St. Petersburg Region.
5. Conquest, *The Great Terror*, 199–204.
6. P-17014, List 5–7, FSB Archives of St. Petersburg Region.
7. P-17014, List 10, FSB Archives of St. Petersburg Region.
8. P-17014, List 11, 13–14, FSB Archives of St. Petersburg Region.
9. Catherine Merridale, *Night of Stone: Death and Memory in Twentieth-Century Russia* (New York: Viking Penguin, 2001), 2–5.
10. "Жители Курской области, репрессированные в 1930–1950 годы" ["Residents of the Kursk Region, Repressed in the years 1930–1950," http://gorenka .org/index.php/zhertvy-repressij/8210-zhertvy-politicheskikh-repressij -kurskoj-oblasti-kos-ku.
11. "Возвращённые Имена: Книги Памяти России" ["Return of the Names: Book of Memories in Russia"], http://visz.nlr.ru/person/book/t1/4/110.
12. Shkarovsky and Cherepenina, *History*, 298.
13. "'Open List': Woldemar Bogdanovich Wagner."
14. Tatsenko, Pastor, and Schwan, "Bruder Bruno."
15. "May God Preserve You...," Tanya Ryumina.
16. Dagmar Zeksel, "Воспоминания о Пасторе Курте Муссе" [Memories of Pastor Kurt Muss], in Уроки Гнева и Любви: Воспоминания о Репрессях

(1920–80 гг.), Выпуск 5 [*Lessons of Hate and Love: Remembrances of Repression (1920–80)*, Volume 5] (Saint Petersburg, Russia: B.I., 1993), 15–16.

17. P-12690, List 3–4, FSB Archives of St. Petersburg Region.

18. P-12690, List 4, FSB Archives of St. Petersburg Region.

19. Zeksel, "Memories of Pastor Kurt Muss."

20. P-12690, List 5–7, FSB Archives of St. Petersburg Region.

21. "Жертвы политического террора в СССР" ["Victims of Political Terror in the USSR"], last modified December 13, 2016, http://lists.memo.ru/index13.htm. Anne Applebaum's *Gulag* has an interesting note related to executions in Karelia, and quite possibly, Muss's and Meier's labor camp: "On September 20, 1937, a fairly typical day, the troika of the Karelian Republic sentenced 231 prisoners of the White Sea Canal camp, Belbaltlag. Assuming a ten-hour workday, with no breaks, less than three minutes would have been spent considering the fate of each pris-oner. Most of those condemned had received their original sentences much earlier, at the beginning of the 1930s. Now, they were accused of new crimes, usually connected to bad behavior or a poor attitude to life in the camps. Among them were former politicals—Mensheviks, Anarchists, Social Democrats—and a former nun who 'refused to work for the Soviet authorities.'" Applebaum's research paints a clear picture of how Muss and Meier were put on the conveyor belt of Soviet justice, their sentences rubber-stamped in a transparent attempt to do away with the "former people." See Applebaum, *Gulag*, 107.

CHAPTER 30

1. Fond 7384, Delo 160, List 8, St. Petersburg State Archives; P-34994, List 80–92, FSB Archives of St. Petersburg Region. Andrievsky was accused of slandering Soviet power, conducting anti-collective farm agitation, praising the life of workers in czarist Russia and carrying out counterrevolutionary conversations about the new constitution. His ultimate fate is uncertain, but he was finally rehabilitated by the Russian state in 2001.

2. Fond 7384, Delo 160, List 11, St. Petersburg State Archives.

3. P-32706, Volume 1, List 3, FSB Archives of St. Petersburg Region.

4. P-32706, Volume 1, List 4, FSB Archives of St. Petersburg Region.

5. P-32706, Volume 1, List 7, FSB Archives of St. Petersburg Region.

6. P-32706, Volume 1, List 9, FSB Archives of St. Petersburg Region.

7. P-32706, Volume 1, List 115–17, FSB Archives of St. Petersburg Region.

8. P-32706, Volume 1, List 118, FSB Archives of St. Petersburg Region.

9. P-32706, Volume 1, List 119–20, FSB Archives of St. Petersburg Region.

10. Jansen and Petrov, *Stalin's Loyal Executioner*, 73.

11. Jansen and Petrov, *Stalin's Loyal Executioner*, 94–95. Between October 1936 and February 1937 alone, Yezhov oversaw the arrests of 2116 individuals who were accused of working in "anti-Soviet blocks or for hostile governments." See Shearer, 320.

12. P-32706, Volume 1, List 38, FSB Archives of St. Petersburg Region.

13. P-32706, Volume 1, List 147–50, FSB Archives of St. Petersburg Region.

14. Fond 1001, Delo 52, List 10, 104, St. Petersburg State Archives.

15. P-32706, Volume 1, List 147–150, FSB Archives of St. Petersburg Region.

16. P-32706, Volume 1, List 125–126, FSB Archives of St. Petersburg Region.

17. P-32706, Volume 1, List 127, 204–6, 220–27, and Volume 2, List 122, FSB Archives of St. Petersburg Region. Erwin Deters and Ernst Essifer were classmates of Bruno Reichert's at the Peterschule, so that association allowed the NKVD to link them to Bruno and claim that he recruited them for the fabricated German spy ring. As a current graduate student at the Leningrad Industrial Institute and with his past practical work as a student at the Lenenergo plant, Deters was said to have gathered information for Bruno which he then passed along to the German consulate. See List 129–34 of the same file listed above.

18. Fond 7384, Delo 160, List 14, 16–17, 26, St. Petersburg State Archives.

19. Fond 7384, Delo 160, List 12, St. Petersburg State Archives.

20. Fond 7384, Delo 159, List 41, 44–45, St. Petersburg State Archives.

21. Fond 7384, Delo 160, List 16–17, St. Petersburg State Archives.

22. Mikhail Mudyugin, "A Remembrance of Life."

23. Shkarovsky and Cherepenina, *History*, 119–20. The Migle brothers lived with their seventy-two-year-old mother, Maria, in apartment 27 on the Griboyedov Canal embankment in the center of the city, equidistant from St. Peter's on 25 October Avenue and Christ the Savior on Zagorodnii Avenue. The brothers were arrested on October 27. On November 22, the name of the *dvatsatka* chairman of Christ the Savior, Jakov Smigla, was included in the indictment against the Migles, along with parishioners Eduard Vineger, Minna Ravushka, Ottilia Lutova, Aleksey Mikstais, Anna Smirnova, German Ozolin, and Petr and Hermina Jakovlev. Alexander Migle's correspondence with foreigners was noted, including letters to an Edith Spier in America (whose parents lived in Pskov, Russia, where he had once served). It was also observed that he had received food parcels in the past through Bishop Malmgren, most likely the aid that John Morehead had secured. Alexander Migle's visits to the Latvian, German, and American consulates in Leningrad and Moscow were recorded, even though he said his visits were related to church matters. These connections were used by the NKVD when they wrote down Alexander's "confession" on November 9, claiming that Bishop Malmgren and the late Pastor Mikhail

Lapping had recruited him to create a group opposed to Soviet power. On December 7, a typed copy of the charges against the Latvian Lutherans was prepared, accusing Alexander Migle with his brother and fellow parishioners of creating a counterrevolutionary group dedicated to carrying out spying activities and terrorist propaganda among the Latvian community in Leningrad. On December 8, Nikolai Yezhov and the Procurator of the Soviet Union, Andrey Vishinsky, accepted the evidence that the group was spying and acting on behalf of Latvia and ordered all the indicted to be shot. See P-30561, List 4, 79, 81–82, 87–96, 203–210, 272–73.

24. Mikhail Mudyugin, "A Remembrance of Life."

25. P-32706, Volume 2, List 122–23, 144–46, FSB Archives of St. Petersburg Region. Ernst Essifer is not listed among those who were executed, but there is also no mention of him being released.

26. Alexey Uimanen to Matthew Heise, November 2013.

27. Shkarovsky and Cherepenina, *History*, 57.

CHAPTER 31

1. Shkarovsky and Cherepenina, *History*, 57.

2. Shkarovsky and Cherepenina, *History*, 82, 311.

3. E. L. Packer to Cordell Hull, March 5, 1938, RG 59, 861.404/418, National Archives II.

4. Marina Mikhalova, "Family Photograph." Pavlovsk was the hometown of the Mai family, so they most likely found housing easily since Reinhold's mother, Maria, still lived there in the family home. His parents had operated a pharmacy, but his father, Arnold, had disappeared during the Civil War and was presumed dead. Maria raised the boys by herself.

5. Marina Mikhailova, "Family Photograph;" P-87431, List 60–63, 66, FSB Archives of St. Petersburg Region. Wolf Liss's file lists Marta as a sister of Reinhold's, but Tamara Kosetti Mai's granddaughter says she was a cousin. Sometimes Russians refer to cousins as brothers and sisters, so she was more than likely a cousin.

6. P-25625, List 14, 164, FSB Archives of St. Petersburg Region; Marina Mikhailova, "Family Photograph."

7. Marina Mikhailova, "Family Photograph." Leningraders often employed black humor when referring to the DPZ, labeling it as Домой Пойти Забудь: "Forget about Going Home."

8. David Remnick, *Lenin's Tomb: The Last Days of the Soviet Empire* (New York: Vintage Books, 1994), 117.

9. Marina Mikhailova, "Family Photograph."

10. P-25625, List 15, FSB Archives of St. Petersburg Region.

11. P-25625, List 164, FSB Archives of St. Petersburg Region.

12. P-25625, List 174, FSB Archives of St. Petersburg Region.

13. P-25625, List 180–81, 183, FSB Archives of St. Petersburg Region.

14. P-25625, List 183, FSB Archives of St. Petersburg Region.

15. Marina Mikhailova, "Family Photograph."

16. "'Open List': Woldemar Bogdanovich Wagner."

17. P-32723, Volume 1, List 4, FSB Archives of St. Petersburg Region.

18. P-87431, List 1, 4, FSB Archives of St. Petersburg Region.

19. P-87431, List 60–63, FSB Archives of St. Petersburg Region. Not only was Liss blessed with musical talent, but he also served both the Czarist (1915–1917) and Red Army Air Force (1918–1920) as a radio technician. He apparently had served effectively because he was given a small silver medal by the Soviet government for his zeal. Unfortunately, none of this redounded to his benefit. See List 7, 12 of the same file.

20. P-87431, List 60–82, FSB Archives of St. Petersburg Region.

21. P-87431, List 389, 407, FSB Archives of St. Petersburg Region; Энциклопедия Петришуле: Тамара Валентиновна Коссетти [Encyclopedia Petrischule: Tamara Valentinovna Kossetti], last modified October 21, 2017, http://all petrischule-spb.org/index.php?title=Коссетти,_Тамара_Валентиновнаю.

22. Fond 7384, Delo 160, List 30, 63, St. Petersburg State Archives.

23. Fond 7384, Delo 160, List 28, 30, 32, St. Petersburg State Archives.

24. Fond 7384, Delo 160, List 27, 38–41, St. Petersburg State Archives.

25. Fond 7384, Delo 160, List 46, 49, St. Petersburg State Archives; Sebastian Brandt, ed., *Petrikirche—Tserkov Svyatogo Petra [Peterkirche—The Church of St. Peter's]* (St. Petersburg, Russia: Ofset Master, 1998), 3.

26. Brandt, *Petrikirche*, 16–17.

27. Brandt, *Petrikirche*, 43; "В Петрикирхе торжественно откроют новый орган" ["In Petrikirche a Solemn Opening for a New Organ"], IANews, Sept.25, 2017, https://ianews.ru/articles/104295/.

28. "Северный полюс-1" ["North Pole-1"], wikipedia.ru; last modified October 28, 2017, https://ru.wikipedia.org/wiki/Северный_полюс-1.

29. Fond 7384, Delo 160, List 52–53, 63, St. Petersburg State Archives.

30. Fond 7384, Delo 162, List 30, St. Petersburg State Archives.

31. Fond 7384, Delo 162, List 39, St. Petersburg State Archives.

32. Fond 7384, Delo 162, List 40, 43–45, 52, St. Petersburg State Archives.

33. Fond 7384, Delo 162, List 47, 54, St. Petersburg State Archives.

34. Fond 7384, Delo 162, List 55–56, St. Petersburg State Archives.

35. Kahle, *Geschichte*, 142. Theaters would become a popular use for former church buildings, as St. Anne's was reconstructed into the Spartak theater in January 1938. See Shkarovsky and Cherepenina, *History*, 137.

36. Schleuning et al., *Und siehe, wir leben*, 151.

37. P-25625, List 184–87, 194, FSB Archives of St. Petersburg Region.

38. P-40699, List 33, FSB Archives of St. Petersburg Region; Olga Ryumina to Erik Muss. According to Gerhardt, who lived until 2004, he had become a bit of a hooligan without parental supervision, stealing free rides on the trams in Leningrad. Once his uncle Otto saw him from his own car and gave him a "dressing down" afterwards. See Olga Ryumina to Erik Muss.

39. P-40699, List 33, FSB Archives of St. Petersburg Region.

40. Жертвы политического террора в СССР [Victims of Political Repression in the USSR], last modified December 13, 2016, http://lists.memo.ru/index25.htm.

41. Olga Ryumina to Erik Muss.

42. P-40699, List 38, FSB Archives of St. Petersburg Region.

43. P-40699, List 39, FSB Archives of St. Petersburg Region.

44. P-40699, List 40–41, FSB Archives of St. Petersburg Region.

45. P-40699, List 41–42, FSB Archives of St. Petersburg Region. The Yezhovschina, or "Yezhovization," is the phrase often used to describe the Great Terror of 1937–38. Authors Arch Getty and Oleg Naumov think it is a bit of a misnomer since Stalin surely was ultimately responsible, however eagerly Yezhov carried out his instructions. See Getty and Naumov, *Road to Terror*, 491.

46. Marina Mikhalova, "Family Photograph." In 1962, Reinhold Mai's family would be told that he died of gangrene of the lungs in 1942. However, due to the tireless labors of the human rights organization Memorial and its website, "Return of the Names," after the fall of the Soviet Union Reinhold's granddaughter would learn of his 1938 arrest and execution and eventual rehabilitation in 1957.

47. P-40699, List 4, FSB Archives of St. Petersburg Region.

48. P-40699, List 10–11, FSB Archives of St. Petersburg Region.

49. P-40699, List 12, FSB Archives of St. Petersburg Region.

50. P-40699, List 13–15, FSB Archives of St. Petersburg Region.

51. Lothar Tumm Letters—Muss Family Documents.

52. Фонд Последний адрес [Last Address Foundation], Герман Яковлевич Берхдольт [Herman Yakovlevich Bergholdt], accessed April 2, 2017, https://www.poslednyadres.ru/news/news416.htm; Litzenberger, *The Evangelical Lutheran Church and the Soviet Government, 1917–1938*, 338.

53. Getty and Naumov, *Road to Terror*, 475–76.

54. P-40699, List 208–26, 231, 236, FSB Archives of St. Petersburg Region.

55. Getty and Naumov, *Road to Terror*, 256–57.

56. Of the Hansen boys, only Gerhardt lived into old age. Ralf and Meinhardt did not survive the Leningrad Blockade by Nazi forces in 1941. Gerhardt went on to serve on the front during World War II, and after being wounded in battle and due to his German last name, he was evacuated to Sverdlovsk (modern-day Yekaterinburg). After the war he settled in Nizhniy Tagil, just north of Sverdlovsk in the Ural Mountain region, and worked as a chauffeur. With the demise of the Soviet Union, he went with his cousin to the KGB archives where they both learned the fate of their fathers. Gerhardt died in 2004 at the age of eighty-four. See Olga Ryumina to Erik Muss.

57. Shkarovsky and Cherepenina, *History*, 57–58.

58. Jansen and Petrov, *Stalin's Loyal Executioner*, 164–65.

59. Jansen and Petrov, *Stalin's Loyal Executioner*, 181–82, 187–88.

60. Jansen and Petrov, *Stalin's Loyal Executioner*, 211.

61. *The Path of Faith*, 82–83, 89, 106.

EPILOGUE

1. Mikhail Shkarovsky, "Новомученик Пропст Фридрих Ваккер," ["New Martyr, District President Friedrich Wacker], April 8, 2016, http://sdsmp.ru/ns/item.php?ELEMENT_ID=6852.

2. Junker and Arkkila, *Nacht und Neuer Morgen*, 30–33.

3. Maxim Ivanov, *The Lutheran Quarter in Petersburg*, 46.

4. Maxim Ivanov, *The Lutheran Quarter in Petersburg*, 45–48.

5. Brandt, *Petrikirche*, 45–46; Vladimir Izotov, "Немецкая Волна: Петрикирхе: лютеранская церковь в истории города на Неве," in Portal Credo.ru, February 2, 2003, https://www.portal-credo.ru/site/?act=monitor&id=1238.

6. Brandt, *Petrikirche*, 42–44; "Ein Wort über einen Freund," *Der Bote 4*, 2000.

7. "St. Petersburg Martyrology of Clergy and Laity: Evangelical Lutheran Church."

8. Zeksel, "Memories of Pastor Kurt Muss."17. The words in Russian are: Своей нам силой в трудный час, не устоять в напасти, но ратует в борьбе за нас, избранных Божьей власти.

9. "St. Petersburg Martyrology of Clergy and Laity: Evangelical Lutheran Church."

10. Oleg Sevastyanov to Matthew Heise, June 2017.

11. НГ-Религии [NG Religion], "Крутой маршрут архиепископа: Михаил Мудьюгин прошел путь от инженера до архиерея " ["Cool Journey of the Archbishop: Mikhail Mudyugin Path from Engineer to Bishop"], by Архимандрит Августин (Никитин) [Archimandrite Augustine (Nikitin)], March 2, 2005, https://rusk.ru/st.php?idar=10377.

12. Oleg Sevastyanov to Matthew Heise, June 2017. See Mudyugin's preface to the book Мартин Лютер: Избранные произведения [Martin Luther: Selected Works] at http://www.soluschristus.ru/biblioteka/mezhcerkovnye _otnosheniya/predislovie_k_knige/.

13. *The Path of Faith*, 96, 114–16; Aari Kugappi to Matthew Heise, May 2007.

14. Müthel, *I Remember*, 192–93.

15. Lel, "How They Were Trying to Destroy Us," 12, 19; Ryumina, "May God Preserve You..."

BIBLIOGRAPHY

Afanasiyev, A. L., and Y. K. Baranov. Одиссея Генерала Яхонтова [*The Odyssey of General Yakhontov*]. Moscow: Soviet Russia, 1988.

Aleksandrova, E. L., M. M. Braudze, V. A. Vysotskaya, and E. A. Petrova. История Финской Евангелической-Лютеранской Церкви Ингрии: 2011–1611 [*The History of the Finnish Evangelical Lutheran Church of Ingria: 400 Years, 1611–2011*]. Saint Petersburg: Gjöl, 2012.

Anderson, Paul B. *People, Church and State in Modern Russia*. London: Student Christian Movement Press, 1944.

Applebaum, Anne. *Gulag: A History*. New York: Doubleday, 2003.

Borshewskaja, Herta. "Die Errinerungen den Gemeindemitgliedern." *Der Bote* 3 (1997).

Boychenko, Yaroslav. О Лютеранах в России, Нижнем Новгороде и не только… [*Of Lutherans in Russia, Nizhniy Novgorod and More…*]. Nizhniy Novgorod, Russia: Povolzhiye, 2007.

Brandt, Lev. Лютеранство и его Политическая Роль [Lutheranism and its Political Role]. Leningrad: OGIZ Priboi, 1931.

Brandt, Sebastian. "Petrikirche nach 60 Jahren wieder Gotteshaus." *Der Bote* 4 (1997).

——, ed. *Petrikirche*—Церковь Святого Петра [*Petrkirche—The Church of St. Peter's*]. Saint Petersburg, Russia: Ofset Master, 1998.

Braun, Léopold L. S. *In Lubianka's Shadow: The Memoirs of an American Priest in Stalin's Moscow, 1934–1945*. South Bend, IN: University of Notre Dame Press, 2006.

Briem, Efraim. *Kommunismus und Religion in der Sowjetunion: Ein Ideenkampf*. Translated from the Swedish by Edzard Schaper. Basel, Switzerland: Verlag Friedrich Reinhardt AG, 1948.

Brodsky, Yuri. Соловки: Двацат Лет Особого Назначения [*Solovki: Twenty Years of Special Meaning*]. Moscow: Russian Political Encyclopedia, 2008.

Brovkin, Vladimir. *Russia after Lenin: Politics, Culture and Society, 1921–1929.* London: Taylor & Francis e-Library, 2005. Kindle edition.

Brownell, Will, and Richard N. Billings. *So Close to Greatness: A Biography of William C. Bullitt.* New York: Macmillan, 1987.

Burleigh, Michael. *Sacred Causes: The Clash of Religion and Politics, from the Great War to the War on Terror.* Harper Perennial, 2008.

Cassella-Blackburn, Michael. *The Donkey, the Carrot, and the Club: William C. Bullitt and Soviet-American Relations, 1917–1948.* Westport, CT: Praeger, 2004.

Chamberlain, Lesley. *Lenin's Private War: The Voyage of the Philosophy Steamer and the Exile of the Intelligentsia.* New York: St. Martin's Press, 2007.

Chamberlain, Lesley. *Motherland: A Philosophical History of Russia.* New York: Overlook/Rookery, 2007.

Clark, Katerina. *Moscow, the Fourth Rome: Stalinism, Cosmopolitanism, and the Evolution of Soviet Culture, 1931–1941.* Cambridge, MA: Harvard University Press, 2011.

Conquest, Robert. *The Great Terror: A Reassessment.* New York: Oxford University Press, 2007.

——. *The Harvest of Sorrow: Soviet Collectivization and the Terror-Famine.* New York: Oxford University Press, 1987.

——. *Religion in the USSR.* London: Bodley Head, 1968.

Curtiss, John Shelton. *The Russian Church and the Soviet State, 1917–1950.* New York: Little, Brown, 1953.

Dau, William Herman Theodore, ed. *Four Hundred Years: Commemorative Essays on the Reformation of Dr. Martin Luther and Its Blessed Results, in the Year of the Four-Hundredth Anniversary of the Reformation.* St. Louis: Concordia, 1916.

Davies, Sarah. *Popular Opinion in Stalin's Russia: Terror, Propaganda and Dissent, 1934–1941.* Cambridge, England: Cambridge University Press, 1997.

De Wolf, Koenraad. *Dissident for Life: Alexander Ogorodnikov and the Struggle for Religious Freedom in Russia*. Grand Rapids: Eerdmans, 2013.

Diedrich, Hans-Christian. *Sie Gehen von einer Kraft zur Anderen: In Memoriam, Arthur Pfeiffer: 18.8.1897–30.10. 1972*. Erlangen: Martin Luther Verlag, 1997.

———. *"Wohin sollen wir gehen ..." Der Weg der Christen durch die sowjetische Religionsverfolgung*. Russische Kirchengeschichte des 20. Jahrhunderts in ökumenischer Perspektive. Erlangen: Martin Luther Verlag, 2007.

Die Freunde Irma Löweniches. "Ein Wort über einen Freund." *Der Bote* 2 (2000).

Dobkin, A. I., and M. Sorokina, eds. *In Memoriam:* Исторический Сборник Памяти Ф.Ф. Перченка *[In Memoriam: Historical Collection of Memories of F. F. Perchenka]*. Moscow-St. Petersburg: Feniks-Atheneum, 1995.

Dönninghaus, Victor. *Die Deutschen in der Moskauer Gesellschaft: Symbiose und Konflikte (1494–1941)*. Münich: R. Oldenbourg Verlag, 2002.

Duin, Edgar Charles. *Lutheranism under the Tsars and the Soviets*. Ann Arbor, MI: Xerox University Microfilms, 1975.

Dunn, Dennis J. *Caught between Roosevelt & Stalin: America's Ambassadors to Moscow*. Lexington, KY: The University Press of Kentucky, 1998.

Eddy, Sherwood. *Russia Today: What Can We Learn from It?* New York: Farrar & Rinehart Inc., 1934.

Evangelical Lutheran Church of Ingria. Путь Веры Длиного Встолетий Церкви Ингрии: 400 Лет Истории, 40 Лет без Храмов, 4 Веки Возрождения *[The Path of Faith through the Long Centuries of the Church of Ingria: 400 Years of History, 40 years without Churches, 4 Centuries of Rebirth]*. St. Petersburg, Russia: Evangelical Lutheran Church of Ingria, 2012.

Figes, Orlando. *The Whisperers: Private Life in Stalin's Russia*. New York: Picador, 2008.

Fitzpatrick, Sheila. *Everyday Stalinism: Ordinary Life in Extraordinary Times: Soviet Russia in the 1930s*. New York: Oxford University Press, 1999.

Fitzpatrick, Sheila, ed. *Stalinism: New Directions*. Rewriting Histories. London: Taylor & Francis e-Library, 2003.

Fitzpatrick, Sheila. *Stalin's Peasants: Resistance and Survival in the Russian Village after Collectivization*. New York: Oxford University Press, 1994.

Fleischhauer, Ingeborg, and Benjamin Pinkus. *The Soviet Germans: Past and Present*. Edited by Edith Rogovin Frankel. New York: St. Martin's Press, 1986.

Gabel, Paul. *And God Created Lenin: Marxism vs. Religion in Russia, 1917–1929*. Amherst, NY: Prometheus Books, 2005.

Gaddis, John Lewis. *George F. Kennan: An American Life*. New York: The Penguin Press, 2011.

Georgiyevskaya, Elza. "Церковная Жизнь Москвы в 20–30-е Годы" ["Church Life in Moscow in the Years 1920–30"]. Наша Церковь [*Our Church*] 3–5 (1996): 60–63.

German, A.A. Немецкая Автономия на Волге, 1941–1918 [*German Autonomy in the Volga, 1941–1918*]. Moscow: MSNK Press, 2007.

Getty, J. Arch, and Oleg V. Naumov. *The Road to Terror: Stalin and the Self-Destruction of the Bolsheviks, 1932–1939*. New Haven, CT: Yale University Press, 1999.

Goldman, Emma. *My Disillusionment in Russia*. Garden City, NY: Doubleday, 1923.

Green, Lowell C. *Lutherans against Hitler: The Untold Story*. St. Louis: Concordia, 2007.

Greisinger, Adam. *From Yekaterina to Khrushchev: The Story of Russia's Germans*. Lincoln, NE: The American Historical Society of Germans from Russia, 1981.

Gregory, Paul R. *Terror by Quota: State Security from Lenin to Stalin*. New Haven and London: Yale University Press, 2009.

Haigis, Peter, and Gert Hummel. *Schwäbische Spuren im Kaukasus: Auswanderergeschichten*. Metzingen, Germany: Verlag Ernst Franz, 2002.

Harrison, Marguerite, and William Benton Whisenhunt, eds. *Marooned in Moscow: The Story of an American Woman Imprisoned in Soviet Russia*. Montpelier, VT: Russian Information Services, 2011.

Haynes, Emma Schwabenland. *A History of the Volga Relief Society*. Lincoln, NE: The American Historical Society of Germans from Russia. 1982.

Husband, William B. *Godless Communists: Atheism and Society in Soviet Russia, 1917–1932*. Dekalb, IL: Northern Illinois University Press, 2000.

Ivanov, E. J., and K. K. Sevastyanov. "Die Buntglasfenster der Petrikirche." *Der Bote* (1999).

Ivanov, Maxim. Лютеранский Квартал в Петербурге [*The Lutheran Quarter in Petersburg*]. Saint Petersburg, Russia: Yevropeiskiy Dom, 2004.

Jansen, Marc, and Nikita Petrov. *Stalin's Loyal Executioner: People's Commissar Nikolaiy Ezhov, 1895–1940*. Palo Alto, CA: Hoover Institution Press, 2002.

Johnson, Daniel H. *Loyalty: A Biography of Richard Gustavovich Reusch*. St. Cloud, MN: SunRay Printing, 2008.

Junker, Johannes, and Reijo Arkkila, eds. *Nacht und Neuer Morgen: Die Evangelisch-Lutherische Kirche von Ingrien in Russland*. Gross Oesingen, Germany: Verlag der Lutherischen Buchhandlung Heinrich Harms, 2001.

Kahle, Wilhelm. *Geschichte der Evangelisch-Lutherischen Gemeinden in der Sovetunion, 1917–1938*. Leiden, Germany: E. J. Brill, 1974.

——. *Wege und Gestalt Evangelisch-Lutherischen Kirchentums: Vom Moskauer Reich bis zur Gegenwart*. Erlangen: Martin Luther Verlag, 2002.

Kampen, Hans, and Nina Paulsen, eds. *Dunkle Jahre: Zum Gedenken an die Opfer des 'Grossen Terrors' und der Zwangsarbeitslager in der Sowjetunion, 61–62*. Stuttgart: Landmannschaft der Deutschen aus Russland e.V., 2012.

Kandidov, Boris P. Церковь и Шпионаж [*Church and Espionage*]. Moscow: Government Anti-Religious Publishing Co., 1937.

Karev, V., ed. Немцы в России: Энциклопедия Том 1, А-И [*Germans of Russia: Encyclopedia. Volume 1, А–И*]. Moscow: ERN, 1999.

——. Немцы в России: Энциклопедия Том 2, К-О [*Germans of Russia: Encyclopedia Volume 2, К–О*]. Moscow: ERN, 2004.

Kern, Gary. *A Death in Washington: Walter G. Krivitsky and the Stalin Terror*. New York: Enigma Books, 2004.

King, Charles. *Odessa: Genius and Death in a City of Dreams*. New York: W. W. Norton, 2011.

Klehr, Harvey, and John Haynes. *The Soviet World of American Communism*. New Haven, CT: Yale University Press, 1998.

Knight, Amy. *Who Killed Kirov? The Kremlin's Greatest Mystery*. New York: Hill and Wang, 1999.

Knyazeva, E. E., and G. F. Solovyeva. Лютеранские Церкви и Приходы в России XVIII-XX Веков: Исторический Справочник, Часть 1. [*Lutheran Churches and Congregations of Russia XVIII–XX Centuries: Historical Handbook, Part 1*]. Saint Petersburg: Russia, Litera, 2001.

Kofler, Natalie, and Stephan Reder. Евангелическо-Лютеранская Церковь в Ташкенте и Узбекистане [*The Evangelical Lutheran Church in Tashkent and Uzbekistan*]. Saint Petersburg, Russia: ELTS, 1996.

Kolarz, Walter. *Religion in the Soviet Union*. New York: St. Martin, 1961.

Kolb, Robert, and Timothy J. Wengert, eds. *The Book of Concord: The Confessions of the Evangelical Lutheran Church*. Minneapolis: Fortress, 2000.

Kozlov, Vladimir. "Судьба Протестанских Храмов Москвы после Революции" ["The Fate of Protestant Churches in Moscow after the Revolution"]. Наша Церковь [*Our Church*] 3–5 (1996): 52–55.

Krasikov, P. A. На Церковном Фронте: 1923–1918 [*On the Church Front: 1918–1923*]. Moscow: 1923.

Kretschmar, Georg, and Heinrich Ratke. *The Evangelical Lutheran Church in Russia, the Ukraine, Kazakhstan and Central Asia*. Saint Petersburg, Russia: AO Satis, Der Bote, 1996.

Krieger, Viktor. Translated by Alex Herzog. *Volga German Intellectuals as Victims of Political Persecution*. Lincoln, NE: American Historical Society of Germans from Russia, 2009.

Krylov, Pavel. Ингрия, Ингерманландцы и Церковь Ингрии в Прошлом и Настоящем [*Ingria, Ingrians and the Church of Ingria in Past and Present*]. Saint Petersburg, Russia: Giol, 2012.

Kubistskaya, O., ed. Немцы в России: Энциклопедия Том 3, П-Я [*Germans of Russia: Encyclopedia Volume 3, Р–Я*]. Moscow: ERN, 2006.

Kurilo, Olga. Лютеране в России: XVI–XX VV. [*Lutherans in Russia: 16th–20th Centuries*]. Sterling Heights, MI: Lutheran Heritage Foundation, 2002.

Kurko, Karlo. Финны-Ингерманландции в Когтях Г.П.У. [*Finnish Ingrians in Labor Camps*]. Saint Petersburg, Russia: Giol, 2010.

Lel, Johannes. "Как Они Нас Уничтожали но не Уничтожили" ["How They Were Trying to Destroy Us, but Didn't Succeed"]. Наша Церковь [*Our*

Church] (September 2001): 12–19.

Lemetti, I. M. Советская Ингерманландия [*Soviet Ingria*]. Sotsigrafich. Ocherk, 1931.

Lenoe, Matthew E. *The Kirov Murder and Soviet History.* Annals of Communism Series. New Haven and London: Yale University Press, 2010.

Liebert, Arwid. "Unruhe in Marxstadt." *Der Bote 2* (1995): 26–29.

———. "Unruhe in Marxstadt." *Der Bote 3–4* (1995): 38–41.

Lindes, Harald. "Ёлочка \ Christbaumchen." ["Christmas Tree"]. Website "Архангелиты — дети Немецкой слободы" ["Archangelites: Children of the German Settlements"]. 1997.

Litzenberger, Olga. Евангелическо-Лютеранская Церковь в Россиской Истории XVI–XX vv. [*The Evangelical Lutheran Church in Russian History 16th–20th c.*]. Moscow: The Lutheran Heritage Foundation of Education and Culture, 2003.

———. Евангелическо-Лютеранская Церковь и Советское Государство, 1938–1917 [*The Evangelical Lutheran Church and the Soviet Government, 1938–1917*]. Moscow: Gotika, 1999.

Lorant, Stefan. *Sieg Heil: An Illustrated History of Germany from Bismarck to Hitler.* Norton, 1974.

Lotov, Dmitry. "Слово об Ернсте Херщёлманне: Органисте Соборе Святих Петра и Павла в Москвы" ["Words about Ernst Hörschelmann: The Organist of St. Peter and Paul in Moscow"]. Наша Церковь [*Our Church*] (October 1998): 34–36.

Luukanen, Arto. *The Religious Policy of the Stalinist State: A Case Study: The Central Standing Commission on Religious Questions, 1929–1938.* Helsinki, Finland: Societas Historica Finlandiae, 1997.

MacGillivray, Rev. G. J. *The Anti-God Front of Bolshevism: A Statement of Facts.* London: Catholic Truth Society, 1933.

Marshall, Richard H., Jr., ed. *Aspects of Religion in the Soviet Union, 1917–1967.* Chicago: University of Chicago Press, 1971.

Martsinkovsky, Vladimir. Записки Верующего: Из Истории Религиозного Движения в Советской России 1923–1917 [*Memoirs of a Believer: From* the History of the Religious Movement in Soviet Russia 1923–1917]. Chicago: Slavic Gospel Press, 1974.

Meacham, Jon. *American Gospel: God, the Founding Fathers, and the Making of a Nation*. New York: Random House, 2006.

Merridale, Catherine. *Night of Stone: Death and Memory in Twentieth-Century Russia*. New York: Viking, 2001.

Meier, Theophil. Наследие Лютерв в России: К 400-летному Юбидею Реформации Отмечаемаму Евангелическо-Лютеранскими ОБшинами в России [*Luther's Heritage in Russia: On the Occasion of the Celebration of the 400th Anniversary of the Reformation in the Evangelical-Lutheran Community in Russia*]. Moscow: Gotika, 2003.

Miner, Steven Merritt. *Stalin's Holy War: Religion, Nationalism and Alliance Politics, 1941–1945*. Chapel Hill, NC: University of North Carolina Press, 2003.

Mislin, David. "Beyond Christian Nationalism: How the American Committee on Religious Rights and Minorities Made Religious Pluralism a Global Cause in the Interwar Era." *Religions* (December 16, 2016).

Montefiore, Simon Sebag. *Stalin: The Court of the Red Tsar*. London: Vintage, 2005.

Mudyugin, Mikhail. "Iz Vospominaniya o zhiznii Leningradskikh evangelichesko-luteranskikh obshin pered ikh likvidatsii" ["A Remembrance of Life in the Leningrad Evangelical-Lutheran Congregation until its Liquidation"]. *Journal of the Church of Ingria* 3–4 (December 1993).

Muggeridge, Malcolm. *Winter in Moscow*. Grand Rapids: Eerdmans, 1987.

Musaev, V. I. Политическая История Ингерманландии в Конце XIX–XX Веке [*Political History of Ingermanland at the End of the 19th Century–20th Century*]. Saint Petersburg, Russia: Saint Petersburg Institute of History RAN: Nestor-History, 2004.

Müthel, Edith. *An Gottes Hand: Ein Deutsch-Russiche Lebensgeschichte*. Leipzig: Verlag des Gustav-Adolf-Werks e.V., 2013.

———. Я Помню: Из Петроградн в Петербург через Поволжье и Сибир: Судьба Дочери Пастора [*I Remember: From Petrograd to Petersburg through the Volga and Siberia: The Fate of the Daughter of a Lutheran Pastor*].

St. Petersburg, Russia: Tsentralizovannaya Religioznaya Organizatsiya-Evangelicheskaya Luteranskaya Tserkov, 2015.

Nevalainen, Pekka. Исход: Финнская Эмиграция из России 1939–1917 гг. [*Exodus: Finnish Emigration from Russia 1939–1917*]. Saint Petersburg, Russia: Kolo Publishing House, 2005.

Osipova, I. I. *Hide Me within Thy Wounds: The Persecution of the Catholic Church in the USSR*. Translated by Malcolm Gilbert. Fargo, ND: Germans from Russia Heritage Collection, 1996.

Patenaude, Bertrand M. *The Big Show in Bololand: The American Relief Expedition to Soviet Russia in the Famine of 1921*. Stanford, CA: Stanford University Press, 2002.

Peris, Daniel. *Storming the Heavens: The Soviet League of the Militant Godless*. Ithaca, NY: Cornell University Press, 1998.

Petrone, Karen. *Life Has Become More Joyous, Comrades: Celebrations in the Time of Stalin*. Bloomington, IN: Indiana University Press, 2000.

Philipps, John. *About Myself and Repression of the Germans in South Ukraine*. Translated by Alex Herzog. Fargo, ND: Germans from Russia Heritage Collection, 2009.

Pipes, Richard. *Russia under the Bolshevik Regime*. New York: Vintage Books, 1995.

——. *The Russian Revolution*. New York: Vintage Books, 1991.

Pospielovsky, Dmitry V. *A History of Marxist-Leninist Atheism and Soviet Anti-Religious Policies*. New York: St. Martin's Press, 1987.

Poerzgen, Hermann. *Ein Land Ohne Gott*. Frankfurt am Main: Societäts-Verlag, 1936.

Prokhanov, Ivan. *In the Cauldron of Russia: 1869:1933*. New York: All-Russian Evangelical Christian Union, 1933.

Rappaport, Helen. *Caught in the Revolution: Petrograd, Russia, 1917—A World on the Edge*. New York: St. Martin's Press, 2017.

Reinmarus, A., and G. Friesen. Под Гнётом Религии: Немцы-Колонисты СССР и их Религиозные Организации. [*Under the Wrath of Religion: German Colonists of the USSR and their Religion*]. Moscow: Government Publishing Co.,1931.

Remnick, David. *Lenin's Tomb: The Last Days of the Soviet Empire.* New York: Vintage Books, 1994. Kindle edition.

Richert, Sigismund. *Russland! Russland! Und die Lutherische Kirche?* Erlangen: Martin Luther Verlag, 1934.

———. *Tod und Morgenrot in Russland.* 4th ed. Erlangen: Selbstverlag des Verfassers, 1937.

Richman, John. *The United States and the Soviet Union: The Decision to Recognize.* Raleigh, NC: Camberleigh and Hall, 1980.

Robinson, Robert, with Jonathan Slevin. *Black on Red: My 44 Years inside the Soviet Union.* Washington, DC: Acropolis Books, 1988.

Roemmich, Heinrich. "Die Ev. Luth. Kirche in Russland unter der Sowjetherrschaft." *Heimatbuch der Deutschen aus Russland 1961.* Stuttgart: Die Landsmannschaft der Deutschen aus Russland, 1961.

Roemmich, Heinrich. *The Rose and the Sickle: Survival of the Lutheran Church in Russia.* Edited by Oscar Sommerfeld. Translated by Frederick Lenz. Saskatoon, SK: Division of Communication: Evangelical Lutheran Church of Canada, 1984.

Roepke, Claus Juergen. *St. Paul, Odessa: Kirche, Gemeinde, Glaube, Partner: Festschrift zur Wiedereinweihung der Kirche.* Lindenberg, Germany: Kunstverlag Josef Fink, 2010.

Roslof, Edward E. *Red Priests: Renovationism, Russian Orthodoxy, and Revolution, 1905–1946.* Bloomington, IN: Indiana University Press, 2002.

Satter, David. *It Was a Long Time Ago and It Never Really Happened Anyway: Russia and the Communist Past.* New Haven, CT: Yale University Press, 2012.

Schleuning, Johannes, Heinrich Roemmich, and Eugen Bachmann. *Und siehe, wir leben!: Der Weg der evangelisch-luthersichen Kirche Russlands in vier Jahrhunderten.* Erlangen, Germany: Martin Luther-Verlag, 1977.

Schlögel, Karl. *Moscow, 1937.* Translated by Rodney Livingstone. Cambridge, England: Polity Press, 2012.

Schmidrina, Ludmilla. "Ein Jahr in Wiedererstandenen Gotteshaus." *Der Bote* 3 (1998).

Schrader, T. A., ed. Немцы в Санкт-Петербурге: Биографический Аспект XVIII–XX гг., Выпуск 7 [*Germans in St. Petersburg: Biographical Aspects XVIII–XX Centuries,* 7th Edition]. Saint Petersburg: Kunstkamera, 2013.

Service, Robert. *Spies and Commissars*. Public Affairs, 2012.

Shkarovsky, Mikhail, and Alexander Bovkalo. "Пастор Курт Мусс" ["Pastor Kurt Muss"]. *Der Bote* 3–4 (1996).

Shkarovsky, Mikhail, and Nadezhda Cherepenina. История Евангелическо-Лютеранской Церкви на Северо-Западе России, 1945–1917 [*The History of the Evangelical Lutheran Church in Northwest Russia, 1917–1945*]. Saint Petersburg, Russia: Dmitry Bulanin, 2004.

Shkarovsky, Mikhail. "Епископ Артур Малмыгрен" ["Bishop Arthur Malmgren"], accessed April 15, 2013, http://spbda.ru/publications/mihail-shkarovskiy-episkop-artur-malmgren/.

Simon, Gerhard. *Church, State and Opposition in the U.S.S.R.* Translated by Kathleen Matchett in collaboration with the Centre for the Study of Religion under Communism. Berkeley, CA: University of California Press, 1974.

Shearer, David R. Policing *Stalin's Socialism: Repression and Social Order in the Soviet Union, 1924–1953.* New Haven, CT: Yale University Press, 2009.

Sinner, Samuel D. *The Open Wound: The Genocide of the German Ethnic Minorities in Russia and the Soviet Union 1915–1949 and Beyond.* Fargo, ND: Germans from Russia Heritage Collection and North Dakota State Libraries, 2000.

Sommer, Erich. *Geboren in Moskau: Errinerungen eines Baltendeutschen Diplomaten 1912–1955.* Munich: Langen Müller, 1997.

Sorokin, Vladimir, and Mikhail Shkarovsky, eds. Санкт-Петербургский Мартиролог. [*Saint Petersburg Martyrology*]. St. Petersburg, Russia: Mir, Association of Vasily the Great, 2002.

Snyder, Timothy. *Bloodlands: Europe Between Hitler and Stalin.* New York: Basic Books, 2010.

Springer, Siegfried. *Dem Himmel in Russland Näher.* Erlangen: Martin Luther Verlag, 2013.

Stackelberg, Natalya. "Кружок Молодых Историков и 'Академическое Дело'"

["Circle of Young Historians and the 'Academic Affair'"]. *In Memoriam: Исторический Сборник Памяти Ф. Ф. Перченка* [*In Memoriam: Historic Collection of Memories of F. F. Perchenka*]. St. Petersburg, Russia: Feniks, 1995.

Stach, Jakob. *Zelle oder Insel?: Eine Frage der Reichgottesarbeit im Zusammenhang mit dem Bolschewismus*. Pforzheim: Albert Zutavern Verlag, 1925.

Stangl, Janice Huber. *Collectivization in the Soviet Union: German Letters to America, 1927–1932*. Fargo, ND: Glueckstal Colonies Research Association in cooperation with the Germans from Russia Heritage Collection, 2012.

Starr, S. Frederick. *Red and Hot: The Fate of Jazz in the Soviet Union 1917–1991*. 2nd ed. New York: Limelight Editions, 1994.

Striks, Olga. "Последняя Конфирмация в Московской Общине Святого Петра" ["The Last Confirmation in the Moscow Congregation of St. Peter's"]. Наша Церковь [*Our Church*] 3–5 (1996): 70–71.

Tatsenko, Tamara, Alexander Pastor, and Hans Schwan. "Bruder Bruno." *Der Bote* 4 (2002).

Taylor, S. J. *Stalin's Apologist: Walter Duranty, The New York Times's Man in Moscow*. Oxford: Oxford University Press, 1990.

Timasheff, N. S. *Religion in Soviet Russia: 1917–1942*. New York: Sheed and Ward, 1942.

Trexler, Samuel. *John A. Morehead: Who Created World Lutheranism*. Whitefish, MT: Kessinger Publishing, 2010.

Tschoerner, Helmut. *Arthur Malmgren—Theologe, Pfarrer, Bischof in Russland und der Sowjetunion*. Erlangen: Martin Luther Verlag, 2012.

——. *Das Ev.-luth. Predigerseminar in Leningrad 1925–34*. Erlangen: Martin Luther Verlag, 2002.

Tucker, Robert C. *Stalin in Power: The Revolution from Above, 1928–1941*. New York: W. W. Norton, 1990.

Tupolev, Boris, ed. *Russland und Deutschland*. 2nd ed. Moscow: Nauka, 2001.

Tzouliadis, Tim. *The Forsaken: An American Tragedy in Stalin's Russia*. London: The Penguin Press, 2008. Kindle Edition.

Ulyanov, N.P. "Судьбы Учителей Петришуле: 20–30 гг." ["The Fate of the Teachers at the Peterschule: 30–1920s]. In Немцы в России: Люди и Судьбы. [*Germans in Russia: People and Fates*]. Saint Petersburg, Russia: 1998.

Vaksberg, Arkady. *Stalin's Prosecutor: The Life of Andrei Vyshinsky*. Translated by Jan Butler. New York: Grove Weidenfeld, 1990.

Viola, Lynn. "The Peasant Nightmare: Visions of Apocalypse in the Soviet Countryside." *Journal of Modern History* Vol. 62, No. 4 (Dec 1990): 747–70.

Volkogonov, Dmitri. *Lenin: A New Biography*. Translated and edited by Harold Shukman. New York: The Free Press, 1994.

——. *Stalin: Triumph and Tragedy*. Translated and edited by Harold Shukman. New York: Grove Weidenfeld, 1991.

——. *Trotsky: The Eternal Revolutionary*. Translated and edited by Harold Shukman. New York: The Free Press, 1996.

Völl, Johann. "Bilder aus der Geschichte einer Kirche unter dem Kreuz," *Heimatbuch der Deutschen aus Russland*. Stuttgart: Die Landsmannschaft der Deutschen aus Russland, 1958.

Völl, Johannes. "Zum Gedenken an Pastor Ferdinand Hörschelmann," *Heimatbuch der Deutschen aus Russland*. Stuttgart: Die Landsmannschaft der Deutschen aus Russland, 1964.

Vossler, Ronald J. *We'll Meet Again in Heaven: Germans in the Soviet Union Write Their American Relatives, 1925–1937*. Fargo, ND: Germans from Russia Heritage Collection, 2011.

Walters, George J. *Wir Wollen Deutsche Bleiben: The Story of the Volga Germans*. Edited by Christopher D. Walters. Kansas City, MO: Halcyon House Publishers, Inc., 1982.

Wells, H. G. *Russia in the Shadows*. New York: George H. Doran, 1921.

Wengert, Timothy J., ed. Dictionary of Luther and the Lutheran Traditions. Grand Rapids: Baker Academic, 2017.

Wentz, Frederick K. *Lutherans in Concert: The Story of the National Lutheran Council: 1918–1966*. Minneapolis: Augsburg Publishing House, 1968.

Yanson, P. M. От Угнетений и Безправий к Счастливой Жизни [*From Persecution and Injustice to a Happy Life*]. Leningrad: Lenoblispolkoma and Lensoviet Publishing, 1936.

Yaroslavsky, F. *Religion in the U.S.S.R.* New York: International Publishers, 1932.

Young, Glennys. *Power and the Sacred in Revolutionary Russia: Religious Activists in the Village*. University Park, PA: Pennsylvania State University Press, 1997.

Zeksel, Dagmara. "Воспоминания о Пасторе Курте Муссе" ["Remembrances of Pastor Kurt Muss"], in Уроки Гнева и Любви: Воспоминания о Репрессиях 80–1920 гг, Выпуск 5. [*Lessons of Hate and Love: Remembrances of Repression 1920–80, Volume 5*]. Saint Petersburg, Russia: V.I., 1993.

Zugger, Christopher Lawrence. *The Forgotten: Catholics of the Soviet Empire from Lenin Through Stalin*. Syracuse, NY: Syracuse University Press, 2001.

ARCHIVES AND LIBRARIES USED

Archives of the Evangelical Lutheran Church in America

Russian State Archives of Saint Petersburg

Federal Security Bureau of Saint Petersburg Region

Federal Security Bureau of Moscow Region

Germans from Russia Archives at North Dakota State University

United States National Archives II

Russian State Library—Moscow, Russia

SUBJECT INDEX

interrogation of, 171–73
arrest of, 180
release of, 194
marriage of, 256
death of, 389
Schwartz, Renata, 156
Seib, Eduard, 231
Seib, Otto, 143, 151–52, 207–8, 240–41
Seib, Woldemar, 231–32, 291
Simon, Oktav, 295
arrest of, 287–88
sentencing of, 293
Shukino-Bodarets, Elena, 163–64
Stalin, Joseph (General Secretary of the
USSR), xiii, 110, 118–19, 128, 130,
141–43, 145, 150, 165, 169, 171, 183,
186, 190, 193, 195, 198, 201–3, 216,
220–21, 245–47, 250–51, 255, 259,
297, 311, 314–15, 317, 321–21, 323,
325–26, 332–36, 340, 444
solidification of power, 121–22
First Five Year Plan, 248
Second Five Year Plan, 243
Kirov murder, 283–84
Stalin Constitution of 1936, 327,
337, 347, 349–50, 355, 363, 366,
368–69, 375, 383, 386, 452
Stalinism, 122, 145, 176, 188, 248, 269,
273, 277, 305, 315, 325–26, 350,
354, 392, 427, 446
de-Stalinization, 220, 322, 382, 386
Sterle, Gotthold, 105,
arrest of, 169
Stimson, Henry (U.S. Secretary of
State), 176, 418, 423–24
Streck, Alexander, 36, 106–8, 209–10,
241, 253, 263–64, 303, 314–18, 375,
395, 403, 432, 440, 442,446–47
arrest of, 321–25
interrogation of, 328–30, 336–39, 346
execution of, 347

T

Tchaikovsky, Peter, 373
Tikhon, Patriarch, 16–17, 26,

arrest of, 42–43
release of, 60–61
Toryassan, Bruno, 83, 169, 227–28, 251,
254, 351, 358, 391–93, 430, 447,
466
Toryassan, Ossip, 303, 319,
execution of, 351
Trexler, Samuel, 7, 63
visit to USSR, 302–3
comment of Morehead's passing,
309–310
Trotsky, Leon (People's Commissar of
Military and Naval Affairs of
the USSR), 20, 26, 32, 65, 128,
283
removal from power, 121
Troyanovsky, Alexander (Soviet
ambassador to the U.S.), 281,
323–24, 327
Tumm, Otto, 138, 172–17, 411, 419,
395–96
arrest of, 169, 230
marriage of, 256
re-arrest and death of, 380

V

Veniamin, Metropolitan, 17
trial and execution of, 42, 45–46
Völl, Johann, 71, 113–16, 212, 402, 408,
414–15, 418
Voroshilov, Kliment (Chairman of
the Presidium of the Supreme
Soviet), 275

W

Wacker, Friedrich, 36, 83–84, 95, 169,
179, 201, 213, 217, 221, 225, 234,
240–41, 371, 410–11, 434, 453
interrogation of, 180
arrest and deportation of, 210–11
release of, 257
execution of, 386
Wagner, Woldemar (Seminary student
and professor), 257, 271, 370–71,
380–81, 434